Giving to Help, Helping to Give

GIVING TO HELP, HELPING TO GIVE

The Context and Politics of African Philanthropy

**Edited by
Tade Akin Aina
& Bhekinkosi Moyo**

Published by Amalion Publishing and TrustAfrica 2013

Amalion Publishing
BP 5637 Dakar-Fann
Dakar CP 00004
Senegal
http://www.amalion.net

TrustAfrica
Lot 87, Sacré Coeur 3 Pyrotechnie x VDN
BP 45 435 Dakar-Fann, Senegal
http://www.trustafrica.org

Copyright © TrustAfrica 2013

ISBN 978-2-35926-020-5 (Paperback)
ISBN 978-2-35926-021-2 (Ebook)

Cover and illustrations designed by Anke Rosenlöcher

Printed in the United Kingdom by CPI Group (UK) Ltd., Croydon, CR0 4YY

CONTENTS

TABLES

FIGURES

CONTRIBUTORS

Tade Akin Aina, currently the Program Director, Higher Education and Libraries in Africa for the Carnegie Corporation of New York, studied Sociology at the University of Lagos, Nigeria, and Sociology of Development at the London School of Economics, and holds a DPhil from the University of Sussex, UK. He served as Deputy Executive Secretary at CODESRIA, Dakar, Senegal from 1993 to 1998, and worked with the Ford Foundation in the Nairobi office from 1998 to 2008. He has also served as consultant for many international agencies on a wide range of development issues such as urban poverty, higher education reform, governance, environment and development. He currently serves on the boards of Winrock International, Seeding Labs, the King Baudouin Foundation, and the Kenya Human Rights Commission among others. Tade Akin Aina has authored and co-edited more than ten books and numerous chapters in books, articles in journals and learned publications.

Kwaku Asante-Darko is currently a Senior Expert on Conflict Prevention at the Conflict Management Division at the African Union (AU) Commission in Addis Ababa, Ethiopia. Prior to working at the AU, Asante-Darko worked as an academic in universities in Ghana, the Kingdom of Lesotho and South Africa and was was a Senior Researcher in the Governance and African Peer Review Mechanism Programme at the South Africa Institute of International Affairs (SAIIA), Johannesburg. His publications cover both policy and academic issues in conflict prevention, mediation, early warning, African indigenous knowledge and literature.

Mohammed Bakari, Phd, is the Head, Department of Political Science and Public Administration, University of Dar es Salaam, Tanzania. He coordinated the research group on Islamic Philanthropy for Social Justice in Tanzania supported by the Ford Foundation Office for Eastern Africa.

Bertha Chiroro is a Research Specialist at the Africa Institute of South Africa, in Pretoria. She has an MPhil. in Political Science from the University of Durham,

UK, she has done research and published on a range of issues on civil society, democracy and governance, gender and elections and political processes in Africa.

Marwa El Daly is the Chairperson of the Maadi Community Foundation/ Waqfeyat al Maadi al Ahleya and author of the first National Study on Philanthropy in Egypt and other major publications in this field. She was selected in 2007 by Ashoka as a Social Entrepreneur from the Arab region in recognition of her efforts in institutionalizing philanthropy and the revival of the waqf endowment system.

Alan Fowler is an adviser to, researcher on and writer about civil society and international development. He is an emeritus professor of the Institute of Social Studies in the Hague, The Netherlands.

Ibrahima Hathie is Research Director at Initiative Prospective Agricole et Rurale (IPAR Senegal). Previously, he was a value chain manager at the USAID Economic Growth Project in Dakar, Senegal. From 1992 to 2009, Dr. Hathie served as a professor and later Director of Studies and Fieldwork at the École Nationale d'Économie Appliquée (ENEA, Senegal). He holds a PhD in Agricultural and Resource Economics from the University of Connecticut, USA.

Jenny Hodgson is the Executive Director of the Global Fund for Community Foundations (GFCF) based in Johannesburg, South Africa. She has been working in the field of philanthropy and development since 1992 in Kenya, Russia, Singapore, Thailand and Uganda. She was Co-Director of the Charities Aid Foundation's Moscow office and has worked as a consultant to the Charles Stewart Mott Foundation, Ford Foundation and Allavida. Jenny has a BA (Hons) in English literature from Emmanuel College, Cambridge and an MA in International Relations from Johns Hopkins School of Advanced International Studies (SAIS).

Andrew Kingman is the Director of Programmes, Fundação MICAIA and Managing Director, Eco-MICAIA Lda, Mozambique. Having completed degrees in politics, economics and international development, Andrew established Village Aid from the UK, working in West Africa from 1990 to 1997. Three years with Charities Aid Foundation to 2000 gave Andrew the opportunity to work with civil society partners in Eastern Europe and Asia, and to engage with the growing social enterprise sector as well as with the evolving world of philanthropy and social investment. From 2000 to 2007 Andrew served as founding Director of Allavida, working on social enterprise, philanthropy promotion and rural livelihoods in East Africa. In 2008, Andrew and his wife (Milagre Nuvunga) moved to Mozambique to establish MICAIA.

Christa Kuljian is a development consultant and freelance writer based in Johannesburg. Originally from Boston, she first arrived in South Africa in 1984 when she worked for the South African Council of Churches and Senator Edward Kennedy. She was the Director of the Charles Stewart Mott Foundation in South Africa from 1992 to 2003. Since then, Christa has written case studies and articles for non-governmental organizations and in 2010 was a recipient of the Ruth First Fellowship from Wits University to write about the refugee crisis at Central Methodist Church in Johannesburg. Christa holds a BA from Harvard (1984), an MSc in International Development and Public Policy from the Woodrow Wilson School at Princeton (1989) and an MA in Creative Writing from the University of the Witwatersrand (2007), and is the author of *Sanctuary* (Jacana Media: 2013).

Halima Mahomed is the Philanthropy Program Advisor at TrustAfrica. Her work at TrustAfrica is directed at knowledge building, outreach and advocacy on African philanthropy, with a particular emphasis on advancing social justice philanthropy. She has previously worked at the Ford Foundation Office for Southern Africa, at the EDGE Institute and, amongst others, as a long-term consultant to the Ford Foundation and the Global Fund for Community Foundations. She also serves on the Philanthropy for Social Justice and Peace Working Group. She holds a MSc in Development Studies from the University of the Witwatersrand – with a research focus on social justice philanthropy in South Africa.

Bhekinkosi Moyo is Director of Programs at TrustAfrica, based in Dakar, Senegal. He holds a doctorate in political science from the University of the Witwatersrand in South Africa. He previously worked at the Africa Institute of South Africa, Tswaranang Legal Advocacy Centre and at the Institute for Democracy in South Africa. He has written and published extensively on governance, democratization and philanthropy in Africa. He has edited several books including, *Africa in the Global Power Play: Debates, Challenges and Potential Reforms* (2007), and *(Dis) Enabling the Public Sphere: Civil Society Regulation in Africa* (2010).

Robert Muponde is Associate Professor of English in the School of Languages, Literature and Media, University of the Witwatersrand, Johannesburg. He has numerous publications on African and Zimbabwean literature and culture. His most notable publications include co-edited works such as *Versions of Zimbabwe: New approaches to literature and culture* (2005); *Sign and Taboo: Perspectives on the poetic fiction of Yvonne Vera* (2002); and *Manning the nation: Father figures in Zimbabwean literature and society* (2007). He is currently researching the politics and representations of the differently bodied individuals and freaks in African culture and politics.

James Muzondidya is a Zimbabwean academic and policy analyst. He is currently the Research Manager of the Zimbabwe Institute, a political think-tank based in Harare. His research interests are in contemporary African politics and development, migration studies and identity politics, and he has published extensively in these areas.

Connie Ngondi-Houghton is a lawyer by training. She was educated at the University of Nairobi and at Yale Law School. She is a leading human rights campaigner and in Kenya and an advocate of the High Court of Kenya. She has worked as Executive Director of International Commission of Jurists and has consulted extensively for charities, NGOs, and donors in Kenya including the Ford Foundation. Her most recent work concentrates on philanthropy in East Africa.

Kayode Samuel is the CEO of Development Alliance West Africa and a visiting fellow at the Institute of Commonwealth Studies, University of London, UK. He is the author of *Political Transition in Nigeria, 1993–2003: Commentaries on selected themes* (Malthouse: 2010).

Mohamadou Sy is the Managing Director of the Institut Supérieur de Développement Local (ISDL) based in Dakar, Senegal. From 1998 to 2008, he was the Director of the Department of Planning and Organizations Management at the École Nationale d'Économie Appliquée (ENEA) in Dakar. Sy has also worked as consultant in organizational development for various international institutions. He is a member of the International Society for Third-Sector Research, The World Bank Rob McNamara Program Alumni and the Réseau Francophone d'Appui au Développement Local, and completing a doctorate on management and higher education governance.

Gérard Tchouassi, PhD, teaches economics at the Department of Economics, Faculty of Economics and Management, University of Yaoundé II, Cameroon. He has published on migration, remittances, diaspora, altruism, philanthropy and development in Central African Region.

Fondo Sikod is professor of economics and Head of Department of Human Resources, Faculty of Economics and Management, University of Yaoundé II, Cameroon. His research and publications are in the areas of globalization, remittances, diaspora, philanthropy and development in the Central Africa region.

Susan Wilkinson-Maposa is an independent consultant and researcher based in Cape Town. She has directed social development and research programmes in Southern Africa for international agencies, consultancy companies and universities. Susan is a specialist in community philanthropy and volunteering. Her current research interests include: the understanding and measurement of civil society from an African perspective, individual giving and volunteering, community responses to children affected by AIDS and poverty and the organisational development of community grantmakers.

Saida Yahya-Othman is an associate professor in the Department of Foreign Languages and Linguistics of the University of Dar es Salaam, Tanzania, where she teaches pragmatics and critical discourse analysis. She has been involved in various projects on religion, democracy, and philanthropy in Tanzania. She was co-editor of *Justice, Rights and Worship: Religion and Politics in Tanzania* (E&D Publishers: 2006) and *Women Writing Africa: The Eastern Region* (Feminist Press: 2007). She has been Head of Department, Associate Dean, Director of Postgraduate Studies and Director of Research at the University. For many years she headed the Research and Publications Committee of REDET, the Research and Education for Democracy project under the Department of Political Science and Public Administration. Her main publications have been in pragmatics and language politics. She currently chairs the Board of the Gender Training Institute at Dar es Salaam, an affiliate of the Tanzania Gender Networking Programme and is working with two others on a new biography of Julius Nyerere.

PREFACE

The past decade has seen a flowering of philanthropic activities across many parts of Africa. Unlike before, this flowering has the distinct character of African agency, energy and engagement. Philanthropy is no longer about narratives of passive, poor and miserable Africans receiving help from rich, fortunate and often Western outsiders. The emerging narratives about philanthropy in Africa are about an increasingly confident and knowledgeable assertion of African capacities to give not only to help but also to transform and seek to address the root causes of injustice, want, ignorance and disease. The narratives are also about the increasing questioning of the role and place of Africans in the world's philanthropic traditions and what constitutes African specificities but also African differences and varieties.

This book is about African philanthropic experiences, their varieties, challenges and opportunities. It is about documenting, investigating, describing, questioning and reflecting on these philanthropic experiences. Because Africa is not a monolithic entity with one single history, cultural, political and economic experience, this book is about the varied modes, forms, vehicles and means in which the philanthropic experiences are expressed. It is a pioneering and ambitious effort in a field and community of practice that is new both in terms of scholarship and in professional practice. Many of the chapters therefore carry with them the burden of reflections, questions, ambivalences and ambiguities that one often finds in an emerging and tentative field, in which the outlines, concepts, frameworks and theories of scholarship and practice are nascent.

As I read through the contributions that make up this book, I sense the tensions of a beginning, as well as a reclamation, particularly in the struggles by the authors to define the subject. Almost every single contribution feels the need to directly or indirectly define 'philanthropy'. There is also the same need to establish the validity of African practices across different periods as being worthy of consideration to be part of the world traditions of philanthropy. At the same time there are strong attempts to present alternative modes of delivering assistance, such as the wide range of pre-colonial, informal and hybrid forms that exist in actual practice across time and places. Of course these efforts, located in a history of the ethnocentric denial of the existence of philanthropic practices in non-Western societies such as those of Africa, are bound to create boundary problems for definitions. These problems exist in this collection. There is also the proliferation of terms and notions such as horizontal, vertical, indigenous, modern, traditional philanthropies. Many of these notions and terms require greater rigour, more and deeper conceptual and analytical work that is bound to grow from the establishment of a vibrant community of practice and thought that this book is hopefully a contribution to.

Another important element of the book is that it has taken some time in its making, bringing together different generations of scholars, activists and practitioners. Since 2006, the editors have systematically identified, invited and secured contributions from both young and older generations of activists and practitioners. They have also attempted to cover various areas and components that define the variety of African philanthropic experience across regions, linguistic and cultural groups and distinct non-Western traditions such as Islam and certain national forms. Important and emerging trends such as diaspora engagement and social justice philanthropy have also been included. This book thus attempts to cover the different aspects of the varieties of African philanthropic experience, such as national and regional studies, the experience of non-Western forms and, of course, specific issues such as equity, poverty and social justice.

As I pointed out earlier, the making of the book has taken some time and effort and there is a story behind that. This book is in actual fact the articulation of more than one initiative or institutional project. It is the coming together of ideas and actions by different actors who cared about, engaged, worked on and in philanthropy in Africa.

It began with the Ford Foundation African Philanthropy Initiative (API), launched late in 1998 and led from the Office for Eastern Africa by its then Representative, Katharine Pearson. The API had a three-pronged approach of encouraging local philanthropy through

i.   foundation building and strengthening. This included working with community foundations such as the Kenya Community Development Foundation (KCDF) mentioned in this volume, to set up and strengthen capacities such as management, resource mobilization such as fundraising and endowments and governance;

ii.   contributing to building and strengthening the infrastructure of philanthropy such as building and strengthening networks, regional associations of grant makers (such as the East Africa Association of Grantmakers) and the growth of civil society support organizations(such as Allavida and Ufadhili Trust, both in Nairobi, Kenya);

iii. contributing to building an enabling environment for philanthropy and civil society through knowledge building and dissemination, policy research and advocacy that encompass legal, institutional and policy frameworks, financial contexts, and the political and human rights terrain in which philanthropic organizations exist.

These three elements were pursued with wide-ranging support across the continent, but mainly in Eastern and Southern Africa, and within a period of about ten years contributed immensely to changing the landscape for philanthropy, particularly in Eastern Africa, where the discourse and practices were particularly affected in a positive manner.

Parallel to these efforts was the emergence of TrustAfrica, which started as a Ford Foundation Special Initiative for Africa in 2001 and later became a fully fledged pan-African foundation in 2006. With the mission of strengthening African initiatives that address the most difficult challenges confronting the continent, and an insistence on African solutions to African problems, TrustAfrica, with an autonomous and developed programme on 'cultivating African resources for democracy and development', took over the project of developing and producing this book. The product is this collection that is a first in the field in Africa for both its coverage and its comprehensiveness. It is also a beginning of what promises to be an exciting epoch for building the field and community of practice for knowledge and work in the varieties of African philanthropic experiences.

In closing, it is important that we acknowledge our gratitude for the support and contributions that ensured the making of this book. Because of its very specific origins, I begin by thanking the Ford Foundation, particularly the Office for Eastern Africa and former colleagues and friends in the Foundation. Our thanks go to Susan Berresford, Barry Gaberman and Chris Harris for their support to the cause of a global philanthropic movement worldwide and African philanthropy at a critical moment of its self-assertion. We also acknowledge with thanks the support of Akwasi Aidoo, Gerry Salole, Katharine Pearson, Adhiambo Odaga, Alice Brown, Emma Playfair, Sushma Raman, Joseph Gitari, Willy Mutunga, Rob Burnet, Milagre Nuvunga, Basma Elhusseiny, Halima Mahomed and Hanna Ahere, all of whom worked across the different Ford Foundation Africa offices on different aspects of the initiative. Our sincere thanks also go to consultants and partners in the initiative – Elkanah Odembo, Anne-Marie Griffin, Jenny Hodgson, Joyce Malombe, Monica Mutuku, Connie Ngondi-Houghton, and Andrew Kingman. This book would not have happened without the dedication and drive of colleagues at TrustAfrica and the intellectual and administrative leadership of Bheki Moyo. Bheki, thank you for your gentle and firm persistence in the midst of all the many other things you had to get done. Also, we would like to say a big thank you to our publishers, Amalion Publishing and its Director, Sulaiman Adebowale. Last but not the least, our thanks go to our families, Bheki and I. Many times, Florence and our children in my case have wondered whether this book will ever be finished and have bravely endured endless hours of reading and re-reading different iterations of the contributions. Thank you for your patience, support and affection.

Tade Akin Aina
New York, May 2012

INTRODUCTION

There is almost never a perfect time for a book. Yet, this book is being published at the right time in Africa's history and context. Today it is almost a cliché to say 'Africa is rising and Africa is more than ever, a destination for investment'. Almost all projections, even by the most pessimistic rating agencies, point to a very bright Africa – an Africa that has become the least risky region for investments, an Africa with a young population and an Africa with fast growth rates and an increasingly growing middle class. All these developments have major implications for philanthropy in Africa.

A decade ago, the landscape was different. Certainly the appetite for African philanthropy was very low and there were few structures that promoted African philanthropy. Today there are different forms of philanthropic institutions and cultures across Africa. One major development has been the establishment and formalization of the African Grantmakers Network (AGN) – a platform created to provide space(s) for collective action, innovation and best practice in African philanthropy. Launched in 2009, AGN has grown in stature and voice. As this book was going to press, the Network had just completed its second pan-African Assembly in Johannesburg focusing on 'Growing African Philanthropy' – a phenomenon I am increasingly referring to as 'African resources'. To be sure African philanthropy is about all resources – human, social, cultural, political, natural and financial among many others.

How these resources are utilized and shared as well as how they contribute to an equitable and socially just world are questions that this book, *Giving to Help, Helping to Give: The Context and Politics of African Philanthropy,* tackles from various traditions and experiences. Another fundamental question the book also explored is centred on the governance of society and the various mechanisms embracing features of solidarity, reciprocity and mutuality – all central tenets of accountability – that different societies have put in place.

The theme of governance speaks very loudly to today's societal challenges around the attainment of sustainable development. We are today engaged in discussions about the ways through which governance can be central to the post 2015 Millennium Development Goals. In our African context, how governance is practised and implemented depends almost entirely on available resources that support its implementation. It is for this reason therefore that we have chosen to pay special attention to the question of African resources in this book. I am convinced that African philanthropy (resources) is at the heart of questions around Africa's political economy and development. We cannot talk about African philanthropy without reference to land, natural resources, and their governance.

For a book conceived about eight years ago, the saliency of the discussion have been particularly prescient. The recent uprisings in Africa, particularly in North Africa and the Arab region due to what some have termed the lack of a governance of development, and the upsurge in dissatisfaction with the extractive industries in Africa, punctuated by the Marikana mine protests and killings as well as the Occupy Movement's attempt to stem the power of corporate Wall Street on the global stage, have brought back the question of resources and equity into currency across the world.

Although this book has undergone various revisions and updates since conception, it is inevitable that it has been difficult keeping statistical figures relevant and up to date and where possible some authors have tried to update their figures. Other authors have requested permission to publish some aspects of their chapters to seize what they saw as the right moment. Robert Muponde's chapter – "'I am well if you are well': Nervous Conditions of African Philanthropy in Tsitsi Dangarembga's Novels" was published in the journal *African Identities* in December 2011. While Mohamadou Sy and Ibrahima Hathie's chapter on 'Institutional Forms of Philanthropy in Francophone West Africa has been published as a report by the International Development Research Centre (IDRC). Thus in the process we have extended our reach beyond what was initially planned.

Through the years, what has become equally important for us is the journey that we have travelled in making this book. Tade Akin Aina states aptly in the *Preface*,

> there is a big story behind this book. For me the story is that of a coming together of various institutions and individuals to plant trees whose shades they might personally not sit under but will be used by generations still to be born. After all my vision for African philanthropy is to be forward looking and preemptive of some of the eminent changes.

Indeed, how I became a student of philanthropy by accident relate to this. I was researching for my doctoral thesis when I shared a panel with an American professor who kept referring to 'philanthropy'. I took an interest in her presentation for it spoke to the same issues that I was studying then but not calling them 'philanthropy'. After our panel, I asked for more details from the professor and it became clear to me that what I was researching was African philanthropy. I knew then that my doctoral thesis would mention the word 'philanthropy' even though the word was not in wider usage in my context then. As they say, the rest is history.

It is in this context that I say this has been a journey worth taking for a number of us. I look back to the years I started writing and talking about African philanthropy when there was little written and marvel at what has changed. Back then there were no sources of data on African philanthropy nor were there any courses offered by institutions of learning on 'civil society', later alone philanthropy; and more importantly African philanthropy. Today we now have a sizeable body of literature in the field. We have moved from philanthropy has a way of life on the continent to having institutions that have been developed particularly to promote philanthropy and increasingly we are seeing more and more of such institutions by rich Africans and celebrities (musicians, artists, sport personalities, etc) as well as former heads of state and government.

The book charts the various phases that the field has gone through in Africa and much more to tell a story of solidarity, mutuality and reciprocity among Africans. It is not a story about financial figures or transactions only – important as these are. It is primarily a story of various beginnings and experiences across Africa. As readers will discover, almost all authors in the book find a need to first define what philanthropy is before addressing its form, character and expressions. This is an indication that we are grappling with a phenomenon that still needs more detailed discourses. In some regions such as West and Central Africa, authors struggled with finding data and material for their chapters – an indication of the fact that this is a new field in those areas both in terms of theorization and practice. Yet in Southern and Eastern Africa, there is already a long tradition in institutional philanthropy and there exists also some literature which authors resorted to. These varieties offer possibilities for further research for academics interested in furthering the field but also possibilities for collaborations for those working in the field.

I therefore have no doubt in my mind that there can be no better time to publish a book on African philanthropy than today. As stated earlier, a lot has changed since the beginnings of this book in Jinja (Uganda) in 2004, particularly regarding statistics, data and some key figures (numbers, size, scope, finances etc), but a lot has also been consolidated and perhaps made even much more clearer for a better understanding of African philanthropy as it relates to other forms of philanthropy universally. Indeed, the growing literature and discourses on African philanthropy in the past decade has added to the understanding and positioning of African philanthropy internationally and among Africans themselves. The proliferation of research on the field has also been accompanied by a steady growth in the establishment of philanthropic institutions across Africa. In my chapter in this book, I discuss the philanthropic landscape in Africa, trends and innovations that have been developed in response to the context, particularly the perceptions about Africa having moved from pessimism to wild optimism. It was this optimism for a better Africa that kept all of us going.

A book like this would not be possible without collaborations and partnerships. Over the last eight years or so, I have worked with colleagues who have Africa in their hearts and minds. It was the Ford Foundation, particularly its Eastern Africa office, that brought a number of us together in 2004 to reflect on philanthropy in Africa. Some of the chapters in this book grew out of the meeting in Jinja. I want to pay special tribute to Tade Akin Aina, who at the time was the Ford Representative and went on to co-edit the book with me. Gerry Salole who was then the Ford Representative at the Southern Africa office invited me to write perhaps my first paper on African philanthropy. And of course Gerry continues to be my mentor today both in his capacity as Chair of TrustAfrica but also as an experienced leader in philanthropy. It is that paper that has kept me writing about this field for many years now.

I also want to recognize the role played by Jenny Hodgson, of the Global Fund for Community Foundations, who initially took the task of editing the first articles that were gathered for this book. I took over the project later on given what we were doing at TrustAfrica with our 'State of Philanthropy project'. Tade has paid tribute to a number of colleagues in the *Preface* whose names I shall not repeat here but save to say 'thank you all'. To the authors of various chapters, thank you so much for the dedication and patience especially for bearing with me for taking this long to finally publish the book. I kept coming back to you for one thing or the other. Without you, there would be no book to publish.

I also want to thank reviewers of individual chapters, especially Tsitsi Dangarembga who read Robert Muponde's chapter based on her two books – *Nervous Conditions* and *The Book of Not*. *Giving to Help, Helping to Give* underwent a rigorous review process particularly through the hands of David Owusu-Ansah, Professor of History and Special Assistant to the President for Faculty Diversity at James Madison University, USA. Professor Owusu-Ansah travelled the journey with me as we edited the various chapters. Thank you very much Prof. At TrustAfrica, I would like to extend special appreciation to Akwasi Aidoo who has steered TrustAfrica to where it is today. Akwasi has always given staff room to innovate and make a difference. I also want to thank my program and our operations colleagues who made the publication of this book possible. Of course this comes just after we published our first volume on the regulation of civil society in Africa, *(Dis) Enabling the*

Public Sphere: Civil Society Regulation in Africa. It is our hope that this book too will contribute towards policy changes, increased understanding of the field but more importantly towards equipping practitioners and theorists with the necessary tools for their trade. To Jeanne Elone and Harris Ayuk, thank you very much for your usual availability even at short notice to do even the most menial of tasks and for proof-reading earlier versions of the chapters. Fionna Chimpembere read through the chapters and compiled acronyms and identified areas that needed attention. Thank you. Laureen Bertin worked with me previously when we published *(Dis) Enabling the Public Sphere.* She availed herself one more time to copy edit and proof read some of the chapters in this book. And of course our publisher at Amalion Publishing, for taking on the task of bringing to the world one of the very first compilations of works on African Philanthropy. Thank you very much Sulaiman.

I also want to thank the IDRC for funding the West Africa chapter as well as for collaborating with us on many platforms where some of these chapters were presented. We collaborated with the IDRC at the last three International Society for Third Sector Research (ISTR) conferences in Barcelona (2008), Istanbul (2010) and Sienna (2012). In the same breadth I want to extend my gratitude to ISTR for affording TrustAfrica and African researchers on civil society and philanthropy a platform to reflect on their work. During the last three conferences, ISTR has availed to us a full day dedicated to African issues. The result of this has been a special Issue of the ISTR journal *VOLUNTAS* on 'Civil Society in Africa'. I want to thank Margery Daniels for this. The Kellogg Foundation funded the participation of researchers from Southern Africa at the ISTR Conference in Barcelona where some of these chapters were first presented. Last but certainly not least, Tade's family and mine had to bear the brunt of present but inattentive fathers. Our families are our strengths, thank you very much travelling with us all the time.

Bhekinkosi Moyo
October 2012

CHAPTER 1

THE STATE, POLITICS AND PHILANTHROPY IN AFRICA: FRAMING THE CONTEXT

TADE AKIN AINA

Introduction

Philanthropy, no matter how we define it and whatever form it takes, does not operate in a vacuum. It exists and it is expressed in a social and historical context. History, politics, culture and the economy all to a greater or lesser extent define and are defined by the varieties of philanthropic experiences found in any society or group(s) of societies. This is because the act of giving, either to help or transform, is an expression of political and economic relations. The acts and forms of giving are socially constructed and socially changed. They are often expressed and defined by how history has shaped the relationships between groups and individuals and consequently their social positions, access to and opportunities for wealth, as well as material and cultural goods, power and privilege. They are also further determined by the way values and norms of reciprocity, solidarity, charity and domination have been structured, defined, challenged and transformed. In other words, the acts and forms of institutionalized giving and the social relations they carry, are neither innocent nor neutral. They embody, and are implicated in, the economic, social and political structures in which they are found. They also express the basic relations and structures of domination and power in these societies. The philanthropic experience contributes either to re-affirming the structures they are found in, or to questioning the underlying values and norms that allow or define the positions of givers and receivers and produce the suffering, poverty and alienation that philanthropy then attempts to alleviate, palliate or eliminate.

In a fundamental sense, philanthropy is political. It is important that it is seen in its correct sense because such a realization in some ways explains its intricate, complex and often contradictory relationships with political, social, cultural and economic power(s). This chapter explores how acts and forms of giving in parts of Africa are the products and expression of the changing history, politics and economies of Africa and how these different factors driven by both external and internal influences have affected the development of what is broadly termed today as 'philanthropy' in Africa. In doing this, the context is framed and questions are raised. The questions include: How do we situate and explain the relationships between philanthropy and the state and society in Africa today? How do we explain the often complex and contradictory relationships engendered by processes and institutions whose origins had been transformed in a wide variety of ways depending on location, time and political and economic circumstances?

The chapter paints a broad overview of the evolution and changing character and forms of philanthropy in Africa. It also, by situating the different forms and expressions in their specific contexts, attempts to explain or question the prevalence of dominant patterns and forms. But there is need for clarity on this. This is because all the major notions of interest in this chapter can be said to be both complex and in many ways contested. As part of this immediate task, it is important to begin with the geopolitical coverage of Africa. The geopolitical entity that is Africa is complex and diverse – culturally, ecologically, economically and politically. This diversity applies to how different forms of political and social organizations that exist at different places across the continent have changed over time. These range from societies organized as pastoralist to agrarian; absolute monarchies to tributary states and/or organized within varying degrees of complexity as segmentary lineages, age grades, age sets and village societies; to simpler forms of organization of hunters and gatherers (see Middleton, Tait and Bohannan 1958; Fortes and Evans-Pritchard 1970).

As with geographical locations of groups, Africa has been the site of many 'great migrations'. Multiple forms of political organizations, cultures, languages and even the historical and cultural transitions vary. Any meaningful reference to what constitutes Africa must therefore be located in its shifting historical and geopolitical contexts. Given this important point, it is obvious that this chapter cannot provide comprehensive coverage of what we refer to here as the 'African experience'. What is done, however, is to recognize the limited nature of both available knowledge and research on the evolution of philanthropy in Africa. Such a premise helps to provide the beginnings of analyses and raises questions and issues that can provide a basis for further research and the development of the subject as a field of study. To do this effectively, it is necessary to step back and clarify the concepts of state and politics and the place of philanthropy therein.

State and politics

The 'state' and 'politics' are closely interrelated notions that refer to specific institutions, practices and actions around the organization and deployment of institutionalized power and domination in society. However, attempts to understand them are often coloured by ideologies and political beliefs that in several instances lead to theories and conceptualizations that are faulty and not universally applicable, because the theories and concepts themselves are subject to challenges such as ethnocentricity and are often biased towards western models and thinking about what these institutions and practices are or should be (Mustapha 2006). According to Mustapha (2006:3), the state is the organization of public power. This is a definition that recognizes the centrality of the state in the arrangement, the deployment of power and domination, and the attendant social relations in the public arena. It also presupposes the understanding that there are collective players such as social and political groups located at different points within the hierarchy of the socioeconomic structure which work through different institutional mechanisms such as political parties, voluntary associations, ascriptive political organizations based on criteria of birth, age, sex or race, and/or other structures of domination expressed in different modes of governing. These different players conduct 'politics' – in other words, they undertake the struggles for control of the means whereby power is used, or/and occupy an advantageous position in the relations and structures of power and domination. This is often about power relations or the control of strategic resources, both material and human (Aina 1997:419). As Mustapha (2006) has pointed out, the nature of such politics and their outward manifestation has changed in Africa since colonial times, although its underlying pattern of domination has not significantly changed.

However, within the realm of politics, there are counterpoints that themselves also constitute political struggles. These challenge the tendency towards domination and they need to be pointed out here. The counterpoints include the struggles for emancipation and freedom from real or perceived domination, repression and exploitation. Of course there is also resistance, the struggles that emanate from a refusal to surrender or submit to the structures of domination and exploitation. Resistance takes many forms and can be covert or overt, direct or indirect or even involve the construction of an entirely alternative 'public' and world view from that of the formal ruler or colonizer (Ekeh 1994), that becomes a systematic form of subversion of dominant power and authority.[1]

The struggles for domination, resistance and emancipation often take place at the formal institutional levels, but the terrains of such actions extend beyond the formal publics to arenas that are informal and less structured than the domains of government and the state. Therefore, when considering domination and resistance, we often find different layers of formal and informal expressions that different social actors use to structure their multiple realities. Because politics expresses, defines and often represents the nature, dynamics and contradictions of forms and levels of social order, it is an important element of all institutions and social relations, and, as will be seen, it is an important element for philanthropy.

Philanthropy

The question then is, when referring to 'philanthropy' in Africa, what comes to mind? Is it the act of giving, the vehicles of giving, the social relations of giving and assistance, or the more recent arena of voluntary development actors? It is important to ask these questions because, like the notions of the state and politics, there are ambiguities and inconsistencies in understanding the notion. These are further complicated by the dominance of the current era of non-governmental organizations and what has been called civil society organizations. This dominance is actually a more recent occurrence and is in fact limited in terms of its coverage and its relevance for the majority of ordinary African people. What the literature reveals is the changing nature of the use of the notion of philanthropy, from a wide range of forms and acts that embodied the act of charitable giving, to the current functionally specific forms of foundations and trusts (Hall 2006). As in the definition of the state and politics, the attempts to reduce philanthropy to a uniform single expression of the acts and forms of giving and assistance reveals the ethnocentric and teleological thrust of predominantly Western-influenced authors and users.

The notion and practice of philanthropy extends beyond the institutional forms or vehicles that are often seen as the sole defining character. The point here is that philanthropy is best seen and understood not only in terms of the vehicles of delivery but equally in terms of the relations it embodies and the social actions it expresses. According to Schervish (1998:600), an important scholar of the subject: 'Philanthropy is the social relations of care in which individuals (and groups) respond to the moral invitation to expand the horizons of their self-interest to include meeting the needs of others.'

This definition is particularly useful because it does not restrict philanthropy to one institutional or monolithic form or act, as is often found in our modern-day foundations, or to its expression through wealth alone, but rather locates the realm of philanthropy in the acts and modes of giving and 'care' in response to the needs and wants of the underprivileged in society. It therefore does not restrict the definition of philanthropy to the contemporary clichéd notions of 'private giving for the public good' or the deployment of 'private wealth for public benefit'. Again, as positive and meaningful as such sound-bite definitions are, these are extensively contested ideas such as the 'public' and the 'private', as well as the further loaded meaning that accompanies the notion of 'wealth'. In fact, Schervish is uncompromising about what he terms the defining characteristics of philanthropy:

> [I]t is in the social signals it responds to rather than in some formal institutional characteristics such as its tax status, its normative attributes such as being voluntary, or its particular goal such as service to the public good … philanthropic activity is mobilized by the medium of moral or cultural capital in the form of symbolic expression of need (Schervish 1998:600–1).

Proceeding from Schervish (1998), philanthropy is understood as the social relations of care expressed in a diversity of forms and acts of giving through which individuals or groups transcend their self-interest to meet the expressed or recognized needs of others. From the perspective of this definition, it is obvious that we are referring to a phenomenon that is found in many societies where the moral and/or cultural capital include the elements of compassion, solidarity, reciprocity and care in giving to and assisting others. This recognition takes us beyond the sociology of associational life to the wider arena of the social relations of assistance and institutionalized giving.

In relation to politics and the state, philanthropy is the terrain of the social relations of the acts and forms of institutionalized giving and care as derived from the needs of others. It is often intrinsically connected to the nature and dynamics of the dominant social and political order, either through contributing to maintaining and stabilizing it by alleviating and palliative measures, or through questioning its underlying structural inequities through transformational and, at times, subversive and critical interventions. In some cases, we find that the two thrusts of philanthropy, the palliative and the transformational elements, are not mutually exclusive and can be found expressed in the same philanthropic act or form, simultaneously and, at times, sequentially.

By understanding philanthropy in the way we have done, it is possible to see the wider context and range of the ways in which the philanthropic domain interacts with the political domain beyond the mere regulatory functions of the state and governments. We are also able to see philanthropy beyond one specific culturally defined dominant form, lens or institution. We can see its expression across cultures, societies and historical periods. This is the argument that most of the authors in this volume make as they attempt to understand the changing forms of the philanthropic experience in Africa. It is to this context that we now turn to examine what drives it and its changing forms.

Framing the context

Three key elements significantly frame the context of philanthropy in Africa. The first is the general category of needs and wants as expressed in the phenomenon of poverty, thus defining how vulnerable to adversities or how materially deprived individuals and groups are, and what kinds of response mechanisms and social protection and assistance exist for them in their respective societies. The second is the category of injustice and inequality, embedded in the ways many societies are structured and the concomitant social exclusion of many individuals and groups from access to resources that ensure the provision and reproduction of their basic needs and the assurance of their human dignity, for example rights. The third element is the nature of the integration of the societies under discussion into the wider world, either through the ways they are structurally inserted into the global system or through forms of interaction and exposure that can be traced to their experiences of conquest, colonization and other types of relationships of collective domination and participation. This external reality is often the source of imposition or adoption of new ways of seeing and doing things and organizing, including both the political and philanthropic realms. This leads to situations where individual and collective needs are expressed in terms of want and deprivation for which the philanthropic response can be palliative.

Needs can also be expressed as social and or economic inequities and injustices. In such cases, the philanthropic response includes attempts to address root causes and it goes beyond mere alleviation. In this case, philanthropy is transformational. The external factor also often contributes to the distinction between indigenous and foreign forms of interventions and social relations and the emergence of hybrid forms. Hybrids emerge when internal forms and experiences combine with external ones to produce new forms and ways of doing things. In the development of the philanthropic experience in Africa, these new forms can create truly genuine and autonomous forms of philanthropic intervention. Indeed, some of the modern-day practices in philanthropy in Africa are hybrids of pre-colonial and colonial social relations, organizations and practices and their modern adaptations. However, in order to effectively analyze the interaction of the three elements and what emerges as political and philanthropic outcomes, we need to recognize the differences and diversity that are defined by time and place. Periodization or the identification of determining historical periods therefore becomes an important additional element in tracing and situating these developments.

Periodizing the evolution of state, politics and philanthropy relations in Africa

State, politics and philanthropy relations in Africa are neither monolithic nor similar across the continent. The evolution of the institutions and how they are related varied with the history and place of the different societies in Africa. Another important aspect of the variety in the evolution has to do with how internal structures and institutions interacted with significant external forces. Indeed these interactions, such as the noteworthy events of the slave trade and the colonization process, had a significant influence on the political and economic developments in the history of the continent.

Colonization is a major watershed in the history of African societies and can be used here as a defining boundary for establishing key periods of African economic and political developments. Proceeding along these lines that highlight the importance of the colonial experience in African history, it is possible to identify the following periods: the pre-colonial period, the colonial period, the period of independence and national development, and the current period of economic liberalization and globalization.

This periodization applies to most parts of the continent in most of its details, with the exception of a few national societies which, although they never experienced formal colonial rule, were nevertheless either subjected to attempted conquests by European powers or were incorporated into their spheres of influence. Examples of such national entities are the Kingdom of Ethiopia and the repatriated slaves' Republic of Liberia. The analysis in this chapter will be guided by the defining characteristics of this periodization and how the societies themselves were organized, both in relation to, and in response to, important events and dynamics in the periods.

State, politics and philanthropy relations

The terrain of state, politics and philanthropy relations has been studied more from the perspective known as state–civil society relations or state–NGO relations (non-governmental organizations) (see, for example, Ngunyi and Gathiaka 1993; Hulme and Edwards 1997; and Kiondo and Nyang'oro 2006.) However, the terrain is not limited to either the narrow domain of philanthropy or the wider one of civil society. In its existing situations, it includes sectors such as politics, the economy, and the communities and social groups at play in society (Cohen and Arato 1994; Chandhoke 2007). Within this wider interplay we see that the state, politics and philanthropy interact in a context that is continuously changing. The transformation is due to the changing nature of politics and society and how these are defined by the interactions of social groups and communities, as well as other political groups and the state. Of course, this interplay is also affected by external factors such as the nature of the international and global economy and political influences.

While all these factors affect and drive the relations between the state, politics and philanthropy in different societies in Africa, it is important to point out the nuanced elements of the diversity and variety of philanthropic experience in each particular context and the extent, density and proliferation of different philan-thropic forms. An overview of these will be appropriate here.

What is often referred to as 'indigenous philanthropy' comprises local grassroots giving and care built on internally derived practices of mutual aid, reciprocity, solidarity and social obligations. These are often expressed in rudimentary organi-zational forms and are not significantly structurally different from other institutions of lineage, kinship or ethnic affiliation. They are also not functionally specific in being singularly devoted to offering care and assistance, but rather perform several functions, ranging from those that are in convivial and leisure groups to those in economic and occupational activities such as guilds and trade, small-scale credit, and craft associations. There are also those that carry out healing and religious or spiritual cult activities deriving from pre-colonial conventional spiritual cults, heal-ing societies and occasionally syncretistic religious groups organized at micro-scale in villages and towns. They offer healing, succour, sanctuary and volunteer support for their members and others in need. Most of these structurally undifferentiated forms of philanthropic expression are not specific only to Africa; forms such as these have been identified in the evolution of the philanthropic experience of other societies, see Hall (2006) for the experiences of the United States).

These groups tend to be more or less effective with regard to their delivery of care and support in relation to the social needs of their constituencies, and are exemplified by mutual aid groups, burial societies, healing societies, grassroots trade associations, the local credit associations that are precursors of today's micro-credit movement, and convivial groups. They often meet their constituents' needs horizontally in terms of relationships between equals and peers. This ele-ment has come to be the predominant character of what has been called 'African philanthropy', as pointed out by various writers, and in this volume by Ngondi-Houghton and Wilkinson-Maposa. Given the contemporary situation in the evo-lution of philanthropic experience in Africa, it is best described as 'grassroots or 'bottom-up' philanthropy.

There are also the more or less complex associational forms more often con-nected to the coming of the colonial era. This era gave rise to a complex mix of grassroots initiatives and emerging hybrid experiences. Some of these were grafts of the indigenous experiences with externally introduced forms from a variety of sources such as Islamic, Western European or oriental/Asian origins. This broad category includes diverse forms such as home-town associations, village develop-ment groups, church and mosque charity groups, social service or leisure clubs, and the more contemporary charitable trusts set up by families and individuals, politicians, entrepreneurs and business persons, such as the East African Asian philanthropists that were well chronicled by Gregory (1992).

Another group of philanthropic actors is composed of foreign transplants with distinctive and more intentionally structured organizational forms, values and practices. These were set up specifically as charitable organizations, relief organizations and as human development organizations promoting volunteering, public service and duty. They include the Boy Scouts movement, the Rotary and Lions Clubs, the 'Y' Movement for youth, and relief organizations such as the Save the Children Fund and the Red Cross. Iliffe (1987:199), in his study of the history of the African poor, discussed the role and relations of some of these relief, welfare and service institutions with the African poor in the early days of colonial rule.

There were also the functionally specific international philanthropic groups and large private voluntary organizations. The key philanthropic institutions, mainly the private foundations that began operating in Africa during the colonial period, such as the Carnegie Corporation of New York, the Ford Foundation, the Kellogg Foundation and the Rockefeller Foundation, engaged in interventions that promoted research, scholarships and education. These philanthropic foundations were also involved in the provision of technical assistance and capacity- and institution-building for economic and social development in the early period of independence. They supported a wide range of activities addressing the alleviation of poverty or the promotion of social policy. In the more recent post-colonial era, these foundations have addressed issues relating to human rights and social justice. Of the private voluntary organizations, there were the relatively larger organizations such as CARE, PLAN International, Africare and World Vision, many of whom came to play a larger role in relief work, service delivery and development contracting in Africa in the late colonial and post-colonial eras. These were all important players, co-existing in different mixes depending on the specific context and location.

Most of these international organizations – including the conventional foundations, the different operational agencies of the United Nations, the wide array of multilateral financial institutions such as the World Bank, and the regional development banks and bilateral agencies that are mainly aid institutions of European and North American governments – have come to be broadly grouped under the highly contestable notion of 'donors'. This is because their 'giving' is seen as non-reciprocal and unidirectional, while African nations, governments and communities, on the other hand, have been seen mainly as recipients and beneficiaries of aid and philanthropy, without giving back. This is neither true nor real and serves only to reinforce myths of African helplessness and relative lack of agency in finding solutions to the problems that confront them.

Proceeding from the changing nature of these interplays between the state, politics and philanthropy, and building on previous work (Aina 1997:427), the state, politics and philanthropy relations may be broadly classified as follows:

- Co-operative / supportive relations;
- Coercive / oppositional relations;
- Neutral / indifferent relations.

This broad classification of the range of relations is not evaluative, since relations and interactions can be either negative or positive and can at times be indifferent and/or neutral, depending on the nature of the state and the dynamics of politics. Hulme and Edwards (1997:11) in their work on state, NGO and donor relations provided an elaboration of the use of these classes: 'This conceptualization views relationships between NGOs, States and donors in terms of bargaining and nego-tiation, although at times coercion is a possible strategy'.

The relations between the state and the non-governmental sector in general involve strategies of bargaining and negotiations and of course coercion, strug-gles and resistance. A wide range of relations is possible under the broad classes provided here. As stated in an earlier work:

> Under co-operative/supportive relations we can have promotive, integrative and co-optative interactions … Under coercive/oppositional relations we can include hostile, repressive, adversarial, extractive, competitive and exploitative interac-tions, while the class of neutral and indifferent interactions includes deliberate or unconscious neglect, ignorance, or inadequate knowledge about the other party or the sheer lack of capacity to do anything with or for the other party (or parties) (Aina 1997:427).

These patterns of relations and their points of intersection with the different key institutions of interest here are expressed within the context of the defining moments of the periods as stated above, namely pre-colonial, colonial, independ-ence, and the post-independence era of liberalization and globalization. We also need to remind ourselves that the relations and points of intersection are not unilateral, simple or consistent at all times and in all places, even within the same society. They vary with the types and scales of philanthropic experience, the loca-tion, whether rural or urban, and the extent of linkages with the external world, its politics and its economies.

The pre-colonial period

Discussing the range of philanthropic experiences in pre-colonial Africa is very often limited by the absence of data and available historical records. However, there is excellent analysis available, not directly focused on philanthropy in all cases, from which a broad picture may be extracted. The works of Feierman (1998), Iliffe (1987) and Ekeh (1994) all provide useful insights and starting points for more in-depth examination. We utilize aspects of these contributions here and from them extract patterns of the relations during the pre-colonial period. It is important to note, however, that of these three authors, only Fierman focused explicitly on the philanthropic experience. Ekeh was discussing the evolution of public finance and the public realm in Africa, while Iliffe's concern was with the history of the African poor. Even so, each author provided significant insight into the evolution of philanthropic experience and its relations with the state and politics at the time. Feierman perhaps provides the necessary cautionary point about the data, given the paucity of written sources on this period of the philanthropic experience.

In a seminal article that significantly questions the often ethnocentric and western conceptions of philanthropy and philanthropic organizations, Feierman relates the phenomenon to the social relations of assistance, noting the multiple and shifting nature of publics, the importance of reciprocity and solidarity in the process of giving, and the often extensive social continuity between individual and personal giving. Feierman also stressed the face-to-face personal relations and the relatively limited social distance that often accompanies collective and institutional assistance in societies of this period in Africa. Feierman identified four principal forms of giving and assistance, namely:

- those based on kinship reciprocity;
- giving through associations such as ritual and healing societies;
- assistance provided through institutions such as shrines and sanctuaries; and
- religion-based charity, predominantly alms giving (by rich and poor alike) found in early Christianity and Islam in parts of Africa.

In all of these, Feierman understood both the implicit and explicit politics involved in giving and assistance. These included:

- issues related to the preservation of dominance and privilege;
- the existence of patronage and patron–client relations around chiefs, men of power and wealth (the African 'big men');
- the protection of the weak in certain societies against the misuse and abuse of power through philanthropy-like institutions such as sanctuaries and shrines, that provided safe havens with some kind of 'immunity' from political harassment, along with assistance and help; and generally,
- the asymmetrical power relations that exist between the giver and receiver but mitigated in different circumstances by the norms and practices of solidarity, obligations and reciprocity.

The role of the state and its relations to politics took different forms depending on the nature of the public organization of political power. In centralized systems with overt and sharply differentiated political institutions, the state, in the form of monarchies and kingdoms, regulated and guaranteed the security of institutions such as sanctuaries, healing cults and societies, shrines, churches and mosques. They also defined the regulation of practices related to care, alms-giving and donations such as *sadaqat*, *waqf* and *zakat* in the Islamic societies, and the place of religious institutions in providing care, such as in the case of pre-colonial Kingdom of Ethiopia aptly discussed by Iliffe (1987). In the case of acephalous, less centralized and concentrated political systems with less differentiated organization of public power, institutions such as lineages, age grades and sets regulated and organized social relations and were the basis of kinship-based reciprocity, obligations and solidarity. This did not mean that the less centralized societies did not manifest hierarchy and social stratification as well as poverty and severe social exclusion – they did.

Iliffe (1987), in demonstrating the empirical sophistication and attention to detail of the accomplished historian, provided us with the evidence of the history of the relations and politics of care of the poor in Africa. In examining the Islamic-dominated societies of the African Sahel, the Christian Kingdom of Ethiopia, the pastoralist societies of Eastern and Southern Africa and the sophisticated and complex societies of the Igbo and Yoruba of Western Africa, Iliffe's tapestry of the conditions and care of the poor is multi-coloured and multi-layered. It is a narrative that makes no attempt, except in its theme, to seek the consistencies of social actions and practices in these societies, highlighting the contradictions and amalgam of exploitation, political expediency and at times cruelty along with the compassion, religious injunctions, obligations and reciprocity contained in these societies. He pointed out how varying forms of politics excluded the poor and the needy but, equally, how culture and religion provided care, sanctuary from persecution and want, and in some cases opportunities for social mobility and incorporation for the marginalized such as slaves and outcasts. Of course, the work did not escape being a European narrative of these conditions and one often comes across nuancing and interpretation that would have benefited from a more robust engagement of the 'non-colonial library' that oral sources or other primary African sources – as embodied in manuscripts in Amharic, Arabic or other African languages that can be found in Timbuktu and other depositories in East and Sahel Africa – would have provided.

Ekeh (1994) provided the necessary explicit link with the organization of state power, the public realm and the adaptive mechanisms of resistance and social reconstruction of care and assistance that one later found in the colonial and post-colonial societies. Building on the landmark contributions of his earlier works on 'Colonialism and the Two Publics in Africa', Ekeh (1975) showed the relationship of pre-colonial politics and the state for the emergence of the individual, the public realms and public finance in Africa. He showed how the slave trade and the consequent organization of social and political life in terms of slave raids, wars and insecurity, and the externalization of economic relations, affected African pre-colonial political systems and the place of the individual in society.

For Ekeh, these were not innocent and necessarily idyllic societies to be romanticized but rather terrains of conflicts and conquests, domination and resistance for long periods entering in to centuries. Politics in these societies was not often the communitarian or communal relations often invented in the writings and imagination of many writers. Also, most of the economies were driven by want and large numbers of poor people seeking refuge from externally-induced wars and raids and often existing in situations of dislocation and vulnerability to ecological and political disasters. This was the context of most eighteenth and nineteenth century African societies, ravaged by centuries of Transatlantic and trans-Saharan slave trade, European trade wars and conquest expeditions, and deeply weakened and disoriented on the eve of Western colonization (Ekeh 1994:237–9). This period and its highlights are significant because of the continuities, adaptations and of course the transformations from them that colonial societies involved. It is also helpful in seeing the linkages between the various forms of 'indigenous philanthropy', assistance and care, their organization, politics and the cultures of counter-publics and resistance that emerged from Africa under colonialism. The facts of mass poverty and the evidence of continuous systematic dislocation and disruption of the patterns of economic and political evolution of many parts of Africa in the pre-colonial era explain some of the processes and modes of organizing that we see later in the colonial and contemporary periods in Africa.

The colonial period

Although the ideologies of the Western colonizers in Africa proclaimed the 'pacification of Africa' and a 'civilizing' and westernizing mission, the result of the colonization enterprise at its onset comprised mainly conquests, wars and desolation (Zeleza 1993). Colonization involved the re-organization of societies and economies for colonial production in plantations, mines, and peasant agriculture and coerced public works to build colonial infrastructures in many parts of Africa. These dislocations and reorganizations created new forms of production, livelihoods, resistance movements, allegiances, co-optations, collaborations, coerced responses and different kinds of urban living and relations from the pre-colonial existence. Thus, apart from the importation and adaptation of foreign forms of care and assistance, Africans had to invent and re-invent modes of adaptation to their new conditions, resulting in extensive adaptations, new creations and, in many cases, the hybridization of values, practices and institutions. While old needs and vulnerabilities were in many cases exacerbated, new needs and wants arose as part of these dislocations, adaptations and transformations. Philanthropy, as the organization and relationship of care and social assistance in relation to needs, also changed, and was adapted and re-invented in a variety of forms.

In discussing the colonial experience, Feierman (1998:21) noted that:

> The political context of philanthropy changed radically during the years after co-lonial conquest, and so the forms of philanthropy necessarily changed also. Colo-nizing Europeans attacked all forms of autonomous African power. To the extent that they succeeded they brought an end to independent authority of big men and lineage heads, chiefs and kings, powerful healers and shrine mediums. After colonial conquest ... philanthropic institutions ... were transformed. The centralization of power under European government control led to the redefinition of the fields of political force within which ordinary people lived their lives.

The colonizers also introduced or expanded the presence of new and 'foreign' players and communities into the African context and constructed new structures of dominance, wealth, power and privilege. Apart from bringing European settlers and western forms of philanthropic practice, they also brought with them new cultural and racial groups such as the Asians in Eastern Africa (Gregory 1992) and the Syrians and Lebanese (Levantines) in Western Africa (Crowder 1968:293–8) as labour, merchants, civil servants, teachers and other types of intermediaries. The new groups brought with them their customs, cultures and religions and also their own philanthropic practices.

It must be reiterated that for the 'native' Africans the colonial experience was not all about surrender and submission to European rule – there was much adap-tation and 'hidden forms of resistance' that expressed themselves in new forms of organizing urban colonial life, in the emergence of syncretistic religious movements and the construction of new political organizations and symbols. The narratives of European anthropologists on colonial urban life, voluntary associations and social networks were testimony to the resilience and innovations of the colonized ordi-nary Africans who reorganized to resist, support and encourage each other as they encountered the new colonial societies (Little 1965; Mitchell 1969).

Ekeh (1994:240) provided an impressive description of the relationship between the emergent colonial state and African society and individuals:

> But the relationship between the emergent colonial state and African society was distant. First, the colonial state did not crave nor need the values from indigenous African societies for its existence. On the contrary, it sought its legitimation from justifying its conquest on grounds that African societies were primitive and needed re-shaping – a point of view pressed home by its companion Christian missions. The colonial state was virtually *a deus ex machina,* looking down somewhat con-temptuously on African societies from its Olympian heights. Second, from the other side, Africans regarded the colonial state along with its alien functionaries

with ambivalence. There were indeed no moral linkages between the colonial state and African societies.

Ekeh points out that, as a result of this distance and alienation, the African retreated to the 'world' of his native ethnic group and kinship system for his 'political and cultural spaces'. From these spaces, the African constructed some of the important social formations we know today. Either as hybrids or inventions, this is most likely one of the plausible origins of some of the institutions that provided care and social assistance to African peoples and communities in the colonial era, such as the 'mutual aid' groups, the 'merry-go-rounds', the 'burial societies' and 'hometown associations' that authors such as Moyo in this volume refer to.

Ekeh's (1994:240–1) main concern was to show the construction of an alternative public realm by the colonial African. This 'public' he called the 'primordial public'. This was an alternative locus of cultural and moral organizing with its own social and economic validation and political legitimacy. This public provided the colonial subject's 'counter-public' and helped to mobilize resources for care, social assistance and what came to be called development projects such as the provision of scholarships and the construction of public amenities and utilities in their home towns. For Ekeh, the terrain of the colonial public also explained the colonial subject's resistance to the coercive colonial public taxation system that was seen as alien and exploitative. The alternative public provided a different domain for the Africans and a different platform for levying contributions for projects that were defined as more relevant and related to the communities' defined needs.

We see examples of this today not only in the contributions to self-defined 'harambees' and the horizontal fundraising of communities through contemporary African foundations such as the Kenya Community Development Foundation (KCDF) (Lukalo-Owino 2008c), but also in discussing how community members are levied for contributions – or what in today's parlance is known as fundraising and resource mobilization – for these ventures, where Ekeh introduced the idea of 'community and ethnic taxes'. He located these actions in the realm of the alternative or primordial public finance. For anyone familiar with the community fundraising mechanisms of African voluntary associations or the levying by community fund builders so well described by Lukalo-Owino in her book on the KCDF, we can see that these actions are more in the terrain of 'local philanthropy' than that of 'public finance', even where such may carry undertones of community pressure.

Ekeh (1994:242), however, expressed the following view:

> What makes the political sociology of colonialism so remarkable is that such methods of colonial taxation provoked a parallel form of taxation that has the full attributes of contributions by citizens rather than impositions by a superordinate colonial authority. The colonized Africans were busy making their own arrangements

with their kinsfolk on how best to protect themselves from dangers arising from circumstances they did not fully understand, and how to improve their community and collective fortunes in the new world of colonialism. Taking advantage of the new colonial cash economy, many communities and whole ethnic groups taxed themselves to build schools, health facilities, and to award scholarships to their young members in efforts that in some instances, in southern Nigeria at least, rivalled or even surpassed the colonial taxes.

The phenomenon described above seems to be that of the 'home town' or 'village development association'. If that is the case, they definitely were more a part of 'philanthropy' than of 'public taxation', although they were operating from an alternative public than the colonial publics. Indeed, these associations performed many other social and political functions and had different relations to the state and politics in different parts of colonial Africa (Little 1965; Mabogunje 2000). When they built roads and hospitals and offered scholarships to community members, they were part of the colonial 'community development' project and were therefore acceptable to the colonial authorities in a set of collaborative and co-operative relations (Iliffe 1987:200–2).

When these groups became the platform for the mobilization of nationalist politics demanding political independence or expressing strong criticism of racial oppression or discrimination, the relations became hostile and oppositional. When they quietly performed social welfare functions, paying school fees and hospital bills, arranging burials, contributing to the expenses for school fees and childbirth, providing loans for businesses and international scholarships for worthy indigenes or even repairing the roofs of village schools, the relationships were often neutral and/or indifferent.

However, this last point requires an important qualification. The colonial era gave rise to several new forms and domains of indigenous participation in social life for Africans, including in politics. There was the co-optation of some groups and individuals into the colonial administration through various forms of appointment to public office or as colonial operatives and intermediaries. One such infamous appointment was the externally imposed position of chiefs, particularly among communities whose pre-colonial social structures did not include or define such hierarchies. These were the 'warrant chiefs', a phenomenon found across the colonies and well described by Afigbo (1972) for Southeastern Nigeria. In other examples, the *de facto* authorities and geographical domination of some of the pre-colonial traditional rulers, such as the Yoruba and Buganda kings, or the Hausa-Fulani Emirs, received recognition and validation even beyond their pre-colonial levels and boundaries.

Other forms of incorporation into the colonial administration included employment in the colonial forces – the army, police, prisons, customs and immigration, or as interpreters and court clerks. All of these positions defined an administrative collaborative status and, depending on how hostile the context was to the colonial project, Africans who held these positions had a wide range of relations and interactions with their communities. It must be said, however, that the British colonial authorities were shrewd when it came to the composition and use of the security forces. They often recruited from specific communities that were defined as being culturally fierce and warlike, who were then deployed to keep the peace and do policing work far away from their own homelands.

Colonial politics also produced new indigenous players in the form of an emerging breed of African politicians. These were in the main 'the nationalist politicians' and their precursors who fought the colonizers and demanded independence and self-rule for the African countries. These politicians, in challenging the colonial civic public, mobilized their support from the primordial publics, religious bodies, trade unions, and the nascent African political parties. They also took advantage of local and indigenous associational life, cultural symbols and institutions, and social networks. These institutions helped the politicians and their parties with fundraising; organizing meetings and membership drives; sharing local information and intelligence; and providing clandestine sanctuary and safe havens when required, particularly during the 'wars of independence' such as the Mau-Mau period in Kenya or the nationalist struggles in Southern Africa. In many cases, these networks and institutions were more than they appeared. From the solidarity and philanthropic platforms of hometown associations, burial societies, *harambee*, religious voluntary associations, ethnic and pan-ethnic cults and secret societies, they provided political platforms and even organizational settings for the new struggles for resistance and/or incorporation that the colonial context demanded. Thus the lines between care and giving, social assistance and political organizing and activism were crossed many times during the period of the nationalist struggles in the colonial period. This is not a matter of great surprise, as the struggles were led at many levels by the same types of individuals who demonstrated great energy, important entrepreneurial skills, organizational competence, and a high degree of community engagement.

But the colonial setting was a diverse setting. As noted earlier, there were other groups, such as the Asians in Eastern Africa and the Levantines in West Africa. Gregory (1992) has provided a detailed chronicle of the extensive Asian philanthropy in Eastern Africa. In discussing the presence of Asian philanthropy, Gregory (1992:9) observed that:

> the persistence of private philanthropy is illustrated in the contrasting ideals of
> Gandhi and the Tatas, the one deeply spiritual, founded in Indian religious traditions,

and the other practical and pragmatic, a result of India's industrialization – provided two models of benevolence to the South Asian immigrants in East Africa. Because of the peculiar nature of the East African environment, as will be seen, most of the philanthropic leaders among the immigrants combined the two ideals. Contrary to the trend in other parts of the world, the pronounced transformation in ideology and methodology of assistance to the needy that was embodied in the welfare state and professional social work was to have very little impact on the East African Asians.

Indeed, Gregory's last sentence in the quote above applied to not only the South Asians of Eastern Africa, but also to most indigenous African populations. Thus individuals, groups and communities that fell into the dominated category of colonial subjects had to fend for themselves using hybrids of their own indigenous institutions and practices, as well as practices acquired through foreign contacts. For the Asians of Eastern Africa, who have been part of waves of migrations to the Eastern African coast dating back as far as the fifteenth century, religious mores and harsh economic conditions both at home and in Eastern Africa provided the motivation for self-help. 'Through self-help mostly in the form of voluntary monetary contributions, they provided on a rudimentary level most of their own educational, medical, social and recreational facilities and services' (Gregory 1992:37).

Furthermore, like the Africans, what constituted their philanthropic practices were hybrid, diffuse and not functionally specific, or specialized only in the delivery of philanthropy. It needs to be said that Asian philanthropy, given its long history at home and the fact that some of its institutions were established by wealthy persons and families, tended to be more focused on pure philanthropy than some of the smaller-scale indigenous African practices and institutions. They contained many similar features, such as being managed by family members, being driven by communal or indigenous values, and they were responses to the changing conditions and societies that the founders and beneficiaries of these institutions found.

For the Asians:

> there were many other Asian organizations concerned with philanthropy. They were designed primarily for other purposes and assumed charitable functions to meet needs that were not addressed by the colonial society ...Some organizations ... which served the Asian community at large and, in most instances, provided assistance also to Africans, Arabs, and Europeans without distinction of race or creed, were created especially for charitable purposes (Gregory 1992:47).

However, Asian philanthropy in Africa was political in many ways. Some aspects of it supported anti-colonial activities and raised funds to support the civil disobedience and passive resistance campaigns led by Gandhi in India and South Africa (Gregory 1992:82). Some of the leading philanthropists, such as Hassanaly Rattansi, were openly critical of the racial discrimination and colour bar that was a characteristic of the settler colonies of Eastern and Southern Africa (Lukalo-Owino 2008b:20–1). The relations of these with the colonial state were often ambivalent and not always consistent. They were co-operative when it was deemed necessary, but predominantly oppositional, particularly when it became clear that nationalist politics in some of the colonies was on the rise. Gregory (1992:56–7) identified these political links as:

> Being family trusts owned by wealthy families and individuals, some of the Asian philanthropists such as the Aga Khan, the Medhvanis, struggled to maintain a positive relationship with government. The leaders of the business families played prominent roles in the Chambers of Commerce and on the Boards of Government parastatals.

Thus the colonial setting provided a fertile ground for the flowering of Asian and African variants of the philanthropic experience defined by the conditions of colonial rule and caught up in the political and economic relations that were prevalent.

Apart from the Asian and African efforts at philanthropic giving, there were examples of work by European missionaries that continued with the charitable traditions of the religious groups (Iliffe 1987:195). There were also the beginnings of what Iliffe called 'secular institutional charity'. These included European international organizations that were engaged with philanthropy, but they did this mainly from the perspective of relief and/or the emerging notion and practice of economic development.

On the secular charities, Iliffe noted thus:

> Secular institutional charity was a colonial innovation but it grew slowly. Initially the flow of funds was from Africa to Europe. In March 1918, the British Red Cross was reported to have received over £50,000 from Nigeria. Only gradually was the pattern reversed. The Red Cross, founded in 1863, was the world's first international charity and the first to establish itself in Africa, where it appears to have initiated medical work after the First World War.

Other secular players in the field of care and social assistance during the colonial period included the North American private foundations such as the Carnegie Corporation of New York, the Ford Foundation and the Rockefeller Foundation. Along with the multilateral organizations of the newly created United Nations Organization, these offered social assistance but with an emphasis on the notion of 'development'. We turn now to 'development', as a notion that was and remains significant in framing the context.

Enter development

'Development', a nebulous and highly contested notion, entered the international public political parlance from around the end of the Second World War (Rist 2007:485) and from then on changed the language of transitions of nations and the thinking and practice of international philanthropy. Along with a variety of prefixes, such as 'social', 'economic', 'human', 'community' and 'sustainable', it has become one of the most widely used notions to describe in the main the transitions, or hopes about transition, of non-Western peoples to versions of Western modernity that assumes some degree of economic growth and productivity and the presence of an array of social, political and economic institutions predominantly modelled on the forms and values of Western capitalism. The weakness of capitalism to address inequality and economic exploitation or to effectively provide for the weak and marginalized led to the inclusion of further prefixes such as 'social' and 'human'. More recent recognition of the threats of unbridled capitalism to the earth's environment and ecosystem and its 'sustainability' has contributed to the addition of the popular prefix of 'sustainable' development. Theoretically, 'development' has undergone several critiques of its various forms and practices, their ideological and political underpinnings and their consequences for African society, economy and politics (Aina 1993). However, what is important in the understanding of the evolution of philanthropy is the powerful transformational project and imagery carried within this notion, and how it affected the deployment of both philanthropic and non-philanthropic resources in a new era of international assistance and aid that began with the end of the Second World War and the creation of the new United Nations Organization and its many agencies.

Indeed, both the UN and what can be called the 'development phenomenon' appeared on the world scene together, and 'development', along with peace and human rights, provided the United Nations with a raison d'etre. The idea of development was enshrined in the UN Charter in 1948, and the organization soon commissioned significant global reports on the world economy that were tremendously progressive for their time in attempting to address the key problems of labour relations, world trade, productivity, and the nature of economic underdevelopment. The UN was also central in promoting and disseminating some significant ideas that attempted to address the issues of national and international equitable development, such as the 'Basic Needs Approach' and the 'Redistribution With Growth' view.[2] The UN helped to promulgate and promote in 1961 what was known as the first 'Development Decade', and many of its key agencies carried forward the ethics, ideals, goals and practices of the different documents, outcomes of major global conferences and ideas that were enshrined in the development decades and after (Emmrij, Jolly and Weiss 2001; Ghai 2008). The driving force of the UN behind the development process and phenomenon provided the frame for the interventions of governments and philanthropies in Africa in the 1950s, 1960s and 1970s, culminating in the Millennium Development Goals of the early twenty-first century.

The 1980s and large parts of the 1990s were troubled periods for Africa with regard to its many economic and political crises. These problems, with considerable internal origins, did not help the development efforts of the countries on the continent but, as Ghai (2008:770) pointed out, the failures of the 1980s and 1990s were as a result of the international pressures on policies reflected in the dominance of right-wing economic orthodoxy:

> The 1980s marked as they were by the onset of the debt crisis and the Thatcher and Reagan policies that emphasized deregulation, privatization, the markets and the private sector constituted a severe setback to the UN agenda for development that evolved in the 1960s and 1970s. In the realm of ideas and policy, the center stage was occupied by stabilization and structural adjustment programs initiated by the Bretton Woods institutions. The UN agencies were largely eclipsed. They ended up either endorsing the policies of the financial agencies, or at best offering low key critiques of policies relating to debt servicing and stabilization.

We have paid some attention to some of the key highlights of UN ideas and interventions here because they constituted an important frame to the context of development thinking and practice and the whole terrain of 'development aid', which many aspects of philanthropy in Africa reacted to or constituted parts of, in terms of dominant trends and countertrends. The philanthropic experience in Africa in the colonial and post-colonial periods was influenced in many ways by development thinking and practices, in both its conventional and critical alternative modes.

Another element was internal to the development of the more functionally specific and organized philanthropic world. This had to do with the struggles to move from the pigeonholing of philanthropy within the realm of 'charity'. Development offered several philanthropic institutions the opportunity and rationale to move towards the notion and practice of 'strategic philanthropy' or 'scientific philanthropy', giving rise to a new professionalism and an emerging sector (Hall 2006:42). The new professionalism and focus in philanthropic practice in the early to mid-twentieth century in the United States initiated the debates on the distinction between helping people and solving problems as the main basis of difference between charity and philanthropy. 'Development' was largely associated with 'solving problems', perhaps of large-scale proportions.

Coleman (1995:11), in his posthumously published work on the experience of the Rockefeller Foundation in university development in the third world, has traced part of the impetus for American foundations to promote 'development' to the policy position stated in President Harry Truman's inaugural address of January 20, 1949 and 'the Four Point legislation' which emerged in 1950 with: 'its explicit and unqualified declaration that the economic development of under-developed areas was a national policy of the United States'. Coleman further stated that:

> The early pioneers in this endeavor were the American private philanthropic foundations. In 1926 the Carnegie Corporation initiated a program of support of educational development in British colonial Africa. By 1941 the Kellogg Foundation had commenced its program of fellowships in Latin America. And the giant of them all, the Ford Foundation came on stream with its Overseas Development Program in 1950. However, the major actor on a global basis since its founding in 1913 had indisputably been the Rockefeller Foundation (Coleman with Court 1993:11–12).

The adoption of a new kind of philanthropic work that is transformational, and that facilitates the transition of non-Western peoples from their poor and 'backward' situations to the nirvana of western capitalist modernity, both possessed an ideological allure and provided a professional anchor for the emerging distinction between 'charity' and philanthropy for the private foundations and the new field of practice. The four most important American foundations that carried out significant and important work in Africa had the twin elements of 'development' and the internal drive towards greater human relevance and grantmaking effectiveness as key motivations.[3]

For instance, in the case of the Ford Foundation work in Africa, Young (2003) situated it in the recommendations of the Gaither Report of 1949, which laid the framework for the Ford Foundation's subsequent programme restructuring. Young (2003:21) stated that:

> The trustees had specified that the study committee should devise a plan for future programming that reflected the trustees' sense that the time had arrived for the Foundation to shift its focus from ameliorating the effects of social problems to addressing their causes...

> This shift in the Foundation focus, begun in 1950, had by 1956 borne a good deal of fruit, not least in terms of geographic expansion. Until 1956, the year the Foundation sent its first mission to Africa, its connection to Africa was grounded in domestic programs, including International Affairs (IA) and International Training and Research (ITR).

These varying concerns between the different types and levels of philanthropic interventions and their engagement with the 'development' phenomenon defined their relations with the state and politics. This can be seen across the colonial and post-colonial periods in the activities of the large international private foundations, the interventions of the smaller local family foundations and voluntary associations, and the work of the village development and hometown associations. Alongside religious beliefs and values, as well as ethnic and cultural prerogatives, was always the factor of 'development', seen as human capital formation, collective self-help, individual transformation or the provision of services and facilities for communities. However, both in the colonial and post-colonial contexts, 'development' became a platform for what, in most cases, was a set of collaborative and co-operative relations between most of the philanthropic organizations, both local and international, and the post-colonial states. Oppositional and hostile relations resulted from 'doing development' in cases where intentionally marginalized and excluded communities, such as certain ethnic, cultural or religious groups, were assisted by their own autonomously organized institutions or by external bodies that not only reduced the impact of their exclusion but also drew attention to their plight. Such cases, examples of which are discussed in this volume by Bakari, often led to hostile relations between the state, the dominant political groups and the philanthropic organizations involved in providing such aid.

For the British colonial state, in their African and other colonies, 'development' either as economic development or community development was about colonial peoples helping to transform themselves or reduce poverty without much stress being placed on the British Exchequer. Iliffe showed that the British colonial authorities were not keen on social welfare in their African colonies until the 1930s and after the Great Depression. They left the care of the poor to the African indigenous care system, the Asian philanthropists, and the missionaries. However, from the 1937 riots in the West Indies, the whole issue of poverty and how best to address it gained a new political urgency and led to the start of rudimentary official colonial welfare activities. Most British experts felt the real problems in the African continent were the need for economic development and village improvement for the colonies. Furthermore, with the growing threat of the nationalist struggles for independence, fuelled by the success of India's independence and the collective confidence and reaffirmed sense of injustice by colonial subjects – who saw and in some cases fought in the Second World War on the side of the allies – the colonial rulers felt the pressing need to act to address poverty in the colonies.

Among the results was an emphasis on 'community development' (Iliffe 1987:201–2). In terms of politics, Iliffe pointed out that 'it (community development) merged easily into a "hearts and minds" strategy to wean colonial subjects away from emerging nationalist movements'.

Community development became a notion widely adopted even by the African colonial subjects, who adapted their indigenous philanthropic modes to raise funds and mobilize resources for its implementation in their villages. It remains a powerful notion, a point recognized by Iliffe (1987:201), who argued that:

> It must not be implied that community development was misconceived. It was a successful British invention which even the French imitated. But it had a price, and

that price was neglect of the very poor, who were those least able to take advantage of self-help programmes.

This weakness that Iliffe pointed out remains today and the need to effectively address it drives the multiple, diverse and often questionable array of interventions that have come to constitute the 'development process'. The rise and fall of the nationalists, the collapse of their nationalist projects, and the endless search for 'development' constitute the key elements for framing the evolution of philanthropy in post-colonial Africa.

The post-colonial period

Although authors like Ekeh have questioned whether any important changes occurred between the colonial and post-colonial contexts with regard to the functions of core institutions such as the state and the economy, in their colonial but slightly modified modes, it is important to recognize the fact of important transitions in the shift from one phase to the next. This fact does not deny continuities, but they were connections in which the interplay between inherited structures and emergent social agents provided spaces for political manoeuvres. The extent to which the spaces were taken or not taken and the reasons for these decisions and actions continue today to constitute the disputed annals of African contemporary history.

As has been highlighted in the discussions above, 'development', along with the struggle for political independence, can be seen as one of the frames that provided the bridge between the colonial and post-colonial periods. As soon as it was clear in the late 1950s that political independence for most of the colonies was on the horizon, the language of 'development' became a dominant discourse among the nationalist politicians, the new governments and the international agencies that supported them. Locked into this language and its varying, often ambiguous, practices were the different types of indigenous philanthropic efforts that attempted to address the needs of their constituencies as they perceived and defined them and as the available structures and politics allowed them. The chapters by Bakari and Yahya-Othman in this volume extensively address these experiences and the tensions that they embodied in the Tanzanian context. The Tanzanian experience is replicated in many different ways across the continent in the early post-independence period.

The post-colonial period cannot be understood without reference to the politics of the colonial transition and the process of constituting the post-colonial state and the economy. As already pointed out, the 'nationalist' political elites led the transition from the colonial to the post-colonial dispensation. They were a diverse and varied group of political leaders who formed alliances and coalitions with organizations of peasants, traders, workers, civil servants, teachers and even ex-soldiers of the colonial army to fight for formal political independence, and to take over the political system and occupy the apex of the structures of power, wealth and privilege that was vacated by the outgoing agents and functionaries of the colonial state.

There is substantial literature on the nature, dynamics and project of the colonial state in Africa and we need not provide a rendition of the exploitative, humiliating and often brutalizing social relationships embodied in the encounters of the majority of Africans with the colonial state. Indeed, as the colonial archives have become open to the public after the mandatory years of embargo, a new genre of literature by some non-African scholars has emerged about the painful history of brutality, violence and devastation wreaked on African societies in Kenya, Congo and the Horn of Africa (Wrong 2000, 2005; Hochschild 1998; Elkins 2005; Anderson 2005). It is these state structures and apparatuses that the nationalist elites took over, maintained and even perfected the use of, in building and consolidating their own political power, wealth and the search for a hollow prestige and legitimacy. In their transition to power, there was in most cases scarcely any statement or specification of the need to reform or reconstruct the state and politics, transform the economy and rebuild a society devastated by the ravages of colonial rule, the prevalence of poverty, disease and ignorance. Instead, the leaders chose to receive an uncritical notion of development and a less than democratic and inclusive leadership trajectory. As in the colonial period, the state sought to appropriate, manipulate, incorporate or exclude several key institutions, groups and modes of organizing available in society on a large scale. Philanthropy, particularly the indigenous forms utilized and promoted by a majority of the peoples, was not excluded from this process.

The Kenyan experience with *harambee*, an indigenous approach to self-help and mutual aid, is illustrative of this tendency. The story is that of the appropriation of an early colonial mode of communal self-help by the post-colonial politicians as a means of mobilizing 'development' and promoting political clienteles, patronage and corruption (Kanyinga 1995; Transparency International Kenya 2001; Wanyonyi 2004; Government of Kenya Task Force on Harambee 2003). However, what needs to be remembered was that the *harambee* ideal was an expression of the heady optimism that marked the nationalist transition from the colonial era into the era of early political independence, and the reclamation of collective self-confidence and hope manifested in the political project of the new indigenous elites.

This was also the era of the affirmation of African authenticity, marked by the statement of political vision and goals as found in the various testimonies and writings of the nationalist fathers such as Kwame Nkrumah, Julius Nyerere, Kenneth Kaunda, Obafemi Awolowo, Léopold Sédar Senghor, Jomo Kenyatta, Tom Mboya, Sékou Touré, and Nnamdi Azikwe. Most of these leaders, who were modernists in their orientation, sought added legitimacy from indigenous or nationalist ideologies of collective mobilization, self-reliance and nationalism as machines for pushing their nations forward and for their nation-building projects. *Harambee*, formally declared as a national 'approach' by President Jomo Kenyatta, was one such mobilizing and ideological mechanism, as was the '*Ujamaa*' of President Julius Nyerere or the African Socialism of Kenneth Kaunda of Zambia. The *harambee* approach was an affirmation of this kind of politics of culture. However, the nationalist project, particularly with regard to both its nation-building and economic development projects, was essentially flawed in certain basic aspects, and it was to encounter both political and economic crises at the end of the 1960s and the beginning of the 1970s.

The economic crisis was triggered by the decline in commodity prices and the petroleum oil price increases in the early 1970s, leading to severe balance of payments deficit and dwindling foreign exchange surplus crises for the economies. This led to a serious fiscal crisis of the state, resulting in its increasing incapacity to effectively fund development, either in terms of its commitment to the wide range of productive activities that the post-colonial state has become involved in such as the ownership of banks, factories, farms and plantations, or in terms of the extensive commitment to the provision of social services and utilities or subsidies to productive sectors in manufacturing and agriculture. As a result, the African states were not in a position to guarantee favourable economic returns and livelihoods to the majority of their citizens while simultaneously ensuring the incorporation of their growing urban middle and working classes into mainstream economic activities. This led to increased disillusionment on the part of the majority of the population, and growing protests by an increasingly vocal urban elite, students, workers and other groups within the new nationalist dispensation.

Just as crises developed on the economic front, so also were there signs of increasing problems in the political arena. The fiscal crisis of the state, an increasingly restive population, and the fragile consensus of an array of loose elite coalitions beginning to unravel, led to attacks on the flawed nation-building projects that were modelled around a seemingly homogeneous nation state of the European example. The nation-building strategy failed to recognize the plural make-up of most of the new African nations and the delicate ethnic and religious balance constructed from the colonial project that brought together many different nationalities in various combinations within newly defined geopolitical boundaries, but without the construction of a sufficiently organic whole or the building of a viable institutional framework for ensuring consensus, protecting and integrating minorities, and managing dissent and conflict.

The late 1960s and early 1970s saw what has been called the 'disintegration of the nationalist consensus'(Nyong'o 1989) and the gradual growth of authoritarian rule expressed in the one-party states and military regimes that were found all around the continent in the 1970s and 1980s. In the creation of the authoritarian regimes, all institutions of national engagement were appropriated and compromised in the pursuit of personal rule, political patronage and clientelism that sought to enshrine or perpetuate the post-colonial rulers.

With its institutionalization as a state project, the *harambee* system in Kenya became a victim of the mobilization and appropriation of the increasingly authoritarian and corrupt system that grew with the rise of political authoritarianism in Kenya. As students of the phenomenon have pointed out, the *harambee* approach in Kenya was one example of how the state, politics and philanthropy interacted in the process of social and political mobilization in an African context. As pointed out in the *Task Force Report of 2003*, there were different forms of *harambee* – namely, public, group and private. The public type was that in which collections were made and funds raised for public projects and the provision of social and other services. The private form involved people giving to help others who needed to pay for school fees, hospital bills, rites of passage such as burials, weddings and childbirth or any other such predominantly private needs. The group *harambee*s were mainly hybrids of private and public forms in which social groups such as women and youth raised funds to provide support for individual or collective needs (Task Force Report, 2003:40). The Task Force Report pointed out that there were many beneficiaries of *harambee*, ranging from the vulnerable poor to the elites through contributions to overseas scholarships and the political elites. It noted that, even though it was abused, the *harambee* system provided an avenue for both horizontal assistance and for the rich to assist the needy, thus promoting a culture of philanthropy in Kenya (Task Force Report, 2003:x).

The *harambee* system is of interest here because it covered the whole spectrum of indigenous philanthropy as discussed in this chapter, with regard to its use as 'giving to help', 'giving to resist and to collaborate' politically, and also 'giving for development'. It also had the element of 'levying' that Ekeh (1994) mentioned in his discussion of the alternative public.

Kanyinga (1995:99), who had carried out a study of the system in the mid-1990s, showed clearly how this inclination towards levying was perverted into outright coercion by provincial officials in Kenya in raising funds for local-level development:

> Throughout the country during the last days of single party rule, and apparently still in some KANU-dominated zones, the provincial administration played a key role in 'implementing' *harambees*. In Taita Taveta some residents asserted that before multi-partyism, chiefs sometimes on instructions from the DO (District

Officer) would determine how much each household should contribute to given *harambees*. Subsequently the chiefs and sub-chiefs went from house to house collecting the money.

Indeed, the story of the *harambee* system is the story of the passages in the life and evolution of an African indigenous system of giving. It began as an autonomous expression of voluntary giving and assistance in forms other than monetary, manifested in self-help and mutual aid in the early colonial days, and was utilized as part of the nationalist resistance struggles (Task Force Report, 2003:1). It was then taken over by the nationalist politicians, who used it to mobilize resources ostensibly for development. They appropriated both its cultural symbolic value and its material element, including incorporating it in parts of legislation (Task Force Report, 2003:29–31). This way it lost significant aspects of its horizontal and communal nature as the elites and the wealthy used it to contribute to political projects and efforts, a situation that became more brazen in the 1970s and 1980s. It then became increasingly perverted, using coercive mechanisms for fundraising from poor people, and becoming an instrument of vote buying, political patronage, clientelism and outright corruption in the diversion of public funds and the absence of accountability and transparency.

This led to increasing calls for reforms and regulation, culminating in the establishment of the Task Force by the Kibaki-led National Rainbow Coalition (NARC) Government that came to power in 2003, after about forty years of rule by the nationalist party, KANU. The perversion of politics and the erosion of the major institutions of public life in many of the African states were complicated by the emergence of what has been called the 'era of crisis and adjustment' in African contemporary history.

From the latter part of the 1970s several African nations entered a phase of extended economic decline, accompanied in certain areas by drought, famine, severe ecological degradation, debt, political instability, conflicts and the imposition of economic adjustment policies. Economic decline and the debt crisis constituted the most critical elements of this era, and economic liberalization and stabilization policies, aggressively promoted by the Bretton Woods Institutions (in particular the World Bank and the International Monetary Fund) through a battery of conditionalities including reforms around deregulation, liberalization and withdrawal of the state, were seen as the immediate solutions. In the context of this crisis, the world also witnessed a major change in the configuration of global politics with the collapse of the Soviet Bloc in the late 1980s and the abrupt end of the Cold War. This political event provided the space for a new impetus on political liberalization, a renewed call for electoral and multi-party democracy, and the entry into the global and national public arenas of the 'importance of civil society', seen mainly through an increased role for non-governmental organizations.

This era provided the wide array of African and international non-state actors – including both local and foreign philanthropic institutions – an expanded space for interventions and the promotion of a new set of social justice discourses such as democracy, peace and human rights. These discourses were not only pushed by local African political and social groups involved in the democratic struggles to overthrow or remove their authoritarian rulers, but also by international agencies including the UN bodies, international foundations and the Bretton Woods Institutions, who introduced and appropriated the notions through their narrow and technocratic definition and promotion of what they called 'democratic governance' or simply governance.

Again, the frame for philanthropic support and intervention experienced a different impetus and dynamic beyond the previous concern with 'development'. The demands for electoral democracy, political pluralism, public accountability and transparency led to changes in the language of social mobilization, philanthropic organization and formation, and the practice and ideology of aid. This had implications for the role of both local and international philanthropy and their relations with African states and politics. Indeed, many of the major international foundations, along with the dominant players of the 'donor community', modified their agenda to take on these elements of rights and democracy as their key goals and mission in Africa (Zeleza 2004).

It is important here to clarify the point about the modification of what has been called the 'donor agenda' in the late 1990s. The emphasis on the modification is not a denial of the 'liberal' or 'social justice' agenda of some of the private foundations and that their founding mission committed them to the promotion of democracy, peace, knowledge, understanding and justice, but rather that the international donor context now favoured the space to more assertively affirm and promote the liberal agenda on the world stage, albeit within the constraints of a more conservative and neoliberal global economic platform. The philanthropic institutions were now more empowered than in the early days of political independence to distance themselves from inept, corrupt and authoritarian actions of governments and politicians, and to openly support what were once politically risky interventions in the fields of human rights, reproductive and sexual rights, political pluralism, and freedom of information. Part of the process of promoting pluralism and giving voice to minorities and previously excluded groups involved the need to strengthen what was called civil society presence and its supportive infrastructure in the form of a critical mass of activist and knowledge-building organizations, as well as service and support intermediaries. Organized philanthropy, constructed in the western model or transplanted from its soil, was seen as one major approach, and it involved a process known as foundation building. The effort included two key impulses, the first being the promotion and seeding of community and community development foundations modelled on the North American experience (Malombe 2000), along with the encouragement of general purpose or special interest foundations at either the national or continental levels. In Africa in the 1990s, three private foundations, two operating mainly in Southern Africa, the Charles Stewart Mott Foundation and the Kellogg Foundation; and the third, the Ford Foundation with a wider continental reach, were involved in these efforts that focused principally on the promotion and growth of the philanthropic sub-sector of the non-governmental sphere.

The Ford Foundation in fact had a continent-wide initiative, the Africa Philanthropy Initiative, run mainly from its Office for Eastern Africa in Nairobi, Kenya, that ran from 1997 to 2004. This initiative provided support and encouragement for strengthening the old trusts and foundations set up by families; and participated in helping to set up new community foundations and some specialized social justice foundations. It also supported the establishment of intermediaries that promoted debates and awareness of corporate social responsibility, the promotion of corporate philanthropy, and the creation of support organizations working on training and improving the craft of grantmaking. Another area of support within this initiative was the creation of regional associations of grantmakers such as the East Africa Association of Grantmakers. Utilizing a battery of interventions that included institution capacity building, peer learning, training fellowships, study visits and scholarships, support for endowment building, public communications and dissemination, this initiative contributed in no small measure to influencing the quality and quantity of interventions in the operations of local philanthropy, particularly in Eastern Africa.

The work of the large international private foundations in this area was of course part of the redirection of donor funding from direct support to African governments and public sector institutions that occurred in this period. With the shift from support to governments by the donor community to support for 'civil society' and non-governmental organizations, the era of crisis and liberalization saw the massive growth and transplantation of non-governmental organizations, including philanthropic institutions, in Africa.[4] This growth in the era of crisis and adjustment in Africa was also a worldwide phenomenon, as explained by Hulme and Edwards (1997:5):

> The rise of NGOs and GROs on the world scene is an important phenomenon which has implications for the development prospects of poor people, for the future of these organizations themselves, and for the wider political economy of which they form a small but growing part. The rise of NGOs is not an accident; nor is it solely

a response to local initiatives and voluntary action. Over the last fifteen years, and particularly since the end of the Cold War, development policy and aid transfers have been dominated by what Robinson (1993) calls a 'New Policy Agenda'. This Agenda is not monolithic; its details vary from one official aid agency to another, but in all cases it is driven by beliefs organized around the twin poles of neoliberal economics and liberal democratic theory.

It is in the context of this agenda that we witnessed the massive growth of the non-governmental sector in many African countries and the pressure from both the governments and non-governmental sides for the establishment of different forms of regulatory regimes. While governments were alarmed and appeared keen to track and control the resources that came into the NGO sector, the NGOs were more concerned with struggles to simplify and liberalize registration in the sector, with tax relief and incentives and the promotion of their rights as related to freedom of association, movement and organization.[5]

With the growth of the conventional human rights movement and the mainstreaming of its language and different varieties of discourse into activist practices and even media activities, governments have become increasingly tense over attempts at scrutinizing their development, welfare, rights, fiscal, security and other efforts. The demands for public accountability and transparency and for freedom of information have increased and have complicated the relations between the state, politics and philanthropy. The international foundations are increasingly engaged in funding difficult programmes and causes and many of them support what has been called advocacy issues. At the same time, they are also large-scale supporters of scholarships, fellowships, university development, the re-thinking of adjustment and globalization policies, and in some cases major basic education and health programmes.

Lodged within the same philanthropic institution, large or small, local or international, are different tendencies and patterns of interaction with governments and politics, depending on the issues. While some governments would welcome HIV/AIDS intervention in terms of care and delivery of services, they are often tense with regard to issues of advocacy around stigma, sex work, same-sex relations, intravenous drug use, the status of girls and women, sexual violence, and the conditions of prisoners. Yet all of these issues, along with the medical aspects, constitute what can be called the minimum standards in intervening in this field. Thus, the relationships have become more complex and cannot be discussed in terms of binary opposites.

Practitioners in the field also recognize the range of engagement with government and politics at different levels. For instance, specific philanthropies working on service delivery or related issues might find that they have very positive co-operative relations with local authorities while their relations with national authorities might be oppositional, for example, if they combine service delivery with advocacy around budget transparency. State, politics and philanthropy relations have become more complex and nuanced at several levels and with the different forms of philanthropy since the era of crisis and adjustment in many African nations. However, this conversation would be incomplete without some discussion of two more contemporary issues that frame contemporary practice. These are the revision of the most drastic elements of the neoliberal agenda in economic policies, and the emergence of a new global framing of development goals – the Millennium Development Goals (MDGs).

On the first point about the weakening of what has been called the 'Washington Consensus', which was the market-driven neoliberal economics largely imposed on African economies in the 1980s, there has been strong evidence of increasing impoverishment and a decline in all indicators of the Human Development Index, the UNDP indicators of human well-being that are widely applied. In the 1980s, 1990s and the early 2000s, particularly, it became clear even to the Bretton Woods Institutions such as the World Bank that the war against poverty was being lost. For instance, *The Index of Global Philanthropy* (2007:9) reported that:

> The World Bank found that poverty was either not reduced, or even increased in 14 of 25 surveyed countries that have received loans since 1990. In 2007, the Canadian parliament found that poorly designed projects, lack of local leadership, and ineffective aid institutions failed to improve the lives of Africans.

A further detailed analysis of the inter-institutional and global politics involved in the universalizing of adjustment policies in the Third World has been provided by a group of eminent chroniclers of the United Nations' intellectual history. In reviewing how the promotion of economic adjustment and liberalization eroded the gains of the United Nations' Development decades, they declared:

> Twenty years down the road, it is more and more recognized that orthodox policies have three basic traits. They are crisis-prone. They are deflationary. And they stimulate the spirit of speculation. The crisis-prone system is obvious from the 'lost decade' of the 1980s that was followed by the Tequila crisis in Mexico and Argentina (1994–95), the Asian Crisis of 1997–99, the Russian debacle in 1998, and the Brazilian crisis in early 1999. In between, we witnessed attacks on the British pound ('the billion of Soros'), the Italian lira, and countless other currencies. Joseph Stiglitz – until December 1999 chief economist of the World Bank and formerly chairman of the Council of Economic Advisers (CEA) under President Bill Clinton – came to the conclusion that financial and capital liberalization can be an important source of macro-instability and financial shocks (Emmerij, Jolly and Weiss 2001:131).

It was obvious, beginning with the critique of adjustment by the United Nations Children's Fund (UNICEF) in the 1980s, that adjustment was not reducing poverty and that there were still important roles for states and governments, as well as social policy, in the development process. These positions were further buttressed by the arrival on the world stage of India and China, whose economic development processes were not singularly driven by neoliberal orthodox doctrines. The conventional wisdom of the economic orthodoxy was beginning to be eroded.

Thus, the 'donor' community began to modify its position again and return to some investment in public institutions and social policy, and social development issues like health and education. At the broad global level, the UN regained its leadership in contributing to the direction of development through its enactment of the Millennium Development Goals and the mobilization of the world's nations in attaining these.

The MDGs emerged from the UN Millennium General Assembly of 2000, at which

> nearly 150 heads of states pledged to do their utmost 'to free our fellow men, women, and children from abject and dehumanizing conditions of extreme poverty'. The Millennium Development Goals translate this pledge into eight goals and 18 concrete quantified targets with a deadline of 2015, to cut poverty and hunger by half, to achieve universal primary education, to empower women and promote gender equity, to cut child mortality by two-thirds and maternal mortality by three-quarters, to halt and begin to reverse the spread of AIDS and other major diseases, to halve the number of people without access to clean water and sanitation, and to develop a global partnership for development.[6]

Although the commitment of government donors, particularly those of the richer countries, to meeting their different pledges has been questioned, the MDGs platform became a new and useful frame for interventions to pursue development and fight poverty on a major scale. Its clear goals and identifiable and measurable indicators provided a new basis for partnerships between governments, the international aid institutions and the variety of private philanthropies working not only in service delivery but also in advocacy. This platform, in spite of its many weaknesses and the opportunism that it has sometimes generated, has provided a new consensus for global discourse on development.

It is a frame that one encounters in discussions ranging from the interventions of a community foundation in a small rural hamlet to the programme framework of large global foundations. With regard to its relations with the state and politics, this framework is once more giving rise to complex realities where it allows for not only collaboration and co-operation with governments and political leaders, but also provides the basis for oppositional and at times hostile engagements when targets are not being met and states and their officials become obstructionist.

As we talk about this era, the era of the early twenty-first century, we also begin to see new dynamics and trends in the philanthropic arena that are influencing the African context. There are increases in the formation of corporate philanthropic institutions as these companies made significant profits in the early part of the century. The notion of 'foundations' is also becoming generalized and universalized, as mega-foundations such as the Bill and Melinda Gates Foundation regularly receive press and media coverage for their investments, interventions and innovative practices.

As the *Index of Global Philanthropy* (2007:5) glowingly characterizes this emerging approach:

> The striking trend in overseas philanthropy is that of 'new age' donors using new technologies to cut down on the cost of delivering assistance – financial services firms, donor-advised funds, the 'for-profit philanthropy' of Google.org, the philanthropic arm of Google.com, corporate 'cause-related' marketing, and immigrants sending money back home through customized bank accounts, credit cards, and cell phones. The mobile phone as a purse may be the developing world's Industrial Revolution for creating prosperity. The new age donors are hands-on. They want to participate directly in the design, operation and measurement of their endeavours. They want to see results and create real and lasting partnerships with people and institutions overseas.

While the early private foundations avoided media publicity and self-promotion, there has been a clear shift as the new foundations and philanthropic entrepreneurs aggressively promote themselves. A significant element of these developments is the change in practices and driving ideologies already mentioned above. The new philanthropies being the product of a new generation of successful business people in banking, finance and information, communications technology is often managed along business lines and intentionally crosses the lines between business and philanthropy, a situation that Edwards (2008) has described as 'philanthro-capitalism'. As the *Index of Global Philanthropy and Remittances* (2008:6) explains in a recent review:

> Whatever it is called – social entrepreneurship, philanthro-capitalism, venture philanthropy or the latest label by Bill Gates, creative capitalism – the lines between business and philanthropy continue to blur. This trend in philanthropy has been dubbed the 'double bottom line' or making money and helping a charitable cause at the same time. In fact, the terrain of practice is replete with new names and ideas that include notions such as 'social franchising' and 'social investment', the problem here being an uncritical application of the notion of the 'social'.

This tendency is increasingly expressed in Africa, and in some countries, like Kenya, new circles such as the 'social investment forum' have been created. Indeed, the 2008 edition of the *Index of Global Philanthropy and Remittances* has devoted an unprecedented amount of space to analyzing the African trends.

Again, from the perspective of this chapter, the phenomenon of the 'new international philanthropy' and the attendant changes in the structure of monetary transfers, particularly the growth of 'remittances' from Africans overseas, require a careful situation situating carefully in its their multiple and complex political and economic contexts in terms of the nature and dynamics of power relations and the ultimate questions of who benefits and what is addressed. This is more so with regard to the discussion of philanthro-capitalism and the crossing of business and philanthropy boundaries. In contexts of regulatory agencies and infrastructures, where many African countries are weak, it is important to emphasize the need for greater scrutiny, accountability and transparency of these approaches before we succumb to the euphoria of their often hyperbolic claims to 'opportunistic innovations'. This is because the history of many African societies has included histories of unbridled exploitation by cavalier and 'new frontier' entrepreneurs and opportunists, both local and foreign. It will be most unfortunate if philanthropy becomes another such vehicle.

Conclusion

In this chapter, we have attempted to explore an important but often neglected aspect of the phenomenon of philanthropy – how it is very much determined by context and what roles politics plays in the determination. In this case, our efforts have focused on tracing the contexts and significant moments and issues that frame the evolution of philanthropic giving in Africa. In contextualizing the process and phenomenon, we have endeavoured to show its complexity, diversity, occasional ambiguity and ambivalence, and its embodiment of often contradictory tendencies.

What is evident and is implicit in most of the contributions in this volume, is that there is more than one philanthropic and humanitarian tradition beyond the often promoted Western forms and traditions. This does not deny some universalisms based on the facts of the psychic unity of humankind, but it does challenge a monolithic, unilineal and often teleological construction of the varieties of human experiences. Neither does it deny the usefulness of adaptation and importation of ideas and processes in a world in which trans-national contacts and mobility have been ongoing for several centuries. In engaging the role of politics and the relationships between the state, politics and philanthropy, the important elements of contexts and historical specificity come into the analysis and assist and permit a deeper and more nuanced understanding of the evolution of the phenomenon of philanthropy in Africa.

As has been shown in this chapter and in many of the contributions to this volume, politics and philanthropy intersect and are connected in many ways. This is expressed in the mission of philanthropies, the circumstances of their establishment, the nature, distribution and modes of access to wealth, opportunity, power and prestige in societies, and even in the way seemingly sovereign and autonomous national entities engage themselves. Of course, there are many other technical, managerial and technocratic elements to organizing philanthropy, such as the issues of management, resource mobilization and sustainability, accountability and transparency, effective grantmaking and programming, ethics and values. But it is important to always remember the significance of the politics of philanthropy and the relationship between philanthropy and politics, not only because these factors are always there, irrespective of what the managers may say, but also because they shape and are shaped by how philanthropic traditions evolve and interact. This chapter has sought to contribute to the framing of these issues, not by providing answers but by posing questions as part of a necessary preliminary step to understanding the evolution of giving to help – and helping to give – in Africa.

Endnotes

1   In fact, resistance was a major element of colonial politics, and its different aspects have been well documented in what has been called the resistance literature in African history. See, for instance Ranger (1970) and Isaacman and Isaacman (1977:31–62).

2   For a more comprehensive discussion of the contributions of the United Nations to some of these important ideas, see Louis Emmerij, Richard Jolly and Thomas G. Weiss (2001), *Ahead of the Curve? UN Ideas and Global Challenges,* Bloomington, Indiana University Press.

3   See Young (2003); Coleman with Court (1993; and Jefferson Murphy (1976).

4   This was the period when some of the most developed African philanthropic institutions, such as the African Women's Development Foundation (AWDF) and the Kenya Community Development Foundation (KCDF), were founded. It was also the period of the growth of the philanthropic service institutions and grantmakers' associations.

5   See Ngondi-Houghton (2008) for an example of the regulation discourse in Eastern Africa.

6   See Sakiko Fukuda-Parr (2004), 'The Millennium Development Goals: The Pledge of World Leaders to End Poverty Will Not Be Met with Business as Usual', *Journal of International Development,* 925–32, Vol. 16 (7), pp. 925–6.

CHAPTER 2

TRENDS, INNOVATIONS AND PARTNERSHIPS FOR DEVELOPMENT IN AFRICAN PHILANTHROPY[1]

BHEKINKOSI MOYO

Introduction

This chapter is a discussion of the many manifestations of philanthropy in Africa and how it seeks to address the promotion of well-being – well-being taken to mean total development. No doubt, philanthropy and development are not new phenomena in Africa. Neither are they divorced from the questions of humanity's quest for total development. For its part, philanthropy is intrinsically embedded in the life cycle of birth, life and death of many, if not all Africans (Moyo 2009). At any one given time, one is either a philanthropist or a recipient of one kind or another of benevolence. Though not a common or even user-friendly concept in Africa, philanthropy is a phenomenon perhaps best captured by the notions of 'solidarity and reciprocity' among Africans and some of the features that accompany relation-building. As a result, therefore, culture and relation-building are central attributes in defining what philanthropy in the African context looks like. By the same token, an African's dance with the contested and contradictory trajectories of developmental processes goes a long way back to pre-colonial times. Since then, Africans and their continent have been a laboratory for trials and errors on development frameworks. Africa might continue being the testing ground for more trials if no deliberative action is taken to reverse the trend. Till today the development question has not been settled. Any attempts to settle it have normally resulted in the abandonment of the African culture in pursuit of an externally carved solution. In this theatre of trials and tribulations, philanthropy – local and external – has not been a neutral spectator. As Douglas White (2010:62) writes, 'philanthropy commands a lot of money and it plays a major role in the financial success of charities'. One might add that because it commands a lot of money and influence, philanthropy is never a neutral actor in any setting. There are motivations and intentions for philanthropy. At times this has been for the good of humanity but at times this has been to the detriment of human progress. Indeed, donors or rather philanthropists give for particular reasons, and they are all motivated by different things: giving back to their communities; driven by political, social and religious beliefs, or because they have been asked to give. But overall, philanthropy – or, when reduced to a narrower meaning – charity 'serves and has always served an important strategic social function by mediating between the needs of the disadvantaged and the resources of the privileged' (O'Halloran 2007:30).

Hence, from time immemorial, philanthropy as understood to mean the 'love for humanity' has always been practised by Africans in their different and unique contexts. Understood mainly as giving or helping – or, even better, more encapsulated as solidarity and reciprocity, this entailed collective or individual efforts towards a social or public good. This conception of good was not divorced from questions of welfare, well-living or well-being – understood today more in terms of sustainable, people-driven and inclusive development. However, due to analytical influence and frameworks primarily from the West, philanthropy in Africa or, to be more specific, African philanthropy has sometimes been wrongly and maliciously defined as indigenous or informal. Yet African philanthropy is in fact the foundation on which an African's life and his or her development revolve. It is the foundation upon which modern institutions are built or get their inspiration and identity. The bifurcation between informal and formal misses the central point about African societies: that one is an extension of the other. In other words, rather than talking of informal and formal forms of philanthropy, it is much better and conceptually appropriate to talk about horizontal and vertical forms of philanthropy (inadequate as this framework might be) – what other scholars of philanthropy have called 'philanthropy of community' and 'philanthropy for community'. The first has as its foundation African philosophies, while the second is externally induced.

Conceptually, it is dangerous to define African philanthropy as informal or indigenous as this relegates everything 'African' to the informal realm because at the centre of the African's identity is this aspect of solidarity, reciprocity, giving or helping for a social good. The other reason why it is inappropriate to do so is because it relegates African philanthropy to the periphery of the mainstream or recognized modus operandi, yet African philanthropy is actually at the centre of the universal meaning or even practice of world traditions of philanthropy. In fact, African philanthropy is foundational to an African's upbringing or life as a whole.

This is more eloquently described in the Zulu saying: *Umuntu ngumuntu ngabantu*: You are because I am. And as explained by Marcel Mauss;

> The pattern of symmetrical and reciprocal rights is not difficult to understand if we realise that it is first and foremost a pattern of spiritual bonds between things which are to some extent parts of persons, and persons and groups that behave in some measure as if they were things. (reproduced in Feierman 1998)

In other words, one's existence is intrinsically linked to that of others. In most African societies, one is defined as poor only if one does not have relatives or people he or she calls relatives – social or biological – and not because one lacks money. It is in this context that today's philanthropic expressions and manifestations, particularly in Africa, need to be understood as they intersect with development and questions of well-being. Menkhoff (2010:138) could have been writing about an African society when he said, 'Philanthropic givers can range from the widow with two mites and the man in the street dropping spare change into a tin can thrust at him, to multibillionaires like George Soros and Bill Gates.'

This chapter discusses these intersections between philanthropic innovations and partnerships, well-being and development in Africa. It has four sections. The first gives a general background to the concept of well-being as it relates to questions of development. The second gives a snapshot of the landscape of philanthropic practice in Africa, paying attention to philosophies underpinning giving, helping, reciprocity and solidarity. It locates this discussion on the new forms and trends of philanthropy that have taken place over the last decade in Africa and how these have devised innovative strategies for addressing well-being. These include such strategic innovations as impact investing, leveraging, strategic grantmaking, peer-learning, online giving, collaborations and advocacy among others in an attempt to interface and interact with key development actors in the continent. The third discusses some of the existing collaborations and partnerships that philanthropic institutions have developed between themselves and other development actors. The fourth pulls everything together to identify new forms of knowledge that are emerging out of these innovations, collaborations and partnerships. It also identifies implications for policy options on questions of well-being, philanthropy and development in Africa. And, finally, it talks about the implications for the twenty-first century agenda for promoting well-being.

The examples that are given throughout the chapter are illustrative, due to all the multiple varied forms philanthropic institutions and practice in Africa. So, for example, we try to briefly discuss impact investment in corporate philanthropy, given the major role the corporate sector plays in development.

Development and well-being in Africa

On development

Africa has come of age. It is a continent that was once described by *The Economist* magazine as a 'Dark or Hopeless Continent'. This was due to incessant and protracted conflicts – most of which still persist today. A number of African countries are still under the scourge of civil conflicts. Increasingly also are conflicts caused by the dramatic changes in the climate, making climate change the most popular Achilles heel for many African countries. In addition, Africa continues to record the highest records of human rights abuses. The paradox is that, while many countries in Africa have democratized and adopted pluralism and multi-party systems, their political elites pay lip-service to the culture of democracy. Political instability remains a threat to the well-being of African citizens – more often exacerbated by electoral politics and resource scrambles. This has had ramifications for economic performance. But even those countries that have performed well, recording such growth rates as 6 per cent or so over the last decade, have not translated their growth into tangible effects on the well-being of their citizens. Inequality still remains very high and the number of poor people has increased exponentially. One of the ticking bombs in Africa is the phenomenon of unemployable graduates and the increasing number of helpless youths. This raises serious questions not just about the question of the sustainability of the growth rates that Africa continues to register, but also the model of development that Africa adopted.

In the African political sphere, governance deficits are threatening the gains made so far, especially in the economic performance of such countries as Botswana, Liberia, Namibia, Mauritius, South Africa and Zambia among other performing states. The increasing repression of human rights advocates, the deterioration of the rule of law and the general decline in governance standards and adherence to principles of democratic culture are some of the fundamental negatives that are reversing the gains made particularly over the last years. The state is still fragile, corruption is endemic and basic freedoms are eroded daily in Africa. Clearly this has serious implications for the overall well-being of citizens. Their ability to choose values that they subscribe to is highly compromised by this state of affairs. This disconnect between citizens and their rulers has led to serious protests, particularly in North Africa, for basic rights, accountability and decent conditions of living. Further, the poor governance system in Africa has also contributed to Africa being the least peaceful region in the world.

These developmental challenges confronting Africa have implications for social development and efforts on alleviating poverty. There is a widening gap between the poor and the rich across Africa. Access to health, education, water and sanitation remain pressing social issues across Africa. This is further compounded by the always volatile food prices. As a matter of fact, the whole of Africa is currently food security risky and most countries are vulnerable to climate change. This has repercussions for the promotion of well-being and what role each development actor assumes. It also puts into sharper focus the kind of strategies and innovations that are needed to respond adequately to the threats to well-being in the twenty-first century. These fault lines in the social and cultural spheres such as social ills, illiteracy, poverty, social injustice and inequities among others are widening with great speed. All these are threats to well-being as expounded in Amartya Sen's Capability Approach Framework, which defines it as 'the ability to live well across all spheres of life' (Clark 2005:1340). This approach refers to both 'mental and material aspects of development in addition to many other substantive freedoms which are not covered by the limited notions of utility and opulence that once defined well-being' (ibid.).

At the same time, however, there is serious movement in Africa that no longer sees Africa as the hopeless continent but rather as a continent of hope. Writing for the Africa Progress Report, Kofi Annan said:

> What was termed the hopeless continent ten years ago has now unquestionably become the continent of hope. Hope that strong growth rates will translate into jobs, incomes and irreversible human-development gains; that the continent's enormous wealth will be used to foster equitable and inclusive growth and generate opportunities for all; that economic transformation and social progress will drive further improvements in democratic governance and accountability as the middle classes grow and demand more of their politicians and service providers; and hope that rulers who abuse their power to enrich themselves at the expense of the poor and of democratic processes are, at last, seeing the writing on the wall (Africa Progress Panel 2011:6).

Today Africa is increasingly being defined as the 'Land of Opportunities'. For example, a report by the *Wall Street Journal* (Sept 19, 2011) illustrates the map of Africa from Cape to Cairo with all kinds of opportunities that investors can reap if they came to Africa. The map had more opportunities than risks, in many ways confirming what is increasingly becoming the norm, that Africa is the next frontier for investments and development. According to the IMF, Africa is poised to grow in 2012 by 5.8 per cent.

Indeed, Africa might be seen today as a new frontier for development, but this has 'not translated in progress being measured in tangible improvements to people's lives' (Africa Progress Panel 2011:8). People's well-being has not been improved. There currently exists a disconnect between economic performance and social progress. The growth rates are of low quality. These are not accompanied by the much-needed 'structural transformation and diversification' to achieve well-being outcomes. Neither do they translate to equitable human development and public services (ibid:11). As the Africa Progress Report points out:

> Driven by capital intensive extractive sectors, the current type of economic growth has little positive impact on employment and income levels and virtually no effect on employment-intensive sectors such as agriculture. It is hardly surprising that despite a decade of strong economic growth, poverty remains pervasive throughout the continent (ibid.).

To match economic performance and social progress it is therefore imperative that African leaders accelerate economic diversification and structural transformation – failing that, growth will be meaningless. But it is also important to address the totality of a person or society's well-being from a political economy perspective. So critical is the political economy of Africa that it cannot be divorced from the interventions that have been made to address Africa's challenges as well as the different strategies that have been adopted to harness the opportunities that Africa presents today. Likewise the role that different development actors play in Africa to address equitable and inclusive development cannot be isolated from this political economy. It is here, therefore, that philanthropy finds itself so intricately interspaced with Africa's cultures, knowledges, institutions and normative frameworks that its discussion as it relates to well-being cannot happen outside the intricacies that exist between development and African philosophy. Our understanding of well-being therefore rests squarely on the African creed; 'I am because you are'.

On well-being

While this chapter is not dedicated towards defining 'well-being', it suffices to state that its definition has been contested over the years. There are different dimensions of human well-being comprising the material and non-material assets, resources and experiences (Edwards 2011). There are some scholars, for example, on the one hand who have narrowly seen it as referring to notions of utility (happiness, desires, and fulfilment) and opulence (income, commodity command). On the other hand, others like Amartya Sen have viewed well-being as much more broader and substantive. Sen remains the dominant scholar to have dedicated a much bigger framework to understanding well-being in his writings. His articulation of well-being is thus both a 'critique of the traditional notions of development that conflated well-being with opulence and utility' (Clark 2005:1341) and a development of a framework that prioritizes capabilities or what he terms 'substantive freedoms that people have reason to value'. In strengthening this framework, Deneulin and McGregor (2010) stretch the capability approach to include what they call 'the telos of living well together – expanding the social conditions in which it is possible to live well in relation to others in society' (ibid:503)'. In other words, while Sen's well-being is individually oriented, these scholars see an intersection between individuals and societies. Hence in their view, a much more nuanced capability framework is one that 'situates human beings and their well-being at the end concerns of economic and social processes' (ibid:514). It is one that 'makes people subjects of their own lives'. This was well captured by the Report by the Commission on the Measurement of Economic Performance and Social Progress (Stiglitz, J.E., Sen, A. and Fitoussi, J.P. 2009) when it stated that 'Current well-being has to do with both economic resources, such as income, and non-economic aspects of people's life (what they do and what they can do, how they feel, and the natural environment they live in).'

In the African context as elsewhere the concept of well-being is not static. It is one that adapts to new contexts and their demands. Its dynamism is determined by the political, economic, cultural and social developments. This understanding and realization means that our view of philanthropy's role in this regard should be one that addresses different dimensions in different ways and over very different time frames (Edwards 2011:9). Michael Edwards synthesized this very well when he stated:

> Some foundations value short term improvements in material well-being over every other indicator, while others are preoccupied by long term systems change. Some are prepared to trade off democratic participation in order to get things done, while for others 'getting things done' is the task of democracy itself. Some are happy to focus on extending the poor people's participation in the current structure of the economy, while others are want to transform it in order to address the future challenges of climate change and consumption (ibid.:10).

This is echoed by the Southern Africa Trust, a grantmaker based in South Africa focusing on regional frameworks to eradicate poverty; well-being should be approached and addressed from a multidimensional perspective involving the tackling of poverty of the whole person as opposed to a narrow focus on economic performances and incomes. Further, well-being should be addressed systemically, targeting how societies are structured and how they relate to each other, including transforming power dynamics. And thirdly, addressing well-being should adopt a regional approach, as opposed to statist frameworks that focus only on national development without taking into account how economic and social relations cut across the board.[2] The link between well-being, development and philanthropy is best nuanced by the values of solidarity, reciprocity and caring that African societies espouse. Below is a short discussion of the African philanthropic landscape and how it relates to the promotion of well-being.

African philanthropy landscape

In its etymology, philanthropy has to do with the love of humanity, making the link between well-being and philanthropy natural. Yet the large philanthropic resources within and from outside Africa have not given birth to a reduction in inequality, dictatorships, poverty or social injustices. For the most part, some forms of philanthropy, especially the externally-induced ones, have remained very rigid, failing to adapt to the changing and complex demands of well-being. For its part, the various forms of philanthropy in Africa have responded differently, based on philosophical or even ideological and religious underpinnings, to giving and helping. It is therefore important that a short discussion of the philanthropic landscape in Africa is discussed here so as to provide both the framework and context for the subsequent sections on philanthropic innovations and collaborations in promoting well-being.

For many years there has been a characterization of the philanthropic landscape in Africa in general as that comprising both horizontal and vertical forms of philanthropy. Because the term 'philanthropy' is not that popular with the people in the continent, and neither is it useful in capturing the different nuances of what exists, the emerging body of literature on philanthropy in Africa prefers to define philanthropy as 'help' or 'giving' (Wilkinson-Maposa et al. 2006) or solidarity – something that Wilkinson-Maposa et al. call the philanthropy of community. Here, philanthropy refers to giving by many, particularly the marginalized or the poor, to other poor individuals of their community. More often this form of philanthropy has both cultural and linguistic underpinnings – hence usually taking on expressions such as cooperatives, rotation and savings clubs, communal collective efforts and burial societies (Moyo in MacDonald and De Borns 2010:263).[3] Locating philanthropy in Africa within the reciprocity framework, Feierman (1998:4) wrote that:

> Sub-Saharan Africa in the centuries before colonial conquest was a region where voluntary giving was, in a majority of cases, grounded in reciprocity, and yet where inequalities existed, where kindly help was as double edged as it is in the philanthropic West – a peculiar combination of caring and dominance, of generosity and property, of tangled rights in things and in people, all in a time and place where the strong would not let the weak go under, except sometimes.

He went on to describe the various dimensions of this reciprocity, saying;

> In many places, the model for generous giving was that of apparent caring for children, so that even strangers might be taken in and defined as children. This way of giving care to the poor grew out of a perceived need for numerous and fruitful descendants – a need partially grounded in the religion of the ancestors as practiced in many societies in Africa (ibid.).

Other forms of this reciprocal giving include traditional systems of cooperation, mutuality and solidarity. These remain active today across African societies, 'primarily in rural areas as well as in informal economic settings'. Among these are rotating savings and credit associations – popularly known as stokvels in South Africa but found everywhere across Africa. More often a group of people come together and pool their resources for a later redistribution. Beyond the savings and credit elements is the central value of mutual assistance. Burial societies are another form of African solidarity, which initially played the role of cultural and societal compliance with rituals associated with death, especially for those who die far from their ancestral homes. They have today incorporated a somewhat micro-insurance aspect to them; beyond the communal fundamentals of sending off the dead to the land of ancestors, burial societies now serve as financial backers for the bereaved. There are also other mechanisms for sharing labour-intensive ventures such as farming, house construction, harvesting or any other activity that might need mutual work sharing. Known as *ilima* ('coming together to help those without') among the Nguni-speaking people, this practice is widespread across Africa. Writing on cooperatives, Jurgen Schwettman, ILO Deputy Regional Director for Africa, said:

> These ancient traditions have been adapted to modern times and applied to the conditions of the urban informal economy of many African countries. Modern examples include those female traders from West Africa who pool their resources to send one of them to China to buy merchandise in bulk for all of them, without any written agreement (2011).

All these forms of philanthropy or solidarity (burial societies, stokvels, rotating savings clubs, cooperatives etc.) are bound together by a certain form of social capital which acts as a social control mechanism. Regardless of the amount of money involved, large or small, members of these formations are protected by social capital as opposed to any written legal instrument. Working cooperatively is something inherent in their lives. According to the ILO, Africa is home to more than 70 million members of cooperatives.

These cultural underpinnings provide the foundation upon which institutional philanthropy – another form of philanthropy in Africa, understood to mean private foundations, trusts, corporate foundations, family trusts, community chests and more recently community foundations –is built and formed. This form of philanthropy is understood as vertical in nature, referring to giving or helping by few to many – usually by the rich or High Net Worth Individuals (HNWIs) to the poor. This form of philanthropy should not be understood in isolation of that practised by the poor philanthropists. For doing so disempowers the poor by placing them under the mercy of the rich philanthropists. By so doing, the reading of the rich philanthropist in isolation of the poor takes away the poor's agency and the very fact that the poor are philanthropists in their own right, and that they are subjects of their own lives, as the capability framework provides. Research is increasingly showing that giving is not an exclusive domain of the wealthy (Everatt and Solanki 2005; Wilkinson-Maposa et al. 2006). In other words, everyone is a philanthropist in his or her own right. Writing in *Global Philanthropy,* Tamzin Ractliffe argued:

> There is in South Africa and Africa broadly, a deep rooted tradition of giving and mutual helping. It is perhaps these terms that are best able to describe the philanthropic activities of the large majority of the populace. Indeed 'giving' resonates much more strongly within South African society on a broad level, covering every day acts of kindness as well as planned giving by ordinary people within and between communities (2010:237).

The question that remains is whether vertical and horizontal philanthropy actually meet? Very seldom do these meet, and where they do, for example in South Africa where banks attempted to scale up stokvels, the defining features of horizontal philanthropy gave way to the vertical ones. The result was, of course, the fragmentation of the social capital in favour of more structured and legal frameworks. This is an area that still needs attention: how to use horizontal forms of philanthropy as the foundation for the vertical expressions of modern-day philanthropy.

The point though is that, till recently, foundations were mainly those of an international nature, primarily American and European. These were not linked to the cultural and philosophical foundations of solidarity, giving and helping that Africans expound. Most focused on grantmaking mainly to civil society and the private sector around such areas as development, governance, human rights, community development, HIV/AIDS, and peace and security among others. But they did not nuance their promotion of well-being or whatever it is they were addressing in ways that took into account the African approach and understanding of well-being. As addressed above, human well-being has many dimensions, and only an approach that values cultural and social dynamics can adequately respond to the needs of the African setting. As new ways of giving develop in the philanthropic sector, mechanisms for connecting horizontal and vertical forms of philanthropy will be needed. Fortunately, there have been some changes in the continent as a result of this realisation. For example, a number of international donors have moved their resources to their African counterparts to handle and manage them in ways that are context-specific and sensitive. There has also been an upsurge of African foundations right across the continent, such as TrustAfrica, African Women's Development Fund (AWDF), Southern Africa Trust (SAT), Mo Ibrahim, Nelson Mandela, TY Danjuma, Tony Elumelu, and Youssou Ndour among many others. Some of these foundations have been created and supported by international foundations. However, a number of those receiving money from outside have very strong values and orientation towards what is good for the continent as opposed to just being delivery channels of western actors, or rivers through which any water flows. Of importance is that these African-rooted foundations have an understanding of the continent and this determines what money they take and how they shape and deliver their programmes.

Others, like the the TY Danjuma and Tony Elumelu foundations, are African founded and funded. These are established by ultra-rich Africans, now popularly called the High Net Worth Individuals (HNWIs), most of whom made their money from such sectors as mining, financial services, construction and telecommunications. These include the likes of Mo Ibrahim, Tony Elumelu, TY Danjuma, Tokyo Sexwale, Patrice Motsepe, and many others. The 2011 World Wealth Report states that the HNWI population increased exponentially in 2010 and this increase was also reflected in Africa. According to a Barclays Wealth Report (2010:2–3), 'philanthropy among the high net worth individuals across the world is set to increase with individuals likely to give more both in terms of money and time…These individuals tend to give a portion of their resources to causes that are meaningful to them.' The increasing size of the middle class across Africa also means that more and more of such individuals will be setting up their own foundations as a way of giving back to their communities. According to the analysis of the 2011 World Wealth Report done by Dalberg, there are between 1600 and 2000 HNWIs in Africa, and Africa's HNWI population is the fastest growing in the world (11.1 per cent between 2009 and 2010, compared to 8.3 per cent global average).

The main challenge, however, with this group so far is that it generally tends to support issues that address only the tangible side, or rather the material dimensions, of well-being and not the non-material aspects such as governance, social justice, body integrity or issues related to policy reforms. There are exceptions. The Tony Elumelu Foundation, for example, supports governance issues around private sector development. The Foundation is also leading efforts to catalyze further investments in African management education, and to provide private sector support to transformational African governments. The Mo Ibrahim Foundation supports governance reform initiatives through the Mo Ibrahim Index and the Presidential Awards. But generally, most HNWIs support issues that have material expressions such as schools, health, building clinics, roads and buying materials such as wheelchairs, books, and computers among others. More often these individuals are driven by short-term needs of the poverty-stricken contexts, as opposed to long-term questions of policy and the environment under which well-being can be tackled substantively. In addition, short-term results drive the giving of these HNWIs. Questions of measurability also determine where they spend most of their resources. It is easier to show a school or count the number of desks and computers than it is to prove that policy change has indeed taken place. At times it is also because these HNWIs do not make the connection between how they made their profits and the general policy and governance environment. When approached for support for questions of governance, human rights, etc., they normally pose the question, what is in it for me? This displays the disconnection between their success and the general policy and governance environment which most of these other non-material aspects of well-being seek to achieve.

There is also a widespread increase in the establishment of foundations that are set up by politicians such as former heads of state and government (for example, Nelson Mandela, John Kufour, Thabo Mbeki, Joachim Chissano and Kenneth Kaunda among others). While these might not be as financially endowed as those set up by HNWIs of the likes of Elumelu and the Danjuma, they nevertheless have built their foundations on the basis of the influence that they exert, especially at the policy level. This is now a trend and, as such, more of such foundations will be formed as more and more heads of state leave incumbency.

Sports and other celebrity personalities such as footballers, musicians and artists have also created their own foundations right across the continent, and these focus on issues that are dear to their hearts. These normally support sport-related projects. This is another area where more could be done, given the numbers of athletes, soccer stars and artists who are making billions of dollars either locally or internationally. These can be linked to community foundations – another phenomenon that has seen an increase in Africa since the early 1990s. There are today more than 15 community foundations across Africa.

Table 2.1: Summary of philanthropic expressions in Africa

Horizontal Forms of Philanthropy	Vertical Forms of Philanthropy
Burial societies	Family foundations and trusts
Hometown Associations	Corporate foundations, including Corporate Social Investments (CSIs).
Rotating Savings Clubs	Individual giving including religious giving (alms, zakat, etc.).
Cooperatives	Community foundations and chests.
Stokvels, harambees, merry-go-rounds, etc.	Operating and private foundations, e.g. AWDF, TrustAfrica, etc.
Mutual aid, including labour-intensive activities such as house construction, ploughing, etc.	HNWIs and their foundations, including venture philanthropy.
Traditional loaning of cattle for milk and farming usually by a local rich person, etc.	Foundations set up by politicians, athletes, artists and other influential individuals.

Foundations – whether family or corporate or even operational – have always been the biggest constituents of institutional philanthropy in Africa. But as stated above, there are other forms of philanthropy, as summarized in Table 2.1.

The highest concentration of foundations is still in Anglophone countries, mainly in Southern Africa (South Africa), East Africa (Kenya) and parts of West Africa (Nigeria and Ghana). Although there is no existing research that explains why this is the case; anecdotal information suggests that it is partly due to the different colonial experiences and the fact that major philanthropic expressions, particularly foundations, have their history in North America and Europe, whose geopolitical interests are in Anglophone Africa more than Francophone or lusophone Africa. In addition, there is less literature on philanthropy in Francophone Africa than there is in Anglophone settings. But new foundations are being set up in these previously neglected areas. North Africa, for example, particularly in Egypt, has developed some foundations.

The majority of these philanthropic institutions maintain that their work is geared towards addressing questions of well-being. The Kenyan-based philanthropic entity the Kenya Community Development Foundation (KCDF) views threats to well-being as simple issues, as access to basic things such as education, health, food etc. Janet Mawiyoo of KCDF argues that:

> For many, once these simple and basic needs are addressed, it becomes easier to make choices on what to do or value. It is the basic issues in one's life that the Foundation addresses because the majority of people are not in a position to make choices, due to their conditions.[4]

As a result, KCDF looks at the overall issues affecting a person rather than narrowly boxing its programmatic thrust to specific thematic areas. This way the Foundation has kept its agenda and focus open enough to respond to community needs. For example, one of the issues that has resonated across Kenya has been the demand for educational scholarships, particularly for children whose parents cannot afford or those children who are orphaned. This has led to the development of an Education Fund which addresses access to education. As Mawiyoo notes:

> In areas where poverty is extreme, it is impossible to talk about well-being unless you are able to be responsive to basic needs that are fundamental such as human rights, health, food, water, shelter, education, etc....The Foundation thus finds itself in a situation where it is not enough to work to influence government policy, it has to engage communities to think about long-term ways of addressing such concerns among them and among vulnerable groups in their midst. Making programme support flexible to address such matters is therefore critical. In this process, KCDF has recognized that developing and building grassroots governance is very critical as a long-term way of ensuring that communities have capacities to engage government and other actors on the ground for their benefit.[5]

In a similar manner, the Foundation for Civil Society in Tanzania also views the threats to well-being around the lines of access primarily to education and health. According to the Foundation's CEO, John Ulanga, these two areas impact heavily on citizens' capabilities.[6] And the AWDF, based in Accra, uses the women's rights lens to examine well-being and citizenship. The Fund argues that the women's constituency has been part of the framing of the questions of well-being and the shift from the mere focus on economic performance to other encompassing indicators, social, cultural, etc. The Fund's Director of Programmes, Sarah Mukasa, stated so eloquently this point by saying:

> The marginalisation of African women through exclusion and discrimination has impacted negatively on the well-being of communities, nations and the continent. Whatever area it is (whether environmental, economic or otherwise), unless approached through the experiences or conditions of these marginalised women, we will still be in the same position in another 50 years. [7]

Mukasa continued to emphasise that

> Unless there is an ability to live the spirit of Ubuntu – humanness, as opposed to differentiating (read discriminating) on the basis of gender in our relations, we will have the same conversation in another 50 years.

What is very clear is that well-being is multidimensional and different entities emphasise different aspects depending on their contexts or ideological, even philosophical, orientations. Some, like KCDF, view their interventions as addressing primary needs such as access to food, education and health. There are some like the AWDF that approach well-being from a particular framing and political consciousness. Yet an organization like SAT approaches well-being from a regional, systemic and multidimensional perspective. This implies that to properly get a full meaning of well-being or something closer to it, one needs to look at the aggregation of these institutions as opposed to a singular dimension. In many ways this is an indication of the complexity of the construction and meaning of well-being in a context that is beset by a mixed array of challenges that encompass both first- and second-generation rights. Because these institutions define well-being and its threats differently, their strategies and innovations also differ, as we discuss below.

Innovations in African philanthropy

Africa is a land of experiments and innovations. A lot of creativity takes place across board. Philanthropy has not been spared either. In an insightful article, Menkhoff (2010:137) writes that:

> All forms of philanthropy are (today) experiencing unusual changes. The first is borderless philanthropy. The second is e-philanthropy and the spread of giving, enabled by technology, in innovative ways. The third is philanthrocapitalism, with

the ambitions, and the resources of business entrepreneurs and their many ideas, ambitions and resources for increasing social impact. The fourth is collaborative philanthropy, as givers and even governments seek to collectively create greater social impact.

He argues further that all these trends are motivating the rich and the not-so rich to give more and in new ways, thus powering philanthropy, leading it toward an exciting and, sometimes, surprising future. As a result of these innovations, there has over the last decade or so been an increase in private capital flows. For example, during the global economic meltdown, private flows outpaced the official development spending. According to the *Index of Global Philanthropy and Remittances* published annually by the Hudson Institute,

> Private and voluntary organizations contributed US$12 billion in private funding to the developing world in 2009, a slight increase from US$11.8 billion in 2008. Of the total amount, regionally 33% went to sub-Saharan Africa, and 4% went to the Middle East and North Africa (2011:12).

This was due to the new sources of money that included philanthropic investment firms, impact investors and the use of innovative forms of financing such as KIVA (Africa Progress Panel 2011:51). Online giving is one innovation that has occurred in philanthropy with the advantages of wider reach and being responsive. In addition to the benefits of online platforms is direct connection between donors and recipients by such entities as KIVA. These platforms KIVA and DonorsChoose, for example, provide instant matching services for donors and beneficiaries (Menkhoff 2010:143). Established in 2005, KIVA allows people to lend money through the internet to microfinance institutions across the world, which in turn lend money to small businesses. In 2010, KIVA had distributed since 2005 over US$110 million in loans from over 630,000 lenders and donors.

Huge donations by a few rich individuals have also changed the face of philanthropy globally and in Africa. Donations such as those from Bill Gates and Warren Buffet have had huge influence on policy and practice of philanthropy in particular and development in general. In Africa huge sums of money endowing foundations such as the Tony Elumelu and TY Danjuma are also redefining the meaning and direction of philanthropy. If more private-sector individuals establish foundations, impact investing will be the norm in Africa as it has already resonated with a number of organizations. And because these are locally funded, they have the flexibility to fund development differently without having to negotiate political interests with their donors. The trend of locally-funded foundations is set to increase given the rise in local giving especially by the middle class.

Mass giving is also on the increase especially for particular causes such as disasters or humanitarian situations, such as the recent famine in Somalia and Kenya.

The Gift of the Givers is a South African-based emergency relief philanthropic entity that has responded swiftly to such needy places as Haiti, Japan and Somalia. The Gift of the Givers has had to work through the Department of International Cooperation in South Africa to channels its resources across borders. While internationally there is an increase in borderless philanthropy, the legal and institutional frameworks for cross-border philanthropy have not been updated to meet the times. The Kenya for Kenyans initiative is another example of mass giving, a trend and innovation in philanthropy that addresses some of the elements of well-being. And in 2010, when Haiti was hit by a disastrous earthquake, a group of African civil society organizations and philanthropic institutions under the leadership of Graça Machel in collaboration with TrustAfrica, SAT, CIVICUS, AWDF and the African Monitor among others pooled resources together towards the people of Haiti. One of the powerful resources was the solidarity that Africans from all walks of life showed towards Haitians. Financial resources were also gathered through online giving, tele-smses, individual giving and direct banking. This was an example of collaborative philanthropy for an international cause.

> Grantmaking is another tool that most of the philanthropic groups utilise. Most of these are very strategic regarding how they make their grants. The AWDF, for example, recognises that grantmaking can be exclusionary. This is so particularly to make the life of philanthropic organizations easy, for example, by giving small grants or not giving grants to groups that are not organised along traditional conceptions of an organization, etc., yet these constitute the largest population of Africa. Sixty per cent of AWDF's grantee profile consists of women's organizations whose annual budgets do not exceed US$100,000.

According to Mukasa (op cit.):

> This requires greater investment by AWDF in technical assistance, capacity building, outreach and a flexible approach to grantmaking which to some may appear costly and time consuming. Nevertheless, this constitutes the majority of women's organising on the continent particularly in rural communities. As an organisation seeking to support women's rights organising in Africa, it would be remiss to exclude this sizeable constituency, which is for the most part excluded from the traditional grantmaking organisations which are increasingly adopting the 'larger, fewer' strategy (larger grants, fewer grantees = greater focus and impact). These investments are at the community level. But these women are then linked with the national discourses through the provision of a platform to showcase contributions, achievements and to express issues of concern. This enables them to influence national dialogues on legal, economic or political issues.

Capacity building is another area of on-going innovation that philanthropic groups are engaged in. The continent as a whole has embarked on capacity development as the way to achieve development effectives. The Nepad Capacity Building

Framework of 2011 is perhaps the continental blueprint that most institutions refer to in addressing their needs and those of their constituents. The AWDF has embarked on capacity-building through movement-building approaches that encompass various sectors. For example, the AWDF is the hosting organization of the African Feminist Forum (AFF), a program initiated by African feminists to craft an autonomous space for reflection and agenda setting. The AFF has been widely recognised as an innovative and effective mobilization tool and methodology. The other movement-building dimension is that of engaging with the popular culture. Through the African Women in Film Forum, AWDF has convened a number of key actors, producers, writers and distributors in the 'Nollywood' (Nigeria) film industry to examine the negative and discriminatory portrayal of African women in these popular movies. [8] TrustAfrica's grantmaking strategy is also geared towards the provision of technical assistance in addition to institutional and project funding particularly for its civil society partners in crisis countries such as Liberia and Zimbabwe. In Zimbabwe, for example, TrustAfrica has facilitated the establishment of an NGO House and Arts Factory where civil society formations will access subsidized state-of-the-art services. In Liberia, TrustAfrica has focused on strengthening the capacity of civil society to engage in the post-conflict reconstruction and policy engagement. And the Tony Elumelu Foundation builds the capacity of African enterprises for good governance. It is through such efforts geared towards building the infrastructure for social change that some aspects of well-being are addressed.

Private-public partnerships are also increasingly being adopted by the philanthropy sector. In Tanzania, at least in the two areas of access to health and education, there have been innovations that express new ways of doing things. In health, for example, in the last three years, an initiative called Medical Women Association of Tanzania (MEWOTA) was established to respond to early detection of breast cancer. Appealing to the citizens, MEWOTA partnered with a private television station to mobilise resources to fund the campaign. So far the association has raised more than US$300,000.00 from individuals, corporations, etc. [9] Perhaps what this shows is that people give to a clear cause. Still in health, a hospital run by an NGO, the Comprehensive Community Based Rehabilitation Treatment, has been raising money in partnership with Vodacom, Barclays Bank and other corporations to treat disabled children and women with fistula. According to Ulanga, none of this money was raised from foreign sources. And in the field of education the Foundation for Civil Society has given seed funding to communities as catalytic funding for bringing communities together to set up village communities to mobilise resources for community developments such as scholarships.

This approach is more or less what KCDF also does for communities and what the Tony Elumelu Foundation does for entrepreneurs. According to Mawiyoo:

KCDF encourages communities to mobilise resources and the Foundation matches whatever the communities would have raised. The Foundation currently houses 20 community funds amounting to US$1 million from ordinary people, most of whom are hometown associations. These communities decide how they want to use their resources and which areas they want to address. If for example, their Fund is for scholarships, the community members select the children they want to support using a criteria they develop themselves. Further these communities have used the money to establish income generation projects that allow them to address other well-being issues such as health, youth, women, etc. KCDF has in the past provided incentives for communities interested in building small endowment funds for issues they are passionate about. A number of communities have opted to build such funds for education for orphans and other vulnerable children. KCDF still offers incentives to communities who want to raise money for things that matter to them but not to funders, e.g. a dormitory for girls, etc. This is meant to encourage communities to continuously consider resources from among themselves and not feel that they can only do stuff with money from outside.[10]

Social investments are new ways through which a number of philanthropic organizations are doing business today. GreaterGood, for example, is a philanthropic organization based in South Africa which from onset was established:

In order to address the need for information to strengthen civil society, to grow the connections between communities and people and to facilitate and encourage giving activities of all kinds; building a philanthropy of community, whilst at the same time creating the infrastructure, database and information that would ultimately also respond to the needs of the corporate sector wanting to engage more meaningfully with the imperatives of social investment (Ractliffe 2010:238).

As a result, GreaterGood also offers advisory services for social investment. In addition, GreaterGood provides '

a range of ways for connecting people with their communities (such as giving time, goods, skills, knowledge, reward points and money). At the heart of this approach is the message that everyone has something to give. Following out of this, GreaterGood created the South African Social Investment Exchange (SASIX) in 2006. This is a platform that helps CSI managers through pre-screening, social investment analysis as well as monitoring and evaluation of impact. By the beginning of 2010, SASIX had brokered commitments of around ZAR250 million (approximately US$26 million) in social impact financial investment (ibid.:241).

Impact investing is a popular strategy that a number of social venture philanthropists, including the Tony Elumelu Foundation, are making use of. Venture philanthropy is a relatively new trend but albeit growing very fast. This concept originated 'among business people who, after having achieved economic success mainly in the private sector, were looking for ways to use not only their money but their business skills and expertise to address social issues and community needs'

(Johnson et al. 2005:39). The term can also be used loosely to mean all forms of charitable endeavours that involve risk-taking, innovation and entrepreneurship (O'Halloran 2007:52). More specifically, this form of 'philanthropy supports social entrepreneurs with scale-up potential'. Venture philanthropists or their followers have criticised conventional philanthropy, mainly foundations of investing in programmes and projects rather than in non-profit infrastructure, capacity building and entrepreneurial talent (ibid:52). As a result they have urged foundations to innovate and make use of the six strategies from venture capitalism, namely i) deploying risk management tools, ii) creating performance measures, iii) developing close relationships with their investments, iv) investing more money, v) investing over long periods, and vi) developing exit strategies.

Defined as generating financial returns, which can range from producing a return of principal capital to offering market-rate or even market-beating financial returns, while solving social or environmental challenges, impact investment is not necessarily a new phenomenon, as the Dalberg Report (2011) shows. But it is a buzz right across Africa. In West Africa, for example, the highest concentration is in Ghana and Nigeria but overall there were 207 impact investors in 2011 during the time that Dalberg conducted the survey. Of these, 86 were microfinance institutions, 68 were venture capital funds, 18 were Development Finance Institutions (DFIs), 12 were foundations and 23 were institutional investors (ibid:24). Overall these had invested US$3.2 billion across various sectors.

Impact investing is, however, still not fully developed and as such there are some challenges that could hamper its success. For example, in most of these countries the skills gap is still a major area to be addressed. And so is the legal and institutional framework for impact investing. As detailed in a Special Report on Impact Investing by the Rockefeller Foundation;

> As with any nascent industry, the current framework for impact investing is still very basic and fragmented. There are only a limited number of independent third party sources of information or investment consultants; there is a complete lack of clearing houses and syndication facilities; and a common language for impact investing is yet to emerge. All this makes it difficult to communicate opportunities, successes and failures and greatly increases transaction costs for investors.[11]

The good news, however, is that the Global Impact Investing Network (GIIN) is developing some of these necessary legal and institutional frameworks, including the monitoring ones to make it easy for the field to use a common lexicon. Another challenge associated with impact investment is that of absorptive capacity. According to the Rockefeller Report, there are currently very few businesses with proven investment models. Thirdly, liquidity is a common and predominant challenge across Africa for impact investors. But these challenges can only make the industry stronger and more exciting as the world progresses more and more towards greater usage of technology and business models. To be sure, impact investing will not replace old conventional philanthropy but it will certainly unravel it a bit and complement it. In an interview with GIIN, Tony Elumelu, the founder of the Tony Elumelu Foundation, stressed the point that impact investing is new to Africa and that most of impact investment in the continent is conducted by foreign organizations. However, given his foundation's position in Africa, he hoped that it would become a resource for networking and partnerships for impact investing in Africa. And highlighting the opportunities presented by impact investing, Elumelu said:

> As impact investing grows in Africa, it can influence traditional investors in Africa to be more aware of the social and environmental effects of their investments. By driving the concept of impact investing, the private sector will see that there is a lot of money to be made in Africa not only by providing services to middle and upper class Africans, but also by providing services to the poor, such as investing in low-income housing, agriculture aggregation, education and low income health-care to name a few. We are at a tipping point now as there are billions of dollars coming into Africa through private investment. That's why it is important that a significant portion of this new capital is deployed in ways that are intentionally about impact investing.[12]

Clearly the emergence of new philanthropists who are hands-on and seek to be more responsive to the changing and complex Africa are also making significant changes to the face and practice of philanthropy. In many ways this is helping change perspectives on Africa from being seen as a charity case to seeing Africa as a place for innovation and success. Elumelu summed it well when he said:

> In the coming years, impact investing has the potential to truly transform the continent. Those of us pioneering impact investing field in Africa are not only making investments, we are also engaging and supporting important partners who can help impact investing grow. As an African entrepreneur, I hope to show African entrepreneurs that they can make money while also truly touching the people who live at the base of the economic pyramid.[13]

Endowment building is another area that African philanthropy has adopted. The concept of an endowment is not new in Africa. In most traditional societies a granary was used to store resources for later needs. Also, family names were and still continue to be used as memory and legacy. Only family names can keep alive the lineage. For a number of these philanthropic groups, the question of sustainability is one that they seek to address through building endowments. The AWDF, Mandela Children's Fund and KCDF among others have all established these funds so as to sustain their interventions. Others like the TY Danjuma have personally financed their own endowments. These endowments enable these groups to engage in policy advocacy and other areas of lobbying that cannot be funded from outside. TrustAfrica and SAT, for example, are involved in advocacy efforts towards protecting the space for civil society in Africa. Politically this is a minefield, and matters are made worse if such efforts are funded from outside Africa. Endowment building will help make the agenda local and legitimate.

Perhaps the most important innovation and strategy is that of collaborative philanthropy alluded to above. Realising the power of transformative partnerships is an innovation that for years to come will define how relations are made. In many ways, this is in response to the realization that addressing well-being is not something a single institution can tackle alone. There is need for collaborations that transform the status quo. This discussion is taken below.

Transformative collaborations and partnerships

Building strong relationships between different types of groups as opposed to developing the well-being of one group over others is fast becoming a must do in the continent among philanthropic actors. Neville Gabriel of SAT sees this as one of the priorities of his organization as it builds a value chain of relationships especially for policy change.[14] SAT has developed strategic partnerships with key civil society actors, the business sector, intergovernmental agencies and, more importantly, with the media across the region and continentally.

The issue of partnerships is further taken up by the Africa Progress Panel in its 2011 Report:

> effective cross-sectoral partnerships can make it possible to overcome challenges that are too difficult or complex for one organisation or sector to address alone. Partnerships can also make efforts more effective by combining resources and competencies in creative ways.

As noted by Menkhoff (2010:144):

> Even the Bill and Melinda Gates Foundation, one of the world's largest foundations with total assets of US$30 billion, has worked actively with other foundations. There is a realisation that today's challenges and their scale require the power of partnerships and diversity of talents than only an alliance with other organisations can bring.

Partnerships have been established by African philanthropic entities at a global level with such platforms as the European Foundation Centre, WINGS, Synergos, the African Grantmakers Affinity Group and the Foundation Centre among others. However, the single most transformative partnership they have done since 2009 is to collectively come together and establish a network in Africa dedicated to their common experiences, visions and expertise. This platform, the African Grantmakers Network (AGN) emerged as a result of the need to reposition and clarify Africa's position in global relations as well as critically develop efforts to unite Africa's response(s) to global challenges of well-being. The formation of the

AGN has the potential to function as a platform for diverse philanthropic actors and institutions for the development of the continent. Such a platform or network will collate views and ideas; amplify African perspectives and methodologies; conduct mapping studies to understand the terrain; and hold dialogues and convenings to catalyze ideas and collectively identify needs and strategies to address them. Launched after a series of many consultations in 2009, the AGN is a platform that aims to

- establish systematic mechanisms for fostering learning, sharing, exchange and collaboration among Africa's burgeoning grantmaking community;

- harmonize current and existing informal attempts to have a continental body that brings together ideas, skills and people working on philanthropy;

- build on regional associations such as the East Africa Association of Grantmakers (EAAG) by providing a platform for cross-regional learning and exchange;

- conduct a number of studies that will deepen the sector and institutions' understanding of the philanthropic terrain, for example grantmaking landscape, in Africa;

- build a participatory platform for broader engagement with development processes;

- hold regular convenings on philanthropy and other related development issues;

- conduct studies related to building a knowledge base and evidence-based grantmaking;advocate for an enabling tax/fiscal environment in African countries;

- become a resource for stimulating giving including from the corporate sector and the diaspora (Moyo 2009).

So far the AGN has managed to hold its first inaugural assembly, where it brought together more than 200 grantmaking or philanthropic institutions in Africa to set the agenda for the AGN. Today there is a serious move to position the network as the premier pan-African platform for philanthropy in Africa, offering membership services, capacity building, outreach and philanthropic advisory services to different groups of philanthropists.

In addition to the AGN are philanthropy circles and forums, including regional networks. Across Africa, philanthropic institutions have created networks or platforms to collectively respond to issues that affect them from a national, thematic or even regional dimension. In Nigeria, for example, the TY Danjuma Foundation in partnership with other philanthropic entities in the country holds an annual philanthropy forum to address the landscape in Nigeria. In the inaugural session, the country's President, His Excellency Goodluck Jonathan. committed to setting up a commission that would look into the regulatory framework for philanthropy in Nigeria. In South Africa, the Philanthropy Circle is a forum where national issues affecting philanthropy are addressed. In Liberia, the Philanthropy Secretariat was developed to coordinate donor funding primarily to the government. And in East Africa, the EAAG holds annual assemblies to take stock of the landscape in the region. Unfortunately, the Southern Africa Grantmakers Association fragmented and died a few years back. These platforms are critical as they give participants 'voice'. According to Neville, 'voice' is an important part of well-being. In most of these platforms, there is an increasing realization that there is a need to celebrate African philanthropists. Awards feature prominently in these forums, examples include SAT's 'Drivers of Change' and Inyathelo Awards among others.

Table 2.2: Summary of innovations and partnerships in African philanthropy

Innovations/strategies	Partnerships (collaborative philanthropy)
E-Philanthropy (online giving, direct connection between donors and recipients, new social media, etc.)	Global partnerships (such as with WINGS, EFC, AGAG, etc.)
Cross-border (borderless) philanthropy	Local partnerships including:
Philanthrocapitalism (social investments, venture philanthropy, impact investing, social stock exchanges, etc.)	African Grantmakers Network
Advocacy and lobbying including awards celebrations	Philanthropy circles, forums etc.
Huge donations – fewer recipients	Regional associations of grantmakers
Mass giving including diaspora giving	Philanthropy secretariat(s)
Grantmaking	Joint programming
Capacity building including movement building	Public–private partnerships
Public–private partnerships	Secondments (staff, etc.)
Endowment building	Joint funding and fundraising

Other partnerships are at the level of individual organizations. For example, TrustAfrica – a pan African foundation based in Dakar, Senegal – has since its establishment prioritized partnerships with local African institutions and other development actors. For example, with SAT, a number of collaborations such as joint funding, publications and staff exchanges have been conducted since 2008,

resulting in collective outputs. The Tony Elumelu Foundation improves the competitiveness of Africa's high-growth private sector businesses while introducing
some of the world's brightest young business talent to executive suites across
Africa. It also partners with Tony Blair's Africa Governance Initiative on the Blair
Elumelu Fellowship Programme that supports transformational governments by
strengthening the private sector's role in economic transformation. Each of these
foundations has developed partnerships based on mutual respect, credibility and
reciprocity. In the coming years, investing in partnerships will increase in importance, as will impact investing.

Pointers for new knowledge and policy implications for promoting well-being

This chapter has discussed the various expressions of philanthropy in Africa and
how each of those manifestations relates to well-being. Clearly, there is no one
dimension to philanthropy and neither is there one aspect to well-being. Different
actors address well-being differently based on their contexts, structures, orientations and beliefs. Despite these different nuances and perspectives, a number of
trends stand out that have implications for the promotion of well-being and policy
development in the twenty-first century. The following paragraphs pool out some
of those trends in order to offer pointers for policymakers, philanthropic institutions and other development actors.

First, there is a new way of practising philanthropy in Africa, one that builds
on solidarity, reciprocity, giving and helping from local sources. The emergence
of locally established and funded foundations and the fact that from Tanzania to
Kenya to South Africa, individuals, corporations, etc. give to public and private
causes is a reaffirmation that Africans are givers naturally. There is hope that Africa
can support her own developmental needs as well as define her own trajectory.
Till such time that Africa finances her own development, well-being will remain
elusive. The challenge, however, still remains that in most of the African countries
there is no legal and institutional framework for philanthropic practice. Perhaps the
African Grantmakers Network's real relevance would be to cultivate the culture
of philanthropy for social justice and other forms of development inclusiveness
among policymakers by establishing necessary policy frameworks as well as to
motivate among African citizens – individually or collectively – giving towards the
well-being of societies and their peoples. This calls for dialogue and collaboration
between citizens, their formations and the sphere of public authority (the state)
in fashioning African-led and supported initiatives and frameworks.

Second, Africa has unique philosophies and cultural foundations. These underpin
the different expressions of philanthropic practice. Africans' well-being therefore

---

Box 2.1: Collaboration and solidarity in 'crisis' Zimbabwe

As early as 2007, TrustAfrica responded to the political and economic crises in Zimbabwe through projects that sought to strengthen the vibrancy of civil society and its capacity to respond to those crises. So when Zimbabwe Alliance – a consortium of donors interested in funding Zimbabwe – was born, it made sense for TrustAfrica to collaborate for a number of reasons. First, to avoid duplication of effort. Second, it was in line with TrustAfrica's approach of collaboration, dialogue and consultation. Third, it further bolstered what TrustAfrica was already doing in Liberia – another post-crisis country – where it collaborated with Humanity United to strengthen civil society to contribute towards the reconstruction of Liberia.

TrustAfrica saw itself playing a critical function in Zimbabwe Alliance. Because of its existing projects in Zimbabwe, it brought knowledge, experience and political consciousness. In addition, TrustAfrica's staff – from operations, grantmaking and programming – were all involved in the identification and implementation of projects. The Zimbabwe Alliance would thus benefit from a low overhead and be able to disburse most of the resources to partners, as TrustAfrica staff were already covered by its core funding. TrustAfrica had also developed and expanded its internal systems so that the Alliance could be assured that its resources were in good hands and would be disbursed after rigorous due diligence.

In addition, TrustAfrica's pan-African reach meant that it had developed networks across the continent which helped provide the necessary solidarity, movement-building and partnerships to deal with politically charged situations. Finally, TrustAfrica attempted to match in part the resources from Zimbabwe Alliance, financially and in kind.

Perhaps it is too early to say definitively whether the collaboration has been worthwhile, but the signs are that it has. TrustAfrica has pooled resources, and indications are that more members will join and increase the grantmaking budget. Like all other collaborations, TrustAfrica and the Alliance had to learn about their individual and organizational cultures, approaches and principles: what to compromise and what not to compromise; what to prioritize and what to leave for later. In many ways, it has been an opportunity to deepen understanding of particularly identities and principles. The collaboration with Zimbabwe Alliance has also enabled to tighten Zimbabwe projects and connect all collective partners there under the banner of the Alliance. And if the political climate worsens, there is a network through which to build a stronger resistance. Only partnerships and collaborations have the potential to address the underlying causes of political and economic malaise in a country like Zimbabwe. And civil society is key to such an intervention.

---

cannot be separated from these cultural and philosophical foundations. Utilising Sen's capability approach, it means Africans have to take the lead in promoting their own well-being. This implies that all forms of philanthropy or development actors that are not aligned to these foundations are bound to miss out on the nuances of

African well-being. In many ways this calls for a review of the development trajectory that Africa adopted, one that does not prioritize local institutions, knowledge and perspectives. This calls for serious investment on strengthening local institutions, systems and normative frameworks. The new HNWIs are well positioned to fund development differently in Africa. Not only can they provide leadership in this area, they are also influential individuals who can champion policy agendas for well-being in Africa. For this to happen, philanthropy in Africa has to forge a partnership with the different types of HNWIs and policy influencers to address well-being questions in Africa. Rather than focusing on their differences and the methodologies they employ, it is time now for these to collectively respond to the challenges facing the continent and the world, such as climate change, democratic deficits, inequality and other forms of exclusion.

Thirdly, the sure and fastest way to address well-being is the need for development to be driven by the people concerned. And yet ironically it takes a long time for a project to be people driven. This implies that for policymakers and development actors alike there is a need to invest adequately in participatory frameworks, just as much attention is given to material aspects of human well-being. Questions of capacity building, infrastructure development, leadership development, governance reforms and education become more critical than projects-based investments. As discussed earlier, one of the strong aspects of social venture philanthropy is that it prioritizes building the infrastructure for social change. This is likely to grow and get resonance among many African institutions. For policymakers, this requires creating an enabling environment for social investments. And for conventional philanthropy, this means learning from some of the principles that have made venture philanthropists successful. And as for the venture philanthropists, it requires humility to accept that not everything needs a business model.

Fourth, there is a danger, especially as a result of HNWIs and the private sector still not funding or supporting social justice questions, that the notion of well-being can be narrowly simplified to mean tangible questions of access to water, education, health, etc. but not address the wholeness of a human being. As this chapter has tried to demonstrate, human well-being comprises both material and non-material aspects; and as such, focus should be given equally to all its dimensions. Because increasingly wealth is concentrated among a few HNWIs, who also are primarily from the private sector, there is a tendency and perhaps rightly so given their background to be reductionist and seek solutions for social challenges in the business models that have made them successful. To be sure, there is a role for this approach but it must not replace the other forms of philanthropy that have existed over years and addressed such challenging and complex questions as social justice, democracy, the media and increasingly now socioeconomic rights. For policymakers this is a call for an appropriate environment for all forms of philanthropy to thrive in order to meet the ever-changing dynamics of well-being. For philanthropic actors there is a need to build mechanisms for complementarity, collaboration and new ways of tackling inclusive development.

Fifth, no one organization or individual can address human well-being holistically, not even Bill Gates or Warren Buffet. Even these have seen the need to forge partnerships in order to strongly respond to the needs and demands of societal and individual well-being. It is for this reason that the establishment of the AGN and the other regional and national philanthropic platforms is crucial in moving Africa forward. Increasingly it is becoming very clear that the lines between the business sector and philanthropy will be closed and both will partner with governments to address pressing developmental questions in Africa. There is a dire need to prioritize transformative partnerships, most of which are driven by new technologies, innovations and the passion for a progressive continent. Nothing seals these partnerships better than the spirit of solidarity and reciprocity underpinning African relationships. Thus impact investing encompassing venture philanthropy, online giving and strategic philanthropy, among others, will complement in effective ways other forms of philanthropy in Africa in tackling development and well-being.

Endnotes

1 This chapter was originally prepared for the Bellagio Summit, an initiative of IDS, Rockefeller and Resource Alliance. Permission to reproduce this updated version was granted by IDS.
2 Interview with Neville Gabriel, Executive Director, Southern Africa Trust. Midrand, 12/10/11.
3 For a very detailed discussion of philanthropy in Africa, see Moyo, B. (2009; 2010) in the *Encyclopaedia of Civil Society* and also in *Global Philanthropy*.
4 Interview with Janet Mawiyoo, Executive Director: KCDF, 20 September 2011: Bellagio Rockefeller Center.
5 Janet Mawiyoo, op. cit.
6 Interview with John Ulanga, CEO: Foundation for Civil Society in Tanzania, 20 September 2011: Bellagio Rockefeller Center.
7 In-flight interview with Sarah Mukasa, Director of Programmes: AWDF, 23 September 2011: SN Brussels to Accra.
8 For more details of AWDF, see www.awdf.org
9 John Ulanga, op. cit
10 Janet Mawiyoo, op. cit.
11 See 'This is Africa' — *A Special Report on Impact Investment* by The Rockefeller Foundation.
12 See *Investor Spotlight*: 'The Tony Elumelu Foundation', http://www.thegiin.org/cgi-bin/iowa/investing/spotlight/225.html, accessed 2011/10/13.
13 Ibid.

14 Gabriel, op. cit.

CHAPTER 3

"I AM WELL IF YOU ARE WELL": NERVOUS CONDITIONS OF PHILANTHROPY IN AFRICAN CULTURE[1]

ROBERT MUPONDE

Introduction

In this chapter I propose to deploy the optic of culture, specifically in the context of gift-giving and gift-receiving, to examine the conditions and potentialities of philanthropic practice in Africa as it is represented in the two novels of the much-acclaimed Zimbabwean writer Tsitsi Dangarembga. Her first novel, *Nervous Conditions* (1988), has been read tropistically as a gender-sensitive narrative which explores the tensions and hopes attendant on the emergence of African girlhood into liberated personhood. What has absorbed critics, male and female, is the spectacle of the girl child's struggle against odds, patriarchal and colonial, and the ever-looming figure of the benevolent patriarch Babamukuru (her Big Father), who obliquely recalls Pumblechook's philanthropic and ironically vindictive and blackmailing gestures in Charles Dickens' *Great Expectations*.

What has therefore escaped critics is the tradition of philanthropy in African culture which is predicated on the often abused philosophy of hospitality and mutual care and dependency as encapsulated in the Shona response to a greeting, '*tiripo kana muripo-o*' (I am well if you are well). This seemingly phatic response to a greeting sets social conditionalities that are mutually binding. But these conditionalities, the very props of good neighbourliness, have to be understood within the ever-shifting and taxed matrices of the culture undergoing coerced change. Tsitsi Dangarembga's second and successful novel, *The Book of Not* (2006), revisits and critiques the impulse of indigenous philanthropy as embodied by Babamukuru, her uncle, the same character who enabled her female narrator's liberation and education in *Nervous Conditions*, but who now sets stultifying traps for her in the guise of generosity and free-spirited giving. *The Book of Not* seems to suggest the dangers associated with an uncritical appreciation of in-house or indigenous practices of philanthropy which masquerade as self-upraising projects.

This chapter, therefore, uses the lens of the novel to launch a critical examination of these trapping manifestations of goodwill, and what informs their world view, and points towards what might be considered alternative cultures of giving and receiving as adumbrated in the two novels as well as in the practices figured in African folklore. It is hoped that by examining these cultural spaces, the question 'which world view defines philanthropy' might be reached and speculations about African complex reactions (if not sometimes cynicism) to philanthropy-as-development might be rethought. In the course of the chapter, I will reflect on three Shona folkloric views on giving and receiving and their consequences in the two novels.

i.   *Ukama igasva hunozadziswa nekudya/karere mangwana kagokurerawo* (relations are empty vessels that are filled with sharing / raise him today he will raise you tomorrow);

ii.   *Tsitsi dzinotsitsirira/ kupa kunenge kuramwa/kutuka* (kindness/generosity kills / a generosity that is like throwing away or insulting);

iii.   *Chisi chako masimba mashoma; mombe yekuronzerwa igama wakaringa nzira.* (you have no power over what is not yours or what is given as a gift; you milk a borrowed cow with your eyes locating the escape route).

Patriarchal largesse: *karere kazokurerawo* (raise one who will raise you tomorrow)

'Babamukuru' means the Big Father, one's father's elder brother, who assumes the role of Father over the whole family. He is usually the first born in the family. 'Uncle' does not give one a clear sense of this man's power, influence and responsibilities in Shona culture. It is this Big Father, a highly educated headmaster at a mission school in colonial Zimbabwe (Rhodesia), who takes upon himself the responsibility of uplifting the family of his poorer young brother Jeremiah. The story of his largesse, and the destruction of social bonds that his altruism entails, is narrated by Tsitsi Dangarembga over the space of two novels, *Nervous Conditions (NC)* and *The Book of Not (BN)*. Both novels tell the story of a young woman's struggle for education and visibility, and the subsequent collapse of her vision and ambitions, as well as that of her Big Father's social upliftment project. The first novel opens with the death of Tambu's brother, who had been first chosen by Babamukuru as the object and instrument of his charity and upliftment project. It ends with Babamukuru's own daughter Nyasha's near-death as a result of a nervous breakdown.

The second novel opens with the violent beating of Babamukuru by the guerrillas ('elder siblings' as they are called in the novel) for sending Tambu to a whites-only school. Tambu's own sister Netsai loses a leg when she steps on a grenade at the scene where Babamukuru is being beaten by the guerrillas. The novel ends with Babamukuru in a wheelchair, having been crippled by a stray bullet during the inaugural celebrations of Zimbabwe's Independence in April 1980. It also ends with Tambu more uncertain about what it means to be a 'new Zimbabwean', having lost the initial impetus to search and provide for 'the good and human' which goes beyond 'only my own calamities' (*BN* 246).

In both novels, there is an attempt to define what Tambu calls '*unhu*', the good and the human, and this is done in conditions that test what it might mean to be good and human in times of social stress and disorder. This is a time of war and change, a time of emergencies, national and familial. Tambu herself is yoked to Babamukuru's upliftment project by default, because Nhamo, Jeremiah's son, had died inexplicably in his teens without having fulfilled Babamukuru's vision of emancipating his young brother's family from degrading poverty through education. In choosing Nhamo, Babamukuru had at least two ideas in mind.

One idea is that, in a situation of poverty and oppression where, as Jeremiah puts it, 'You can't dream! You can't dream!' (*NC* 45), 'These children who can go to school today are the ones whose families will prosper tomorrow' (*NC* 45). Sending a child to school then becomes an insurance policy against the uncertainties of the family's future. The child's education becomes communal property. Babamukuru, for instance, realized at some point during his own missionary-aided studies that 'even more than myself my whole family needed my qualification' (*NC* 45). He therefore chooses to educate Jeremiah's son Nhamo in order to replicate his efforts, hoping Nhamo would see his own pursuit of education as a 'duty to do'. There is something missionary about his magnanimity: it is not only about a sense of duty to his clan, but a sense of obligation to reciprocate and repay a social debt. The missionaries who educated him taught him to endure and defy hardships, and to stand as a good example of magic of hard work and unstinting benevolence, and reproduce the teachings about giving freely and teaching a man how to catch fish. He embodies the religious devotion to an unquestioning but strategic benevolence which he puts to the service of his own civilizing mission. He becomes, in a way, the power of charity writ large in his homestead, which stands as his special area of attention. 'He didn't need to be bold any more because he had made himself plenty of power; Plenty of power; Plenty of money; A lot of education; Plenty of everything' (*NC* 50), as Tambu and his clan see him. This idea of plenty-as-power enables him to make decisions for the entire clan about who benefits from his philanthropic and social upliftment project. It also enables him to devise and spell out the agenda of development to be followed by the beneficiary of his largesse.

The second reason Babamukuru chooses Nhamo is not only because of his sense of power, and the 'plenty' it brought with it, which enabled him to determine the destiny of each individual in the homestead, but a desire to advance a specific male agenda. It is a charitable act undergirded by the designs of a patriarchal order. This is because Babamukuru had reckoned:

> Looking at the family as it stands today, … I see that the problem is with Jeremiah. Tete [Auntie] here is all right – her husband is able to take care of her and her children. Thomas [another brother] is also in no trouble – he may not have a degree, but his teacher training is a solid qualification. The family does not go hungry.… The real worry is your branch, Jeremiah. (*NC*, 45)

Prosperity of the homestead entails rescuing the male folk, so they in turn can raise children and provide for their wives, and hence ensuring that the homestead is 'well' too.

Nhamo reads the gesture of the giving hand in the same terms as Tambu his sister. He sees intimations of power and plenty in the giving hand, which he sees himself inheriting and exercising over his siblings, and possibly parents later on in life. Thus the power of the gift destroys the receiving hand. It is a gift given without enough safeguards on the part of the giver as well as the receiver. Nhamo is lost to his family as soon as he leaves the homestead for Babamukuru's mission house. The gift he receives from Babamukuru propels him out of the orbit of the family. He immediately devises ways of avoiding coming home and at some point loses his mother tongue altogether (*NC*, 53). Whereas Babamukuru's education in the UK, itself a gift from the missionaries, does not induce a sense of alienation in him, but commits him more to a sense of a healthy, well-developed community, Nhamo's acquisition gives him a momentum that alienates him from his family. The power he begins to exercise over his siblings is that of a bully, even though he is still at primary school level.

This is contrary to the demeanor of Babamukuru, who acquires a quiet, benevolent power from the life of the gift he receives from the missionaries. Nhamo therefore offers us one way of thinking about gifts and charity that destroys individuals and societies who are recipients, because the purposes of that charity are not made binding on the individual, and there is no tracking device to detect when deviations from the purposes occur. Nhamo's example of a deviant recipient of charity also goes to show the conflict between communal aspirations and individual values. Where Babamukuru and the clan thought the elevation of Nhamo would mean the elevation of the whole community, Nhamo only saw his own flight

from poverty and depressing social conditions. By the nature of colonial education itself, which emphasized individual effort and excellence and competition,
the norms of communal cohesion and development could not be guaranteed by
advancing a single individual through an individuating educational process. It was
a contradiction in terms which only Babamukuru was able to overcome when
he placed his qualification on the altar of communal aspirations. That too meant
Babamukuru understood the giving of a gift as sacrifice, and he saw clearly how
sacrifice and self-interest may combine to give an overpowering sense of altruism
in the engineering of society.

Nhamo's death should therefore be seen as a necessary sacrifice of the individual
in order to spread the gift widely and equitably. His death closes the chapter on
possible corruption that may occur when gifts are deposited in the hands of those
who will not reciprocate in expected ways, or are ill equipped to reciprocate. The
gift becomes an unmitigated burden from which one seeks urgent relief. Nhamo's
death can be viewed as a retirement of a bad social debt. For Nhamo's mother,
Babamukuru's gift to her son and family disrupts, devitalizes and atrophies her life
as a poor woman. It conjures the stillbirths that characterized her married life. She
rebukes Babamukuru and his wife:

> 'First you took his tongue so that he could not speak to me and now you have taken
> everything.... You bewitched him now he is dead.... You and your education have
> killed my son.' (NC 54)

The gift from Babamukuru, and the charity it stands for, instead of representing
brighter opportunities on the boil for her, resemble the power of witchcraft to
transfix a life and turn social bonds into instances of bondage to an inescapable force.
Her four babies, 'three of them sons, had died in infancy' (NC 51), succumbing to
the mysteries of nature and biology. Nhamo is abstracted from her by a more po-
tent force, 'plenty' money and education, represented by a more consolidated and
modernized patriarchal position such as Babamukuru occupies in the colony. The
gift he provides is as much a despoiler as it is a colonizing one, causing and bearing
all the debilitating symptoms of nervousness associated with colonial education.

The offer of the same gift to Tambu, the sister, is an attempt to revitalize and
re-engineer social progress through an alternative medium. It has very little to do
with Aafke Komter's (2005:3) understanding of modern society's desire to create
solidarity through gift-giving, where 'gifts still create and maintain social bonds,
thereby continually contributing to the revitalization of society'. It has more to do
with ideas of individual self-perpetuation: the desire to create more binding ties
between giver and receiver in order to control the ways in which social relations
might be reproduced and configured. The stylistics of giving and receiving underline
one simple fact of the omnipotence of plenty. Tambu argues:

> 'When you have a lot of anything it makes you feel good to give a bit of it away. I knew that because when I had a tickey from Babamukuru I could buy six *fet koeks* at break. I felt like a saint when I gave my friend Nyari two. That was why Babamukuru was always so kind and generous'. (*NC* 50)

An equation is soon set up: plenty equals giving where giving equals saintliness. Or another arithmetic: plenty is saintly when it equals giving. It becomes a compulsive ritual, a mindset which responds to the pressure to give because giving is a performance of saintly generosity, and hence what is good and human. The same compulsion to give sets up terms for future ritualistic behaviour where the fact that one once received compels one to give. But giving is not a boundless oceanic gesture; it is highly selective and constricted. The gift is offered to one who has the potential to return it, and give it more life. So a community of givers and receivers, in which gifts circulate, is carefully chosen and cultivated.

> 'That was why he did all he could for everybody and in this case had singled out Nhamo for special promotion, as he had been singled out by the good wizards at the mission.... I understood that that made him [Nhamo] the logical choice for Babamukuru's project'. (*NC* 50)

Hierarchies of giving

A community creates hierarchies of giving. The giving is unidirectional. It is from one with authority to another without authority. This authority does not only inhere in resources, but in age and race. A white missionary ('good wizards', as Tambu calls them) gives to a black boy, and the black boy in turn, when he has made use of the gift received from the good wizards, and is himself in a position of privilege and authority as a headmaster at a mission school, also gives to another black boy, who is in circumstances similar to his own when he was a boy. This hierarchy of giving is underwritten by an ethos which seeks to make the idea of giving a game of power and privilege masquerading as voluntary charity. The social investments made in this chain of giving and receiving ensure the perpetuation of this hierarchy as it begins to install itself at the heart of society as a tradition. The young boy does not give to those who already have, or those who have already given him. One gives not because one can. Giving is an enactment of power, a gathering of privileges, as well as a recognition and consolidation of hierarchies.

Babamukuru can only give to his young brother's family, not to the white missionary's family. It seems to be against the grain to return the gift to the authoritative other who enabled one's privileges in the first place. It seems a reversal of roles, a social coup. This is contrary to Shona custom, which says '*kandiro kanoenda kunobva kamwe*' ('you give to those who give you') or '*ukama igasva hunozadziswa nekudya*' ('relations are not fulfilling unless there is sharing of gifts and food'). There seems to be something wrong in gifts that flow in one direction: downstream. What they do is that they create an expectation among the less privileged, such as Jeremiah and his wife, a sense of entitlement to gift-receiving, that they need not give, but receive. That it is perfectly acceptable to expect the elder to give to the younger person, the powerful to the powerless, without questioning the content of what is given, and how it is given. It is only Nhamo's mother who questions what her son is given.

The giving by the powerful and privileged becomes a matter of rote learning in the ways they exercise their authority and privileges and elderhood. It is not necessarily a desire to benefit humanity. It is a necessary sacrifice to maintain the hierarchy of giving (including the giving of orders) where: 'To give is to show one's superiority, to show that one is something more and higher' (Mauss 1954:72).

Gifts as orders to perform

It is not far-fetched to think of gifts in such a hierarchy as orders to perform in certain expected ways once indebtedness is foisted and acknowledged. In the case of Babamukuru, he is indebted to the 'good wizards', and the works of his ordered charity should be rendered visible by his own recruitment of Nhamo into his project. Nhamo is expected to perform certain tasks in order to satisfy conditions of the gift contract. He is compelled by necessity as well as the allure of a possible life of plenty to accept the contract. Thus, the giving back to Babamukuru he can do is mandatory servitude to his immediate family. Babamukuru went through the same apprenticeship of giving when he supported his brother's family while he was study-ing in the UK. It is a form of martyrdom, self-abnegating in order that the other might receive and live. Nhamo is of course the wrong candidate, the interview of him by Babamukuru had not been based on his being 'older than [Tambu] and much more advanced academically' (*NC* 50), as Tambu initially thought, but on the fact that he is a boy, a male, and a potential Father of the family like Babamukuru. It is a gift that will circulate in approved circles. The gift is an instrument that establishes the orbit and direction of social energies of the receiver. Camouflaged as a token of compassion and generosity, it is 'obligatory and interested' (Mauss 1954:1) as an instrument of creating in the receiver what Charles Rzepka aptly called 'the emotional currency of gift-indebtedness' (1995:175). It is a feeling and obligation that is carefully and systematically induced, just like the idea of patriotism or filial piety. If well taught and well managed, it creates networks of patronage and alliances.

Thus, the hand of Babamukuru does not give freely in this regard, because the gift does not fall freely into the receiver's palm. He is constrained by antecedent practices of male giving, which make the giving of particular gifts a specifically male activity and privilege. Nhamo's squandering of the gift can be seen as resistance to both this practice of giving as well as its prescriptions. Nhamo fails to live up to the idea of a loyal boy who will become Father. He abandons his homestead, the one he is supposed to take care of, denounces his father ('I shall no longer be Jeremiah's son' (*NC* 48) and becomes aphasic. He loses the language that should carry the values filigreed to the gift he receives from Babamukuru. He dies because he will not be able to innovate and continue the tradition, authority and politics strapped to the gift. He cannot be male enough. He dies in infancy, metaphorically, because he would have ruined the social and metaphysical investments attached to the gift. It is a preemptive death.

Babamukuru's is a gift that kills if its edicts are not observed. It is not a gift that seeks to transform the individual in order for him to perform roles differently. It is a gift that seeks to conserve those roles, and make them more predictable and more efficient in terms of producing predictability. Nhamo, like Babamukuru, was supposed to be educated in order to take care of a homestead, by which is meant women and children. By giving, Babamukuru sought to reproduce himself in Nhamo, because 'to give something is to give a part of oneself' (Mauss 1954:10). Babamukuru gives more than a part of himself. His giving is part of the technique of load-shedding of future social responsibilities to the extended family. It is a way of decentralizing the art of cultivating gift-indebtedness. This is in order to animate and effect the folkloric wisdom of gift-giving which exhorts charity in others because '*karere mangwana kanozokurerawo*' ('raise him/her today he will raise you tomorrow'). The gift is a bidding. It is an expectation. Nhamo dies because he is no longer living on the terms of the gift. It is a constraining and imprisoning gift. It requires a measure of self-denying martyrdom which only Tambu is capable of enduring. She carries its burden across the space of two novels. It can also be argued that Nhamo dies because of his growing misanthropy, which threatens to staunch the circulation of obligatory social energies of which the gift is a vector or conduit.

Is it a boy, is it a girl?

Babamukuru's choice of an heir to the gift first offered to Nhamo is as limited as Tambu's choices when confronted with the offer to revive the gift. For Babamukuru, the choice of heir is already made for him because Tambu is as hard working and intelligent as Nhamo before her. She is older than all the children in the family, thus placing her next in line to receive the gift. But she is a girl, meaning in Shona culture she is not the most obvious person to be recipient of patrimony, as girls are often considered passers-by in the family. Tambu's father puts it succinctly when the matter came up for discussion concerning whether Tambu should benefit from Babamukuru's 'scholarship' scheme. 'Tambudzai's sharpness with her books is no use because in the end it will benefit strangers' (*NC* 56) when she gets married.

The idea is to keep the gift circulating within the family. Yet Babamukuru must give Tambu a chance:

> You are correct, Jeremiah,... but I will not feel that I have done my duty if I neglected the family for that reason. Er – this girl – heyo, Tambudzai – must be given the opportunity to do what she can for the family before she goes into her husband's home. (*NC* 56).

So, Tambu will have to 'pay back' before she can be allowed to move on. These conditions were never placed on Nhamo, the boy, for as a man the repayment period only comes to an end when another boy child is anointed to take the place of the 'giver'. Giving is inherited, and as an inheritance it is passed down a certain line. Babamukuru inherits this 'giving' from the 'good wizards', whose criteria for choosing him included the fact that he was 'performing exceptionally well at school' and that he 'was diligent, he was industrious, he was respectful' (*NC* 19). All this was in spite of the fact that he put in 'a full day's work on the farm' (*NC* 19) at the mission during the day and attended classes in the evenings. But more important, 'They thought he was a good boy, cultivable, in the way that land is, to yield harvests that sustain the cultivator' (*NC* 19).

The receiver of charity must exhibit certain attributes that reflect the character of the giver, one who preaches austere, humble living.

Through self-abnegation and diligence:

> My uncle became prosperous and respected, well enough salaried to reduce a little the meagerness of his family's existence. This indicated that life could be lived with a modicum of dignity in any circumstances if you worked hard enough and obeyed the rules. (*NC* 19)

There is one lesson to be learnt about this type of gift: its rules have to be endured and obeyed (*NC* 19). The potential receiver has to have the prerequisite qualities, bendable to the giver's sway, that match the giver's philosophical projections of outcomes. Babamukuru is a perfect specimen to receive the gift: diligent, intelligent, pliable, and productive in approved ways. But he is not a dogmatic learner, because the dogma of giving that he learnt from the 'good wizards' is not assiduously committed to memory. His own attempt at being missionary by passing on the gift is flawed, and is therefore bound to disappoint. For instance, he chooses Nhamo on the basis of his being a boy in the family and someone with the potential to resemble Babamukuru in the acquisition of book knowledge as well as in the sharing of a common background of poverty. He chooses Tambu on the basis that there is no Nhamo, and no other boy in the family, so he might just as well do with a girl who shows intellectual promise. He does not look at the receiver's potential to be cultivable and pliant. The charity Babamukuru received from the missionaries is calculated to produce well-meaning ideological clones. His own form of charity produces rebels, because it alienates the individual from his or her formative experiences and aspirations, creating a disconnection between individual initiative and his benefactor's goals.

While Babamukuru himself has a Christ-like acceptance and endurance of austere life, he rises from and above it, and hugs it intimately as a source of his strength. He uses the talismanic powers of the gift he received from the missionaries to transform a life of deprivations into a visionary life of generosity. On the contrary, Nhamo, the boy he anoints as receiver of his gift, as soon as he makes his escape from the impoverished homestead into Babamukuru's mission house:

> All this poverty began to offend him, or at the very least to embarrass him after he went to the mission, in a way that it had not done before. Before he went to the mission, we had been able to agree that although our squalor was brutal, it was uncompromisingly ours; that the burden of dispelling it was, as a result, ours too. (*NC* 7)

So, Babamukuru has not learnt something about human agency and choice. He has also not learnt that the contract implied by the receiving of the gift is only binding in situations where the receiving individual or community shares similar values with the giver, or has the propensity to comply with its implied commands.

Tambu would have us believe that, having been appalled by Nhamo's renegade character, she would do better if placed in his position. It does not happen that way, and she never gets to fulfil her contract with Babamukuru. Tambu herself is very much like Nhamo, only more poetic and effusive in her expression of personal gratitude to Babamukuru's offer. In spite of her mother's objection to this offer, she writes: 'I was triumphant. Babamukuru had approved of my direction. I was vindicated!' (*NC* 57).

She had wanted to go to school, at some point cultivating her own plot of maize in order to sell the maize to raise money to go to school. She wanted to be someone else. 'I decided it was better to be like Maiguru [Babamukuru's wife, holder of MA degree], who was not poor and had not been crushed by the weight of womanhood' (*NC* 16), especially after facing discouragement from her mother, who thought that because of the 'poverty of blackness on one side and the weight of womanhood on the other' all Tambu could do in the circumstances 'is to learn to carry your burdens with strength' (*NC* 16).

Thus father and mother had already limited for her what was possible to dream, only allowing her opportunities to taste defeat, as her mother grudgingly says to her father when allowing her to cultivate a plot of maize in order to raise her own fees: 'Let her try. Let her see for herself that some things cannot be done' (*NC* 17). When she gets into Babamukuru's car, on her way to the mission school, 'in the front seat beside him' (*NC* 58), she writes, 'My horizons were saturated with me, my leaving, my going' (*NC* 58). About her parents, she writes:

> My father, as affably, shallowly agreeable as ever, was insignificant. My mother, my anxious mother, was no more than another piece of surplus scenery to be maintained, of course to be maintained, but all the same superfluous, an obstacle in the path of my departure. (*NC* 58)

About her siblings:

> As for my sisters, well, they were there. They were watching me climb into Babamukuru's car to be whisked away to limitless horizons. It was up to them to learn the important lesson that circumstances were not immutable, no burden so binding that it could not be dropped. (*NC* 58)

The rupture has already taken place. Her climbing into the car and being 'whisked away' accentuates the climax of the disintegrating forces that have all along been prising the individual from the social glue that bonded her with family and community. Returning Tambu to this corroded family and society will be comparable to regression. It will be synonymous to making her an anachronism in her own self-modernizing life trajectory. 'When I stepped into Babamukuru's car I was a peasant' (*NC* 58). That is her point of origin. As a vector, and explorer, her ends are clearly limned. 'At Babamukuru's I expected to find another self, a clean, well-groomed, genteel self who could not have been bred, could not have survived, on the homestead' (*NC* 59). Clearly, there is a desired disjuncture between the past and the now which erases traces to the point of origin. Babamukuru had not anticipated this capacity to aspire in his charities. It is the promise of the elsewhere that the gift holds that sways Tambu, and Nhamo, and not obligations to repay. Holding his charity inflexibly to the edicts of his gift is tantamount to hostage taking. Yet taking the gift without the intention to repay, as Nhamo does, amounts to mugging the almoner.

Tambu refers to her movement from her father's house to Babamukuru's house as 'my transplantation' (*NC* 59), a telling concept in our attempt to understand the way Tambu views the transforming and uprooting nature of Babamukuru's gift. It is also possible to reflect on this transplantation as cause of the social malaise that the gift amplifies. Tambu's own initiative of growing maize in order to educate herself had only been appreciated by her teacher Mr Matimba, who helped her sell the maize in town where she raised ten pounds, enough to see her through school for two years. Babamukuru's intervention, though welcome, disrupts this self-driven and self-generated mode of self-help, and stymies its momentum by abducting the agent from processes of self-uprising. His intervention, which does not take into account Tambu's own vision of herself had she paid for her own education, takes away Tambu's initiative, and makes her an object of his own self-help agenda, and ultimately his dependant.

Thus, there is a clash of ideals and aspirations: what Tambu wants to be, and what Babamukuru wants her to be. So, at the end, Tambu becomes a trickster character, deploying tactical subservience as a technique to ensure her personal dream to approximate Maiguru's hitherto misconstrued social standing triumphs. Nhamo lacked tact. The only difference between Nhamo and Tambu is that Tambu endures the gift, maps out own way of transforming the gift into a tool with which to hone her own vision of herself in the world, and is patient and circumspect: 'Having developed well I did not foresee that there would be reason to regress on the occasions that I returned to the homestead' (NC 59). So, unlike Nhamo, she continues to show tactical commitment to the homestead when she visits it, without raising suspicion about her motives, although sharing Nhamo's sentiments and revulsion.

It is therefore not a question of is it a boy or a girl, but rather of the nature of the gift. It is a gift made in circumstances where it cannot be refused. Tambu herself has no choice in the matter: there is no school to go to after her present grade; as a girl she could easily be overlooked, as once happened when the family ran out of money and chose to make her stay at home while the boy Nhamo went to school. Babamukuru's own experience of gift-receiving is a compelling example of a predicament that he replays when he presents his own gift later on to Tambudzai.

> Babamukuru was appreciative of the opportunity that had been offered; and further, to decline would have been a form of suicide. The missionaries would have been annoyed by his ingratitude. He would have fallen from grace with them and they would have taken under their wings another promising young African in his place. (NC 14)

So, like Babamukuru before her, Tambu realizes that the gift being offered her can be given to another, so has to be seized and made use of while its currency was still good. It is a question of seizing the moment in a situation characterized by non-choices.

Gifts that kill (*tsitsi dzinotsitsirira*)

Babamukuru offers the gift in a situation that compels him to be kind and generous. He had not only benefited from his own peasant mother, who supported him in his early years as a boy, but from strangers. Above all, his upbringing and position in the family makes him heir to the homestead, as the Big Father. But the realities of a cash economy make it impossible for him to dole out unlimited amounts of cash and other goods to his extended family. He has to find a proxy to do his bidding and extend his influence on the homestead. Thus he has to subdue Jeremiah's family, which is already at the mercy of nature, by acts of kindness-as-control. The 'scholarship' he offers to Tambu after Nhamo's death cannot be limited to his idea of benevolence. It is a technique of social control as well as self-capitalization. It unmans Jeremiah by usurping and thwarting any suggestion of initiative he might have had to rescue his family from poverty, and reduces him to a fawning, uncreative, hero-worshipping, spineless and indolent dependant. The more he worships Babamukuru, the more Babamukuru's own respect of him as an individual and a man diminishes. He is incapacitated and infantilized by Babamukuru's charitable acts, and is spoken to by Babamukuru as well as his wife in terms that recall an adult addressing a child. At some point, Babamukuru forces Jeremiah and wife to go through a white wedding, all for the sake of demonstrating that he has the money and the will to make them follow his whims.

Tambu soon learns about the malice behind Babamukuru's gift and her own mother's attempt to ameliorate her sense of the family's gift-indebtedness to Babamukuru. In this section, I want to limit my comments to the idea of gifts that kill both giver and receiver, and how retributive justice is achieved by both parties. In the process, I will comment on how the gift and the charity associated with it become acts of recognition, atonement and exculpation.

It is in *The Book of Not* that these ideas are most clearly articulated. What Helmuth Berking (Berking and Camiller 1999:viii) thought of the tendency of gift-giving practices to 'hierarchize and stratify' does not create solidarity (Komter 2005), but 'bonds of symbolic violence' (Berking and Camiller 1999:ix) As a result, there is resentment and social disintegration where gift-giving was intended to be regarded 'as the glue that keeps people together, whether by mutually identifying and sharing certain norms and values, or by contributing to some common good or both' (Komter 2005:2).

The lines of friction in a top-down gift-giving practice are identified in *Nervous Conditions*. First, Tambu's mother resents the idea that her son is taken to a mission school where he acquires social tastes that drive a wedge between him and his mother and father; she resents again the fact that her daughter will be taken to the same mission to take the place of the dead son. She believes that all this is happening because she is poor, and can therefore have no say over what happens to her children and her home. Jeremiah, while applauding Babamukuru's actions because they take away the burden of providing for his own family, is bitter when Mr Matimba, helps Tambu to sell her mealies in order to raise school fees. Pointedly, he says:

> 'Does he think he is your father? ...[H]e thinks that because he has chewed more letters than I have, he can take over my children. And you, you think he is better than me' (*NC* 24).

This is a situation where 'The recipient cannot shake off a suspicion that he has placed his autonomy in peril' (Berking and Camiller 1999:8), because the receiver of charity feels degraded by his own sense of powerlessness. In *Nervous Conditions*, Jeremiah attempts to reinstate his sense of self-worth through a show of aggression to Mr Matimba. In *The Book of Not*, Tambu's mother can only recuperate her dignity and power through aggression and extortion. She orders the beating and maiming of Babamukuru by the armed guerrillas on trumped-up charges that he is a traitor to the liberation struggle. First he sends Tambu to a white school, against her mother's wishes, where:

> I was proof of my uncle's dubious spirit. For why would a man select a school for his child where the education was superior to the education given to the children of other people? A school that would not, unlike other schools in areas where guerillas battled for independence, be closed? (*BN* 6)

Second, Tambu's mother instances David Cheal's argument that 'gift giving is as much a part of the struggle for existence in the modern world as is any other form of behaviour' (1988:ix). She wants him punished and killed, not only because he has taken her two children away from her, but because the illusion of 'plenty' that Tambu reads off Babamukuru's education and magnanimity remains only a tantalizing and envy-inducing illusion for Jeremiah and his wife. What would have completed a satisfying picture of being well catered for by a powerful deity is held in abeyance indefinitely. Tambu's mother explains to her daughter:

> 'Look at the way Samhungu has put a fence round his place!' she exclaimed enviously about our neighbours. 'Don't think the working Samhungus, the ones with jobs haven't helped their poor relatives! They have helped! They have made the Samhungus here in the village safer with that fence because of all these things that are going on around us! But we, your mother and father here, we are left to the mercy of the open like that by Babamukuru as if we are forest animals. In spite of all that money of his! Don't think people don't see it, Tambudzai! People see it. They ask where people put all the things they have if no one sees it coming home to other people!' (*BN* 7–8)

Having put himself in a position to provide, Babamukuru is sacrificed for his half-measures. The 'fence' here is a metaphor of total independence, prosperity, control and security, which Babamukuru could not provide, having mooted the outlines of that dream, and partly animated it by his patronage of the Jeremiah family. This is an instance where the receiver of charity now expects to live on the same terms as the giver. But having encouraged Jeremiah's indolence and dependence, and thus his inability to provide the labour for his own dreams, Babamukuru must now pay with his own life the sins of a benevolence that neutralizes and kills the initiative of the receiver. It is only Tambu who understands the dilemmas ensconced in

Babamukuru's own rags-to-riches narrative enabled by missionary charity: 'It had a moral too, a tantalizing moral that increased your aspirations, but not beyond a manageable level' (*NC* 19). Babamukuru is able to cap his ambitions, and work for them. Jeremiah and his wife do work, though by extorting alms from Babamukuru in order to live their dreams, which they cannot cap.

Babamukuru caps his ambitions in order to live large and vicariously through acts of charity. He sees in Tambu not only a proxy in his attempts at lifting the burden of supporting the large homestead off his shoulders, but a living instrument of his personal ambitions to transcend his own professional and personal circumstances. He makes his hidden strategic altruism clear when he explains to Tambu how disappointed he was with her failure to pass her A-Level examination according to his expectations. Tambu, who was studying sciences at A-Level, represented a hope that at least someone he had helped, 'his daughter', would not become a mere teacher, like him. His own daughter Nyasha seemed a write-off, frenetic and disobedient, and was quickly replaced in his scheme of things by Tambu, hence the reason for raising the bar for Tambu, whose ambitions he had earlier restricted to manageable levels. Tambu is the avatar of Babamukuru's repressed ambitions: 'Shouldn't a child, one who is intelligent, want to become more than her parents?' (*BN* 185).

His sense of being betrayed is doubled by his recollection of how Tambu's mother wanted him killed by the guerillas. It is something he kept away from Tambu, only telling her because she had failed him, and therefore deserved to be punished by being told of her parent's murderous treachery.

Babamukuru seemed to view his support of Tambu, after being betrayed by Tambu's mother, as an act of reparations, and Christly penance and suffering for the good of humanity. 'Babamukuru had not minded all his sacrifice and suffering as long as I behaved myself' (*BN* 191). Behaving well meant having to live up to the symbol of his success story, as well as an instrument of reparations and exculpation between the feuding families: 'I could not face the scar, the old wound which I knew, without wanting to know, was there beneath my uncle's long-sleeved white shirts. And Babamukuru had hoped for me, like some kind of holy child, to wash away the hostile blood that had caused his wounds' (*BN* 187), a swab to wash away the hostile blood between clans.

He had also hoped to use philanthropy as expiation, to make up for having taken Tambu and Nhamo from their mother, because he hoped that Tambu would get a scholarship to study in the UK, as he did.

'She will leave all this behind her, and when she qualifies, it will all be forgotten. Jeremiah and Mainini there will live comfortably when Tambudzai comes back. What is upsetting their hearts will disappear, because of the good work of their daughter' (*BN* 180), he reasons. When he couldn't achieve these objectives, he turns into an abuser, directing his pent-up hatred and frustrations against Tambudzai, and eventually disowning her, because 'you have shown that what others want of you is of no interest to you! I just want you to remember when you do these things; I shall not provide anything else to help you!' (*BN* 191).

Thus these acts of kindness can be withdrawn, because Tambu has no power over what cannot be claimed as hers (*'chisi chako masimba mashoma'*) and she should have known better not to feel cosy in the arms of charity because, when milking a borrowed cow, you should check that your escape routes are clear all the time. Babamukuru also realizes that he cannot fully possess what is not his: Tambu is another person, helping her does not make her his project or daughter.

In Babamukuru's mind, Tambu has morphed into everything her mother represented: treachery, avarice, malice and ingratitude. With one blow, metaphorically speaking, he destroys the project of his philanthropy, and moves to curtail her horizons by declaring that 'Even if you qualify for university with what you have, you will not qualify for a decent profession' (*BN* 193). Indeed, there are ways in which Babamukuru's wounded charity makes him begin to morph into the image of Tambu's mother as well: 'It was very strange to me to hear Babamukuru beginning to talk in a way that was so similar to my mother' (*BN* 193). Charity is just the flip side of misanthropy, given the intensity of hate engendered by the botched 'cultural invention of reciprocities and relationships' (Berking 1999:ix) that deepen bonds of violence, instead of lessening it. Charity can easily turn into a desire to harm if not fully appreciated by the giver and the receiver. In any case, the cynicism that Marechera instructs us to adopt vis-à-vis the receiving of charity might as well hold sway: 'Any good you get from people you'll have to pay for later' (1978:8).

Conclusion

Dangarembga's novels provide us with ways of thinking about philanthropic practices in Africa and in the world by using the lens of the gift-as-charity in a self-help project as initiated by Babamukuru. It becomes clear that the power structures which are animated in the act of charitable giving do create bonds of violence, instead of solidarity, where inequalities are exacerbated instead of being lessened. Charity sometimes deepens these inequalities that bedevil any kind of project which assumes that philanthropy necessarily induces positive development. As we have seen, there are often clashes between the receivers and givers, all to do with largely overlooked aspirations and initiatives of the receiving as well as giving communities. The world view of the receiver is very important, and more participatory and deliberative democracies need to be instituted so that the receiver of philanthropic aid does not feel insulted and disempowered, ironically, by the act of being upraised.

A recognition that charities might not necessarily want to develop in the ways devised by the giver is important, as overlooking that fact, and not devising ways of matching project to aspirations, creates alienation and frustration, some of it which shows through the vindictiveness with which charities, and even givers of charity, sometimes show to each other, when strategic interests in the gift clash. African folklore abounds with warnings about how to receive, and how to create cultures of giving and receiving that don't kill or create an abusive dependency. The good and the human, 'I am well if you are well' which Tambu attempts, is possible where the good does not oppress and repel the other.

Endnote

1   Another version of this piece is published as an article "'I am well if you are well': Nervous conditions of African philanthropy in Tsitsi Dangarembga's novels" in *African Identities,* Vol 9, Issue 4, 2011, pp. 387–400.

CHAPTER 4

TRADITIONAL PHILANTHROPY IN PRE-COLONIAL ASANTE

KWAKU ASANTE-DARKO

Introduction

It is not easily discernible that different cultures perceive philanthropy differently. The difference in perception is due to two main factors. First, different people usually create different socio-economic customs and practices to respond to their respective environmental and experiential realities. Second, the translations of concepts and practices developed from these respective culture-specific responses do not always find equivalents in other cultures. Thus, translations from one culture/ language into another do not always find the words, practices and contexts that correctly and accurately reflect and refract all the nuances of meanings implied in the word being translated. This difference is similar to the type of reality one sees, for instance, in the fact that when a funny story or a joke is translated from one language or culture into another it may lose almost all its fun.

It is, therefore, not surprising that different cultures could have different understandings of notions and practices such as profit, business, greed, investment, conscience, development and their antonyms. These notions certainly do not have the same meaning, value and importance in all cultures. This fact makes 'the dictatorship of relativism' an expression with conflicting meanings. The sociolinguistic limitations imposed on the transcultural rendition of culture-specific notions and practices affect the effectiveness of international philanthropic action in more than one way. Thus, granted that translation is an exercise in transcultural approximation and is often attenuated by the element of cultural specificities, one should expect that philanthropic discourse – whether it is for the purposes of theoretical analysis, field research, decision debate, or policy implementation – is bound to be heavy-laden with the dominant meanings, attitudes and preferences of the culture and times of the speaker or writer. In feudal England, for instance, 'aid' referred to the amount of money paid by the poor tenant for the benefit of the rich feudal lord on occasions such as the wedding of the lord's daughter or the knighting of his son. Thus, the essential nature and effect of the practice expressed by the English word 'aid', far beyond any declared intents, was that which must make the poor poorer and the rich richer.

The fact that different cultures have different perceptions and, therefore differing definitions of the giving and receiving of assistance makes philanthropy a cultural construct in both its conceptual and empirical aspects. It also has implications for the type of normative motivation, institutions and methods that propel philanthropic action in a given community. Such differences in cultural and personal preferences affect the manner in which philanthropy is defined in terms of its objectives, milieu, methods, actors, management, effects, and the evaluation of its success or failure. For example, Edward Grubb's perception of philanthropy emphasizes the culture-specific individualistic rather than the communitarian in philanthropy when he notes:

> The typical philanthropist is a prosperous person who gives up a large share of his life to the work of improving the lot of his fellow-creatures. ... It is especially characteristic of those societies that are called 'individualistic,' i.e., in which ideals of personal liberty make a strong appeal to the average person. Where the rights of the community over the individual are powerfully felt...there is less call for philanthropy; it is to the community, organized in the State, rather than to wealthy individuals that men naturally look for the redressing of human wrongs (Grubb 1917: 837).

The above opinion implicitly discards or at least marginalizes the existence of philanthropy in milieux such as pre-industrial agrarian communalistic societies like pre-colonial Asante, which, from time immemorial, have practised philanthropy in which the philanthropist did not necessarily have to be an individual and prosperous in an economic system which is predominantly monetary and individualistic, and with a belief system centred around organized religion.

It is the candid contention of this chapter and article that philanthropy can be and has been practised by a group of modest ordinary citizens offering their service of labour, insight, knowledge, time and skills for the uplifting of the needy in communalistic communities. For that purpose it is important to reiterate that, in determining what constitutes philanthropy, different cultures put different emphasis on elements such as the modes and levels of commercial or monetary activity within the community concerned; the intentions and expectations of benefactors and beneficiaries, and the nature of historical and current relations that linked them; the type of belief systems and sociopolitical organization of the community concerned; the areas of philanthropic activity and the methods deployed, as well as the attitude of the state towards individual efforts at uplifting the poor. Thus, far and above any pretensions of universality philanthropy will remain a cultural construct. It should, therefore, not be surprising if, in the workings of international philanthropy, givers and receivers cautiously discern each other's motives and continuously renegotiate some central issues.

Understanding the fundamental transcultural perceptions and differences in philanthropy, therefore, essentially advances the effectiveness of contemporary international philanthropic action for the reason that Peter Dobkin Hall (2006:7) inadvertently observes as follows:

> The history of philanthropy offers useful lessons to contemporary decision makers in foundations. Insulated from market pressures and most other forms of accountability, officers, directors, and managers are prone to believe themselves free of the past as well. ...if today's philanthropic leaders wish to avoid repeating the past, they would do well to learn from it.

Dobkin Hall is obviously referring not only to those aspects of history which should not be repeated, because he cannot be unaware that there are some aspects of history which should be repeated, the good ones. Thus, one way of learning from the past in order to avoid repeating its undesirable aspects will be to research the philanthropic models of other cultures with the view to infusing positive aspects from local sources to address the hindrances that militate against the excellence of the international philanthropic endeavour.

Asante philanthropy and its sociophilosophical precepts

Currently, the key hindrances to effective international philanthropic action in Africa are more normative than institutional. These norms differ from those that inspired philanthropic action in pre-colonial Asante which, I argue, can inspire some solutions to the difficulties of international philanthropic action in Africa. In looking for what can be learned from traditional philanthropy of pre-colonial Asante it is necessary to underline that the key principle of pre-colonial Asante philanthropy was partnership and long-term development which prioritized some areas of economic and social activity as needing immediate attention and heavy and sustained input.

Four key factors determined the peculiar nature, scope, objectives, organization, outcome, and contemporary relevance of this philanthropy. The first was the nature of Asante communal organization which gave the responsibility of the upkeep of the individual to the *abusua* or matrilineage. The second was the fact that the means of exchange in economic transactions – *sika* (gold and cowries; also translated as 'money') – was limited such that a lot of exchange and services were offered in kind rather than in monetary terms. The third was that Asante customs

and attitudes towards the poor (poverty) and the rich (riches) required that philanthropic assistance be offered both from the rich to the poor and vice versa. They
realized that even the most secure and affluent person could need philanthropic
assistance at certain times and in certain aspects of their lives: 'Obiara nni h ɔ a
ne ho so no akwank ɔ' – (Nobody suffices unto himself for a journey) is a popular
Asante expression in this regard. Thus, riches were not intrinsic to the rich, and
poverty was never deemed intrinsic to the poor. Ebereɛ dane – (time changes) and
Bibiara tumi si – (anything can happen) were popular Asante maxims expressing
changes in fortunes. This conviction engendered an attitude which barred any pretensions of condescension on the part of the one who offers assistance. The fourth
was the pre-colonial Asante state policy towards the individual accumulation of
wealth. Contrary to the falsehood according to which the communal ownership
of property in pre-agrarian African communities made everybody equally rich
and equally poor and, therefore, stifling of initiative and personal advancement,
individuals were encouraged to accumulate wealth and titles were officially given
to those who were successful in this venture. The pre-colonial Asante conception
of poverty would find a notion such as 'per capita income' to be so misleading and
absurd to the point of being meaningless.

The Asante concept of poverty

In his assessment of the nature of the economic life of pre-colonial Asante, Mc-
Caskie (1995:37) notes that:

> The general picture, then, for the eighteenth and nineteenth centuries, is of a mixed
> rural economy in which fully established subsistence farming was the dominant
> mode of production. The availability of cultivable land and the productive capac-
> ity of agriculturists guaranteed that Asante society … was not subject to cycles of
> massive deprivation, and cannot remotely be classified as an economy of general-
> ized want and hunger.

It is important to underline that in such an economy poverty would consist chiefly
in not having direct access to land and the resources and produce thereof. There
were certainly service professions generally called *paa* (it covered the offering of
courier services as well as working as a hired farm hand and in mining) but they
were mainly the domain of the poor because one needed land in order to successfully engage in commercial activities such as the production of kola, snails, pottery,
soap, perfume and oil. The poor and poverty were, therefore, synonymous with
privation of land and its resources. So important was the land factor in pre-colonial
Asante economic thought that when a people were conquered they were not dis-
possessed of their land, instead they retained their land and only paid vassal tribute
in the form of gold and people mainly.

Likewise, those whose lands were not productive enough to make them self-sufficient in food production were also deemed to be poor. Their dependence on others for food meant they needed to exchange their own goods and services, and whenever the exchange was not in their favour, they ran into ɛka – debt or indebtedness, which in pre-colonial Asante was generally symptomatic of *ohia* – poverty. *Ahiafo ɔ* (poor people – singular: *ohianii*) were usually urban dwellers with little or no access to land and no skills to enter any profitable economic ventures. Their rural counterparts were also a people who worked as bonded labour on mines and farms which predominantly benefited others. Usually such people had no relatives or had long severed their link with the extended family whose responsibility it was to cushion their woes.

Pre-colonial Asante social organization made the welfare of the individual the irrevocable responsibility of both the nuclear and extended families. For that reason, I will consider philanthropy in pre-colonial Asante as a disinterested and an unwritten contractual assistance offered by individuals or groups to *persons other than family*. Thus, I consider a philanthropic act among pre-colonial Asante to be one in which there is no nuclear or extended family relationship between beneficiary and benefactor. In this context, acts such as a parent paying for the upkeep of their own child or the child of a family member, or assistance to a sibling or parent, or contributing towards the funeral of a member of one's family were not acts of philanthropy. Thus, in pre-colonial Asante help within the family such as contributing towards the naming, marriage, and funeral rites of a family member or making significant contribution to their upbringing and their acquisition of skills constituted a duty rather than an act of charity or philanthropy. Additionally, I will somewhat suggest that the benefactor had no intention of getting commercial, political, or social patronage or advantage from the *duty*.

A close look at the belief system of pre-colonial Asante reveals that the fundamental motivation or the willingness to assist the poor and bring them out of poverty was partly due to the fact that the pre-colonial Asante considered that the set of factors which concur to put the poor in a condition of want had a dual origin. One was internal and the other external. The internal ones included those partly caused by humans or the socioeconomic arrangements put in place by society. These ranged from unintended injustices occasioned by differences in the aptitudes of individuals, ill luck, ignorance, which often produce either timidity or its anti-pole of reckless daring. The external factors would comprise of those caused, the Asante said, by inexplicable causes of destiny (*nkrabea*/hyɛbrɛ), or by wicked spiritual powers and evil relatives in league with evil spirits, offended or vindictive ancestors, gods and other invisible powers. It was because the poverty was caused partly by socioeconomic arrangements that the community had the responsibility of helping those disfavoured by it. The right to such help was often summarized and pinned on the basic obligation of human solidarity in sayings such as *Nipa hia mmoa* – a human being needs help – i.e. a social being cannot do without the help of his/her fellow humans, or the saying: *Nipa nua ne nipa* (literally, a person is a person's brother/sister. Equivalent of: be your brother's keeper).

In addition to these explanations of social organization, destiny and human solidarity, the pre-colonial Asante held that individuals, and sometimes families, differed in economic talent just as they do in athletic, military, musical, leadership, intellectual and altruistic capabilities. The community believed that different individuals did not have the same ability to perceive and utilize economic opportunity or to commute their situation, location, and acquaintances to economic advantage even when the playing field is level. They, however, would have held in ridicule and contempt any behaviour or ideas that looked like the theory of natural selection, where the disadvantaged and maladjusted were only 'helped' to perish. Thus, solidarity was admonished just as achievement was lauded and merit commended to urge all and sundry to embrace hard work. For example, the state organized ceremonies for the exclusive and explicit purpose of honouring and conferring titles on individuals who through hard work accumulated great wealth. A state ceremony was held at which their wealth in gold, goods, houses and family members was publicly displayed. Thereafter such a person was conferred the title of *Ɔbrempon* (great man) or *brempomaa* (great woman) and his/her appearance in public was always heralded by an attendant holding an elephant tail – *mmena*.

Though the welfare of the individual was traditionally the responsibility of the immediate and extended family in pre-colonial Asante, orphans, widows, strangers and the sick that faced destitution were offered assistance by individuals and groups other than their family. They also helped those who needed assistance owing to the natural forces of old age and death. The assistance was given as a *temporary* help to get them *permanently* back on their feet. The attitude towards philanthropy, thus, contained the paradox and duality characteristic of many a pre-colonial Asante perception of reality. Thus, while socioethical maxims enjoined people to practise help to the needy, they equally admonished the needy to get off dependence and to eschew any way of life that would let them need philanthropic assistance. Proverbs, maxims and injunctions, such as the following, had the essential meaning of urging groups and individuals to live honourable and independent lives: '*Bɔ bra pa*' – (live a good life), '*Abusua ne wo bra*' – (the family is your life; i.e. the type of recognition, respect and honour that your own family will accord you will depend on the kind of life or success you achieve); '*Obra ne nea w'abo, enyɛ deɛ wo wɔfa ab'ɔ* – your life is what you have accomplished, not what your uncle has achieved; '*Woforo dua pa a, na yepia wo*' – it is when you are climbing a fruitful/good tree that people will push you up i.e. in the hope of benefiting from the fruits thereof or not being troubled by calls and troubles you should and could have avoided).

In this regard hard work and living within one's means were principal precepts of upbringing among the pre-colonial Asante. Habits such as borrowing, idleness, laziness, malingering, and gluttony, which could lead to indebtedness, dependence, pawning, and even enslavement, were frowned upon with all the contempt they deserved. The famous proverb: '*Ahia me na hwɛ me, nti na obi yɛɛ akoa*' (Rattray 1952:157) (I am in want so take care of me, that is how someone ended up enslaved) cautioned against a reckless lifestyle. Such recklessness was consequential, since pre-colonial Asante had a system of collective family responsibility in which the entire family was responsible for a debt incurred by one of its members. Thus, in the practice known as *awowa*,[1] a creditor could demand as surety the custody of a member of the debtor's family to work for the creditor until the debt was settled (ibid:153).

It is important to clarify that the emphasis on self-reliance and independence and hard work did not preclude acts of goodwill and solidarity. One must note the observation of Peter Akwasi Sarpong (1974:67) in this regard that among the Asante: 'In many instances to refuse a gift amounts to a declaration of enmity, and to neglect to show gratitude is no less offensive.'

Strangers and people other than family could benefit from such acts of largesse for which the actor '...expects visible results of what he does to others, and if these will come to him in the form of praise, reciprocal rewards, health, escape from danger, riches, he is contented (ibid)'. This material disinterestedness largely accounted for the successful or affluent as well as the modest and the poor themselves using their resources, labour, and riches to improve the conditions of the needy. Through maxims such as *Sika frɛ bogya* (literally, 'Money calls blood', meaning money rallies people, blood being a metaphor for 'people'), the society drew members' attention to the extraordinary ability of wealth and its use for solidarity as a magnet that assembles or draws people together and keeps the community in peace. In others such as: '*Mefrɛ sika, sika nngye me so, mefrɛ bogya*' (I call money, money does not respond, I call blood/human), the Asante underlined the fact that human happiness is an end in itself, and the acknowledgement that wealth must serve that purpose. Riches for riches sake were, thus, discouraged and the poor also had philanthropic responsibility towards anyone who needed assistance to restore dignity and independence by their participation in communal self-help endeavour.

In these transactions no reciprocity was anticipated beyond the general progress of community, and indeed humankind. What was expected to be paid back was the assurance of friendliness, goodwill and gratitude rather than any certain and tangible material gain. Pre-colonial Asante philanthropic expression was not primarily to lay foundations for anticipated commercial deals. More importantly, neither the recipient nor the donor intended to perpetuate a philanthropic relationship. This was because to the poor who acquiesced to poverty, poverty and want were considered as *animguaseɛ* – shame or humiliation – and to the helper who sought to exploit the poor, *kwaseabuo* – swindling or cheating – constituted a stigma not only to the individuals but to their extended family members as well. Thus, the consideration of the dignity of the poor was central to the set of considerations that motivated philanthropic acts in pre-colonial Asante.

There should be no poor among you ...²

This consideration for the dignity of all meant that in pre-colonial Asante the ultimate objective of philanthropy was to ensure that no one needed philanthropy. This paradox empirically dictated that those factors that caused individuals and groups to be in a situation where they needed assistance from persons other than family were identified with the view to addressing them definitively. The pre-colonial Asante directed much philanthropic effort at addressing the causes of those factors that led to want and philanthropy such as accidents, diseases, illness, weakness of personal character, indebtedness, violence, unjust discrimination, and the effects of war. Among the primary duties of the king, as chief priest of the nation, was to offer propitiations to the spirits and ancestors to ward off any such hard luck. Their philanthropy equally manifested a cultural dynamism which constantly addressed the negative aspects of sociopolitical arrangements and belief systems such as taxation on deceased estate, slavery and exploitation which could, and sometimes did, lock up sections of the community in a state of dependence on the goodwill of others. Pre-colonial Asante philanthropy was, thus, an effort that sought to provide for the victims of setbacks. Some widows, war victims, the aged, orphans, the sick, lone strangers etc. came to find themselves in a situation where they needed assistance from benevolent and more fortunate individuals, communities and groups of citizens. This assistance was supposed to restore the needy to normal life in dignity and independence, rather than drowning them into dependence and indignity. They sought to abolish philanthropy by abolishing poverty. From this perspective, to wish to be permanently a philanthropist in pre-colonial Asante would have been tantamount to the abominable mischief of the undertaker, the grave digger or the coffin maker who pray that their business should grow.

The fact that the Asante apportioned the causes of want between socioeconomic and spiritual factors implies that they saw two main ways in which philanthropic action should restore the poor to normal life. The first was the alteration in the socio-economic orientation of the individual and society, and the second was the propitiation of whichever spirits could be behind the physical economic failures of the poor individuals or groups concerned. Thus, appeals for good state policies on one hand and good individual/group conduct always complemented each other in the fight against want. An official text of the state talking drums cautions against unnecessary fiscal austerity by the state. This text, entitled *Ɔman fotoɔ* (National treasury) notes: '*Piredwan sisi dantuo mu, / na yɛrehunu amane*' (Packets of gold are sitting in empty rooms, while people are suffering) (Nketia 1974:99).

Philanthropy in Asante was, thus, halfway between right and privilege. This is because even when the causes were attributed to social structures and, therefore, conferring a quasi-sympathy or right to assistance from people other than family, the average pre-colonial Asante generally considered it a humiliation to live on hand-outs or at the mercy of another. Even disaster relief was accepted with the understanding of anticipated reciprocity – a voluntary and tacit undertaken on the part of the recipient to do likewise should the present donor be in a similar situation of need in future. Embedded in this attitude was the principle of fairness, such that the element of dependence was, thus, removed and assistance was essentially considered as partnership of equals in mutual dependence. Help was giving as a means of bringing people out of difficulty since the pre-colonial Asante considered dependence as a form of humiliation. The rich were cautioned in several social art forms such as songs to be respectful towards the poor. Thus, lines expressing ideas such as the following were typical of sarcastic folk songs which admonished caution: '*Osikani, woanya wo sika a, / Ma ohiani aboa na!*' (Nketia 1949:33) (Rich man, you have got money, but do not disturb the sleep of the poor man, unless you think he is a beast).

Areas and forms of philanthropy in pre-colonial Asante

The benevolence offered to the needy in accordance with the precepts and considerations mentioned above was seen in areas including medical services, education, legal reform, and the provision of public infrastructure, food supply, and defence. The socioeconomic organization of pre-colonial Asante was predominantly agrarian in the sense that the procurement of goods and services involved few monetary transactions. In this predominantly subsistence milieu, philanthropic empathy was expressed in gestures such as visits of sympathy, voluntary labour, and the provision of farm produce and other materials which would otherwise have been purchased in a system where monetary exchange is abundant. Though such services were mostly rendered on occasions such as floods, bereavement and other disasters, rite of passage, and festivals, they, nonetheless, had permanent institutional existence and structures for their operation. Here, I will look at the examples of health, education, and socio-legal reforms.

Health

In pre-colonial Asante, philanthropic health services revolved around the work of three types of practitioners and their associated centres. It is significant in this regard that Rattray (1929:39) notes: 'the Ashanti makes a distinction between the following: ɔkɔmfoɔ (priest); the sumankwafoɔ or dunseni (the medicine-man); and the Bonsam kɔmfoɔ (witch-doctor)'. These were private setups with hardly any interference of patronage from state authorities, except to prevent abuse and punish charlatanism.[3] In addition to his role as diviner and controller of social norms, the ɔkomfoɔ, who headed a shrine, exercised the primary function of a healer. Thus, individuals and groups who volunteered donations of money, food, and other produce from farming, hunting and gathering to his or her shrine knew that they were contributing towards the upkeep of the needy who depended on the shrine for their upkeep. Medical care offered to the sick was virtually free, except for a little sum of money offered as asida (thanks) to the shrine by the person whose illness required that they stayed several months or longer at the shrine. At these places, bruises, boils and rheumatism were considered as minor ailments and generally received free treatment.

The beneficiaries of such medically-oriented philanthropic gestures could be large communities. McLeod (1981:38) notes that:

> A few villages seem to have grown up around the temples of major gods to shelter supplicants and to house the drummers, cooks and other people who served the god and its priest. The social make up of such villages was unusual for they contained men and women from many different areas who had come, perhaps with one or two kinsfolk, to seek the aid of the god. Such villages probably provided long-term refuges for people afraid that their relatives were causing them mystical harm.

Residents of such villages would normally take part in communal service for the upkeep of the village or community as a way of contributing to the upkeep of the work of healing offered by the shrine to the community. Money was not offered but the necessary infrastructure needed for the community to continue, such as safe and clean paths, the hauling of goods from the harvest fields, making of handicrafts and the construction of houses for new arrivals were also offered voluntarily.

Education

Philanthropic activity was not only confined to aiding the sick and destitute. Much of the educational functions in pre-colonial Asante were philanthropic and took the form of folklore performed by historians, poets, actors, musicians and dancers. At such activities the history, values and customs of the community were passed on to younger generations. Concerning the functions performed by such groups and the nature of their pedagogical influence, Alan Dundes (1965:227) notes that:

There are many diverse functions of folklore. Some of the most common ones include aiding in education of the young, promoting a group's feeling of solidarity, providing socially sanctioned ways for individuals to act superior to or to censure other individuals, serving as a vehicle for social protest, offering an enjoyable escape from reality, and converting dull work into play.

These functions were offered in a manner as to impart skills, protection, and up-bringing to needy orphans as well as giving counselling and support to widowers, the bereaved, the impaired, and the aged who had no family to care for them. Ruth Finnegan (1994:351) notes the pedagogical significance of these practices when she notes concerning the stories told during such sessions that they are:

> a comment, even a satire, on human society and behaviour. In a sense, when the narrator speaks of actions and character of animals, they are representing human faults and virtues, somewhat removed and detached from reality through being presented in the guise of animals, but nevertheless with an indirect relation to observed human action …. The foibles and weaknesses, virtues and strength, ridiculous and appealing qualities known to all those present are touched on, in-directly, in the telling of stories and are what make them meaningful and effective in the actual narration.

Thus, often these meetings at which artists performed produced songs in which the socially vicious such as bad leaders, the lazy, and the arrogant rich were castigated. It is equally significant to note that some of these appeals could inadvertently, if not plainly, serve to undermine some social institutions and beliefs, such as *awowa* and slavery, to which sections of the community could be subjected. It must be underlined that in spite of the general participation it often enjoyed, these were activities initiated and organized by individuals and groups disinterestedly seeking the welfare of fellow humans other than family.

It is particularly significant to note that though children's education benefited immensely from such collective communal effort geared largely towards upbringing (*nteteɛ*), this assistance was largely gratuitous. Thus, Rattray (1929:13) notes, for instance, that 'an especially naughty or unruly child might be handed over to the care of someone who was well known to be good at managing young children'.

It must, however, be explained that abuse of this system was prevented and the insistence was on personal responsibility and self-reliance rather than outright dependence on communal nurturing and mentoring for one's children. An incident retold by Rattray (ibid:13–14) illustrates this emphasis:

> There is a well-known story in Ashanti of a mother who handed over a bad child to King Kwaku Dua I [b. ca. 1797, d. 1867] to be trained. When she returned later to inquire after it, she was informed by the King, 'I ordered the executioners to kill the child'. 'But,' exclaimed the mother, 'I sent you my child to be trained.' 'Yes,' said the King, 'that is how I train children'.

The enduring worth of this story does not reside in whether or not the incident really took place. Rather, it consists in some two key deductions that can be made from it. The first is that there must have existed in pre-colonial Asante a normal practice of benefiting enormously from communal assistance for the upbringing of one's children – by friends and neighbours (especially the elderly who remained at home while others went to work) at no monetary cost to the biological parents. The second is that the Asante realized the need for constant vigilance to ensure that this philanthropic practice was not overstretched to condone alienation, indolence and the shirking of parental responsibility in the upbringing of children. The meaning of the above story is, therefore, that pre-colonial Asante philanthropy served to promote self-reliance as the prime objective. Philanthropy among the pre-colonial Asante could not condone the pushing of the limits of collective (family, or commu-nal, or national or international) responsibility too far. The underlying pre-colonial Asante principle which the king in the story must be seen to be defending is that nothing that ends in dependence or worsens the condition of the receiver (in this instance, the alienation of a child from the mother) can be called help. The popular Asante expression ɔdomfo kumfo (from adom = grace and kum = kill – the one who has gracious or benevolent intentions, the implementation of which eventually brought disastrous results) addresses this reality and cautions against it.

Socioeconomic reform

Pre-colonial Asante philanthropy did not only seek to safeguard the existing edu-cational and medical order, but equally introduced novelty. One such novelty was the deployment of legal reform to philanthropic ends. It took the form of lobbying for the abolition of customary and legal statutes which directly or indirectly per-petuated or worsened the condition of the poor, or stifled any economic growth from which they might eventually benefit. 'Ayiboadeɛ', – a practice whereby upon the death of a fabulously rich person, the state imposed an enormous tax on his or her lands, gold, and servants – was one such institution reformed through philanthropic action. The ostensible reason for the imposition of ayiboadeɛ was to cater for the price of organizing a befitting funeral for the deceased, whence the name – Ayie – funeral, boa – help, deɛ – thing. The tax portion so imposed was called 'awunyadeɛ' – that which the state gets upon the death of a wealthy person. Its direct effect, which was very much resented, was that it prevented the relatives and helpers of the deceased from benefiting from the riches of their kin or master.

Also practised in close cooperation with ayiboadeɛ and awunyadeɛ was the cus-tom whereby a chieftain who suffered financial misfortune had some of the areas under his/her jurisdiction, including the inhabitants thereof, either translocated to another area or placed under the authority of another chieftain. For the inhabitants, this transfer to a new location or authority often meant the loss of years, if not a lifetime of labour and resources invested. Their plight often worsened. The reform which abolished these centuries-old practices was philanthropic in the sense that those who initiated it targeted the harm that it did to the community in general and the poor in particular. The abolition commenced at a meeting in Kumase in June 1888, when those supporting the candidature of Akwasi Prempeh against that of Yaw Atweneboana in a succession dispute for the position of *Asantehene* (King of Asante) demanded that they would offer military support to Akwasi Prempeh on condition that, upon victory, the state would not only enact legal reforms abolishing the practices of *ayiboadeɛ* and *awunyadeɛ*, but would also restore property so seized in the past by the state to their rightful original owners. Soon after the assurance was given and formalized through customary ceremony, Akwasi Prempeh's faction triumphed by the end of July, with the forces of his contestant seeking refuge in the Gold Coast Colony at the coast. The promise, having been made under Asante oath, was effected and reinforced in the following year by further demands by the beneficiaries that the new law be made irrevocable. This was adhered to at a meeting in a place called Ahyiamu. The essence was described by a group of traders thus:

> In order to assure Ashanti people of the annulment of this law of taking percentage of any deceased's property, Nana Prempeh [Agyeman Prempe] deputed his sister by name Nana Akua Afriyie and his brother named Nana Agyeman Badu, to Ejisuhene [*Edwesohene*], the then powerful King was to drink fetish that Nana Prempe should never at any time ask for any estate of any deceased Ashanti man.[4]

The request for an end to these practices illustrates the Asante belief that being deprived of one's lands, resources and income is the root cause of poverty, hence their belief that helping the poor meant dismantling the system that made them poor and kept them poor. This reform had two key ramifications that enhanced philanthropy and improve the conditions of the poor. First, it accelerated the loosening of state control on the resources of affluent individuals. Second, it facilitated the appropriation, expansion and stricter enforcement of an important ancient precept to cover the poor and slaves, and created solidarity and commitment to the state. This was the law surmised in the existing popular maxim: ' *Obi Nkyerɛ obi ase* ' (no one should disclose the origins of another). It is said to have been introduced under the *Asantehene* Opoku Ware I (d. 1750). It sought to unite and cement the inclusiveness and equality of all Asante states and districts whether they were part of the union before they defeated the Denkyira Empire or joined it thereafter. The offence was called *Asekyerɛ*. It forbade the evocation of the pre-Asante appurtenance of any Asante state.[5]

With the push for equality and with Asante abolishing slavery, the implications of strengthening this law found extension in the equality of all citizens. By extension, this maxim forbade, by law, any Asante to declare the foreign or slave origin of another Asante. It was punishable by death by decapitation. It sought to instil the idea that no Asante was more of an Asante than the other irrespective of race, height, skin colour, and creed etc. It equally prevented the alienation, exclusion, and exploitation of such integrated groups and individuals who were formerly considered as being of non-Asante extraction. Reindorf (1895:51) noted in this regard an Asante 'national law' that:

> Whoever dares tell his son: these people were from such and such a place, conquered and translocated to this or that town was sure to pay for it with his life. Neither were such people themselves allowed to say where they had been transported from. Considering these captives as real citizens, any rank or honour was conferred freely on them according to merit, but not otherwise.

This reassurance engendered by this law created a sense of belongingness and raised levels of commitment to work and enhanced the creation of wealth. It effectively abolished bondage with a logic akin to the one that Jean Jacques Rousseau (1980:22) expresses as follows:

> 'Le droit d'esclavage est nul, non seulement parce qu'il est illégitime, mais parce qu'il absurde et ne signifie rien. Ces mots *esclave* et *droit* sont contradictoires. Ils s'excluent mutuellement.'

Some pre-colonial Asante philanthropists

The emphasis on group or communal organization of agrarian Asante should not be allowed to obscure the fact that the pursuit of such collective interest was guided by a complex built-in mechanism which accommodated and lauded individualism and private pursuits. For example, the flourishing of trading activities[6] led to the rise of individual men and women who accumulated wealth enough to attract a retinue of willing attendants and beneficiaries. Notable among them in pre-colonial Asante were the famous Yamoa Ponko and Kanin Abena Toprefo. Ivor Wilks (1975:694) notes concerning the latter that:

> Purchasing land, she founded the new village of Wioso and established a market nearby with the permission of [the Asantehene] Osei Kwame. When the Asantehene honoured her by visiting the market in person, she is said to have presented him with 125 peredwans of gold dust, and the councillors who accompanied him with 30 peredwans.

The vivid memories of her acts bring to mind another woman, the proverbial Amoa Wisi, who, Asante tradition says, had thirty children of her own and went ahead to adopt thirty others. The saying: '*AmoaWisi a ɔwo abaduasa, kɔgye abaduasa abayɛn*' is still a popular saying evoked to praise philanthropic acts by both men and women.

The philanthropic essence of the activities of these individuals is that they offered access to land to the poor and gave them the chance to create families of their own.

The private effort to address the plight of the poor equally appealed to a king as well. The largesse of the Asantehene Nana Kofi Kakari (1867–74) earned him the appellation *Akyɛmpɔ*, a term which McCaskie (2002:297) rightly notes implies 'A liberal, benevolent person: a benevolent distributor of gold and largesse: the term connotes buying popularity as well as practicing philanthropy ... [it] was a byname or epithet applied to the Asantehene Kofi Kakari.'

He further explains that:

> From his palanquin, he freely scattered packets among the Kumase crowd, each one containing a small measure (*suru*) of gold dust. It is said that he spent his early life in comparative poverty, and that he wept when he saw the amount of gold that had been bequeathed to him as *Asantehene* by his predecessor. Certainly, he is known to have disbursed much of his inherited wealth, – which was state and not personal property – to his individual favourites and concubines. It is said that he justified his behaviour in redistributive terms: 'There is this much gold', he is said to have observed on examining the state treasury, 'while people suffer amidst hunger and poverty'. ....His many fiscal derelictions were among the charges preferred against him when he was removed from office in 1874. (ibid:69)

What are we to make of these gestures of a king who had faced relative financial privation as a child and had wept at the sight of the enormous amount of gold bequeathed to him on his ascension to the throne? It can be seen first as a commitment to the alleviation of the plight of the poor, and then as an appeal to the wealthy to go and do likewise. By distributing gifts of gold to all and sundry, he was breaking the tradition which made the receipt of gold from the king a prerogative of chiefs. In other words, the king must have sympathized with the need for the Asante state to alleviate the plight of its poor. Nonetheless, he must have equally realized that, because the state was the guardian of the *status quo*, any overt official legislation emanating from the occupant of the highest state office, the Asantehene, would have been tantamount to subversion. It is significant to note in this regard that his sympathy with the landless urban poor had led him to argue that the rich bear the cost of the 1872 war, contrary to standard practice which customarily required the imposition of *apeatoɔ* (war tax) on the general population.

The dynamism of Nana Kakari's introduction of philanthropic practice to the royal milieu, whatever its limitation, corroborates the observation of McLeod (1981:85) concerning the vibrant nature of pre-colonial Asante society: 'There is evidence to show that throughout Asante history old forms were increasingly elaborated to meet the needs of a society of growing complexity.' And philanthropy was no exception as individuals were to take advantage of new demands and change trends in existing mores and fortunes to advance the dismantlement of an anachronistic institution. Thus, Asante culture was never static; it was a community in which change was the only permanent thing. For instance, the term *atetekwaa* (an anachronistic person, from *tete* – ancient – and *kwa* – person) was used to describe a person who held on to practices and attitudes which the majority of the community deemed to be obsolete and obscurantist, out of fashion, anachronistic and retrogressive. This dynamism of pre-colonial Asante culture could, thus, facilitate the advent of innovations that were by and large philanthropic.

It is also significant in this regard to underline that the continuous pressure of the pre-colonial Asante philanthropic drive and the demands of the underprivileged and the poor for the improvement of their condition indicates that the communalism of pre-colonial Africa in general, and of Asante in particular, did not by any means preclude a socioeconomic stratification of sharply conflicting and contending economic interests within one and the same community. Thus, the activities of philanthropists naturally had a nibbling effect on the *status quo* which the pre-colonial Asante state authority and its entrenched vested interests were supposed to maintain, or at least change only on their own terms.

Response to European philanthropic gestures

The imperative to change things only on its own terms partly explains the reaction of the pre-colonial Asante state to overtures made by European traders and missionaries. For socio-political and economic reasons pre-colonial Asante responded unfavourably to European appeals to introduce 'formal education' and Christian beliefs and practices to Asante. Thus, the Asante believed that the introduction of European values and their settlement in Asante could only be for the economic advantage of Europe, a point which concurs with the perspective of Charles Dickens that: 'the history of all African effort, hitherto, is a history of wasted European life, squandered European money, and blighted European hope – in which the generous English have borne a great share.'[7]

Second, the Asante judged that European values would be disruptive of and repugnant to the political and social stability of their way of life. More importantly, pre-colonial Asante beliefs would have considered the reception of gratuitous assistance from others as demeaning when there was a way to honourably relate to them through hard work and trade. The Asante argument in this regard is epitomized by the comment made by Kwabena Awua (1843–88), commander of the Asante army, thus: 'Your God is not like our God...if you send in twenty missionaries, you will not get one Ashanti man to be a Christian. It is trade we want, only trade we cry for.' Asante repugnance for Christian values, it must be explained, was partly justified by the untoward behaviour of some two Asante royals whom the King had sent to be trained in the European way of life. It was reported that:

> In 1844, Kwaku Dua Panin complained that these Christian-educated *ahenemma* often committed 'acts of lewdness'; that they were guilty of 'much excess such as criminal intercourse with married and unmarried women'; that they arbitrarily flogged people 'in a most unmerciful manner'; and that their conduct was generally 'scandalous' and 'of the worst possible character'. All of this was far beyond the bounds of any behaviour that might probably be characterized as *mpoatwa*, and it left the Asantehene with 'a very unfavourable impression, as to the probable effects of education' (McCaskie 2002:138).

Thus, fearing foreign domination and social degeneration, pre-colonial Asante rejected foreign help and chose to base its relationship with Europe on fair and mutually beneficial trade instead. Concerning the trade in gold, Barbot (1971:12–13) observes that in the 1680s gold exported from the Gold Coast reached 8,000 marks (12/2 tons). He notes that:

> Of this quantity the Dutch generally have one fourth parts, when there is generally peace among the Blacks, and all the passes are open and free. The English have a fifth or better. The rest is divided among the French, the Danes, the Brandenbergers, the Portuguese and the interlopers of those nations.

The Asante did not see any need to put themselves at the philanthropic mercy of these traders and wanted to prevent the sociopolitical disruption that could come with the influence of European education. The principle was independence, rather than the humiliation of dependence and assistance.

Implications for modern philanthropy in Africa

What clearly come out as the essential traits of philanthropy in pre-colonial Asante are its communal effort to abolish poverty within the community as well as a policy of trade and partnership and self-reliance vis-à-vis outsiders. Thus, their philanthropic activity in medical services suggests that developmental priorities were determined by the needs of the poor receiver rather than the interest of the rich donor. Likewise, the enactment of laws that abolished *awunyadeɛ* and the limitations put on the collective assistance for child upbringing, for instance, implies a preference for only a limited role of the state in private accumulation of wealth *by citizens* and an emphasis on individual responsibility for poverty alleviation. Likewise, the participation of the poor in philanthropic activity underscored the conviction that the fortunes of the poor could and should change for the better, confirming the belief in the basic equality of all humans irrespective of fortuitous material circumstances.

The centrality of the element of anticipated reciprocity implied that philanthropy as practised in pre-colonial Asante was essentially a partnership in which it was those directly affected by the problem, and not the giver, who determined what constituted assistance, and how much and what type of assistance they required. This implies that any imposition of purportedly *universal* solutions would be in total disregard for the real needs of the needy. Thus it would, for instance, be an aberration if a community agreed that it needed electricity, and drew its plans for implementation, only for some donors to dictate that they would rather help provide assistance for the construction of gutters and latrines, which in *the donor's opinion* were what the community needed. Finally, the Asante preference for trade as the key determinant of their relations with foreigners underscores the fact that, as far as dealing with foreign nations was concerned, local industry and fair trade, rather than foreign investment and assistance, constituted the cornerstone upon which pre-colonial Asante founded its solution to poverty and its prevention. It, therefore, underscored the need for philanthropy to encourage forms of independence.

These traits of Asante philanthropy generally stand in contradistinction from those that underlie the general *modus operandi* of international financial organizations today, and which is certainly applicable to the current operations of international philanthropic action. It is an attitude which Lourdes Arizpe (1998:22) rejects thus:

> Western ethnocentrism has customarily been employed as the implicit basis of thinking about development. The paradigm equating development to modernization and modernization to Westernization has long been, and still is, the conventional wisdom, although it has been recognized that there are several alternative strategies of development.

It is curious that for five decades after the Second World War a lot of the operations and methods of international philanthropy have been accepted mainly because they are Western perspectives. Their general ineffectiveness in addressing the developmental problems of Africa has led to a situation which President Harry Truman once described when he noted:

> More than half the people of the world are living in conditions approaching misery.... Their economic life is primitive and stagnant. Their poverty is a handicap and a threat to both them and to more prosperous areas....
>
> I believe we should make available to peace-loving people the benefits of our store of technical knowledge in order to help them realize their aspirations for a better life. And in cooperation with other nations, we should foster capital investment in areas needing development...
>
> This should be a cooperative enterprise in which all nations work together through the United Nations and its specialized agencies whenever practicable. It must be a worldwide effort for the achievement of peace, plenty, and freedom. [8]

Clearly, President Truman speaks of concerted international moral responsibility for acts which would have eliminated philanthropy in favour of long-term development. It was to offer the technology of industrial know-how and investment to the needy, and ensure their permanent self-reliance. The rich were to be motivated by a reward of peace and a sense of fulfilment derived from accomplishing a moral responsibility. Alas! Instead of a design which responds to Truman's scheme of balancing self-interest (peace) with the development of the poor (moral compulsion), contemporary philanthropic effort has been a curious one, centred on self-interest and the reducing of the poor to a permanent philanthropic case, such that Ian Smillie and Larry Minear (2004:2) could note accordingly:

> the moral necessity of humanitarian action is no longer self-evident and has become a matter of debate... Today, aid and human rights organizations spend vast amounts of time and energy making a timely case for humanitarian action, framing need in terms of national security rather than of moral compulsion.

Smillie and Minear go on to present the contemporary crisis in international relief and philanthropic action in these terms:

> The simple humanitarian idea that people in extremis have a right to relief and protection is thus subject to a host of countervailing and intrusive forces. Some are political, reflecting the international and domestic policies of would-be helpers. Some are economic, reflecting the self-interest of helpers delivering what they have in their cupboards rather than what desperate people need. Some are such a mishmash of politics, economics, commercial calculation, guilt, and solidarity that making sense of them is almost impossible. (ibid:9)

This difficulty of current philanthropic action points to two key facts. First, donor effectiveness and/or recipient development will be better realized if stakeholders in philanthropic practice – donors, governments, recipient communities – prioritised the concepts, perspectives, and methods recommended by the poor, rather than preferring the sovereignty considerations of governments and the economic calculations of international donors. Second, much policy must benefit from the insight of existing and local culturally inspired models of philanthropy.

I must underline that this appeal that the insight of traditional systems of philanthropy is necessary for the success of the present search for effective philanthropic regimes does not imply a wholesale return to pre-colonial models, since that is neither feasible nor desirable. Culture contains in itself a duality of continuity and change. All cultures and customs which we defend at any time are themselves reformed versions of some older ones which existed at some immemorial past. Traditions are recreated by such continuing reworking and adaptation, such that modernity is also a culture which will one day be replaced in response to crucial future needs. Taking inspiration from past practices and beliefs to revamp existing ones is, therefore, consistent with the dynamism of culture, underscoring the position that:

> 'we do not intend to revive the past as it was....We want to integrate into modern life only what seems valuable from the past. Our goal is neither the traditional African nor the Black European, but the modern African.'[9]

At the international level, the principal need of philanthropic action today should be to help dismantle those structures that create and maintain the dependency, exploitation and indebtedness of the third world. Pre-colonial Asante had a principle and practice of communal ownership. This principle might not be totally reconstituted to solve current problems to effect a nationalization of natural resources; nonetheless, it can inspire a model of ensuring that communities benefit directly from these resources by having shares in the companies that extract their resources. Thus, philanthropic efforts can buy investment shares for communities, if not individuals. The profits accruing from such investments could then go directly into schemes that alleviate poverty, ensure affordable schooling and public transport services to the community.

The release of Africa from the international encumbrances that create and sustain poverty should allow for the development of local methods of poverty alleviation and wealth creation. The grassroots economic organizations such as the *susu* and *tontin* systems in West Africa will find space to develop to meet the challenges of development in education and health.

Conclusion

This chapter has explored some aspects of the cultural/historical Asante perspective on the multifaceted and complex subject of philanthropy. Consequently, I gleaned the philanthropic perceptions of pre-colonial Asante from a set of normative, institutional, sentimental, and ethical facts that lie beneath the manner in which the Asante perceived poverty and their measures and motives for eliminating it. The assessment consisted of a largely descriptive exploration of the practices and underlying beliefs and motivations that sustained the philanthropic practices of pre-colonial agrarian Asante. I have, thus, underlined that the social organization and political system of pre-colonial Asante possessed knowledge, practices and concepts which in times past inspired and can still feed into the search for methods and concepts to eliminate contemporary poverty. This has helped to clarify some of the otherwise murky but significant connections between traditional knowledge, philanthropy and socioeconomic development in the current fight to eliminate poverty.

I have indicated that most of the nature and objectives of the philanthropic acts in pre-colonial Asante are embedded in the normative, institutional, sentimental, and ethical notions and structures that underlie the beliefs and practices that determined how and why the Asante tackled poverty in the specific way they did. In saying that traditional perceptions and practices must feed into current philanthropic activity, my intention is neither to castigate the efforts of international donors nor to reject all governmental intervention as totally inimical to the philanthropic effort in Africa. This is the reason why I have refrained from presenting pre-colonial philanthropic ideas and practices in idyllic terms. More importantly, I have not advocated for a wholesale return to old social organization or beliefs of pre-colonial Asante. Rather, I have emphatically underlined that the idea of philanthropy as helping the needy to permanently abolish the conditions that put them in need, must be the central objective of current philanthropic actions.

I am proposing that researchers, policymakers and workers who are directly involved in philanthropic activities in Africa trace and explore the current belief systems of respective communities in order to comprehend the values, attitudes, definitions, and significance that these respective communities attach to the practice of aid and philanthropy. This will help enhance the effectiveness of aid by indicating what objectives to prioritize and what programmes to put in place.

Endnotes

1. Rattray notes concerning this practice in pre-colonial Asante: 'There are many survivals of a communistic state still in evidence; it is seen in their system of land tenure, and in that the private debts of one person are recoverable from the entire family of that person. This last is a relic of collective responsibility of the whole clan for the acts of a single member' (Rattray 1952:163).
2. *The Holy Bible*, Deuteronomy Chapter 15 verse 4. New International Version, Struik Christian Books, Cape Town (2005:209).
3. Charlatans were usually tried and sentenced to death and executed at a shrine called *Diakomfoɔ*.
4. NAG, Kumase, File 113/1908, Kofi Sraha and others to Chief Commissioner (Ashanti), dd Kumasi, 1 October 1930. Cited in McCaskie (1995:72).
5. For this state level, see 'The Invasion of Asante by Abirimuru', and the accusation against 'those from Denkira'.
6. Notes on the nature of Asante multiple trade routes.
7. *The Examiner*, 19 Aug. 1848, pp. 531–3 (Reprinted as 'The Niger Expedition' in Miscellaneous Papers.) Coutt, lot. cit. Cited in Norris (1978:99).
8. From point number four President Harry Truman's Message to the US Congress on January 20, 1949. Cited by Bauer (1981:275).
9. 'Ntu Editorials', cited in Davidson (1964:79).

CHAPTER 5

HORIZONTAL PHILANTHROPY AMONG THE POOR IN SOUTHERN AFRICA: GROUNDED PERSPECTIVES ON SOCIAL CAPITAL AND CIVIC ASSOCIATION[1]

ALAN FOWLER & SUSAN WILKINSON-MAPOSA

Introduction

There is a recognized lack of study of and knowledge about philanthropic behaviour rooted within Africa. This chapter presents recent comparative research in four countries of Southern Africa in a bid to redress this gap. Findings from the study show that people who are poor self-generate and rely on prosocial behaviours between each other: they demonstrate what we call 'horizontal philanthropy'. This practice is lived as an indigenous system of helping with interactive dimensions of: interdependence between needs and help networks; the range of capitals valued and used in transactions; the conventions and rules employed; the motivations involved; and a normative moral philosophy that guides prosocial behaviour. Each horizontal philanthropic decision and act can be understood as a combination of these dimensions.

The conceptual relationship between philanthropy, social capital and self-formed associations provides an analytic framework for further probing the empirical evidence. The framing concentrates on fundamental principles of giving and receiving assistance: altruism, reciprocity and cooperation. These principles underpin the indigenous system. Their distribution in help relationships appears consistent with stable, non-competitive relational strategies found elsewhere. Assistance is collaborative, and pooled arrangements complement inter-personal help relationships.

This chapter applies this new understanding about this type of philanthropic behaviour in Southern Africa to debates about social capital. More fundamentally, this understanding is employed to move forward a conversation about the very notion of an 'African philanthropy' as opposed to 'philanthropy with African characteristics'. The critical analysis applied here identifies four topics that would merit in-depth interrogation for advancing an African narrative of philanthropy as a valuable contribution to post-colonial knowledge.

Effective development relies on understanding and purposefully modifying political, economic and social relations and their interdependent processes of change. To serve these ends, the past decade has witnessed an active exploration of the concept, definitions, theories and applications of social capital. Results have served as a source of development policy, as an operational framework and as a guide to investment in poverty reduction in and beyond Africa (Woolcock 1998; Woolcock and Narayan 1999).[2]

Within this context of thinking about social relations, this chapter draws on re-sults of original research employing a new and distinct lens: the prosocial behaviour among poor people in Southern Africa. In doing so it argues that people who are poor live embedded forms of helping each other which constitute a neglected but enduring system of self-directed 'horizontal philanthropy' with distinct character-istics.[3] This organic form of helping is probably found elsewhere on the continent. Evidence of how this system operates has implications for re-addressing debates about social capital as well as pointing at directions to improve development per-formance. It also offers a way of testing western discourse on 'philanthropy' from the perspective of generating post-colonial knowledge and indigenous categories of understanding.

A further feature of the current development decade is a conscious effort to enlist a wider array of actors, sources and types of development assistance. The UN Global Compact with businesses and active encouragement of Public Private Partnerships are but two examples. Perhaps less noticed, but no less significant, are efforts to mobilize domestic resources in developing countries by the encourage-ment of local philanthropy and giving.[4]

One strategy adopted by a number of American philanthropies is to promote the establishment of community foundations. It is beyond the scope of this chapter to detail the substance and evolution of a global movement advancing this model (Sacks 2004).[5] Suffice it to say that a community foundation should be locally con-nected, characterized by its proximity to those it mobilizes resources from, and close – if not answerable – to those it is meant to serve. A community foundation is also intended to be enduring or sustainable, typically because of finance in an endowment (Milner and Hartnell 2006).

However, worldwide efforts to transfer what was originally an American philan-thropic invention for the wealthy to other contexts gave rise to critical concerns. In particular were challenges to assumptions about the life world and 'philanthropic' understanding and practices of those in other countries who are intended to both contribute to and gain from a community foundation in their vicinity. A major proponent of community foundations, the Ford Foundation, therefore decided to re-illuminate the terrain of giving and receiving in developing countries that was previously the preserve of anthropologists (e.g. Mauss 1954). The result was finance for a research project with no predetermined operational objectives which could – subject to the findings – be introduced in a further phase. Applying principles and methods of grounded research, between 2002 and 2005, country-based teams investigated and analyzed the 'philanthropic' or horizontal helping behaviour of individuals within the poorest strata of Mozambique, Namibia, South Africa and Zimbabwe. Of particular interest for a developmental concept of social capital are findings with respect to the principles of poor-to-poor assistance, allied to individual decision-making processes.[6]

Following a discussion of terms and the establishment of an analytic framework in section two, section three describes the research and its limitations. Section four details findings about five dimensions of help, leading to a description of horizontal philanthropy as an indigenous, living prosocial system. The relevance for social capital and self-organized associations is discussed in section five.

Section six deepens the analysis by directly addressing the idea and nature of an 'African philanthropy'. What might it mean and what language and concepts are required to communicate its essence? The reasoning employed to answer this question leads to a contentious conclusion, namely, that the moral ethos and com-moditized practices used by the 'philanthropic industry' of the West are further from the original meaning of philanthropy than what exists 'horizontally' on the African continent. In addition, it poses for debate the issue of an African philan-thropy versus philanthropy with a distinctive African character.

A short conclusion reiterates the potential significance of generating knowl-edge about indigenous practices and lived reality on the continent for reaching the objectives of which this volume is an important step.

Philanthropy, social capital and association

Philanthropy in and of Africa is in search of self-understanding. To further this quest, this section uses and problematizes concepts found in prevailing western-inspired discourse on non-competitive relations that underpin helping others. The conversation of interest relates to social capital and the functioning of collaborative associations. This section has two purposes. First, to establish categories against which research findings can be tested in terms of their relevance and meaning. Second, is to identify Africa-specific concepts that may contribute to and complement efforts to ascertain an indigenous comprehension of 'philanthropy' that is locally rooted rather than reflective of foreign interpretations.

An apparent straightforward tie between an enquiry on philanthropy among the poor and social capital lies in their non-competitive value base. However, a problem with philanthropy as a contemporary concept is that the term has been stretched in so many directions and so inconsistently applied as to be beyond consistent definition (e.g. Wright 2001). Further, the word is not directly translatable into the vernacular languages that research needed to employ. Consequently, bearing in mind context-specific, psycho-linguistic interpretations (Herriot 1970; Vygotskii et al. 1986), a term familiar to all informants – help – was used throughout the field study.

Helping is typically attributed to moral sentiments, commonly expressed through practices of philanthropy and principles of altruism, generosity, volunteering and reciprocity. Western-derived discourse typically makes the following less than definitive distinctions between them. The Greek etymological roots of philanthropy are to be found in 'philos'– liking, fondness or love, and 'anthropo' – humanity or humankind. Its contemporary western expression – often with tax encouragement – is practical benevolence, for example by contributing to general well-being or welfare. Driven by compassion, guilt, a sense of justice, patronism or similar emotions, philanthropy has become a legalized system of non-state resource distribution for the public good from people or institutions with high net wealth. In this sense private/individual assets are made public/collective in a way that society (lightly) regulates and regards as meriting economic incentives.[7]

Altruism is akin to philanthropy as a prosocial motivation and principle that promotes the well-being of others, where 'one person's utility is positively affected by another person's welfare' (Axelrod 1984:135). It is a behaviour that can be distinguished from drivers of duty or loyalty. According to Margolis (1982:15), as long as the free choices a person makes in allocating resources is *regarded as benign*, the effects of benefiting others or society do not diminish what is attained for oneself. An altruistic act need not have a zero or negative outcome for the giver. It can also be a highly personal transaction. Altruism can motivate, but differentiate itself from, modern philanthropy. It is but one in a repertoire of relational principles that is not formalized as a practice of resource transfer according to prescribed public norms and rules.[8]

Generosity is a prosocial or other-serving motivation for helping. Its principle reflects a self-interest that commonly translates into charity. It is typically driven by emotional empathy. The reward is that the perceived value of the gift to one less well placed is understood to generate a larger proportional benefit than the loss to the giver. There is a positive sum outcome which creates self-value to the donor.

In the west, a common expression of generosity is volunteering, typically the unpaid, freely given allocation of time for the benefit of others beyond direct family and/or relatives (Dekker and Halman 2003). It assumes that there is no obligation or coercion to give or deny one's time or effort.

Reciprocity is a (often time-displaced) mutually self-interested exchange with expectation of an agreed return. There may be an element of barter. What is given may be matched by something different but of acceptable equivalence. Reciprocity can be general. That is, the return is not specific but found in the overall improvement in the environment that results for the giver. More often, it is quite specific as an ethical principle underlying personalized human transactions and is important in bonding people together. Indeed, reciprocity is a virtually defining feature of social capital. Through this principle of relating, trust and reputation are built, as are like-minded groupings that may or may not evolve into formal, publicly recognized civic organizations and business firms.

The research terrain of people who are poor in Southern Africa does not necessarily correspond to assumptions implied in these formulations. For example, transactions of relevance are between parties of similar low wealth. There is a presumption of volition or free choice about helping that may or may not be valid in all contexts and cultures. The notion of volunteering is premised on wage employment that is unlikely to be in play with the majority poor of the continent. Consequently, the nature of philanthropy in Africa cannot be assumed, *a priori*, to correspond with these principles – generic as they may seem – or how they are lived. Nevertheless, examining the concept of social capital and processes of association helps set up a framework and questions that lead to insights about what (part of) African philanthropy looks like and how it works.

Literature typically distinguishes three types of social capital – that which *bonds* people into (homogeneous) groups; that which *bridges* (heterogeneous) groups to other groups; and that which *links* groups to other types of institutions. Within groups that are connected or bonded as (disbursed) networks there may be any number of individuals who provide and enjoy bridging and linking capital, for example to institutions with aid-based resources.

Social capital is a function and product of interconnected networks of reasonably stable, enduring and valued social relations. There are differing schools of thought about how this intangible capital is generated. For Robert Putnam (1993, 2001) capital resides in, and is an outcome of, the collective of social relationships. It derives, in part, from the moral imperatives and values – particularly trust – that reciprocity embodies and relies on. For Nan Lin (1999, 2001) social capital is more

contractual.[9] It is to be found in the aggregate of expected return on the investment made between individuals within the network and their links to resources
in markets. Do embedded arrangements of help relationships in Southern Africa
have anything to say about this difference? An answer is offered later.

From an analytic perspective, the interface between philanthropy and social
capital highlights an interpretative problem. At issue is whether or not the complete range of non-competitive 'helping' principles has a bearing on social capital.
Or is it exclusively the principle of reciprocity that applies, implying equivalence
in the value of that which is transacted? But, is this condition always required?
Can other principles that underlie helping also contribute to social capital, and
does this occur? Put another way, can definitions premised on *purposes* rather than
the normative (trust) and structural (network) attributes of social capital bring
other principles of help into the frame? For example, Lin's functional definition of
social capital (1999:31) includes return in terms of the social credentials that non-
reciprocal principles can equally generate. The Southern Africa research detailed
later addresses this issue.

The research also provides insights about conditions under which personalized
help transactions limit what can be achieved in terms of reducing vulnerability
such that collective arrangements are created and relied upon. This process is
described in the theoretical work of Mancur Olson (1971) and Eleanor Ostrom
(1990) on collective action and goods. Their analyses suggest a two-step process
beyond individualized exchanges. First is self-organized collaboration. As long
as each individual's interests are sufficiently satisfied by the benefits of collective
endeavour, the group will sustain itself. Depending on resource constraints, effective collaboration can attract new members and hence growth. However, at a
certain scale, a limit of interactions is reached where the informal rules required
to maintain social relations can no longer work effectively.

Consequently, at a non-predetermined stage there is an alteration in the relative cost-benefit experienced by members for the collective goods produced. This
is the moment where the group splits or formalization ensues, which is a common path to external visibility and access to vertical resources. In development
parlance, innate community arrangements and practices become 'formalized'
grassroots organizations which can seek to register as such and even strive to
become non-governmental organizations. The way that these dynamics show up
is relatively unexplored terrain but potentially vital for a project – of which this
book is part – that 'seeks to define in very clear ways what "philanthropy" is and
the form it takes in Africa.'[10]

The foregoing provides an analytic framework which 1) interrogates philanthropy as a concept with an African expression derived from principles of helping

attributed to social capital and 2) distinguishes the expressions of help relationships involved. We now turn to the research undertaken.

The research

The research project applied the grounded theory methodological approach (Strauss and Corbin 2008). This entails that analytic categories are not presumed from the outset but are elicited from the information gathered. Nevertheless, boundaries must be set that are meaningful in relation to the core focus of the enquiry. In this case, one boundary was established by excluding state support – pensions, unemployment payments and the like – as a form of help to be considered. In addition, a decision was taken not to quantify the value of help. Other research indicated the substantial methodological demands of this type of enquiry that were beyond what was possible or required at this stage.[11]

A grounded approach calls for as broad a spectrum as possible in terms of respondent types, again bounded by as few as possible presuppositions about the variables that may have a bearing on their selection. Statistical representivity is not in play. Breadth of respondent life conditions and experiences of poverty allowed interrogation of qualitative data for recurrences, patterns and emergent properties that are more robust.

Research proceeded in such a way that a landscape of help among the poor could be constructed from below for each country. To this end, first a basic set of what, who, why and when questions where employed. Second, respondent selection was determined by observable individual and group properties. Focus groups were the primary data collection method, supplemented by secondary data and key informant interviews. A simple but powerful initial analytic framework was employed around three fundamental features of all helping relationships: the actors involved (A), the content of the transaction (T) and the motivations concerned (M). The use of Nvivo, text-based analytic software, permitted a systematic review of all focus group narratives – translated from vernacular – for, amongst others, the relative prevalence of sub-categories within A, T and M individually, distribution of pairing, and relative presence of ATM combinations. Text analysis produced additional categories that respondents employed to describe and explain their help relationships.

Research questions

It was necessary to identify what 'help' means for people who are poor and, from here, how poor-to-poor assistance features in their lives. The following questions formed the core of focus group sessions.

• What is help?

- Who do you help and who helps you?
- What forms of help are used for what purposes?
- Why do you help?
- Has help changed over time?

A focus group session was ended by means of summary construction of giver and receiver matrices. Types of help arising from the discussion were placed on the horizontal axis, and sources of help, i.e. actors, were located vertically. In each resultant cell, participants were asked to indicate its relevance, its importance, the frequency with which the combination occurred and, finally, if the transaction was typically premised on ascription (having to) or volition (wanting to).

Respondents

Poverty in Southern Africa and elsewhere has many faces (Maxwell 1999). It is absolute and relative between and within countries and is differentially experienced by types of people at different life stages. Some 52 per cent of the 80.9 million population in the research countries survive on less than US$2 a day. In each country, national data on poverty distribution and human development indicators (United Nations 2005) were used to determine preliminary locations for interviews. At selected sites, socioeconomic details for potential respondents were elicited. Where necessary, wealth-ranking exercises were used to reach a final participant selection.

Focus groups reflecting diversity in poverty situations and experiences were realized through combinations of the following respondent attributes: age, gender, living location – urban or rural, and type of livelihood. Table 5.1 shows the breakdown in terms of the first three. Recognising contextual differences such as relative degrees of urbanization and industrialization, livelihood was approached in a country-oriented way. For example, subsistence farming and fishing is more economically significant in Mozambique than in Zimbabwe, where mining and large-scale farming dominate the formal economy. Country teams used their local knowledge and previous research to identify common ways in which poor people survive. In total, 17 livelihood types were included, not all of which were investigated in every country. They can be grouped in the following way.[12]

- *Petty trading*: hawking, newspaper selling.
- *Rural subsistence*: farming, livestock holding and fishing.
- *Service provision:* sex work, casual labour, car parking, guarding and washing.
- *Financial dependency*: receipt of remittances, begging.

Typical across all livelihood types was precariousness, low earnings and general insecurity of both incomes and assets. In all, 677 respondents took part in 87 focus group discussions.

Emergent analytic categories

Periodic meetings with research teams reviewed accumulating data for signs of oft-occurring responses, phrases and stories that were indicative of systemic categories, frames of reference and processes. These were critically examined and decisions reached about inclusion in Nvivo coding. Data produced the architecture for qualitative analysis, which contained eight major categories and subdivisions.[13]

i.   *Actors* – who is giving or receiving help, including (non-)family, local institutions such as mutual assistance groups, semi-formal and formal civic associations, and support organizations such as NGOs and churches.

ii. *Transactions* – types of material and non-material content.

iii. *Imperative* – reasons for requesting help.

iv. *Impulses* – driving principles for help responses, including values, ascription and volition.

v.   *Rules* – conventions attending a transaction, including eligibility criteria and conditions/expectations attached.

vi. *Practice* – hypothesized and experiential responses as well as change in helping experienced over time.

vii. *Force fields* – respondents' references to wider determinants of help behaviour including socialization and socioeconomic and political factors.

viii. *Quotations* with illustrative power.

Matrices produced by focus groups were overlaid to show the prevalence of ATM variables and combinational properties: relevance, significance, frequency, and volition or ascription as motivations. This preliminary filtering directed attention towards more prevalent categories and combinations. Associated narrative analysis provided information about patterns of connections, indicated directions of causation, illustrated decision-making processes and, eventually, established a reasonably coherent picture of the dimensions that constitute philanthropy of community as a complex behaviour described below.

Limitations

Resources set a limit to the number of focus groups and their distribution across the four countries. Nevertheless, the data produced did not indicate response variations significant enough to suggest that greater numbers of focus groups would have produced a vastly different help landscape. Research at the base of society in

Table 5.1: Focus group breakdown

Country	Number of FGs	Location		Gender		Age					
		Urban	Rural	Female	Male	18<	18–24	25–49	>50	Mixed	Unknown
Mozambique	18	10	8	10	8	0	0	3	4	10	1
Namibia	18	10	8	9	9	1	2	11	4	0	0
South Africa	32	16	16	17	15	4	6	14	8	0	0
Zimbabwe	19	12	7	6	13	1	4	10	4	0	0
Total	87	48	39	42	45	6	12	38	20	10	1

four countries involved 47 ethnolinguistic groups with interviews in 11 languages. Translation to English invites errors of comprehension and interpretation. Random sample checks using third-party re-translation from English back to vernacular captured most, but probably not all, mistakes.

A larger source of possible error stems from different interpretations of categories used by respondents and possible overlaps that are not easy to spot or tease out. An important example is the use of the term 'neighbour', which may or may not be family as well. This problem is confounded by sociocultural and linguistic variation in who is and is not understood as family. Here, the anthropological expertise of country research teams ensured awareness of this and similar issues of potential inconsistency across research sites.

Finally, operational conditions in a country like Zimbabwe – where logistics are difficult and research is treated with suspicion by the authorities – presented particular challenges of access and process. Error identification and prevention was addressed by periodic site visits, self-reflective, joint quality control meetings of teams, a peer review of draft country reports and triangulation of data contained in group narratives and the summary matrices. Overall, there are no compelling grounds to consider the findings unsound.

Findings: philanthropy of community

To reiterate, the research was not directed at social capital *per se*, and produced findings that cover broader, albeit overlapping, terrains. This section concentrates on research results, while section five deals directly with the relationships between horizontal philanthropy and social capital.

Findings are presented in two parts. First, patterns exhibited by the data are described and reviewed. Results are then discussed in terms of the components of help between the poor as a relational system. More detailed and comprehensive analysis is available in the full research monograph Wilkinson-Maposa et al. (2006).

Features and patterns

For respondents, help is 'the giving and/or receiving of something to satisfy or alleviate a need, a problem, a difficulty, a sense of deprivation or a lack of something, be it a tangible good/asset or ability' (ibid.:36).

Associated with this definition, help is a daily lived reality and necessity, not an exceptional event. Asking for help brings *no stigma*. *Offering help* without being asked is commonplace. No matter how little you have you give – *the act is as important as the quantum involved*. Helping brings positive feelings that can be its own (spiritual or moral) reward. To qualify as 'help', *assistance cannot be exploitive or demeaning*. A recipient must *be deserving*. This attribute is principally judged by an individual's helping behaviour within their possibilities. Preference is given for seeking help from people who understand one's situation by virtue of a *shared condition or experience,* rather than from outsiders.

Table 5.2 shows the country findings for the most active givers and receivers of help, as well as the dominant types of content. The figures indicate propensities extracted from the primary focus group matrixes and narratives.

Table 5.2: Prevalence of major types of actors and transactions (percent)

		Mozambique	Namibia	South Africa	Zimbabwe
Actors	Family	55	36	17	22
	Non-Family	38	59	38	57
	Informal Association	2	2	32	4
	Formal organisation	5	3	10	15
Material transactions	Money	25	33	35	31
	Clothes	27	20	25	25
	Food	48	47	40	44
Non-material transactions	Knowledge	1	32	24	40
	Physical/ Manual	98	40	60	52
	Moral/ Emotional	1	28	16	8

In terms of actors as givers and receivers, South Africa exhibits a much greater role of informal associations in the help landscape with diminished reference to family, whereas Namibia and Zimbabwe stand out for reliance on family actors. Reasons for this are not clear. Relative differences in the degree of modernization, ethnic composition, the structure of economies, urbanization and human displacements stemming from apartheid and mining may lead to greater reliance on more formalized helping structures exhibited in South Africa and Zimbabwe.

Nevertheless, there is similarity in terms of the modest role played by informal community associations, such as savings, cultural or recreational clubs, and more formalized organizations such as NGOs and churches. Interpersonal help predominates. One explanation from text analysis is the importance of physical proximity and affinity – by blood or a shared identity through livelihood – in helping and being helped. However, as detailed below, types of and reasons for need also play into the selection of who to approach and who merits help.

Transactions are split between material and non-material content. Data indicate a higher prevalence for material over non-material transactions in Mozambique and Namibia, with the reverse for South Africa and Zimbabwe. While Mozambique stood out in that material assistance was ranked five times more important than non-material, both categories of help were considered to be significant.

Food is consistently the most significant content of material help, followed by money and then clothes. Providing physical support and manual labour are the most common forms of non-material help.

Motivation proved particularly complex and difficult to analyze. Typical triggers or reasons for helping are:

i.   *unexpected events*: births deaths, emergencies

ii.   *shortages*: clothes, food, water

iii. *vulnerability*: worsening poverty, deprivation and asset depletion

iv.   *periodic and foreseen*: seasonal shared labour

v.   *opportunities*: income-generating investment, working capital

These triggers can be further refined in terms of people's short-term and strategic approaches to coping with poverty and uncertainty. Triggers, or the why of assistance, are associated with two major types of content transaction: normal/small/quick and urgent/large. The consequences of this distinction are discussed below.

But, triggers – situations when help is initiated – are not the same as motivations traceable to principles of altruism, reciprocity or collaboration. Narrative review indicates a propensity distribution between these drivers of 10–15, 60–65 and 20–25 per cent respectively. The former – understood by the poor as compassion and pity – is often reserved for strangers or for those that cannot help themselves. Regarded largely as receivers and not givers, these include the poorest of the poor, orphans, the elderly and the disabled. Cooperation involves benefiting from doing together what cannot be done alone.

Within respondents' livelihood, survival and coping strategies, helping is more often exhibited as reciprocal exchange. Local idioms illustrate that reciprocity brings its own reward: *Lokwooko ohali shikula lokuulu* – The one arm follows the one of the leg – i.e. the one that gives is also given to. Reciprocity means that payback can be spread over time – effectively redistributing a giver's assets. If the receiver behaves as required, vulnerability is reduced because risk is spread, making reputation central in decision-making described below. However, reciprocity does not necessarily increase assets. It acts as a form of 'welfare', preventing slippage further into deprivation. Collective action involved in pooling resources is secondary. Conforming to Olson's (2006) thesis, group collaboration affords the prospect of collective gain, to give movement or escape out of poverty.

Assistance spans a broad typology. Examples are: 1) a donation, such as time for supporting orphans; 2) a subsidy, where a normal, expected return is foregone; 3) a fee for service, typically a token of appreciation; 4) a loan, where return is required; 5) a sharing, such as information or application of a skill, neither of which is depleted by the act of giving; 6) redistribution from a public asset, like a chief's grain store; 7) a collaborative endeavour for joint, even if unequal, gain; and 8) as intervention or intercession on someone's behalf.

Modest variation in responses was seen across focus groups of different genders, ages and (urban–rural) locations. Intra-gender help is favoured over inter-gender help. Whether a transaction was considered to be help or not also showed differences related to engendered divisions of labour. Urban locations exhibited importation of rural helping practices, however, assistance is more monetarized. Affinity is more oriented towards those with similar livelihood coping strategies and the physical proximity of neighbourhoods and density of dwellings.

Finally, the choice of conditions to be applied in any one transaction is a product of complex decision-making described in the following section. How the above factors combine to co-construct philanthropy of community is discussed next.

Philanthropy among the poor – five dimensions

While dedicated research would help to thoroughly test the findings, analysis points to systemic relations operating between the variables described above. The system, defined as philanthropy of community (PoC), has five dimensions, each with different properties and functions. First is type of need as a co-determinant of the giver–receiver network selected. Second is the range of capitals involved. Third are ways in which motivations interact with the purpose of assistance. Fourth are the conventions or rules applied. Finally, surrounding and underpinning all other dimensions is a particular moral philosophy. While each dimension may be found in social relations related to non-help interactions, the distinctiveness of PoC (in Southern Africa) derives from their combination and properties emerging from them. Each dimension is described. Their interplay is explored by taking a decision about a horizontal philanthropic act (HPA) as a unit of analysis.

Dimension 1 – interplay of needs and networks

'In life it is impossible not to have helped.'[14]

Unmet needs or unresolved problems are a quintessential aspect of poverty that drive people to seek and provide help to each other. Poor people differentiate help in terms of needs that are 'normal' or those that are 'urgent'. Normal needs are typically small, regular and frequent, including daily use, short term and gap filling. These demands can be planned for and anticipated and the size is manageable in terms of a drain on assets. Such needs are often satisfied through individual reciprocity, and the return is quick.

Urgent needs are immediate and unplanned for or unanticipated. They are usually generated by emergencies such as fire, flooding, death, accidents and drought. The poor also see urgency in terms of dangerous levels of debt or financial constraints that, for example, prevent marriage because of an inability to meet a brideprice. While perhaps lower in frequency and more ad hoc, urgent needs require a rapid response and can demand a significant contribution in relation to available resources. The size of demand in proportion to an individual's asset base may require a group or collective response that can be spontaneous or premeditated. Typical in the latter case is collective creation of a risk-reducing strategic reserve – e.g. a burial society, or a savings and credit group with jointly managed resources that can be called upon under agreed conditions. Country comparisons suggest that both the degree to which such collective arrangements feature in help patterns and the associational modality involved vary. The formalization of help relationships tends to correspond to purposes that should improve life circumstances rather than prevent deterioration in well-being, a spectrum explained in more detail later.

Both individual giving and pooling draw on and co-create help circuits. Access to assistance is gained through a personal set of connections or networks that mobilize resources and address needs. The network involved is shaped by the interplay between the type of need and the nature of affinity – blood and social identity or physical proximity between the actors – as well as individual reputation. In other words, help networks are needs based and multiple. They may or may not include more institutionalized sources of assistance, such as informal associations and more formal organizations.[15] In this respect, depending on the nature of the need, networks may be simple arrays of individual connections or contain complex combinations of actor types.

Dimension 2 – range of capitals

A further aspect of needs and their network-generating effects are the importance that people who are poor attribute to non-material assistance, described previously. While less frequent in terms of transactional content, the value attributed to knowledge, contacts, information, physical and manual assistance and moral/emotional support must not be underestimated. Such assets are not necessarily depleted, lost or foregone through use. In this sense, they help poor people satisfy a reputational requirement to give no matter how little – the act is as important as the content value – which maintains eligibility for assistance, social cohesion and network access.

Dimension 3 – maintenance to movement

Poor people involved in the study judge help in many ways. An oft-cited criterion is whether or not the help is expected to maintain current living status, conditions and prospects – i.e. to prevent slippage into deeper deprivation – or to create movement, that is to increase the possibilities for escaping poverty and better countering adversity. Where political or economic forces and pandemics like HIV/AIDS are a continual source of livelihood insecurity and downward pressure on assets, the developmental significance and impact of maintenance-oriented help is often overlooked.

More readily treated (by outsiders) as developmental behaviour are help trans-actions that carry the potential for increasing or diversifying economic assets or other capitals and widening the scope of life to increase people's opportunities. The inclination of poor people to allocate resources in this way is mediated by their experience of returns on doing so. A case in point for many respondents was the diminishing value of investment in children's education that did not generate a benefit through improved access to employment or other sources of livelihood.

Dimension 4 – conventions, rules and their application

People who are poor help each other and are helped according to unwritten yet widely understood conventions, customs, rules and sanctions. They are not static, but continually updated transaction by transaction. The help system is premised on the axiom 'no matter how little you have you give', which itself rests on a moral philosophy described in Dimension 5. It functions by means of experiential feedback that co-determines the reinforcement or attrition of a network's value to those within it.

In operation, the horizontal help system rests on a decision-making process. First, a trigger arises and a potential transaction is initiated – help is asked for or offered. A request is screened for appropriateness and actor eligibility. If the result of this screening is positive, informed by a motivational principle, a help transac-tion is selected as a combination from the eight options described previously. In a fourth step, actors establish an agreement on the terms or conditions that will apply. Finally, over time there are reputational rewards for conforming to conventions and rules and there are sanctions for not doing so. Sanctions may be individual in terms of decreased eligibility for assistance from the chosen source in the future. When a person's non-compliance becomes systematic or has wider effects, such as threatening social cohesion, they can be corrected by an acknowledged authority – such as elders or age cohorts – and in the extreme isolated, excluded or rejected.

Dimension 5 – moral philosophy of the collective self

'You can fail to give because you don't have anything to offer; you are poor. But when you can't give you feel pained by the fact that you don't have something to offer to make you *a human being among others* (emphasis added).'[16]

The above quotation, and similar expressions to be found in the narratives, point towards a moral philosophy among respondents that requires re-calibration of western metrics of selfless or selfish behaviour that are premised on Durkheim's 'anomie' and individualistic choice. The philosophy of *ubuntu* – I am because you are – rather than the Descartian axiom of I think therefore I am (Masamba Ma Mpolo 1985), provides a different behavioural proposition and interpretation of help among the poor in Southern Africa.

Essentially, *ubuntu* is a theory and philosophy of collective self with strong spiritual and symbolic connotations (Mbiti 1991; Louw 1999). Denying help to another is to deny one's own identity as a human being. The 'moral sentiments' among respondents co-define the normative underpinnings of social capital. They stem from deeper wellsprings of reciprocity than western perspectives of non-exploitive, networked action might recognise. As a philosophy of collective self, *ubuntu* should not to be reified or overestimated as a foundation for cooperation. Indeed, it is argued that today in South Africa, political appeals to *ubuntu* are often manipulative (Marx 2002). Nevertheless, the respondents' moral framework invite re-interpretation of what self-interest and selflessness actually mean if 'self' is a collective property. In such a philosophy of collective identity, help is never selfless – which creates problems with the concept of altruism if defined as a selfless act.

Decision-making

Deciding to undertake a horizontal philanthropic act (HPA) involves a large number of variables, uncertainties, assessment of risk and an estimate of the behaviour of the other actor(s) in response. As a way of life amongst the poor, helping involves an almost innate decision-making process.

The data collected suggests that when respondents decide about asking for or giving help, four leading elements are in play. These are: 1) the size and nature of the need or problem; 2) the affinity among the giver and receiver; 3) the reputation and associated level of trust; as well as 4) underlying motivations that affect the giver's calculus.

Types of need – normal or urgent – are appreciated through three dimensions.

i.   F – Frequency: How often the problem or need occurs and hence how often help is actually requested or offered.

ii.   P – Proportionality: How much of a potential giver's own resources (material asset/time/effort) is required to address the need/problem.

iii.   T – Time: The duration of help and period of return.

Proportional demands of normal needs tend to be low and manageable. Often premised on reciprocity, return is typically soon or rapid. However, the bigger and more frequent normal needs become, the less likely a positive response because of a growing mismatch between the imperative to act and the proportional demand made on a giver's resource base. Lending a cup of sugar a day is one thing. Lending a sack of sugar every day is another, and less likely.

Affinity comprises three relational elements – closeness in terms of blood, i.e. genealogy of kinship or family; closeness in distance, i.e. physical proximity, for example to one's neighbour; and, finally, close socioeconomic relations, which would include shared livelihood, sense of identity, or common membership in an association or organization.

An individual's reputation is central in determining eligibility for assistance. This factor is informed in two ways. First, by status – for example, as a mother, elder, headman or political representative – that may imply a particular level of due respect. The second feature is the individual's character – is the person worthy? A common indicator is the degree of trust a potential giver places in a receiver and, hence, the risk involved in embarking on a help transaction. Like trust, a good reputation is built up over time.

Two issues are often at play in underlying motivations: choice and principles. The decision to help or ask for help could be voluntary and informed by free choice, or it could be a function of duty and obligation, for example ascribed by the combination of one's status, affinity and a particular need or problem. The three principles applied reflect altruism, reciprocity and cooperation.

A horizontal philanthropic act can be located within theories of personal choice applied to transactions between people. This behaviour is typically tested by (laboratory) experiments based on game theories applied with economic and other perspectives. Of particular interest are evolutionary theories of social behaviour. They posit that, over time, for all human populations relatively stable normative relational strategies emerge from transactions between agents, exhibiting a ratio of 20:65:15 for free-riding, reciprocity and collaboration respectively (Fehr, Fischbacher and Gächter 2002). Free-riding – or exploitative behaviour – was not the subject of the research. Nevertheless, within helping patterns among the poor – including what is termed altruism – a similar proportional distribution was seen. Further, the patterns observed generally conform to findings of game-based studies undertaken with small-scale societies representing a range of economic and cultural conditions (Henrich et al. 2005), akin to those within Southern Africa.

Both empirical comparisons suggest confidence in research results and suggest implications for defining an African philanthropy.

With this understanding of horizontal philanthropy in its lived practice and relational theory, we can turn to its contribution to debates related to social capital and the formation of associations.

Social capital theory and civic association

Is there such a thing as an African philanthropy? The research undertaken and the theoretical lens of social capital offer pointers to how an answer or answers can be reached, rather than the answers themselves. This section is therefore intended to advance the discussion by, first, applying findings to debates within social capital theory. Second, it will reflect on the associational life of poor people from the perspectives of horizontal help. A third step is to engage with complex issues of language and definition that will need to be addressed in scholarly debates about the phenomenon of philanthropy on the continent. This latter topic merits detailed attention, given in the next section.

Lin (1999) addresses one controversy about social capital – understood by him as an investment in social relations with an expected return that may or may not have economic value. The debate hinges on an appreciation of social capital advanced by Robert Putnam (2000), as a collectively generated value or, proposed by Lin, as an individualistic asset-based property. While both can co-exist, the findings of this research suggest that, for poor people, these combine in a particular way. For respondents, *reputation* is the individual element, three types of *affinity* form the relational tissue, and need-based *networks* express transaction structure which 'holds' collective value over time.

Reputation is personally carried or possessed. It is continually 'updated' by an individual's behaviour with respect to asking for or giving help. The extreme case of reputation failure results in network exclusion and loss of legitimacy or right to claim assets that social capital makes available. Poverty in this region of the world can make exclusion mean the difference between survival or not. Affinity spans an *ubuntu* meta level of shared humanity to very particularistic features of family and kin. A signature feature of horizontal philanthropy is the predominance and significance of personal knowledge of the other – the system cannot function effectively on the basis of anonymity.[17] This study suggests that when applied to the poor, the debate sketched above is resolved through the moral root of horizontal philanthropy where the reputation 'of' an individual acts symbiotically through affinity 'with' others, expressed in relational networks as a collective asset.

A further issue pivots around the degree to which social capital requires relational networks to be dense or closed or open. This debate has a bearing on the emergence and function of civic associations. Closure towards intimate relations, such as family, kin and clan, is argued to be necessary to reinforce trust and the ability to enforce rules – but with attendant dangers of inefficient amoral familism. Higher density of connections generates greater returns from mobilizing resources, giving positive feedback on membership and, hence, reinforcing solidarity. An alternative position argues against the necessity of closure because open networks offer the potential for enhanced access to other asset networks, including those co-constructed to serve shared interests.

> Rather than making the assertion that closed or open networks are required, it would be theoretically more viable to (1) conceptualize for what outcomes and under what conditions a denser or more sparse network might generate a better return, and (2) postulate deduced hypotheses (e.g., a denser network would be more likely to promote the sharing of resources which, in turn, maintain group or individual resources; or, an open network would be more likely to access advantaged positions and resources, which in turn enhance the opportunity to obtain additional resources) for empirical examination (Lin 1999:34).

The debate can be framed in terms of bonding, bridging and linking features of social capital. The former ties and holds a group together, a significant feature of closed networks. Bridging capital extends asset provision and acquisition to other networks operating at similar socioeconomic levels. Linking social capital operates vertically, connecting and transacting through nested socioeconomic layers of wealth and asymmetric asset distribution. As is to be expected, the horizontal landscape detailed by this particular study shows a predominance of bonding social capital.[18] While not excluded, bridging social capital was not significant. However, findings indicate that closed systems are not geographically enclosed, which affects how poor people experience 'community', discussed later.

Using the categories established in this study, respondents' network profiles are set out in Table 5.3. Horizontal help networks that are need- or outcome-based and affinity-mediated, support the perspective expressed in the quotation from Lin. Selection of closed or more open network depends on the makeup of the outcome required in terms, for example, of enhancement or maintenance of social standing, mixed with an anticipated increase in risk-reducing connections.

Horizontal philanthropy would theorize social capital and civic associations as the value of and self-organized vehicles for an array of relational networks operated and used in a particular way. People in poverty choose an appropriate network based on a probability calculus or 'script' that starts by considering past and anticipated outcome(s) of the assistance requested or offered. Experience and learning are used to update scripts after each transaction is completed.

Table 5.3: Network profiles

Network Character	High Affinity	Medium Affinity	Low Affinity
Normal Needs			
Daily / Small	Closed and local	Closed and local	Open and local
Large/Infrequent	Closed and distributed	Indeterminate	Inapplicable
Urgent Needs	Closed and distributed	Closed and distributed	Open and distributed

Notes:

High affinity corresponds to a blood relationship.

Medium affinity corresponds to a shared livelihood system.

Low affinity corresponds to socioeconomic similarity and basic humanity e.g. strangers.

Local refers to close physical proximity, typically neighbourhoods.

Distributed refers to wider geographic network, often linking rural and urban.

In this process, people who are poor make a judicious selection between open or closed, traditional or modern pathways and institutions for accessing assets or solving problems (e.g. Krishna 2002). Against this backdrop of distinguishable African perspectives on social capital, what might this say in terms of an African philanthropy?

African philanthropy – outlines of a critical conversation

Are embedded poor-to-poor help relations found through the research in fact 'philanthropic'? More critically, following the objectives of this volume and the project behind it, what is to be understood of African philanthropy? Is it a distinct category with an essence that can be empirically studied on the continent? Alternatively, is philanthropic behaviour an attribute of all human beings but with particular African attributes? What can research findings and interpretations described above, and from elsewhere, contribute to a necessary, rigorous conversation about the premises implied in these questions? This section offers an outline of what such a conversation might entail in terms, first, of deconstructing language, concepts and mind sets. It sets out a line of argument that locates horizontal philanthropy closer to the Latin roots of the term than today's western 'philanthropic industry'.

Kingman and Edwards (2006) argue that the term 'horizontal philanthropy' is guilty of not just stretching the concept of philanthropy beyond reasonable limits but of degrading and mislabelling behaviours that are better described and valued as mutual aid and solidarity. They therefore plead against using the similar term 'community philanthropy' as a label for behaviours found in the study. Their reasoning draws on, for example, the observation that in Europe, class, trade and professional solidarity arose as cooperatives, mutual companies, lodges and civic welfare associations. These organizations form what is labelled an *economie sociale* straddling the boundary of civil society (Defourney, Develtere and Fonteneau 1999; Fowler 2001; Kay 2006). This system of mutual support is not restricted to people who are poor. The affinities relied upon and transcend family. These collectively-oriented ways of sharing are *not* 'philanthropy' understood as giving or gifting. In the authors' view, such relations are under threat from individualising asset accumulation and should therefore be recognized and valued in their own right.

The ontology of *économie sociale* allies economic activity with normative values of collaboration. It produces a different understanding of the third sector from Anglo-Saxon approaches, which rely on non-profit status (Evers and Laville 2004). While agreeing with the sentiments and intentions of these authors' perspectives, we would argue that the distinction between philanthropy as non-family 'gifting', and mutuality as inter-family support, is not helpful in determining or defining an African philanthropy. In fact, the notion of applying mutuality and solidarity to African social relations should be approached with caution – deeper interpretations of motivations are in play. What does the research suggest instead?

These writers define 'philanthropy' as 'giving outside of one's family' (ibid:43). Obviously the notion of 'family' is itself culturally determined. Family is highly nucleated in old industrialized economies and highly extended in many others, including in Asian Economic Tigers, that are themselves highly industrialized but with many family-owned conglomerates and a stronger social identity reflecting a collective self. Indeed, there is not a necessary linearity between modernization and nucleation of family, which is exemplified in the Japanese collective psychology of all inhabiting one 'house' (Christopher 1983).

In addition, the definition relies on a socioeconomic and political philosophy and mindset separating the 'private' realm of blood relations from the 'public' world of non-family. Such a distinction resonates with western dichotomizations between the self and other. African political economy suggests that a division between public and private is more often a colonially-inspired normative aspiration than a psychosocial reality. It is beyond the scope of this chapter to examine this phenomenon in detail. It is, however, important in a robust conversation to interrogate the meaning and practice of African philanthropy from rich to poor in terms of patronage, power and political systems on the continent.

A further, fundamental, aspect of a conversation about African philanthropy is to unpack the concept of a 'gift'. In a western world view, axiomatic to a 'gift' is the *voluntary transfer without condition or compensation* of an asset or capital that is valued by the recipient.[19] The associated act of 'giving', however, does not necessarily comply with this condition. Rather, elision of 'giving' with a 'gift' – the term 'gifting' is seldom used in philanthropic discourse – sows confusion as to intent, implying that nothing is expected in return. Whether or not giving necessarily translates into self-sacrifice or negative sum game has been discussed in relation to the concept of altruism. It does not. Zero and positive sum outcomes are also possible, meaning some form of 'compensation' is in play. There is always an aspect of 'utility' in giving. But research findings provide a more 'Africanized' analysis of the concept of altruism.

With caveats, horizontal philanthropy is an expression of *ubuntu,* as philosophy of common humanity. This embedded system of helping corresponds more directly with an etymology understood as 'love of humankind' than today's western philanthropy operating as a dichotomized private/public redistributive industry. In fact, we would argue that philanthropy as currently portrayed in the western world has been purposefully mystified to hide the loss of this deeper meaning. Three examples inform this position. First, philanthropy is not without strings and intended returns. As anticipated by Mauss some thirty years ago, 'gifting' in the monetarized West has become a form of contract-based, personalized social investment highly conditional on achieving agreed outcomes. His interpretation of gifting within Africa at that time was of a:

> spirit of gift-exchange... which have passed the phase of 'total prestation' (between clan and clan, family and family) but have not yet reached the stage of pure individual, the money market, sale proper, fixed price and weighted and coined money (Mauss 1954:45).

Implied is an 'inevitable' progression from the millennia-old cultural-linguistic moral philosophy of philanthropy from humanity as collective being to humanity as individual commodity. This need not be the case. Indeed, his reference to 'archaic societies' may have much positive to say about non-industrialized philanthropy and a collective sense of human relations.

Second, western philanthropy relies on fiscal incentives that abet a shift in interpretations of, and investments in, public policy towards the predispositions of (very) rich individuals. In a sense the public realm is progressively privatized. Citizens as determinants of public policy are being marginalized, with growth in philanthropy as a 'recompense'. Could not a love of humanity be better expressed by ensuring that resources are collectively available through taxation to operationalize the public good as the public see it?

Third, while wealth creation improves people's well-being, promoting western-style philanthropy can perversely reward social and other dysfunctions caused by untrammelled capital accumulation and accelerating inequity (United Nations 2005). Obviously, adjudicating the calculus between benefits and costs of market-based capitalism is highly subjective. Philanthropy has not been immune from commodification. Correspondingly, in play is mainstream philanthropy as part of a hegemonic project reflected in a dialectic of private economic extraction for incentivized and individually crafted public redistribution.

We argue that these and other features have semi-detached philanthropy from a 'love of humankind'. A general progression from the linguistic root – with its extreme of personal sacrifice, through death for the good of others, to reification of the living mega-philanthropist – seems to be:

> Gift (unconditional transfer) ➔ Giving (conditional transfer) ➔ Granting (contractual transfer) ➔ Social investing (socioeconomic performance-based transfer) ➔ Venture philanthropy (innovation-based transfer) ➔ Philanthrocapitalism (recycling-based transfer)[20]

The progression is cumulative. One does not replace the other, but can capture and dictate the discourse through which it is all understood. So, where does this locate the practice of horizontal philanthropy observed in Southern Africa?

In the African settings investigated, the poor giver is also a receiver in terms of respecting and reaffirming their own identity as a human being. As a previous quotation infers, not to give is to separate oneself from humanity. A crucial implication is that if the moral philosophy of *ubuntu* as 'the collective self' holds true, giving is an act of 'self-reciprocity', neither selfish, nor self-less. The supposed dichotomy between the two does not hold. Such a framing of behaviour is then not a tautology, but a defining feature of African philanthropy. However, this interpretation of the phenomenon creates dilemmas in terms of altruism. A logical conclusion is that the concept is not appropriate to understand African help inspirations and norms. But Africa should not be seen as lacking 'altruism' as conventionally understood. So, what terminology is to replace this normative aspiration? *Ubuntu* is appearing in the Anglo-Saxon lexicon. Does an equivalent for the moral inference of 'altruism' exist on the continent?

Self-reciprocity also has potential consequences for understanding motivation or drivers to act or not. If self-reciprocity is always there as a 'return' to giving, why is an 'ask' ever refused? One answer is that the person asked simply does not have what is requested, which is self-demeaning. Other possibilities have been discussed in terms of decision-making, such as bad reputation, low trust, etc. Yet another factor affecting the degree to which people can say yes or no is ascription or volition. Findings indicate variations in this factor by country and type of help.

> In some cases, cultural traditions and norms as well as the degree of community cohesion inform whether help drivers are considered by informants to be duty or choice. In three countries, for material and non-material transactions combined, choice is the more prevalent motivation than obligation (Mozambique 80 per cent;

Namibia 65 per cent and Zimbabwe 51 per cent). The outlier to this pattern is South Africa, where duty is more prevalent (60 per cent).

When transactions are disaggregated, obligation is more prevalent than choice for non-material transactions in South Africa (64 per cent) and Zimbabwe (52 per cent) and less prevalent in Mozambique (27 per cent) and Namibia (44 per cent). For two countries choice is the dominant motivation that informs the provision of material transactions (Mozambique 83 per cent, Namibia 72 per cent) while in South Africa choice accounts for 48 per cent and in Zimbabwe 55 per cent (Wilkinson-Maposa et al. 2006:70).

Reasons for these differences were not examined in detail. But it is clear that a complex help calculus is in operation, of which self-reciprocity is one enduring, but not necessarily determining, component. An inference is that a mosaic of help motivations and accompanying decision rules with distinct African characteristics is to be found. But what of the correspondence between the proportional distribution of principles of help found between people who are poor in Southern Africa and those found across the world? This finding would suggest a generic human predisposition with distinguishable geo-temporal expressions rather than an African philanthropy *per se*. Dedicated comparative study would help test this preliminary conclusion against all forms and 'directions' of African philanthropy.

In sum, from a 'limited' horizontal lens capturing the daily lived reality of a large proportion of the continent's population, a conversation and narrative about African philanthropy, or philanthropy with African characteristics, could usefully address at least four fundamental concepts. These are: deeply-rooted appreciation of being human; an identity of collective self; self-reciprocity as an embedded trait of African 'gifting'; and the nature of 'choice' in the mosaic of motivations and associated rules.

Conclusion

This chapter has introduced and applied a new body of knowledge towards constructing a narrative of African philanthropy that can redress the imbalances and shake loose biases of the colonial past. In doing so, we have tried to demonstrate that indigenous philanthropy has something to say about contemporary issues in theories of social capital and collective agency.

Such an undertaking has required us to grapple with the fundamentals of the sort of conversation that will be required to establish an African narrative in its own right, with its own essence. Doing so presents a serious, exciting challenge in terms of deconstructing the dominant language and an implicit world view that does not correspond to the morality and lived reality of many on the continent. We hope that this approach and its content will be a useful resource for the enormous amount of work that still needs to be done, of which this volume is a critical step.

Endnotes

1   This chapter is based on research undertaken between 2002 and 2005 by the Building Community Philanthropy project at the Centre for Leadership and Public Values, Graduate School of Business, University of Cape Town, South Africa.

2   The work of Putnam (e.g. 2001) and others is primarily focused on donor countries' own dimensions of social capital, which are not the concern of this chapter.

3   Employing the concept of 'philanthropy' is a conscious choice. It seeks to challenge and question an assumed moral superiority of giving from rich to poor when, for the latter, such behaviour is often of far greater consequence for their asset base.

4   Published by Allavida in London, *Alliance* is a periodical dedicated to development of philanthropy across the world.

5   In alliance with US Foundations, March 2003 saw the launch of the World Bank Community Foundation Initiative (CFI) that has strategic links to the institution's Community Driven Development programme that, itself, is a tangible product of the Bank's work on social capital (e.g., Bebbington 2006).

6   Subsequent sections of this paper draw heavily on the research monograph produced by the research project (Wilkinson-Maposa et al. 2006).

7   A worrying concern for the public interest is contemporary philanthrocapitalist because the perceived net contribution to the public good may actually be a loss because of the social costs resulting from capital accumulation (Edwards 2008).

8   This section has benefited from arguments found in Uphoff (1992:326–56).

9   Lin attributes social capital with three other functions: information, influence and reinforcement of claims on resources that are recognized as legitimate.

10 Terms of Reference for the State of Philanthropy in Africa, TrustAfrica, Senegal.

11 For example, see work of the Financial Diaries Project, University of Cape Town, http://www.financialdiaries.com.

12 For details see Wilkinson-Maposa et al. (2006:Appendix 1).

13 Ibid: Appendix 3.

14 Focus group of male casual labourers, Namibia.

15 Institutions are understood as stabile patterns, norms, mechanisms, conventions and organizations of a social structure that govern an individual's relational behaviour.

16 Mixed-age female focus group, rural Mozambique.

17 The internet permits anonymity. But for internet-based market exchange systems to operate, establishing a reputation for propriety remains fundamental. For example, eBay uses a feedback scoring system to 'build' and signal the reputation of buyers and sellers. Those breaking the rules can be expelled (*The Economist*, June 11, 2005:64).

18 The research design militated against the capture of linking social capital.

19 Following Bourdieu (2000), we recognise four types of capital: economic, social, cultural and symbolic.

20 See *Alliance Magazine*, Vol. 12, No. 1, 2007.

CHAPTER 6

THE CHALLENGE OF PHILANTHROPY
IN EAST AFRICA

CONNIE NGONDI-HOUGHTON
& ANDREW KINGMAN

Introduction

For the purposes of this chapter we distinguish between 'charity' and 'philanthropy'. We regard philanthropy as a process that begins with the act of giving. Giving is defined as the voluntary transfer of resources from a source to a target recipient for a specific or general purpose. There are two main types of giving, defined on the basis of their purpose. There is the giving whose purpose is to ameliorate suffering or deprivation, or to realize the fulfilment of an immediate pressing need of the intended recipient; and there is the giving whose purpose is to further social causes aimed at transforming society towards restructuring social power grids, enabling people to assert control over their lives, and to participate in their societies in meaningful and effective ways which in turn produce better lives for all. The former is mostly charity, though ameliorative giving can be philanthropy if it is organized, consistent and linked to structural interventions; and the latter is philanthropy. The two are often confused. Charity ameliorates. Philanthropy, if done well, can both ameliorate and eradicate human suffering and deprivation.

Philanthropy seeks to root out causes of poverty, suffering and inequality, and leverages results; it inspires and promotes individual growth as it nourishes human welfare. Charity is an important part of philanthropy, because it is an unexploited potential for the development of organized philanthropy. It represents the potential for philanthropic development that abounds in the element of *compassion* from which charity grows and that of *trust* through which it flows. The practice of charity is itself a resource, that of social capital.

The second element of the process of philanthropy is the conduit level – that which ensures that the resources that are given reach the intended recipients and are utilized for the purposes for which they were intended. This is the resource management and application level that is occupied by civil society. Sometimes, especially in the case of charity, resources are given directly to the desired recipients. However, in most cases givers do not have the capacity to reach directly all their targeted beneficiaries or to design ways of applying the resources efficiently and effectively, hence the need for intermediaries. These conduits are in many cases the initiators of the philanthropy process. They are constituted first, and then they mobilize resources for the achievement of certain goals, or for onward transmittal to smaller groups at the community level.

This chapter addresses in detail philanthropic intermediaries within civil society. Throughout, we assume that *civil society* is at once the collective of associations (such as NGOs, formal and informal groups), the space in which debates about the goals of economic and social development take place, and also a value in itself i.e. a *civil* society is part of the *good* society. Philanthropy cuts across these three elements of civil society. We distinguish between NGOs and other sub-sectors of the associational element of civil society, and indeed argue that greater delineation is required in East Africa between NGOs and philanthropic institutions. We also illustrate how philanthropy, particularly at community level, is inextricably tied up with traditions and cultures and deeply entrenched patterns of economic and social interaction; that it is an important element of civil society as a *process*. Finally, we assume that organized philanthropy and well-resourced philanthropic institutions are an essential foundation of a *civil* society, one that pursues social justice for all and establishes and maintains effective governance at all levels.

Political, economic and social foundations of philanthropy in East Africa

Pre-colonial period

Philanthropic activities are not a new phenomenon in Africa. Even before colonialism, voluntary groups and organizations were part of African culture undertaking cooperative production, distribution, consumption and accumulation, mainly organized around communal or kinship ties (Gariyo 1996). Philanthropic giving, the pooling of resources, and the channelling of these resources were functions of the socio-economic organization of society. Indeed, the very mode of social structuring and of economic operation was based on philanthropic principles of giving to and for others, pooling resources, and distributing those resources to particular recipients through established effective social systems or units. Besides the family unit, an individual belonged to other social groups such as clans, which were also responsible for ensuring that specific needs and concerns of their members were met. These form the earliest examples of non-profit or voluntary organizations in African societies.

The type of economy on which this communal society depended was one characterized by the peasant mode of production, limited social division and exchange based on an affective rationale. This mode of operation has been called the 'economy of affection', which Goran Hyden (1983:8) describes as:

> networks of support, communication and interaction among structurally defined groups connected by blood, kin, community or other affinities such as a religion. In this system, a variety of discrete economic and social units, in other respects autonomous, are linked together. At the core of the economy of affection is the articulation of principles and values associated with peasant or household economics.

Philanthropic structures within pre-colonial society, though abundantly present, were not visible as such, because they were informal and were intertwined with, and therefore concealed within, the lifestyles of these peasant communities (Kanyinga 1999; Hyden 1983:120). Philanthropy was not discernible as a distinct socioeconomic practice, but was rather part and parcel of the communal lifestyle. There were no independent systems or institutions set up to deal purely with matters of charity (Kanyinga 1999). Resources in this type of philanthropy included material goods such as food, clothing, land, livestock, and labour services. Giving was viewed not only as a benevolent inner disposition toward others, but also as a duty and a self safety net (ibid.). Giving to others strengthened and maintained social ties within the units through which the philanthropic resources were generated and channelled.

Colonial period

Colonization undermined many of the communal modes of social organization that characterized the pre-colonial societies in the three East African countries. Social, economic, political and cultural organization was either deliberately disrupted by colonial policies and processes or this happened as a result of those policies or processes. Disruption was caused in a number of ways: the imposition of formal state and formal politics; the formal capitalist economy with its exclusionist and individualistic nature; ethnicization; villagization; urbanization; formal education; contracting in place of trust and reciprocity; individualistic land ownership regimes; division of labour leading to class formations and resultant inequity; misuse of the traditional units of authority such as chieftains and elders; Christianity, Islam, Hinduism and other foreign religions; labour mobility leading to weakening of units of affinity; and racism and resultant inequity, amongst others.

The importance of religion in relation to charity and philanthropy in East Africa cannot be overstated. Christian missionaries introduced the earliest forms of formal charitable organizations. As early as the 1840s, Christian missionaries had ventured into Kenya and began charitable work as part of their evangelization. Christianity preached charity as a virtue, and practised it in its interaction with people. The practice of charity by the missionaries was paternalistic and was manifested in relief and welfare services that they provided to local converted populations through education, health and youth development activities. These activities were carried out within institutions such as the churches, schools, hospitals and health centres and youth clubs. These institutions provided the foundations of formal philanthropy, and the non-profit activity that evolved in the country mostly focused on relief and basic needs provision.

Alongside religion, economic transformation under colonial rule had a dramatic impact on the evolution of philanthropy in East Africa. The core agenda of the colonial administration was the appropriation of resources – including labour, land and other natural resources – for imperial interests. The agenda was pursued through a series of key processes. First, peasantization was implemented through three core strategies: tribalization, introduction and enforcement of agricultural regulations, and through the organization of peasant cooperatives (Mamdani 1996). This process changed social affinity lines and unitization, establishing mainly tribal lines of social affiliation, and de-emphasizing the importance of others such as age, sects, clans and lineages as channels of resource mobilization and distribution. Although the process led in time to the emergence of social justice institutions that fought against colonial rule, coupled with missionary charity it served to undermine the development of more progressive philanthropy based on communal values. A second key process of economic transformation was increased labour migration. This too helped change the nature of local philanthropy, first, by further weakening the social units of affinity that require proximity to work, and secondly, by increasing individualism (through individual engagement with the market economy) at the expense of communal interests.

The scale of charitable and philanthropic activity increased considerably in the 1930s, the period of the Great Depression. Economic hardship in Europe led to a reduction in resources for the colonial administration and in the funds for missions. In turn, this served to stimulate self-help approaches to development. Community development was undertaken to direct and stimulate the production and marketing of colonial products in order to more efficiently respond to the requirements of the world markets (Cowen and Shenton 1996:310). The policy of community development, building as it does on the spirit of communalism and on communal lines of trust that still persisted among the local populations, is therefore not rooted in some fantasy of an imagined post-colonial community of the poor. Its origins are those of official colonial doctrine, entrenched in legislation such as the Colonial Welfare Act (1929) and its successor, the Colonial Welfare and Development Act (1940).

Just as colonial legislation sought to restrict and utilize indigenous philanthropic potential, it also sought to encourage the formation of voluntary organizations within a framework tightly controlled by the administration. A good example is the Uganda Council of Women, founded in 1947 by European women, and funded by the colonial administration as well as by foreign-sourced donations. The Great Depression thus slowed down the philanthropic activities of the non-indigenous populations and groups in East Africa, and directly led to an increase in local philanthropic activities among indigenous populations, under the rubric of community development. The impact of these activities was, however, curbed by the political interests behind the colonial state. To this day, one of the challenges faced by local philanthropy for community development in East Africa has been its gross misuse by local leaders for political expediency. This has tended to stunt its growth and render it unsustainable.

The struggle for independence also helped shape philanthropy in East Africa. Beginning in the 1930s, the agitation for freedom became more intense as soldiers returned from the Second World War from 1945 on. Political activism was channelled through tribal associations and other groups and, in response, the colonial government developed more stringent associational laws and policies for the Africans. This discouraged open formation of African groups during the struggle, and many of those formed after the war were underground, unregistered or loosely organized, publicly presented as simple self-help groups, but with a hidden political agenda.

Philanthropy in East Africa within the colonial period was therefore defined over time by the social, economic, cultural and political events that shaped national development, by the traditional African way of life, and by how these two interacted throughout the period. This process led to the development of several types of philanthropic institutions in East Africa. These include *religious-based institutions* built on the initiatives of missionaries and with resources mainly from abroad, which attracted local resources in the shape of finance and volunteering from the converted populations, who were also their beneficiaries; *self-help community-based organizations* spinning off the hard times of the Great Depression and the Second World War, through colonial initiative and characterized by government control, mostly targeting women and built mainly on local resources; *tribal associations* seeking social justice in response to colonial rule and as a form of resistance to harsh colonial policies and practices, seeking policy change, and initiated by young educated Africans; *trade unions and cooperatives* which were controlled by the state and used for its ends; *foreign or international organizations* such as the Girl Guides,

Boy Scouts and the Red Cross Society, supported mainly from foreign resources and local volunteerism; and *the liberation movement*, channelling resources through existing tribal associations, villages and individuals united in the vision of freedom from colonialism.

Underlying all these types of philanthropic activity were the ingrained *traditional* attitudes and norms, encapsulated in the principles of mutual responsibility and reciprocity, which tenaciously permeated the lives of the African populations, even through the destruction of the traditional units of affinity and the communal way of life of the pre-colonial era.

Post-colonial period 1: Growth and development 1960s–80s

Immediately after independence, the East African governments adopted 'development' as their principal objective. Development was defined in terms of continued growth of the political and economic institutions established during the colonial period. The strategies which the governments adopted for the realization of this goal had direct or indirect effects on the nature of, and the potential for, the growth of philanthropy in each country. Economic growth was the priority for all three countries (Kenya, Tanzania and Uganda) and each received massive injections of foreign aid during this period. In addition, the governments needed to attend to the pressing social welfare needs of their populations. With few resources to apply directly to these ends, however, welfare policy in Kenya, for instance, was the subject of a 'progressive realization' ('trickle-down') approach. To meet the growing demand for basic social services at the time, however, the new government of Kenya, like Tanzania and other African countries such as Ghana and Zambia, sought to re-centralize the African traditional framework and core principles of social living, which had been weakened by colonialism, as a basis for the development of a policy for self-reliance for local communities. They sought to revive the Africanist principles of political democracy and mutual responsibility, which were uniform among all tribes in their countries. This was embodied in the philosophy of African socialism. In the phrase 'African socialism', the word 'African' was meant to convey the African roots of a system which was itself African in its characteristics (Republic of Kenya 1965:2).

In Kenya, the slogan of *harambee* (pulling together) was used to encourage a sense of service. Communities mobilized financial, volunteer and in-kind resources to develop structures for schools, health centres, community water points and social halls, among other things. The government, through local authorities, matched these community efforts by providing teachers, health staff and materials. *Harambee* in this period was a form of community philanthropic practice which was embedded in the state agenda. It was conceptualized, initiated and controlled by the state within the context of the broader development agenda. Over time it became highly politicized and eventually lost the essence of the African spirit embodied in the principle of mutual responsibility. This period, however, represented one of the most remarkable developmental phases of independent Kenya. Within a period of a few years, access to health services and education became effectively universal (Manji 1998:16). The impacts of *harambee*-supported development were reflected in the dramatic improvements in life expectancy, reduction in infant and child mortality, and improved nutritional status of the young.

In Tanzania, government sought not only to apply the principles of *Ujamaa*, but also to restructure society into social units of *Ujamaa* villages in the rural areas, as a means through which to mobilize and channel resources for development. Development was thought of in terms of things, not people. This meant that traditional social units and ways of farming were dispersed in the areas where *Ujamaa* took root, and new lines of relational trust were developed. *Ujamaa* means community, and is derived from the Kiswahili word *jamii*, which means family. In reality it called for the formation and coalescence of new 'communities' and new 'families'. It was a socialist concept whose logic was based on the idea of cooperation and self-help. Its inception in Tanzania, however, did not take cognisance of the already existing units of cooperation within traditional social structures on which it may have been built. It sought to restructure society into other voluntary developmental units. The idea of self-help was, however, not well thought through or implemented. The government provided all the infrastructure and inputs, including unit leaders from outside the communities, and then required the members in the units to work to maximize output. This approach, however, fostered dependency and laziness, and attempts to correct this situation in the 1970s failed. There was little sense of ownership and it was viewed as government help, not self-help. This greatly affected those initiatives that had existed within the traditional social structures, and the persistence of the dependency that resulted from this continues to inhibit the development of community philanthropy in many areas of Tanzania to this day.

Post-colonial period 2: Structural adjustment, self-reliance and the economy of affection (1980s to mid-1990s)

From the late 1970s, East Africa (and Africa in general) experienced an economic crisis caused by an international price, commodity and credit squeeze. This meant that governments could not continue supporting social service delivery on the scale they had before. Resource mobilization at the macro-level became severely constrained by declining export earnings and the mounting debt crisis, thus reducing flows to already disadvantaged rural areas. Rightly or wrongly, this crisis was widely interpreted as evidence that African economic structures and policies had failed and that there was an urgent need to restructure the entire system to avert an economic disaster on the continent. In order to implement these recommendations, the governments needed to borrow. Financial support was accompanied by prescriptions for economic reform by the World Bank and the International Monetary Fund's Structural Adjustment Programmes (SAPs). SAPs emphasized an export-led development strategy, and frowned on 'inward-oriented' development strategies adopted by countries like Tanzania. In terms of resource allocation, priority was given to the most 'developed and productive' regions, economic sectors and enterprises in each country. The results were swift and visible: growing income differentiation; increasing poverty of the majority, including the middle classes; growing dominance of foreign capital in the national economy; and further weakening of the national government's ability to regulate and direct the economy.

At community level, people responded to the crisis in many different ways, through numerous old as well as new forms of groups and coalitions, especially among women and youth. Many local groups and communities developed self-reliant strategies to provide basic subsistence needs, to accumulate wealth for local use, to protect local interests, and to cope with different crisis situations. A growing number of studies indicate the increasing significance and typologies of these local strategies to cope with deteriorating social conditions, drought, and food insecurity. These have included pooling resources towards a communal goal, or to build the abilities of members to better engage the market in accessing their basic needs. The common threads in all of them, however, are those of people brought together by some common need, mostly with some established relationship such as neighbourhood, gender or age group. They range from individuals contributing resources, either to help out one of their own as a once-off exercise or each member in turn; or for a shared immediate need such as building a cattle-dip; or for a future goal such as establishing an income-generating project. At the community level, local self-reliance is therefore constructed on the basis of the community and the market, and is anchored in initiatives of the local people themselves, aimed at using local resources and meeting local needs. These are initiatives in local community philanthropy that point to the continuing importance of the economy of affection.

Neoliberal market failure and the rise of the third sector

The neoliberal economic model that underpinned SAPs assumed that benefits of the model would 'trickle down' to poorer communities and rural communities. The evidence for this is hotly contested, but what is incontestable is that any such trickle-down was very slow, patchy and insufficient. In these circumstances, non-governmental and non-profit institutions stepped in to fill the gap left by both the state and the market. The emergence and rapid growth of this sector was largely driven by the deterioration of living standards in all three East African countries, political repression by authoritarian regimes, and encouragement by, and easy availability of funds from, foreign donors. Local organizations, supported by resources from foreign donors, focused on poverty alleviation, some service delivery, and engaging these repressive governments on legal and human rights issues. This emergent sector was an extension of foreign philanthropy, although the foreign NGOs still commanded the largest volumes of philanthropic resources from the north. International development aid donors had lost faith in the ability of their governments to act as effective channels for development assistance and had found 'reliable' channels in the non-profit organizations.

These organizations also acted as intermediaries for channelling funds to community initiatives. Availability of external funds for communities and the use of 'external' agents to channel the funds interfered to a significant extent with the potential for the development of local community philanthropy that is based on the economy of affection. By offering funds to local groups that had been mobilizing their own resources without thinking of ways of building on this potential, intermediate community development NGOs and international development NGOs were, and continue to be, responsible for killing the initiative for local resource mobilization and local philanthropy, and re-creating and further entrenching dependency on state and NGOs for 'development'.

Donor patterns, sustainable development, and the new philanthropic agenda

In the early to mid-1990s, many bilateral donors began to change both their approach to funding and their priorities in Africa. Sometimes called 'donor fatigue', the changes reflected concern at the limited impact of foreign aid, but they also reflected shifting geopolitical priorities, especially the new importance of assisting Central and Eastern Europe after 1989. At the same time, many donor governments changed to a rights-based (rather than needs-based) approach, challenging NGOs that had essentially been service providers. A general disenchantment with NGOs could also be discerned among many bilateral donors, leading to several new trends: a return to funding through governments; a shift towards contracting (rather than grants), thus opening up opportunities for private consulting firms such as KPMG to access development funding; and decentralizing more funding to country offices. These changes strengthened the 'market dominance' of the larger international NGOs (INGOs) and largest national NGOs, although it also meant that the INGOs saw greater value in registering in East Africa and the rest of the South in order to access decentralized funds and bid on contracts. Leaving aside the ethics of this issue, these trends put all but the largest local NGOs at risk. As a result, there emerged a discourse on local resource mobilization options. To date, however, much of this effort has been restricted to workshops of local fundraising, with uncoordinated and unsustained efforts within a few organizations to raise funds locally.

At the same time, however, there emerged in the early 1990s a new genre of philanthropic activity and organization in East Africa. Seeing the gap that was emerging in regard to local resource mobilization at a time of dwindling foreign support, a number of private philanthropic foundations from the north took up the challenge of initiating efforts to stimulate thought and debate on the issue, and of catalyzing the development of innovative ways of understanding resource mobilization and modes of structuring it. The Ford Foundation was the leading champion of this cause, along with the Aga Khan Foundation. Their initiatives coincided with a growing interest in local sustainability. They also catalyzed the emergence of local organizations to support the development of local philanthropy through enhancing the understanding of the East Africa context, finding ways to cultivate local philanthropy and organizing it for the support of sustainable development. These developments are a growing feature of the philanthropic scene in East Africa today.

Type and extent of organized philanthropy

Comparative data on philanthropy in East Africa

There is limited data on the extent of philanthropy in East Africa, but one of the available quantitative studies from the Comparative Non-Profit Sector Project of Johns Hopkins University[1] includes some useful indicators for each country in the region. It shows philanthropy as a percentage of total revenue of the non-profit sector as follows:

- Kenya: 14% (fees[2] 81%, public sources 5%) of a total revenue of US$270 million

- Uganda: 38% (fees 55%, public sources 7%) of a total revenue of US$89 million

- Tanzania: 20% (fees 53%, public sources 27%) of a total revenue of US$260 million.

The contribution of philanthropy varied considerably by sector, according to the research findings. For instance, in Kenya, philanthropy contributed 49 per cent of revenue of organizations involved in advocacy, 20 per cent of revenue for educational NGOs, and nothing for organizations involved in health. Foundations in Kenya received 86 per cent of their revenue from philanthropic sources. In Tanzania, the contribution of philanthropy across these sectors was very similar at between 21 per cent and 25 per cent. It is Uganda, however, where the starkest difference arose; philanthropy contributed 100 per cent of revenue for advocacy organizations, 99 per cent of revenue for environmental organizations, and 61 per cent of revenue for health organizations. The huge divergence between results for Uganda and the other two countries might suggest the need for revisiting results and checking interpretation by survey respondents.

The research also highlighted the importance of volunteering. Of a total workforce (full-time equivalents) of 290,000 people in Kenya, 114,000 were volunteers. In Tanzania, 250,000 out of 331,000 people in the non-profit sector workforce were volunteers, while in Uganda there were 137,000 volunteers out of a total workforce of 231,000 people. Once the contribution of this volunteer input was included in the financial analysis of the sector, the contribution of philanthropy increased significantly. In Kenya, the figure rose from 14 per cent to 24 per cent, in Tanzania, from 20 per cent to 62 per cent, and in Uganda, from 38 per cent to 52 per cent.

Philanthropic institutions

Trusts and foundations

A foundation can be loosely defined as an independent institution legally established to obtain funds through contributions and the creation of an endowment in order to grant funds for the enhancement and development of people and communities, locally and where possible abroad (Gordon 1993:3). In East Africa, these organizations are typically registered as trusts, such as, for instance, under the Trustees Act (1962) in Kenya, which establishes clear accountability structures, details the powers conferred upon trustees for execution of their duties, and provides specific guidelines governing investments. Some foundations and trusts register under the Companies Act as companies limited by guarantee. In this way, they become part of the private sector and thereby escape the stringent regulatory mechanisms imposed on NGOs. Foundations operating under this definition are recognized as profit-making entities that distribute their profits in accordance with their registered articles and memoranda of association.

Foundations and trusts have provided an attractive legal framework for NGOs in Kenya, for instance, due to the benefits afforded to them. The chief legal benefit is their exemption from income tax provided under the country's Income Tax Act. This exemption recognizes that the work of these institutions constitutes a direct gift to the people of Kenya and, as such, benefits the country in much the same way as the income taxes are meant to do. It also constitutes an implicit government endorsement of their 'charitable' activities: by not taxing trusts and foundations, the government in effect recognizes them as partners in development.

Many organizations in East Africa have used the trust/foundation legal framework to register themselves as charity organizations, especially during the periods in each of the three countries when there was no framework for registration of NGOs, such as in Kenya pre-1990. They are therefore, for all intents and purposes, operating organizations like NGOs with no particular intention of creating endowments or making grants. This chapter is not concerned with these types of trusts and foundations, as they are not seen as being involved in resource mobilization and asset development for development purposes.

Community (development) foundations, community trusts and mini-endowments

In the context of emerging local foundations, a 'community foundation' has been defined as 'an independent philanthropic organization (part of non-profit, non-governmental sector) dedicated to addressing the critical needs and improving the quality of life in a specific geographic area' (Feurt 2000). Five characteristics and interrelated functions that a community foundation performs in service to its community are grantmaking; local resource mobilization; financial stewardship; donor service; and community leadership. An effective community foundation reflects the dynamics, needs and conditions of the community it serves. It should also be rooted in the philanthropic traditions, history and legal framework of the community in which it is located.

The Community Development Foundation (CDF) is a flexible concept, which encompasses a wider group that includes 'community foundations, civil society resource organizations, local foundations or community development foundations'. In general, the term has been used to refer to organizations that combine grantmaking to community-based organizations and NGOs with other forms of support for organizations or the civil society sector as a whole (ibid.). Discussion about the potential of community foundations in East Africa began in the mid-1990s, stimulated in particular by the Ford Foundation. In 1996, Ford supported research, consultation and strategic design and planning processes that led to the establishment of the Kenya Community Development Foundation (KCDF). Ford was joined in 1997 by the Aga Khan Foundation in providing matched funding for KCDF's endowment challenge. In the many years of its existence, the mission of KCDF has changed several times, reflecting its slow and steady evolution and search for an appropriate identity as a local grantmaking foundation. KCDF is now the leading domestic grantmaker in East Africa, with an increasingly diversified funding base consisting of partnerships with several international institutions (including the

World Bank) for managing grants programmes. Securing substantial local funding, however, especially towards the endowment, continues to be a major challenge.

While KCDF is also the only matured community development or community foundation in East Africa, at local level there are increasing numbers of community trusts, and these institutions – along with other local initiatives such as mini-endowments tied to schools (such as the Aga Khan Foundation's Madrasa Resource Centres Programme) – are potentially an important new force for community philanthropy, though there are several key challenges to address if this potential is to be realized. There have been new community foundations in Tanzania as well, that were developed under the aegis of the World Bank. Their success is yet to be evaluated.

Trusts have been popular in Kenya not least because they are relatively easy, quick and cheap to establish. This explains why, amongst the list of registered NGOs and other groups, many have the word 'trust' in their full name, though this usually does not imply that the organization is a grantmaking entity. However, at community level, trusts are being established to manage and grow community assets. They have been particularly popular in environment and natural resources management, but now are also being used as vehicles for local philanthropy and fund development.

A specific example of innovative mini-endowments, referred to above, is the Madrasa Resource Centre initiative of the Aga Khan Foundation. This mini-endowment project was launched in February 2000 and involved 12 schools that had graduated from a two-year programme of support and capacity building by the Madrasa Resource Centres in Kenya, Zanzibar and Uganda. In 2001, a further 26 schools joined the project. Each school that successfully completed the two-year relationship with the MRC was awarded an endowment grant of US$2,500. In addition, school management committees are responsible for raising money from their communities, which is deposited into the endowment fund; upon graduation the MRC matches funds raised on a one-to-one basis. All funds are invested in a centralized way (mostly in Treasury Bills), and the schools get regular income from the profits made as a dividend. This income supplements the schools' finances for regular payments of, for example, teacher salaries. In one review of the project in Uganda, it was found that school committees had raised an average of US$100 in 2003 towards their endowment, though the total varied from US$25 to US$300. Most importantly, the impact on school finances was significant; many schools reported that the dividend received made the difference between ending the financial year in deficit and maintaining a small surplus.

Public foundations

These are foundations that have been set up by the government or public bodies for a broad public purpose. Examples are the Community Development Foundation (CDF), the Kenya Wildlife Foundation (KWF), and the National Fund for the Disabled in Kenya. These make grants and have large endowments initiated by support from foreign and local donors, or by the government. The KWF is also an implementing foundation.

Family foundations

Family philanthropy is not new in East Africa, although it is not widespread and not very public. It is based on bequests by leading individuals in families for community good, such as the Rattansi Educational Trust and the Rahimtulla Trust; or from families and friends of an individual as a memorial to them. Research conducted by Allavida (2005) on trusts and foundations in East Africa revealed many largely dormant family foundations, many of which have existed a long time. Most of these, especially those set up with small amounts of funding, lack the capacity to leverage more funds and to carry out their objectives. An example is the Charles Mukora Sports Foundation in Nairobi, which lacks funds and qualified personnel to grow further. The Rattansi Educational Trust, which is a leader in this grouping, had a strong track record of philanthropy over four decades, but until it began to participate in the East Africa Foundations Learning Group (initiated by the Ford Foundation), it had never really considered its own capacity nor invested in its own institutional development. Many of the most successful family foundations in East Africa (Kenya) are founded by Asian businessmen or their families. The foundations are a way of giving back to the community and are also mostly motivated by religion. The Rattansi family, for instance, are Ismailis. One core belief of this Islamic sect is that 'What you have, has been given you in trust for others', a belief that Mr Hassanaly Rattansi, the son of Mohamedally Rattansi, the original founder of the trust, often expressed.

Corporate foundations

In East Africa these include the House of Manji Foundation and the Chandaria Foundation, set up by the Chandaria group. Many more have since come up, such as those set by by mobile phone companies such as Safaricom Foundation. The former are, however, run privately, and are sometimes viewed as family foundations because the corporations that set them up are family businesses. They give grants to causes of their choice and have not been actively involved in any foundation capacity -building activities. To some extent, they represent an example of the 'silent' or 'invisible' formal philanthropy in East Africa which, because of culture or beliefs of the actors, is carried out privately.

Typology, distribution and capacity of grantmakers

The data here is taken from research undertaken by Allavida (ibid.) on grantmaking trusts and foundations in East Africa. The survey targeted a sample of 160 organizations in Uganda, Tanzania and Kenya. The total number of completed questionnaires secured at the end of the survey was 78. Approximately 35 organizations, understood to be grantmakers, declined to take part in the survey. Given that this set of organizations includes some well-known domestic grantmakers, it would appear that the scale of grantmaking in the region is larger than suggested by the positive survey returns. Of the organizations targeted, 47 did not have grantmaking programmes. Therefore, about 70 per cent of the target group were grantmakers and a 71 per cent response rate from the active grantmakers in the target group was secured.

Table 6.1: Classification and regional distribution

Classification	Kenya	Uganda	Tanzania	Total
Bilateral institutions	8	6	6	20
Multilateral institutions	3	-	1	4
Diplomatic missions	5	3	6	14
Faith/culture-based institutions	2	2	1	5
Family foundations	2	-	-	2
Independent foundations	2	1	1	4
Public foundations	5	-	-	5
Private foundations	6	3	1	10
Local grantmaking institutions	3	1	4	8
Non-governmental Organizations	4	1	-	5
Registered trusts	-	-	1	1
Total	40	17	21	78

Although table 6.2 suggests that almost two-thirds of active grantmakers in East Africa are international, we believe that many of the 35 non-respondent active grantmakers are local. However, the data still illustrates the relatively weak development to date of active local grantmaking foundations.

Table 6.2: Local versus international donors

	Local donors	International donors	Total
Kenya	16	24	40
Uganda	6	11	17
Tanzania	6	15	21
Total	28	50	78

With regard to assets and income, and focusing specifically on local foundations, the research found that 17 had some form of endowment (this included public foundations and those established with a foreign-sourced endowment). However, the scale, type and income-generating performance of the endowment or asset differed greatly from one foundation to another. In a few cases, for example the Rattansi Educational Trust (Kenya) and Social Action Trust Fund (Tanzania), the endowment provided the principal source of funding for grants programmes. It is worth noting that neither institution has a cash endowment: the Rattansi Trust generates income from rent earned on property and Social Action Trust Fund's grantmaking income is derived from interest on loans made to the private sector in Tanzania.

Of the local foundations, 12 reported income from corporate donors and 20 from individuals, though the scale in both cases was limited. For the foundations with substantial grants programmes, the primary source of income was from foreign institutions. The research also looked at different illustrations of capacity as grantmakers. Of the 78 organizations responding positively to the survey, 42 had guidelines available for applicants. Of these, 17 were local foundations. Of the 18 organizations with guidelines available online, all were international funders. Looking at grant size, perhaps not surprisingly, foreign donors had the highest level of average grants, while local family foundations reported the lowest average grant size. As regards staffing, most local foundations had very small numbers of staff, as well as more part-time staff, whereas the international grantmakers were more likely to have ten or more staff. A specific question looking at background of staff found that between 50 per cent and 75 per cent of the staff of local grantmaking foundations had a background in grantmaking although few staff had received any training in grantmaking.

Research conducted in East Africa as part of the Ford Foundation's Africa Philanthropy Initiative found that, of the local foundations, most had poor and underdeveloped governance structures. They lacked effective boards and effective governance policies. All had a board, thereby meeting the legal requirement under the laws of their establishment. These boards varied from two members to 20. Overall, board members did not have the capacity, nor were they socialized, to fundraise. On the contrary, in some instances board members were the ones to benefit from the foundation's/trust's resources through incentives for board attendance. Most boards (70 per cent) were not sufficiently involved and meetings were held infrequently. According to the research there was a lack of clarity within many organizations on the role of the board. Seven (30 per cent) of those surveyed, however, did have boards that met regularly.

Corporate philanthropy

Broadly, there are two types of corporate philanthropy: the ad hoc, reactive and non-engaged type, practised for decades by companies of all sizes, and the more engaged, thoughtful type that is still uncommon in East Africa, but which needs to be seen as part of a growing movement to promote corporate social responsibility (CSR) in the region. The idea of CSR is premised on the notion of corporate citizenship. This suggests that a corporation which derives profits from society has duties and responsibilities to contribute to society's well-being. Corporate philanthropy as a practice of corporate citizenship is characterized by the voluntary transfer of resources, in cash or kind, to support various forms of development activity in the communities where the corporation works, or elsewhere.

The absolute shilling or dollar value of corporate giving in East Africa is not known, but indications are that millions of shillings are given out or otherwise expended in philanthropic gestures by corporations in East Africa each year, and the figure is growing rapidly. There is limited data on exact figures. The estimate on the extent of giving is also based on those that are visible. There are indications that there is a significant volume of philanthropic giving by corporations, especially small-scale enterprises and family businesses that are not visible because they choose not to be for 'security' reasons, or because they are more ethical and religion motivated, or have individual attitudes to 'charity' which do not allow publicity. From the recent Johns Hopkins studies we can estimate that between 4 per cent and 6 per cent of income for the non-profit sector comes from companies.

Corporate philanthropy in East Africa has been visible mainly among transnational corporations (TNCs) and multinational corporations such as Coca Cola, Barclays Bank, Standard Chartered Bank and large national corporations such as the breweries in the three countries. The visibility of corporate philanthropy only from among large national and international concerns should not be taken to mean that it is irrelevant, or that smaller companies and micro-enterprises do not engage in it at all. The largest portion of the corporate sector in numbers and regional distribution is in fact made up of small and micro-enterprises (SMEs).

Many SMEs in East Africa practise some kind of 'silent social responsibility'. This takes a less overt or reported approach, is more paternalistic in nature and is more linked to how a business operates on a day-to-day basis. Research carried out by the Resource Centre for Social Dimensions of Business Practice into the relationship between business and poverty highlighted the significance of CSR approaches by national companies in countries such as Tanzania and Uganda.

SMEs generally have a greater understanding of local cultural and political contexts, more links with local civil society (for instance, as customers) and a greater commitment to operating in a specific area. Family-owned companies in particular, because they are less internationally mobile than TNCs, often exhibit strong ethical and philanthropic approaches.

The most supported causes by corporations in East Africa are health, education and training, children, sports and recreation, and HIV/AIDS. A study conducted by the Kenya Community Development Foundation (KCDF) shows that the social cause that received the highest level of resources from corporations was health, with 19 per cent, children taking 11.8 per cent, and education 10.5 per cent (KCDF 2001). The form of most of this giving is grants for capital initiatives – building a school, providing equipment – reflecting most companies' primary interest in publicity and concrete outcomes. Corporations in East Africa characteristically give either in cash or kind. In 2002, 56 per cent of corporate gifts in Kenya were in cash, and 44 per cent were non-cash (Allavida 2005). Non-cash gifts have included companies' brand name products; relief items such as food, blankets and medicine; and the employees' volunteer hours in community service.

Although most corporate philanthropy in East Africa remains quite conservative and often self-interested, there are examples of more progressive initiatives that take a stronger social investment approach. A good example from Kenya is the Sun 'n Sand Club, Coast Province, a resort owned and run by the Vishram family since 1971. Today, the hotel subsidizes a public clinic, funds an early childhood education programme and makes regular contributions to match donations made by hotel guests (more than US$20,000 raised so far) towards school latrines, water pumps and similar.

While some companies are exploring this progressive approach to philanthropy, others are joining forces under initiatives such as the Private Sector Initiative in Uganda, the Nairobi Urban Trust, and the Private Sector Corporate Governance Trust in Kenya. The Nairobi Urban Trust is an organization established a few years ago by a group of private sector individuals who see it as a way to channel some of their resources into employment-creating initiatives and, at the same time, circumvent the incentives problem that ordinarily inhibits corporate giving. The Private Sector Corporate Governance Trust in Kenya is a group of private corporations from all facets of the private sector including corporations, trade unions, bankers' associations, insurance companies, transporters, parastatals and the government itself, that have come together to promote corporate governance and social responsibility. Its activities include building schools, clinics, cattle dips, roads, and various other facilities. These organizations have the potential to develop into leading grantmaking organizations in the region on the lines of the Philippine Business for Social Progress (PBSP), which is today the largest grantmaking organization in the Philippines.

Individual philanthropy

There is plenty of evidence of individual giving for the benefit of others in East Africa. Most of it is, however, invisible and undocumented. This is because, culturally, the motivation of individual philanthropy in Africa is not public recognition or notice but 'affection' and a feeling of obligation. There is also still stigma associated with conspicuous display of personal or family wealth. While the wealthy are expected to provide assistance to those in need, especially during calamities, doing so in an ostentatious or flagrant manner invites social disapproval. This attitude also emanates from Christian teachings – 'what you give with your right hand, do not let your left hand know'. Giving is concentrated among familial affective units such as extended family and clans, but it is also increasingly prevalent outside the family boundaries.

Since the emergence of a middle class in Kenya in the mid-1980s, the number of people who are in a position to donate money to charitable causes has grown steadily. There is a good deal of wealth held by individuals who would like to share it with compatriots, but who need to be made aware of effective methods of doing so. There is limited visible individual giving by the rich in their communities in various forms such as donations to schools, churches, or through their leveraging other funds through *harambees* and from wealthy friends.

The organizations benefiting most from individual philanthropy are NGOs and cultural and sports associations. This is an indication that even though the number of those giving individually is still small, they find NGOs a viable medium for their giving. It is therefore conceivable that, with increased and better organized cultivation of individual philanthropy, local civil society could mobilize larger donations for their work from among individual Kenyans.

There are also cases of individual giving by the rich. In Tanzania for instance, there are a number of prominent individual philanthropists, such as Reginald Mengi, who is the owner of large interests in media and local industries.[3] He has used a lot of his income to support the empowerment of the Jua Kali sector. After a visit to the Jua Kali sector in Kenya, he gave funds to establish the equivalent on his return to Tanzania. He has also supported the training of management cadres and supported the disabled through fundraising events and by donating equipment. There are others who give, but do so quietly out of choice and do not wish to be known or publicly acknowledged. The low levels of individual giving in Tanzania have been attributed to the effects of *Ujamaa*, and the formal donors. Besides disrupting the social fabric and communal systems of survival, *Ujamaa* also took away the personal motivation for productivity because, under the system, this fell on everyone else. It therefore diminished responsibility for self and for others.[4] Donors soon began to give without requiring any show of equity contribution, hence further diminishing responsibility and self-initiative. This, however, is beginning to change, with donors displaying a preference for those who can show they are already doing something. Furthermore, the fact that donors are beginning to withdraw has been a cause for concern, and there are signs of people trying to do things for and by themselves, especially in community groups.

Diaspora philanthropy

Diaspora philanthropy can be said to be the process by which migrants allocate a certain portion of their remittances to fund development projects in their origin societies (Shuval 2000; Opiniano 2002). There are no reliable statistics on the number of East Africans abroad. One unauthenticated[5] report, for example, states that there are at least 600,000 Kenyans abroad, while others put the number at closer to 1.2 million).[6] Exact figures for the number of Ugandans and Tanzanians abroad are similarly hard to come by. According to the report, Kenyans remit approximately 63 per cent of all foreign exchange that flows into Kenya (including bilateral loans, grants and other aid-in-kind). This remittance is in the form of monetary aid to family members, personal and other investments. Uganda earned over US$499 million in the 2000/01 financial year from nationals abroad. Private transfers from Ugandans abroad peaked in the 1998/99 fiscal year, earning the country USh 940 billion ($539 million). These figures are an indication of the potential that is there for philanthropic purposes in the diaspora.

Although the potential of diaspora for philanthropy has been recognized by leaders in the philanthropy field in East Africa, little has been done to begin exploring and developing it. In the diaspora, there are various forms of infrastructure (social networks) already in existence, which could be developed to facilitate organized philanthropy. There is also recognition by leaders in the diaspora of the potential of development resources which might be mobilized from the diaspora for home development. Efforts, albeit inconsistent, have been made to mobilize resources from members of these networks for causes back home. For instance, Ugandans in North America launched the Uganda North America Association (UNAA) in

1988 to provide a 'structure in which Ugandans and friends across North America can function as one community'. UNAA holds annual conventions in which issues of concern to members and to Uganda are discussed. The UNAA also already engages in resource mobilization activities for development projects in Uganda. The "Homecoming Convention" held in Kampala in 2000 was to also include as part of its core agenda 'tangible support of specific community projects in the country by Ugandans in the Diaspora'.[7] The association has also been planning to start a Students Scholarship Fund for awarding scholarships annually.

Some Ugandans in the diaspora have also organized themselves along ethnic lines. The Baganda, the largest ethnic group in Uganda, have organized themselves in various groupings 'because of the great love of their culture and traditions of their ancestor', as well as the desire to contribute to the development of Uganda, seeking 'to pursue goals that will benefit it'. There were at least seven different Baganda organizations in South Africa, North America, Canada and Sweden at the time of writing, each of them, among other aims and objectives, 'identifying and promoting ideas for developing all parts of Buganda, hence contributing to Uganda's development'.[8]

These organizations, their goals and activities are an indication that there is a firm foundation for the development of diaspora philanthropy. There is, however, a lack of proper information on priority causes, ways of channelling the funds to the targeted beneficiaries, and a mistrust of networks and organizations at home as channels for such funds.

Community philanthropy

Community philanthropy refers to giving that occurs within and because of a group of people coming together or being together for a common cause, or a mutually beneficial cause, or for a cause not mutually beneficial, but which the group supports. It also refers to the organization of philanthropy in ways that facilitate giving and asset development by and for the benefit of specific communities. Community philanthropy is the predominant mode of philanthropy in East Africa. It is the most widely spread geographically, but also across class, culture, and social structures. It is based on the traditional African modes of communal living and reciprocity and mutual aid practices in the economic, social and cultural spheres. It is important to recognize that culture is not static but is constantly evolving, and models of giving that are grounded in cultural practice therefore also evolve. So, traditional forms of in-kind giving can gradually become more complex, often involving financial transactions.

It is characterized by the 'pooling' together of resources by community members. There are broadly two types and motivations of pooling resources or for community giving: *communal causes* and *giving as mutual aid*.

Communal causes

Traditionally, the communal causes form of community philanthropy was common in times of war, insecurity or famine, and in communal cultural festivals or seasonal ceremonies. It has, however, evolved as a result of social, cultural and economic change. In East Africa, the emphasis has switched to various forms of social service provision through collective efforts such as water, roads, schools, health and security from which everyone in the community benefits. It is therefore a form of self-help activity to fill the gaps left by state failure or withdrawal from such provision. Some of these activities may be subsidized by the government or by a donor but the initiative usually comes from the community. There are, however, those that are initiated by development NGOs or CBOs, with the requirement of community participation. The community therefore comes together to pool resources to sustain the project or initiative. This form of community philanthropy is common in Kenya under the institution of *harambee*, and has been the development finance source for social service infrastructural development throughout Kenya. In Tanzania, the government, building on this form of philanthropy, has set up the Tanzania Social Action Fund (TASAF) and, under it, the Community Development Initiative, in which it encourages communities to pool financial resources for development projects of their choice and the government comes in to match the community amount.

Giving as mutual aid

Giving as mutual aid is a type of giving where members of a community contribute to a pool or join in a collective effort for the support of a cause or a person, with the expectation that when their turn comes, others will contribute and come to their aid. Traditionally, this practice was used in agricultural tasks such as planting, weeding and harvesting, and other tasks such as building houses, funeral preparations, and weddings. While some of these practices are still common in some communities, such as *mrimo* in Tanzania (the agricultural task mutual aid) and *bataka* in Uganda (for funeral preparation and process), and both of these in Kenya as well, the focus and nature of the practice has broadly evolved to reflect changes in the economy and society of the region. Previously, these practices were focused on immediate need satisfaction (hand-to-mouth). Small amounts of money were usually collected and immediately absorbed in intended activities. They are now characterized by evolving microfinance and micro-enterprise models commonly known as merry-go-rounds in Kenya, and *upato* in Tanzania.

Volunteerism

Volunteerism is a form of philanthropy because it involves the transfer of resources of time, energy and skill, and the development of social capital. Because it is rooted in trust, it is an expression of social capital, the network of social interaction that allows volunteers to assume some level of reciprocity within the community. From the Johns Hopkins research cited above, we can see the importance of recorded volunteering in the non-profit sector.

Volunteering is strongly influenced by the history, politics, religion and culture of a region. In Africa, volunteerism is based on the long-established tradition of sharing. This tradition is based on the African philosophy of *ubuntu,* which means humanness. Practised through communalism, at its core the concept calls for the preservation, protection and enhancement of the human dignity of every person in the community. In the past, communal living entailed the pooling of resources and labour for the benefit of the whole of society. It was based on the principles of reciprocity, mutual aid and social safety nets. Volunteerism as a social-cultural ethic has also been expressed in other concepts such as *undugu* (brotherhood) and, in the post-independence era, *harambee* (Kenya) and *Ujamaa* (Tanzania).

A large proportion of volunteerism in East Africa continues to be informal, and reflects the communal spirit described above. Some formations of volunteers occur around events and issues such as weddings, burials and local security, while others perpetuate a shared past experience, such as an informal alumni group. Even more formal or institutionalized volunteerism is channelled through religious, educational and health institutions, voluntary organizations (non-profit), welfare clubs and members associations and corporations.

Professional membership organizations/associations, such as the Federation of Women Lawyers of Uganda, the Law Society of Tanzania and the International Commission of Jurists (Kenya section), have established programmes of membership volunteer service provision through, for instance, legal aid clinics, *pro bono* briefs, advocacy demonstrations, fundraising and programme committees, among other types of activities drawing on their professional knowledge and expertise.

Corporations in East Africa have traditionally supported volunteerism by sponsoring activities such as walks, raffles, golf tournaments, and other fundraising cultural or entertainment activities organized and run by volunteers for a social cause. Recent developments within CSR practice have also led to other more proactive and innovative volunteer support activities whereby companies encourage the involvement of their own employees in voluntary work. For example, a corporation may challenge its employees with a shilling-for-shilling match on any funds raised by them through a voluntary activity, organized and undertaken during non-office hours, such as a walk for a charitable cause of their choice. In such activities, a corporation is often able to use its name, visibility and contacts to leverage additional funds towards causes identified by volunteer employees. In other instances, a corporation might encourage its employees to offer their professional services (such as auditing) free of charge to charitable organizations or to community initiatives in the community where they operate. This approach is still relatively new in East Africa and has yet to be fully exploited but it is potentially attractive, as the company need not spend any money at all but simply lend its name and prestige.

An interesting new phenomenon in East Africa is the creation of opportunities for younger people to volunteer in the types of programmes typically only enjoyed by young people of northern countries. The inception of the National United Nations Volunteers (NUNV) scheme on a pilot basis in 1996 by the UNV is one such approach and it has certainly boosted the involvement and participation of qualified young Kenyans in the country's development. The NUNV scheme is playing a catalytic and synergizing role in its support of the use of volunteers in government institutions, NGOs, CBOs and other organizations. They make a significant contribution in important areas such as poverty eradication, gender mainstreaming, environmental protection, HIV/AIDS intervention, humanitarian programmes, providing support to community-based initiatives, facilitating networking and information exchange, promoting human rights, and enhancing peace-building. Another initiative is the South to South Volunteer scheme, introduced by Voluntary Service Overseas (VSO); this enables young people from Kenya to volunteer in other developing countries. By establishing the scheme, VSO is trying to balance volunteer mobility by recruiting volunteers from the south to work alongside their partners in other countries of the south. A further development emerging from this has been the establishment of VSO Jitolee, which intends to work with partner organizations, including governments, to set up a volunteering scheme for new graduates and diploma holders. The scheme is meant to facilitate the transition from school to the world of work. Young graduates and diploma holders will register their details including academic credentials with an organization that VSO Jitolee supports. This information will be passed on to prospective employers, who will place them in their organizations to work as volunteers/interns for a number of months. The benefits of such a voluntary relationship to both the volunteer and the employer are likely to be significant.

Wherever and however it is practised and encouraged, volunteerism is an important component of philanthropy in its broadest sense, and also an important potential resource for the development of philanthropy in its narrower sense. Through volunteering, especially in community initiatives, people are likely to gain a greater understanding of the issues and challenges with which organized philanthropy grapples, and so be more likely to give creatively towards social justice ends.

Social justice philanthropy

'Social justice philanthropy' is the term used to describe grantmaking or philanthropy that aims to address the root causes of social and economic inequalities. For many commentators, social justice philanthropy (also sometimes called 'social movement', 'social change' or 'community-based' philanthropy) is distinguished from other forms of grantmaking by the fact that success is measured not only by where money is given, but also the process by which it is given. The following are four suggested core principles of social change or social justice philanthropy (Goldberg 2003). A philanthropic institution pursuing social justice goals will:

- Focus on marginalized and disenfranchised communities
- Address root causes of their challenges
- Strive to be accountable to marginalized and disenfranchised communities (in addition to its own board)
- Establish inclusive, accessible processes for groups seeking support.

A key distinction between social justice philanthropy and traditional philanthropy is that 'while traditional philanthropy also works to benefit marginalized and disenfranchised communities and to support the root causes of issues, the process, players and analysis of politics and power are what distinguish social change philanthropy from other forms of grantmaking' (ibid.).

Looking at philanthropy in East Africa through a social justice lens is not straightforward. First, a hardnosed analysis of the practice and policy of the region's active philanthropic institutions (as opposed to the broader collective of NGOs) would probably conclude that none could confidently state that it abides by the four core proposed principles set out above. Taking the members of the East Africa Foundations Learning Group (EAFLG) as a sample, those with active grants or funding programmes mostly focus on marginalized groups (though not exclusively). Examples include the Kianda Foundation, which promotes education for girls and young women (although the Kianda School itself provides for all girls, the Foundation's new programmes are all targeting girls who would otherwise miss out on education and opportunities); the Rattansi Educational Trust in Kenya, which provides bursaries to young people who cannot afford school and/or university fees; and the Social Action Trust Fund (SATF) in Tanzania, which provides grants to schools and NGOs for onward support of AIDS orphans. Active foundations outside of the

EAFLG with a focus on disadvantaged groups include the Urgent Action Fund, which supports women in conflict or danger, and HURINET (Uganda), which funds human rights groups. Many other public and private foundations, however, do not focus on the most disadvantaged groups.

Looking at the other three core principles set out above, on the face of it, few active philanthropic institutions in East Africa embody those principles. SATF, for example, funds the provision of school uniforms and books to AIDS orphans, but does not fund work to address the causal factors of the continuing spread of HIV/AIDS, or the persistent discrimination and stigma etc. associated with it. In general, it would be fair to say that the philanthropic institutions lag behind many operational NGOs in terms of targeting root causes of the development challenges they seek to tackle. In terms of accountability to marginalized or disadvantaged communities, few if any active foundations have mechanisms in place (then again, neither would most NGOs). Some of the active philanthropic institutions do better with regard to being accessible to and supportive of groups seeking support. KCDF meets applicants and discusses the process, as does the Rattansi Educational Trust; others with more operational programmes, such as the Tanzania Gatsby Charitable Trust, Private Sector Foundation Uganda and HURINET, interact closely with their grantees and potential grantees.

However, perhaps that particular set of principles is too exacting for the current East African context. At one level, it would be reasonable to argue that all philanthropy aimed at poor people and communities in East Africa is about social justice. Providing a bursary (or even a school uniform) means creating an educational opportunity where one would have been denied, not because of lack of ability, but because of lack of funds. Providing grants to enable micro-enterprise traders to participate in trade fairs (one of TGT's programmes) is an attempt to enable such traders to compete on more equal terms with private companies that have resources available for marketing and fairs; it is thus, in some sense, about equity and justice.

The danger of such an interpretation of social justice is that it weakens the concept and leaves little to distinguish it from other forms of philanthropy. Even if, for now, we worry less about multiple accountability and even about process (though part of reaching out to disadvantaged communities must inevitably mean creating accessible and supportive processes), social justice philanthropy as a minimum must have a focus on root causes, on systemic and power issues, as well as on targeting disadvantaged and marginalized groups. Of grantmakers in East Africa, perhaps only the Urgent Action Fund truly challenges power structures and structural injustice. Its grants seek, for instance, to enable women to access political and civil decision-making processes, to support campaigns for legislation that will empower or protect women, and to challenge social norms that disadvantage women. Happily, the Urgent Action Fund is an increasingly active entity raising its profile in East Africa, thereby providing an important model.

Another important and often-overlooked dimension of social justice and philanthropy relates to the source and investment of funds. If foundations raise funds locally from people and communities of moderate or low incomes, and invest them in managed funds in mostly foreign companies, the return is a trickle-down of low value over many years. It is at least questionable whether this fits within a social justice framework. Issues of social justice and philanthropy are further complicated in East Africa by the challenge of understanding, interpreting and assimilating into the philanthropy mainstream, traditions and cultures of community philanthropy, self-help and activism. Take, for example, tribal associations that emerged between the 1920s and 1950s. Tribal associations were social justice initiatives, a response to the injustice of colonial policies and processes such as appropriation of native land, harsh rule, racism and discriminatory developmental social services policies which created increasing resentment among the local populations, and commercialization which resulted in exploitation and inequity. In pursuing their agenda, the associations became very successful at mobilizing local resources for their activities. In Kenya, associations such as the Kikuyu Central Association, Taita Hills Association, Ukamba Members Association, Nyanza Central Association and North Kavirondo Association played important roles, all supported with resources and volunteerism by the tribal populations. Independent schools, churches and trade unions were also established by a few educated African elite, such as Jomo Kenyatta, Tom Mboya, Ronald Ngala and Daniel Arap Moi in Kenya, most of whom led the liberation struggle and became state leaders after independence (Kanyinga 1999). In Uganda, tribal associations included the Young Men of Toro (YMT), and the Young Basoga and Abataka Association. These associations were set up to protest unfair and excessive taxation, restriction of freedom of movement, unfair wages, and lack of social services, among other forms of oppression and exploitation. The tribal associations and some of the independent social institutions became sites for the social justice movements that grew into the liberation struggles.

Trends, challenges and opportunities for philanthropy in East Africa

This is an exciting time for everyone involved in the promotion of philanthropy in East Africa. New people and institutions are entering the discussion about how to proceed; models and strategies employed to date are being challenged; complex and challenging issues are being raised about the connections between tradition and modernity in philanthropy; new support institutions are emerging and increasingly developing specialized skills and focus; and the infrastructure of philanthropy is consolidating. Governments in the region are seriously considering what role organized philanthropy can play in national development and what sort of enabling environment is necessary.

Trends

There have been three main externally linked or initiated 'drivers' of philanthropy in East Africa evident in the last ten years. First, there has been a growing awareness of the need for NGOs to identify alternative, preferably local, sources of funds to replace or at least supplement dwindling foreign funding. The second driver has been the foundation-building process, initially motivated by a desire to explore the potential in the region of community foundations. Thirdly, there has been increasing discussion about the importance and potential (for society and companies) of corporate social responsibility (CSR) in the region. Here we suggested also that changes in the aid regime and in the type of NGO interventions have acted as a driver for new forms of community philanthropy. The external drivers were largely characterized by foreign models: the community foundation, CSR and corporate citizenship, and 'modern' fundraising techniques. Reflecting the use of external models, strategies employed in East Africa focused heavily on exposure to well-established versions of the models, through either study tours or visiting resource people. In 2004, there was evidence of a wide-ranging reaction to the external drivers and strategies used. There was a new emphasis on understanding local context, moving from the African particular to the universal.

Revisiting assumptions – questioning models – learning lessons

The first important emerging trend is an examination of existing assumptions and a reappraisal of existing models.

- **Looking for meaning and connections, questioning language.** This is a time of reflection in philanthropy in East Africa. In common with other parts of the continent, discussions are under way about the definition of 'philanthropy' for East Africa. As people acknowledge and begin from what they know – the traditions of community solidarity and mutual aid – they are exploring ways of using modern forms of philanthropy that develop traditional mutual forms, or else are seeking to define philanthropy in such a way as to accommodate those mechanisms from other cultures and jurisdictions that are useful to them. The very language of organized philanthropy is under review: for instance, how can we better explain the concept of an endowment to communities of people who live day-to-day? Perhaps we have to begin by describing what we mean, not by stating the term as a universal 'given'. We might then discover what forms of 'endowment' are practised in the community and, starting from this base, we might arrive at terminology with which people in the community are comfortable.

• **Foundation-building.** It is unnecessary to revisit in detail the early stages of KCDF's development, based as it was on assumptions about the appropriateness of the community foundation model and its combination of local resource mobilization for endowment building, good governance and effective grantmaking. This framework provided a useful mechanism for addressing key concepts in any foundation. However, the enthusiasm for particular models undoubtedly swept people and their institutions along and, for some considerable time, hindered serious questioning of the appropriateness of particular strategies (such as endowments or grantmaking). Similarly, the initial (implied) prospect of endowment grants from the Ford Foundation was extremely attractive to the institutions awarded planning grants and led to expectations that have not been – and are unlikely to be – met. It is now clear that none of the institutions supported through the EAFLG will ever make the transition to becoming a 'pure' community foundation. Apart from the fact that the grantees were all established as service deliverers or as grantmakers in a particular sphere, an undeveloped local donor base and low capacity amongst potential grantees/partners makes it more realistic to think that, for certain organizations, grantmaking will continue to go hand in hand with service delivery/operations and capacity building for some time yet.

Some of the lessons learned through efforts to date in foundation-building have already been noted. It is also worth saying, however, that as attention has shifted away from a particular model or strategy, a new and richer conversation has emerged, one that is more focused on balancing the origins, experience, values and goals of local foundations with developing generic capacities for resource mobilization and grantmaking.

Regarding community foundations, or even community trusts, there is now a recognition that the route to establishing such institutions should be organic, evolving out of a confluence of different routes taken by different communities in a society. These routes will be dictated by the socioeconomic, cultural and political contexts of the communities in which foundations emerge or are working. Any development paradigm must take into consideration the culture of the people that it seeks to develop (Moyo 2003). The widespread community units of mutual aid (merry-go-rounds, *batakas, mrimos*), visible throughout East Africa are a result of the increasing poverty from the early 1980s to date that has brought people together to create networks of survival. Though they have alleviated immediate needs, they have not developed solutions to alleviate these needs in the long run. This raises the question of sustainability, which seems to affect most civil society organizations in developing countries. It is in this context that community foundations, and other ways of mobilizing resources to address local developmental challenges in the long term, make sense. They must, however, be conceptualized in the cultural, socioeconomic and political context of the people or the communities that they serve. This is because, when communities own development, they feel empowered and tend to work for the good of the community. A certain degree of connected-ness develops, bonds of trust are cultivated and this usually results in positive developments in the communities concerned (Moyo 2003). There is growing evidence to suggest that the size and density of social networks and institutions, and the nature of personal interactions, significantly affect the efficiency and sustainability of development programmes. Such conditions exist in many East African communities, and community foundations and funds could tap into those pockets to build the financial clout of the community.

- **Grantmaking.** In addition to the local foundations already engaged in grantmaking, the last few years have seen in East Africa growing numbers of NGOs adopting re-granting strategies in conjunction with their foreign donors. There are challenges and opportunities here, but an important point to note is that grantmaking is beginning to be regarded as a distinct process, a particular set of skills, not an activity that can be simply grafted onto other operational programmes. At the same time, there is now recognition, even within established grantmaking foundations, that capacity for grantmaking (skills, knowledge, systems) is very weak.

- **NGOs and fundraising.** NGOs actively seeking local funds can be seen to be the 'demand side' of the philanthropy equation; an effective NGO sector can stimulate local philanthropy. From the mid- to late-1980s, with increasing recognition of changing patterns of aid, there has been a growing emphasis in international development on encouraging local resource mobilization for southern NGOs. This is manifested in training workshops in specific skills, ranging from proposal writing to running a direct mail campaign. The best of these workshops, run by Resource Alliance, brought together expertise initially from Europe and North America, and more recently from across Africa, and genuinely sought to engage with local experience. Nevertheless, there was an assumption underpinning such training that the techniques developed in the north could be replicated and adapted in the south. Today, these assumptions are being questioned. While efforts are under way to professionalize fundraising in East Africa – a much-needed step, given the emergence of many would-be 'fundraising consultants' with dubious experience – greater efforts are being made to document local experience of successful resource mobilization. There is a recognition that many established fundraising techniques are only suitable for the most sophisticated urban NGOs, and that entirely different approaches are needed for smaller groups, particularly those operating in rural areas.

Mainstreaming philanthropy

This is a second key trend in East Africa, with two significant elements being identified within this trend.

- **Institutionalizing methodologies of philanthropy.** This is distinct from establishing institutions. In part, it is a question of process, for example, embedding learning and capacity building without setting up schools. It is also, in part, a question of grounding the conversation about philanthropy, and about standards and certification. Similarly, we have seen how key concepts such as an endowment are entering into mainstream discussion in the context of philanthropy and development at every level, from community to government.

- **Recognition of the importance of an enabling environment.** There has been extensive discussion within the non-profit sector for many years about the importance of an 'enabling environment' for NGOs and for the development of philanthropy. Usually, 'enabling environment' is interpreted to mean laws that support the establishment and operation of NGOs and that facilitate effective governance and accountability, and fiscal incentives for local giving (tax breaks). Many institutions, including Ufadhili (Centre for the Promotion of Philanthropy) and the Aga Khan Foundation, have undertaken serious work to research the potential measures that could be taken, and much of this work has been publicly presented and discussed. This work is now being taken forward by the EAAG, which is planning to establish a specific project or unit to prepare an evidence-based set of recommendations for incentives to present to governments in the region.

  In Kenya, the Government established in April 2003 a Task Force on Public Collections (or *harambee)*. Although the focus of the Task Force, which reported in December 2003, was on the issue of *harambee* – its use, appropriate regulation and so on – it also looked at the broader issues of an enabling environment for philanthropy. Recommendations were made for tax incentives to promote giving, the establishment of a National Endowment Fund and also Constituency Development Trusts, as well as a range of measures to 'cleanse' *harambees*. It is worth noting that the discussion about misuse of *harambees* is an element of a growing public awareness of the importance of an enabling environment for philanthropy.

Infrastructure development

The third key trend we have identified in the region is the development of a third sector infrastructure.

- **Networks, associations and collaborations.** The launch of the East Africa Association of Grantmakers marked an important development in the infrastructure of philanthropy in the region. The Association reflects a desire amongst emerging grantmakers in the region to carve out their niche, support each other in developing capacity, and establish standards for good practice. We already referred to initiatives such as the Private Sector Corporate Governance Trust, a collaborative grantmaking mechanism, and to other similar initiatives. Another new addition to the infrastructure of philanthropy is the Professional Association of Fundraisers, which is being pioneered by the Resource Alliance.

- **Support organizations.** There has also been an emergence of several organizations focused on philanthropy support and promotion. Amongst the indigenous organizations, the most prominent is Ufadhili. The Centre has spearheaded efforts to promote corporate social responsibility, volunteering and the enabling environment, as well as philanthropy more broadly. Two international organizations have entered the sector: Allavida and the Resource Alliance. Allavida focuses on foundation-building, skills development for effective grantmaking, asset development and community philanthropy. The Resource Alliance focuses on building fundraising skills, professionalizing fundraising and seeking to develop indigenous models and techniques for local resource mobilization.

Challenges

This is a time of major transition in the philanthropy field in East Africa. There are many positive trends as set out above, and a range of exciting opportunities. However, there are also some formidable challenges.

Building donor constituencies

Giving in a charitable fashion is widespread in East Africa, either through extended families or other close networks, or through religious institutions, or to well-known charitable appeals and institutions (such as the Heart Foundation in Kenya). The challenge is to strengthen organized philanthropy (especially for social justice). In part, this means improving levels of trust that people have in the NGO sector, which in turn requires NGOs to improve their public communications and their accountability. It also means understanding the potential and importance of creating pools of funding for social investment, whether in the form of endowments or short-term grants funds. It means significantly raising the profile of philanthropic institutions, and it also means developing effective *means* for people to give, possibly including deductions through the payroll, affinity cards and so on.

A challenge specific to the foundation sector is to raise local funds for grantmaking. It is likely that, in time, this funding will come from the corporate sector, so companies will need to be convinced that foundations can add value. This is particularly problematic for foundations because there seems to be a public belief that NGOs raise money for their own operations rather than for disbursement. More generally, while there is limited dialogue about philanthropy, it has not become a major public issue. Media coverage continues to focus on charity – acts of giving by celebrities, fundraising events, or specific appeals – rather than on stimulating a serious discussion about the role and potential of philanthropy. Serious effort is needed to expand a public debate about philanthropy. An important element of this debate is about sensitizing potential donors to care where their money goes, to demand high standards of accountability, but also to start investing more constructively in the most essential aspects of philanthropic endeavour.

Building the resource base

In a philanthropy field that is relatively young, it is not surprising to find that the resource base – of people, knowledge, and investment – is still limited. There are few experienced resource people from the region and so, too often, external consultants are drafted in. Similarly, there is a dire lack of researchers actively engaged in trying to understand and interpret traditions of philanthropy, or to look at external models and how they can be adapted. In both fields, investment is urgently needed to develop the human resource base for philanthropy in the region. A third element is the lack of 'thought-leaders' capable of linking the philanthropy discussion to wider issues of African epistemology.

Linked to these issues of human resources is the limited involvement in the philanthropy sector to date of academic institutions and researchers (with some notable exceptions, e.g. the Johns Hopkins researchers). There has been a tendency in the non-profit sector generally, and the philanthropy field in particular, to use consultants (usually practitioners), many of them foreign, rather than to engage with local academic institutions. Building an academic underpinning for philanthropy can be an important element in strengthening the field.

As a result of the lack of researchers and resource people, primary research remains limited, as do case studies, quantitative data and support materials for local philanthropy. The Johns Hopkins studies are useful and important in this regard but much of the data remains sketchy and derived from limited samples. Specific research by Ufadhili, Resource Alliance, Allavida, Aga Khan Foundation and KCDF has added to the knowledge of the sector, but much more needs to be done.

A challenge specific to the support organizations in philanthropy is to increase collaboration. The resource base for philanthropy promotion is weakened if the few organizations focused on philanthropy only pursue their own agendas. Encouraging signs of collaboration include work on the enabling environment, on research, and on the development of a professional association of fundraisers. However, much more needs to be done to maximize collective efforts.

Finally, additional sources of financial investment are needed, especially now that the Ford Foundation's dedicated philanthropy portfolio has closed. The challenge is to convince the major institutional donors of the strategic importance of investing in the promotion and strengthening of organized philanthropy.

Foundation-building

As noted above, foundation-building efforts are under way in East Africa, but the sector remains relatively weak, especially if compared to the 'top end' of the NGO sector. Allavida's research indicates that there are at least 50 active grantmaking institutions in the region, and many more that are more or less inactive, including a number of family foundations. For the established, active foundations, the key challenges continue to be those of building their funding base (including permanent funds) and their specific skills in grantmaking. These same challenges exist for new and emerging foundations, though the level and type of support needed will differ from that required by the more experienced institutions.

For the support organizations involved in foundation-building, there is a challenge of reaching out to the many inactive foundations, identifying blockages and offering support, as part of expanding the sector. More generally, a key challenge for the foundation sector is to carve out its niche, differentiating itself from other parts of civil society. This is a major challenge, not least because many foundations have developed as operational NGOs, and because they lack the financial resource base to stand apart, i.e. they are effectively competing with NGOs, for both local and foreign funds. Nevertheless, if foundations are to become a significant part of the non-profit landscape in East Africa, they must differentiate themselves. For the foundations that have made a transition to grantmaking from being an implementing agency, the challenge is also to make the internal cultural switch and to start thinking like a grantmaker rather than an NGO.

Part of achieving this differentiation lies in foundations – and particularly the grantmaking foundations – establishing for their sector standards of good practice in accountability and transparency (for example, publishing annual reports and lists of grants); fundraising; and grantmaking. The EAAG can play the lead role in establishing and promoting these standards. Another key element of differentiating foundations is for government to introduce specific registration processes and frameworks for foundations; lobbying on this issue should be a priority for the foundation sector. Another challenge in differentiation for foundations is to match the NGOs in levels of understanding of the causal factors and dimensions of the issues they target as grantmakers. Finally, for foundations seeking to build an endowment, there are many challenges, among them selling the idea of endowment in a context of so much immediate need, and investing and growing the endowment either locally or off-shore (balancing risk).

Enabling environment

The apparent willingness of governments in East Africa to discuss legal and fiscal issues relating to the non-profit sector in general and to the promotion of philanthropy in particular is encouraging. However, securing an effective enabling environment remains a serious challenge. Although there is little evidence to suggest that in low- and middle-income countries, tax concessions lead directly to increased levels of giving overall, key sections of donor constituencies are encouraged, especially larger corporate donors.

Research in East Africa suggests strongly that the lack of tax breaks for company donations is inhibiting corporate philanthropy. In Kenya, for example, many companies undertake community investment initiatives within the framework of 'advertising', for which there are tax concessions. The lack of fiscal incentives for corporate giving ties donations to achieving high profits (not common in difficult economic times) and also inhibits companies from becoming more strategic in their giving. An important challenge for the sector is to make the economic case for tax concessions on donations. Unless it can be shown that the net effect of tax breaks will mean an increase (or at least no decrease) in the fiscus, governments will be reluctant to offer the concessions. Making this case will require considerable research and investment.

Blending the traditional and modern

The need to harness the wellspring of community philanthropy and expand it in scale and scope is a challenge. In part, this is a challenge of understanding – a part of the challenge of increasing knowledge set out above – but it is also a challenge to all involved in promoting philanthropy to question assumptions about models, good practice and meaning. It is a challenge of interpretation, of finding ways to communicate concepts and terms so that common ground can be found. It is a challenge of institution-building too, for the mainstream institutions of philanthropy are ill suited to meet the needs of traditional forms of philanthropy. At the same time, as new institutions emerge, such as community trusts, there is a challenge of establishing appropriate standards of governance, accountability and stewardship.

Conclusion

We conclude this chapter by looking at some of the opportunities presented by the current context.

Innovation at community level

This is where the challenge of blending traditional and modern approaches to philanthropy will be met. The practical need for communities to develop assets which can meet local needs both through returns on the assets (either interest/dividends on funds, or earned income from productive assets) and through leverage (match-funding) is stimulating innovation and institutional development at community level. Models can be developed that do not compromise or destroy affinity lines or communal units of giving, or disrupt sociocultural institutions, but instead create partnerships between communities and intermediary institutions that both preserve identities and ensure local legitimacy. A second level of innovation in relation to community funds and philanthropy is concerned with adding value to single community funds through appropriate investment strategies. One such strategy is that offered by KCDF to community funds that wish to hold their endowment within KCDF's own fund.

Breaking out of the 'silos'

In each of the 'silos' connected with philanthropy – foundation-building, corporate social responsibility, social investment and so on – there are exciting developments taking place. There is a need and opportunity to work across silos in order to maximize impact in promoting and strengthening philanthropy. A good example of this is the growing interaction between the financial services sector and foundations, as the former begins to recognize a potential new set of clients and the latter sees the need for professional services as an important part of its institutional management and stewardship. Similarly, companies seeking more effective mechanisms for their CSR programmes can look to partner with foundations, while a coalition of interested parties across silos will be more effective in seeking legislative and fiscal changes to enhance philanthropy.

Legislative and fiscal change

There is now an excellent opportunity to make progress toward legislative and fiscal change that will enhance organized philanthropy in the region. All three governments in the region are showing a willingness to discuss ways in which, through either of these channels, the non-profit sector's contribution to society can be increased. The presence in the Kenyan Government of former civil society leaders is at least ensuring that issues relating to the enabling environment can be taken forward. With a willingness on the part of government to listen, the opportunity exists for a range of specific, well-researched proposals to be put forward by particular elements of civil society.

Developing dedicated grantmakers

Changes in the nature of foreign aid and development finance (decentralization of funding programmes to country offices of bilateral donors, increased funding for re-granting) should give domestic grantmakers a comparative advantage over NGOs. However, for the time being, many donor agencies automatically look to the NGOs that they have funded over many years and simply shift from project funding to provision of re-granting funds. The opportunity for domestic grantmakers, individually and as a group, is to sell their specific grantmaking capacity – capacity that NGOs rarely have. This requires, of course, that foundations meet the challenge of building their grantmaking capacity, but the potential of securing significant re-granting funds should offer an added incentive.

It is not just foreign donors that could offer significant grants funds to grantmaking foundations. There is an opportunity to offer corporate donors a distinct approach (small grants programmes) to giving, whilst also removing workload from companies in responding to regular requests for support. It is important for grantmakers to build their specialist knowledge and understanding of the issues they are tackling and to develop appropriate staff and board capacity.

Diaspora philanthropy

The East Africa diaspora internationally is a huge potential reservoir of philanthropic investment for the region. Within the region and within countries, the diaspora also offers significant potential for philanthropic contributions to home communities. There is a great opportunity to emulate the experience of non-resident Indians in the United States in giving back to India, and there are many other similar examples in developing models, mechanisms and institutions to mobilize diaspora-giving for East Africa.

Endnotes

1   Data presented at a seminar in Nairobi, 16 March 2004.
2   'Fees' is taken to include fees for service, subscriptions, dues etc. and also management fees charged within development and aid projects.
3. Information provided by Ernest Tarimo of Social Action Trust Fund, Dar es Salaam.

4   Ibid. Most of the interviewees about philanthropy in Tanzania had the same to say about the effects of *ujamaa*.
5   Report does not quote source of the estimated statistics.
6   Kenya community abroad, www.kenyansabroad.org
7   www.bctex.com/websites/unaa/what.html
8   www.bicusa.com/diaspora.htm

CHAPTER 7

PHILANTHROPY AND EQUITY:
THE CASE OF SOUTH AFRICA[1]

CHRISTA L. KULJIAN

Introduction

We must appreciate that all over the world, right down the centuries, there have been great
religions that have encouraged the idea of giving — of fighting poverty and of promoting
the equality of human beings — whatever their background, whatever their political beliefs.
That spirit has lived not only in the world but in South Africa as well. — Nelson Mandela[2]

Nearly two decades after South Africa's first democratic elections on April 27,
1994, the country is in a concerned mood. While it is still important to look
back at past accomplishments, there is a growing emphasis on the many objectives not yet met. The post-apartheid period has seen successful elections at the
national and local level, the development of a new and internationally respected
constitution, and the development of institutions and policies to implement the
new democracy. Despite these significant political changes, apartheid's social and
economic legacy remains entrenched and the majority of South Africa's 45 million
people continues to live in conditions not dissimilar to those of two decades ago.
Access to good quality education, housing, health care and other basic services as
well as jobs remain unattainable for the majority of the black population, close to
60 per cent live in poverty. While there is a growing black middle class, the bulk
of the country's wealth remains in the hands of a small percentage of the population. Given South Africa's great wealth and enormous inequality, is it possible to
eradicate poverty and achieve greater equity? This is the central question to be
explored in this chapter.

In the past several years, scholarly interest in 'social justice philanthropy' has
increased. There are findings which suggest that advocacy and policy development may get to the root of social ills more effectively than basic service delivery.
However, in South Africa, where much effort during the past decade has been on

policy development, donor funds have tended to flow to the larger, more professional and urban-based non-profit organizations. As a result, the smaller, often rural and peri-urban, community-based organizations have lost out. So while advocacy efforts will continue to be central to promoting equity and social justice, an even greater effort will be needed to make sure that the voices of the marginalized are included and promoted in the process.

Throughout South Africa's first and a half decade of democracy, philanthropy has been particularly interested in issues of democracy, governance and political equity. These issues have been paramount, given the fact that the majority of the country's population was disenfranchised. A lot of focus and resources (international and local) were devoted towards sharing information about the Constitution, the workings of national, provincial and local government and the political process. These efforts have been crucial for broadening political equity so that the previously disenfranchised, including women, the homeless, the unemployed, and those living with HIV/AIDS, could theoretically stake their claim.

Yet philanthropy has been more hesitant to squarely address issues of *economic equity,* which is where – given the high levels of poverty and unemployment – the challenge now lies. Economic equity is not the realm in which philanthropic institutions generally feel most comfortable. Philanthropic resources (from the private sector and wealthy individuals) were generated by an economic system that has neither been able to eradicate poverty nor produce the jobs necessary to significantly reduce unemployment. This makes it difficult for these institutions to fund critiques of that system, or to promote creative thinking outside that system. As Rick Cohen, President and CEO of the National Council for Responsive Philanthropy in the USA, says, 'As the products of wealth, foundations and their governing bodies may find it difficult to support a type of grantmaking that challenges the basis of how that wealth was generated' (Milner 2003).

And Emmett Carson argues that 'foundations owe allegiance to the social systems that created them'. As Vadim Samorodov holds, for many years in Russia, 'philanthropy was viewed as a cynical act of capitalism'.[3] To avoid the cynicism, it will be necessary for philanthropy to more squarely address the root causes of South Africa's poverty and economic inequality. This chapter attempts to outline some of the contours around this.

There are five sections to this chapter. The first is a discussion of definitions – particularly 'philanthropy' and 'equity', as well as assumptions about philanthropy, its sources and models. The second explores the South African context, including apartheid history and current scale of poverty. The third briefly considers the relationships between equity, the state, the market, civil society and philanthropy. The fourth reviews certain philanthropic practices and models, and how they engage with the issues and challenges of equity. This chapter, however, does not provide a comprehensive review of the different types of philanthropy as they exist in South Africa. The Centre for Civil Society at the University of KwaZulu Natal did a lot on this through *The State of Giving Project*.[4] The concluding section discusses the limitations of philanthropy and suggests how philanthropy can most effectively address equity issues.

Definitions

Philanthropy[5]

Definitions and perceptions of the term 'philanthropy' differ internationally. *The Collins English Dictionary* defines philanthropy as 'the love of mankind' and 'the practice of performing charitable or benevolent actions'. The modern use of the term emanates from the United States, but is often seen to have elitist and patronizing connotations elsewhere around the world. Ironically, the terms 'charitable giving' and 'charity' are more commonly used and more palatable in the United Kingdom, but they also carry negative connotations elsewhere. In some cases, 'philanthropy' and 'charity' are seen as broadly equivalent terms. In others, 'charity' is viewed as handouts to the poor, while 'philanthropy' is thought to be more 'strategic'. As Joseph Rowntree wisely wrote in 1865, 'Charity as ordinarily practised, the charity of endowment, the charity of emotion, the charity which takes the place of justice, creates much of the misery which it relieves, but does not relieve all the misery it creates' (Burkeman 1999). And Martin Luther King Jr said: 'Philanthropy is commendable, but it must not cause the philanthropist to overlook the circumstances of economic injustice that make philanthropy necessary' (Collins 2001). More recently, Burkeman (2004) wrote that:

> unless philanthropy helps to change the situations that give rise to the need for it in the first place, then it simply reinforces existing power imbalances in society and enables the rich and powerful to feel good about themselves despite the fact that they are doing nothing to effect real change for the poor and powerless.

In South Africa, both terms, 'philanthropy' and 'charity,' hold negative connotations. For example, consider these quotes:

> Philanthropy doesn't engage communities and is considered patronizing. (*CSI Handbook*, South Africa)

> Our organization regards 'philanthropy' as being paternalistic and lacking in a developmental approach to community service. Our challenge in a developing country is to engage in partnerships as opposed to philanthropy. (Volunteer Centre, Cape Town)

The term 'philanthropy' does not have a direct translation in South Africa's eleven official languages. The Building Community Philanthropy (BCP) project at the University of Cape Town spoke of how poor communities mobilize resources by giving and receiving 'help'. BCP used the term 'help' because it is more easily translated than 'giving' or 'philanthropy'. Another working definition for philanthropy is 'private resources put towards the public good'.[6] We must note that 'public good' is not defined and that this definition may imply that all philanthropy is voluntary, whereas in certain cultural circumstances giving is seen as obligatory. Nevertheless, this definition does provide a useful distinction between private philanthropy and public aid.

Equity

The *American Heritage Dictionary* defines 'equity' as 'the state, quality, or ideal of being just, impartial, and fair'. What differentiates 'equity' from 'equality'? One answer is that equality implies that everyone is equal, whereas equity implies that everyone has equal access. In South Africa the term is often used in relation to political, economic, gender, or race relations. This is consistent with the manner in which Amartya Sen (2000) conceptualized equitable human development. He concentrates on the ability of people to improve their lives and to remove obstacles such as illiteracy, ill health, inadequate resources, or lack of civil and political freedoms.

In South Africa, issues of racial equity and gender equity are of central importance, as the black population, and black women in particular, have been historically disadvantaged in their access to the country's resources. Today, economic equity, or its lack thereof, cuts across racial and gender equity as a major challenge to the country's future. HIV/AIDS adds another layer of inequity in South Africa.

There are assumptions regarding philanthropy that need to be brought up-front here and these include, first, that giving in South Africa does not only flow vertically from the wealthy to the poor, but also horizontally. This is confirmed by a 2004 study which found that 'poor and non-poor respondents were equally likely to have given in the month prior to being interviewed – making giving not to be the domain of the wealthy only but part of everyday life for all South Africans, rich and poor alike' (Everatt 2004:i). The report also concluded that volunteering is not the preserve of the middle class, as 23 per cent of the poor respondents said that they had volunteered in the month prior to being interviewed, as opposed to 17 per cent of those who were not poor. It is likely that this trend has not changed in 2012. Second, just as philanthropy is often assumed to be acts of kindness by the wealthy for the poor, so too is the assumption that philanthropy and giving are voluntary. While much of what is termed philanthropy in a Western context is voluntary, in most developing nations it is seen as an obligation and duty (Everatt 2004, 2005; Wilkinson-Maposa 2005).

South Africa's socioeconomic context: Key challenges to equity

While the first democratic elections of 1994 gave all South Africans the right to vote, they did not wipe away apartheid's legacy of widespread poverty and inequality. Inequality, by definition, was promoted by state policies in such areas as education, spatial planning, land use, and labour law. Racism and colonialism took hold in South Africa and shaped social and economic development over hundreds of years and apartheid locked it in place for over half a century. While political apartheid might have ended with the 1994 elections, economic apartheid still exists. Income inequality in South Africa is second highest in the world, just behind Brazil. The African population had 20 per cent of the national income in 1975, and only 36 per cent in 1996, when Africans were 75 per cent of the total population. Seekings and Nattrass (2005) noted that inequality worsened between 1995 and 2000; the Gini-coefficient rose from 0.65 in 1995 to 0.69 in 2000. While these statistics might be outdated, reality is that the status quo has remained.

In assessing inequality, it is therefore important to look not only at current income, but also at acquired assets such as land, livestock, housing, cars, and bonds and stocks. Such assets can be a significant source of income and can provide security in times of unemployment, illness or crisis. In South Africa, the disparity between Africans and whites in terms of wealth (assets) is thought to be much greater than it is in terms of income. Colonial and apartheid policies concentrated wealth within the relatively small white population. Enormous inequality in land ownership and housing stock still exists. Unemployment has been growing in South Africa since the early 1980s, with job losses in the minerals and energy sectors. Recently, jobs in the clothing, manufacturing, construction and the public sectors have all fallen, with almost a million jobs lost between 1994 and 1997. By 2003, the strict definition of unemployment had risen to 28.2 per cent and the broad definition, that includes discouraged workers, had risen to 41.8 per cent. Moreover, formal employment fell from 69 per cent in 1994 to 49 per cent in 2001. In the 1990s there was some growth in the informal sector, including street trading and domestic work, but this sector provides low-income jobs with little security, and growth in this sector stalled around 2000 (Altman 2003:162–76). Unemployment is skewed greatly by race, gender and location. This statistic is one reason for greater rates of poverty among female-headed households and points to the need for support for these families. The same households are most affected by another threat that emerged just as apartheid was coming to an end: HIV/AIDS – which Desmond Tutu calls 'the new apartheid'.

Equity and the role of the state, the market, civil society and philanthropy

The role of the state

The government that took control in 1994 was expected to be the driving force in delivering socioeconomic equality to the poor. The African National Congress's campaign motto calls for 'a better life for all'. The demands on the new South African government were enormous. In its efforts to extend its reach to the entire population, government has confronted some equity issues more successfully than others. For example, there have been some significant increases in access to electricity, clean water, and sanitation.[7] But enormous challenges have remained, including high unemployment, inadequate housing, the need for greater access to quality education and health care in general and specifically in relation to HIV/AIDS. Although the system of social grants offers support to pensioners and single parents, very little reaches the bulk of the poor, whose poverty is as a result of unemployment.[8] Pieterse and van Donk (2002) suggest that 'the absence of a robust redistribution framework that can produce much greater income equality will prove to be the Achilles' heel of the transition project'. If the government does not address these needs sufficiently, it becomes the responsibility of other players to monitor and act as a watchdog to make sure the state is accountable and responsive to the needs of the poor.

The role of the market

It is impossible to address economic inequity without examining the role of the market in economic development. In South Africa, a debate rages on about the government's macroeconomic policy and its impact on the government's efforts at poverty eradication. The African National Congress (ANC) came into power in 1994 promoting the Reconstruction and Development Programme (RDP), which called for extensive spending on health, education, housing and basic services, with a central role for the non-governmental sector. In March 1996, the RDP office was closed and the Growth, Employment and Redistribution (GEAR) strategy was introduced. GEAR put a much greater emphasis on the broad macroeconomic framework, fiscal discipline, reduced debt and social spending. South Africa's democratic government came into power at a time when there was a global trend towards reducing the role of the state. GEAR's reliance on foreign direct investment and the private sector did not result in the rapid growth hoped for by government. Indications are that the latest two macroeconomic plans – the Accelerated Shared Growth Initiative for South Africa (ASGISA) and the New Economic Growth Plan – do not signal a major shift or a striking new approach to development.

Also up for debate are specific approaches to poverty eradication. These include privatization, cost recovery for services, labour liberalization, trade policies, social service programmes including pensions, child support grants and the proposed basic income grant. The government has been strongly criticized by trade unions and civil society for its policy, for example, on cost recovery. Increased charges for basic services such as water and electricity have affected the poor's access to and quality of services (Desai 2002; Kotze 2003). There is a growing consensus that unbridled free-market capitalism is not able to promote an equitable society. In an interview in South Africa in December 2003, George Soros stated 'markets are basically designed to allocate resources on competing private needs but there are some public goods that the markets are not designed to provide and you need to take care of those public goods'.[9]

The role of civil society

The history of the liberation movement in South Africa points to the critical role played by formations outside the state and the market. For example, many churches, women's organizations, youth groups, sporting clubs and civic associations pooled together in the early 1980s to form the United Democratic Front. A large portion of civil society at the time was motivated to bring services to the black population and to bring an end to apartheid itself. Since 1994, civil society organizations have had to redefine their role in relation to the state. The civil society sector is not homogeneous. One of the most striking findings from Swilling and Russell (2002) was that 53 per cent of South Africa's non-profit sector can be characterized as less formalized, community-based organizations. Other studies identified three distinct groupings in civil society, each of which has a particular relationship to the state (Habib and Kotze 2003). These are: 1) small community-based organizations that have limited funding and a limited relationship with the state; 2) larger urban-based NGOs that receive private funding and often partner with government for service delivery; and 3) a growing number of social movements that play a more adversarial role. These social movements are also diverse. They include, among others, the Soweto Electricity Crisis Committee and the Concerned Citizens Group in Chatsworth outside Durban, that both organize against electricity cut-offs The Treatment Action Campaign, as well as Abahlali Basemjondolo, challenges the state's policies on HIV/AIDS and promotes access to anti-retroviral drugs for AIDS sufferers.

Civil society organizations can give voice to the marginalized and they can promote greater participation. However, it is often mistakenly assumed that a strong civil society necessarily results in a stronger voice for the poor. Social and economic inequalities have an impact on the ability of the poor to participate in a political democracy. It is important that philanthropic resources be devoted to strengthening civil society, particularly the poor, marginalized populations and organizations that represent them.

The role of philanthropy and the state

Steven Burkeman (2004) explored the possibilities for a contract between endowed foundations and the state. He suggested that foundations take on long-term tasks because election-conscious governments tend to focus on short-term political imperatives. He also suggested that foundations fund more risky programmes be- cause governments tend to be risk averse. Burkeman made a third point: endowed foundations, being somewhat immune from populism, can fund the protection of minorities. In South Africa, there are relatively few endowed foundations and trusts. Philanthropy is in the form of sources such as corporations, individuals, communal mechanisms, etc.; the concept of endowments has not yet taken stronger roots. Burkeman's points are relevant in reviewing the role of philanthropy in general in South Africa. Philanthropic resources should not be spent on things that the government can do better. Rather, these should address longer-term, more intractable, riskier issues.

Philanthropy could be used to further explore the role of the state in achieving greater equality. As the Commission on Africa Report in 2005 and others have stressed, a weak state and poor governance are not likely to promote development. Private resources can bring creative thinking to the debate on the role of the state in promoting equitable development. As Howell and Pearce (2001) argue, civil society's role is not only to 'defend citizens from the state, but also [to] participate in thinking and debating the common good for a given society and how a demo- cratic state could play a role in promoting it'. If philanthropic resources in South Africa were to promote such a debate, the outcomes would benefit not only South Africa, but also other countries grappling with the same issue.

The state can promote foundations and philanthropy by offering tax privileges. Campaigns throughout the 1990s sought to broaden tax exemption for non-profits and expand tax incentives for giving. Changes proposed by the Minister of Finance in 2000 resulted in an intense period of consultation with the non-profit sector and negotiations with the South African Revenue Services (SARS). The new law came into effect in July 2001 (Nelson 2002). The old law provided tax exemption to a very narrow set of organizations defined as religious, charitable and educational. Most developmental organizations, including those involved in, for example, pov- erty eradication and gender equity, were excluded from the benefits. 'Charitable' was defined as soup kitchens and welfare work, and did not include job creation projects or other developmental programmes. The new law created a new category of 'public benefit organizations'. These organizations qualify for income tax exemption if they carry on public benefit activities, as defined by Treasury. While the old law allowed donors to deduct from their taxable income only contributions to universities, colleges and educational funds, the new law has expanded the activities for which donations are deductible.

There is enormous wealth in South Africa in private hands. As this wealth transfers to the next generation, the South African government would do well to review the estate tax. Instead of letting the money pass on to the next generation of predominantly white South Africans who will inherit their parents wealth, or taxing them so heavily that they try to hide their assets, it would be beneficial to structure estate taxes in a way that would encourage the wealthy to put some of their assets to philanthropy and development.

Philanthropy and equity in South Africa

Philanthropy in South Africa has been shaped, over time, by political pressures and the shifting social context. The roots of philanthropy are multilayered, and vary according to different cultural traditions. This section reviews six types of philanthropy in South Africa: 1) local communal giving mechanisms, 2) other forms of individual giving, 3) corporate social investment, 4) community foundations, 5) other local grantmaking organizations, and 6) international private foundations.

Local communal giving mechanisms

South Africa, as much of Africa, has a rich history of mutual support and assistance. The extended family has provided support and a safety net for many. The principle of 'one hand washes the other' is embodied in burial societies and savings clubs, where common savings are accrued for the inevitable costs that a family must bear. In a practice called *ukusisa* a relatively wealthy family in the community loans their cows to a poorer family for food and milk production. In the practice of *ilimo,* members of a community work together to assist a family with their harvest or to construct a hut. Both of these terms are isiZulu, but the concepts and practices exist in other African languages of Southern Africa as well (Moyo 2004). Another important concept in many African cultures is that an individual does not exist in isolation, but is human because of the individual's relationship with others. Mbigi summarizes the concept well when he writes:

> Africans have a thing called *ubuntu*: it is about the essence of being human; it is part of the gift that Africa is going to give the world.... We believe that a person is a person through other persons; that my humanity is caught up, bound up inextricably in yours.... The solitary human being is a contradiction in terms, and therefore

you seek work for the common good because your humanity comes into its own in community, in belonging.[10]

Other examples of communal savings mechanisms include *stokvels*, savings clubs and burial societies. These provide a way for community members to contribute to a common pot of money with the knowledge that on a regular basis (once a month or once a year) they will be able to draw from the pot. What one gives will come back when one needs it – for purchasing an appliance, paying for school fees, or even having a party when money is in short supply. Below is a brief description of each.

Stokvels

The term *stokvel* is thought to have its roots in the cattle auctions or 'stock fairs' of the English settlers in the Eastern Cape of South Africa in the early nineteenth century, where black farmers and labourers began to exchange ideas and pool their money to buy cattle. The concept of a *stokvel* was then transported to the cities when gold was discovered in the mid-1800s and large numbers of African men went to work in the mines (Lukhele 1990 as quoted in Moyo 2003).

Other historians suggest that *stokvels* were formed by black women who moved to the cities in the 1920s and 1930s, as a means of supplementing their meagre incomes. Some women started to brew beer illegally, and when they were harassed by the police other *stokvel* members would come to their aid. 'In this context, *stokvels* transcended their primary role of circulating money and became comprehensive support systems for members in time of hardship' (ibid.).' Speaking at the launch of the National Stokvels Association of South Africa (NASASA) in 1988, Andrew Lukhele estimated that there were then 4,000 *stokvels* on the outskirts of Johannesburg. Today, the number is estimated to be much larger (Moloi 2001).

Burial societies

The high costs of a funeral can put enormous strain on a family's finances. Burial societies, another form of joint savings, were developed so that a family could ensure their loved ones a proper funeral. People make monthly contributions to a burial society and then draw on the funds to cover such costs as transporting the body from the city to the ancestral, rural home and providing food at the funeral for the community. Over the past decades, the growing HIV/AIDS epidemic has put increased strain on burial societies. In 2002, the Kaiser Family Foundation published a report on the impact of HIV/AIDS, drawing on a national sample of 771 households. The study found an increase in child malnutrition, a growing number of orphans, and family breakups. In addition, the study found that 55 per cent of the sampled households had paid for a funeral in the preceding year, at an average cost of R5,153 (more than US$700 at today's exchange rate), or four times the total household monthly income. Many of the households had experienced more than one serious illness or death in the family.[11] The system, designed to support families in time of need, is now stretched beyond the breaking-point. *Ukusisa, ilimo, stokvels* and burial societies are often referred to when discussing the concept of indigenous philanthropy. Authors, including Zabala (1999) and Moyo (2003), have asked, 'Are these indigenous philanthropic social support systems or are these coping mechanisms associated with attempts at poverty alleviation?'. If someone sets up a scholarship fund for children they don't know, it is considered philanthropy, but if the same person pays the school fees for children within their extended family, it is considered an obligation. Clearly, these types of giving and mutual aid groups serve the needs of the broader community. When exploring how to promote philanthropy, it is crucial to build on these already existing mechanisms. Contacts between these forms of local community giving and larger, more Western forms of philanthropy are limited.

More could be done by local grantmaking organizations, community foundations, and others to build on what exists on the ground. It is surprising how little research exists to document the function and impact of various types of mutual support organizations, such as burial societies and *stokvels*. Research in this arena would greatly inform the rest of the field of philanthropy. Whether mutual support associations have had an impact on equity can be answered in several ways. First, these mechanisms assist people to actively engage in solving problems facing their communities. Secondly, they are 'coping' mechanisms that allow people with few resources to hang on; and it is important not to place more pressure on them than they can bear. Development practitioners see community participation as the first step in putting together effective projects and advocacy campaigns.[12] Yet many NGOs and development agencies often overlook mutual assistance organizations as potential actors in the development process.[13] As Susan Wilkinson-Maposa wrote in 2005:

> The research has uncovered evidence of sophisticated and well-established systems of giving and receiving help in communities battling chronic poverty. The data portrays the poor as resilient and reliable givers who mobilize and redistribute limited resources within their communities through families, neighbours and local associations. Understanding and respecting these systems and their rules and channels and how they vary, could point towards strategies that work more effectively in poor communities to alleviate poverty (Wilkinson-Maposa 2005).

Just as it is important to recognize their existence and their potential, it is also important to recognize, and not to glorify, the strain being placed on burial societies and other mutual support associations. Given prevailing poverty, unemployment and HIV/AIDS, these mechanisms are stretched beyond their means and could be at their breaking-point (Kotze 2003).

There are other forms of giving, particularly individual giving of time, money and goods. In all these, religion seems to play a major role in shaping the form and perhaps content of giving and to what cause. Historically, religious institutions have tended to support the charitable needs of the poor, the sick, children and the elderly.[14] Alumni giving is another area that needs attention in South Africa. Universities do not appear to benefit as much from alumni giving as they do in the United States. A survey conducted by the University of Cape Town indicated that their alumni have a preference for charitable and religious causes, rather than to support large institutions such as universities, museums, and libraries. They perceive support of such institutions as the responsibility of government rather than individuals.[15] Surveys of other institutions would be instructive in gathering a broader sense of patterns and perceptions of alumni giving. Inyathelo, the Institute for Advancement, began a five-year, US$10 million programme in 2006 funded by the US-based Kresge Foundation. The initiative supports four institutions – the University of the Western Cape, the Cape Peninsula University of Technology, the Red Cross Children's Hospital and the University of Pretoria. One of the major objectives is to build local giving to these institutions, especially from individuals, including alumni.[16]

Family foundations

Hylton Applebaum, the Executive Trustee for his father-in-law's foundation, the Donald Gordon Foundation, suggests that individual philanthropy in South Africa is 'an endangered species'. He cited two major reasons for this. First, there are no tax incentives to promote giving as there are in the United States and, second, South African society is 'racially, linguistically, culturally, and politically divided'. Applebaum's comments are focused predominantly on philanthropy from within a group of wealthy, white South Africans. He implies that such individuals may have thrived in the past, but the numbers are shrinking. Unfortunately, the numbers were never that high and few of them have taken the opportunity (as Donald Gordon did) to establish a family trust or private foundation.[17]

Ann Micou's *The Donor Community in South Africa: A Directory* (July 1993) was the first comprehensive donor directory in South Africa. She sent surveys to over 700 individuals, trusts, foundations and companies; 258 (37 per cent) responded, and 24 of these (9 per cent) were individual and family trusts. While corporate donors have figured prominently in the National Business Initiative and the *CSI Handbook*, there is no equivalent source of information about individual and family trusts. *The SAGA Donor Directory 2003/04*, for example, had a section on trusts and foundations, but it lumped international private foundations and local corporate trusts together with family trusts and foundations. The most current source of information is the donor database in the PRODDER Directory online at www.prodder.org.za but again there is no separate listing for family foundations.

Additional research is needed to gauge whether family trusts and foundations resources are addressing equity issues in South Africa. While their number is said to be growing, they generally do not disclose the grants they make. The Ackermans, founders of the Pick 'n Pay retail stores, is another family that has established a family trust. Wendy Ackerman comments, 'We as a family and a company have tended to work in isolation.' While the Applebaums and the Ackermans are relatively open about their grantmaking, her comment appears to confirm that most family trusts in South Africa prefer to work quietly on their own. In addition to the Ackermans and the Applebaums, several black South African businessmen, including Patrice Motsepe, Cyril Ramaphosa and Tokyo Sexwale, have set up their own philanthropic institutions and have since joined the Global Philanthropist Circle (GPC), an initiative of the New York-based Synergos Institute. Tokyo Sexwale, for example, was quoted in the *Sunday Times* in March 2005 saying:

> Black Economic Empowerment is about philanthropy. As my mother says, 'You have one pair of legs, my son, you can't take this money with you.' In the end you are going to leave it behind. So philanthropy is what we do, almost every day. We do so without claiming victories. We give money to schools, we fight HIV/AIDS, we provide university fees, we build clinics, and we build hospitals – both in South Africa and in neighbouring countries.

Given the cultural practices of giving discussed earlier, it is likely that the High Net Worth Individuals emerging from Black Economic Empowerment (BEE) have been involved in giving within their own extended families and communities. There are signs that this approach to giving is broadening to include formalized and institutionalized giving through the establishment of family trusts and foundations. However, progress has been slow. Given their distinct past, emerging from South Africa's formerly disenfranchised population, individuals who have benefited from BEE theoretically could act as role models to establish family foundations with strategic programmes to address clear needs for greater equity. However, such a pattern may not develop, given the standard set by many other South African family foundations to stay small and play it safe.

Has individual giving and family philanthropy contributed to equity issues? Available data and analyses suggest that individual giving efforts are generally neither coordinated nor focused on the root causes of inequity. With few exceptions, family foundations and other forms of individual giving go to charitable and religious causes. The challenge is how such giving can be targeted to support those who are most marginalized and give them a voice in policy development and reform.

Online giving is another area to be explored, as more and more South Africans resort to cyberspace. There is certainly potential for online giving to grow in the future.

Corporate social investment

Corporate giving is one of the largest sources of funding for civil society in South Africa. According to Swilling and Russell (2002), private-sector funding accounted for 25 per cent of all non-profit income in South Africa, compared to an average of 11 per cent in 28 other countries in the study. Despite the fact that they provide significant support, companies remain reluctant to work with the most marginalized, promote their voice and support advocacy campaigns. As of 2005/6, corporate social investment (CSI) funds had gone predominantly to education and training (42 per cent) and health and social development (33 per cent), with the remainder going to a combination of job creation, sports, environment, arts and culture, safety and security, and housing (in descending order of size of contribution).

The total funding from corporate grantmakers in 2006 was R2.88 billion, an 8.9 per cent increase over 2005 and up from R980 million in 1987 when the first tracking of CSI expenditure began. As the *CSI Handbook* (2006:41) stated: 'This appears to be a massive increase, but if one adjusts for inflation, it should be noted that real CSI expenditure over the last decade or so has remained fairly constant and only an 8 per cent increase in real terms since 1987'.

Ironically, it was apartheid and the consequent social unrest and threat to the economy that provided the first real stimulus for CSI. After the 1976 student uprisings in Soweto, several companies banded together to establish the Urban Foundation, which focused on urban development, housing and education in black townships. At about the same time, the Sullivan Principles were introduced, requiring American companies to justify their presence in the country by contributing to local communities. This encouraged more formalized giving by the private sector in general. In 1984–85, the groundswell of opposition to apartheid and the international attention it received brought a further stimulus to corporate giving. Also in the 1980s, in response to the country's economic and cultural isolation, the South African apartheid government offered generous tax incentives to business to sponsor South African sports. South African companies responded by spending about R500 million annually on such sponsorships in the late 1980s and early 1990s.

The Urban Foundation's support of community centres, and education and training in black townships was modest in amount and did little to dismantle the system that kept black people in those townships in the first place. Other efforts to pool company funds – the Joint Education Trust (JET), formed in 1992, and the Business Trust, formed in 1999 – similarly focused more on service delivery, but also looked at institutional change. The Business Trust has developed programmes related to crime, higher education and job creation. To date, there has been no comprehensive impact evaluation of the Business Trust. However, a case study written by its CEO Brian Whittaker begins to set out some of the lessons learned.

Over the past ten years, companies have recognized the impact of HIV/AIDS, and funding for health and social development has increased significantly. Most corporate funding has focused on HIV/AIDS education and prevention, given the government's initial reluctance to recognize the need for anti-retroviral (ARV) therapy. The long-awaited roll out of ARVs began in 2004 and currently reaches only about 20 per cent of those who need it. To cite one example of corporate involvement, Toyota in Durban became one of the first corporates to reach agreement with the Department of Health to serve Toyota's 9,500 employees. Public-sector anti-retroviral (ARV) sites provide initial treatment and Toyota provides counselling, blood tests and follow-up (Whittington Banda 2006).

Most corporate HIV/AIDS programmes emphasize service delivery. Relatively few CSI initiatives advocate major policy reform or fund organizations such as the Treatment Action Campaign that provide a voice for those outside the arena of policy formation. Nor has CSI paid much attention to rural areas or the needs of women. It is relevant to mention that, in the wake of the closing of the Southern Africa Grantmakers Association (SAGA) in 2006, there has been a growing call for corporations to increase their information sharing and collaboration in new ways so as to become more effective. The *CSI Handbook* (2006:156) presented a collaboration tool in their 2006 edition in an effort to encourage greater communication among practitioners working in education, job creation, health and social development.

BEE and CSI

In the wake of the broad-based Black Economic Empowerment Act signed into law in January 2004, the Department of Trade and Industry released a set of BEE Codes of Good Practice and a BEE Scorecard in December 2005, calling for public comment. These were finalised as law in February 2007 and provide specific targets for seven elements of business, including ownership, management and control, employment equity, skills development, preferential procurement, enterprise development and socioeconomic development. While the draft code referred specifically to a CSI component, the final language refers to 'socioeconomic development'. The BEE Scorecard prescribes that companies spend 1 per cent of after-tax profit on initiatives to promote socioeconomic development and 3 per cent to promote enterprise development. There are set targets and expenditure requirements for each of the seven elements that affect an overall BEE 'score'. While one might assume that this is good news for those looking for more corporate resources to address development challenges, some CSI practitioners have expressed concern that the BEE Scorecard will result in companies moving away from strategic thinking to focusing on compliance only. Zinzi Mgolodela from Woolworths states 'Some of us are concerned that many companies will adopt a "tick-the-box" approach', and focus only on what will keep them safe on the scorecard' (ibid.:19). Also, the scorecard refers only to the amount of financial resources devoted to CSI and black empowerment, which has no bearing on whether any of those funds will be used to address the structural reasons for inequality.

Another aspect of BEE worth exploring is the extent to which BEE companies are engaging with corporate social investment. Tokyo Sexwale's Mvelaphanda Holdings set up the Mvela Trust. However, there is limited information available about its mission and programmes. In 2004, Cyril Ramaphosa's corporate group established the Shanduka Foundation 'through which we have committed ourselves to investing R100 million over the next ten years – in projects relating to education, training and small business development' (ibid.:xiv). The Shanduka Foundation runs the Adopt-a-School programme encouraging companies to adopt and support schools in an ongoing way. As of December 2006, it had engaged with 26 schools.[18]

BEE companies not only need to comply with the new BEE scorecard, but they also meet with social pressures from their peers and from those in society who are less fortunate. At this stage, BEE companies, as a whole, are not taking the lead in creating social change with their profits. There are several reasons to argue that CSI does not focus on those who are most marginalized. First, most companies are urban based and their development efforts reflect this. Most CSI spending is targeted towards urban and peri-urban areas, leaving only a third targeted towards rural communities. Given the high levels of poverty in rural areas, these percentages seem to be in inverse proportion to need. Second, 15 per cent of the funds from CSI programmes go to company employees and their families and another 49 per cent on the communities in which the companies operate. The result is that people and communities who have little or no connection to corporate South Africa, as employees or customers, are badly underserved. With the broadly defined unemployment rate at over 40 per cent, CSI is not reaching those who are most marginalized and have least access to resources and information (CSI 2003). Third, the government has promoted the concept of public–private partnerships to address social needs and implement government programmes. Companies are encouraged to partner in order to achieve greater exposure and win government favour. It is unlikely, therefore, that companies will publicly criticize government policy or support local communities and organizations that do so. Fourth, most CSI budgets in the UK and the US are determined by a formula of pre- or post-tax profits. In contrast, most CSI budgets in South Africa are not calculated this way. As a result, budgets are more vulnerable to the arbitrary decisions of management and less likely to be strategically focused. Finally, when it comes to evaluation, companies tend to focus on inputs and anecdotal evidence, with little effort to assess developmental impact, lessons learned and implications for policy reform. Therefore, without giving attention to the weaknesses outlined above, CSI is unlikely to make any significant contribution to greater equity in South Africa.

Community foundations

In the early 1990s, the Ford, Mott and Kellogg Foundations began to explore the potential for community foundations in South Africa. In 1994, Kellogg funded a small group of South Africans interested in learning more about community foundations to visit the US. Later that year, Mott and Ford commissioned a study by the Cape Town-based Foundation for Contemporary Research (FCR) on the applicability of the community foundation model to South Africa. FCR's final report, completed in mid-1995, did not discuss in detail how community foundations could take root in South Africa, but it did suggest that the concept could be viable and was worthy of further investigation. In 1996, the then newly formed Southern Africa Grantmakers Association (SAGA) held a workshop on community foundations and in late 1997 launched a five-year pilot programme to test the feasibility of the community foundation concept in South Africa. From 1998 to 2002, SAGA worked closely with ten communities. The initial model presented to South Africa was predominantly based on the US experience. Over time, several of the fledgling community foundations in small towns and rural areas failed. Those started in the large metropolitan areas of Pretoria and Durban, after seemingly promising starts, faltered as well. The Durban Community Foundation continues to exist, not as a fully independent foundation but rather as a vehicle for local government. The Pretoria effort collapsed. The five-year community foundation pilot programme at SAGA was brought to a close in 2003.

Why so many of the pilot sites failed needs to be addressed, but is beyond the scope of this chapter. By 2004, two community foundations from the pilot remained as the front runners: the Uthungulu Community Foundation (UCF) in Richards Bay, KwaZulu Natal, and the Greater Rustenburg Community Foundation (GRCF) in Rustenburg, North West Province. More have since come up again including the West Coast Community Foundation and the Community Development Foundation of the Western Cape.

How have community foundations impacted on equity? No doubt the role of community foundations in addressing the need for greater equity is a concern in the United States as well as in South Africa. Emmett Carson (2002), in his May 2002 keynote address to the Community Foundations of Canada national conference, stated, 'Community foundations have not always modeled the best practices of diversity and have not always been at the forefront of championing dialogue and action on the most difficult social issues facing the community.'

Carson observed that 'the growing obsession of US community foundations on asset accumulation is shifting the focus of community foundations around the world away from discussions about civil society, inclusive diversity practices, community building and social justice' (ibid.). No matter how much an individual community foundation in Mexico or Brazil, Thailand or South Africa might want to develop an emphasis on equity and social justice, if they do not build any endowment assets, they will get low marks from the international community foundation community, led by the big private foundations in the US and the big associations of foundations in the US, Europe and globally. While South Africans interested in the community foundation model may have been initially interested in how best to address development needs and inequity in South Africa, they ended up focusing predominantly on building an endowment and raising assets.

The community foundation model is appealing and can inspire passion to develop locally controlled institutions that mobilize local resources to address local needs. However, some of the appeal of the model globally is that international donors are interested to promote it. It is important to remember that community foundations are one possible vehicle to promote institutional philanthropy, not *the* universal model of institutional/organized philanthropy (Kuljian 2003). The Global Fund for Community Foundations has embraced this approach and has worked hard to strengthen a range of different organizational types since it was formed in 2006.

Other local grantmaking organizations

European governments and other international donors in the 1980s looked for credible local agencies through which to channel their funds. The three largest were Kagiso Trust, the South African Council of Churches (SACC) and the South African Catholic Bishops Conference (SACBC). Unlike many other countries, South Africa has a history of development funding that flowed to a set of indigenous organizations, as opposed to international NGOs. This history helped to build a set of local South African development funding organizations that continue to operate today, such as Kagiso Trust and the Social Change Assistance Trust. Another aberration of South African history that resulted in the development of local grantmaking organizations was the divestment campaign of the 1980s. As a result of the campaign, several American companies decided to divest and leave behind major endowed funds. Others decided to stay in South Africa but created endowed funds as well. Organizations with endowed funds that were created at that time include:

- Equal Opportunity Foundation (created by Coca Cola) in Cape Town;
- Pretoria Development Trust, the Trust for Educational Advancement (established by the Ford Motor Company);
- Algoa Bay Charitable Trust (also established by the Ford Motor Company); and
- The Zenex Foundation (formerly the Human Resources Trust, then the Youth Development Trust), established by the Xerox Corporation.

These organizations still exist (with Zenex as the most active and prominent the four, but have remained limited in their scope and public profile. This raises the important question: Is establishing an endowment useful when the future governance, leadership and mission of the organization are not assured? Despite good intentions, none of these organizations have gone on to make a major contribution toward equity issues in South Africa. Yet they still continue to exist because endowments give them eternal life. Endowing a grantmaker does not assure that it will remain socially relevant. This should be a lesson to community foundations and other non-profits that build endowments. They must not only focus on endowment building, but must also work to keep their organizations focused on South Africa's most fundamental challenges.

Trends

There are a growing number of domestic trusts and foundations that derive their income from a variety of sources and are diverse in terms of their operations and funding. No information on these trusts and foundations as a collective group has been found in the course of this research. It is therefore difficult to determine whether funds from these sources has increased or decreased over the past decade or whether these funds tend to flow towards the need for greater equity.

The Southern Africa office of the Synergos Institute established a Community Grantmakers Learning Cooperative in 2005. There are close to 30 member organizations from countries in the region including South Africa, Zimbabwe and Mozambique. Some members are local grantmaking organizations that were established to fund community-based organizations in a particular geographic area, such as the Ikhala Trust in the Eastern Cape and the Dockda Rural Development Trust in the Northern Cape. Others exist to fund a particular sector, such as the WHEAT Trust, funding women's rights and women's development, the Aids Foundation to fund HIV/AIDs, and the Nelson Mandela Children's Fund (NMCF) to fund children and youth. NMCF is particularly significant in that Nelson Mandela set an example by pledging a portion of his own income to establish the organization.

There is another set of local grantmakers called community chests, including the Community Chest of the Western Cape and the UBUNTU Community Chest, that have their history rooted in the 1920s and take an approach similar to the United States-based United Way. Yet another set of local grantmakers were initiated by international bilateral funding agencies. The European Union established the Foundation for Human Rights (FHR), that focuses on human rights and access to legal justice, and Themba Lesizwe, that focuses on trauma (sadly, Themba Lesizwe closed in 2007). The British Department for International Development (DfID) established the Southern Africa Trust, with the mission to reduce poverty and inequality in Southern Africa by strengthening the voice of poor people in the public policy process. These local grantmakers offer great potential in the sense that, in name and mission, they focus on equity and rights. Tracking their efforts and documenting their experience will be important. Impact assessments can help assess whether these local grantmakers have had an impact on issues of equity and social justice.

However, there has been limited research on this important set of development funders in South Africa. It would be useful to look more closely at them to assess whether, as a group, they have focused on equity issues. It would be useful to explore what factors affect whether or not such local grantmakers focus on structural change to promote equity. Does it make any difference as to whether the local grantmaker has received support predominantly from private foundations, corporate funders, bilateral funding or a combination of sources? Do issues of donor flexibility, leadership and governance make a difference?

Some large NGOs have been pushed to become intermediary grantmakers, and donors then delegate to them the task of administering funding for smaller non-profits. It is bilateral government donors, predominantly, that have followed this pattern, but some international private foundations are also looking for the best way to cut down on their administrative load. It is important in these cases to guard against 'funding channels quickly turning into funding chains' (Galvin 2000).

Despite the paucity of current research, it appears that local grantmakers have greater potential than corporate or individual giving to address equity issues. For example, these organizations, theoretically, are considered to be more in touch with grassroots needs. Also, by virtue of the fact that many of them fund community-based organizations, they have a more direct relationship to marginalized communities and therefore a greater ability to encourage community mobilization and advocacy initiatives.

Unfortunately, one of these grantmakers, the International Fundraising Consortium (Interfund), closed in July 2005. Its demise was significant because, at its peak, it provided funding support of R30 million annually to 350 organizations across the country. When this 20-year-old organization closed, there was a sense that the country had lost an example of a funder that had begun to reach marginalized communities and was willing to engage with policy and advocacy issues related to equity.[19]

International private foundations

United States private foundations have had a long history of working in South Africa. An early example is the Carnegie Corporation of New York supporting the Carnegie Commission on the Poor White Problem in the 1930s. Support grew throughout the late 1980s and early 1990s. In 1996, the Southern African Grantmakers Affinity Group in the US sponsored research on levels of US private foundation giving in the region. The findings indicated that 43 US foundations were active in the region with expenditures of US$55.4 million, a 27 per cent increase over the US$43.5 million spent in 1994. All but six of the 43 foundations with Southern African programmes were engaged in grantmaking in or related to South Africa and three-quarters of the total US$55.4 million was earmarked for South Africa.[20] The research found that, while several foundations focused on community level programmes, many 'put considerable emphasis on policy analysis and the generation of new policy options in education, health, environmental protection, and other major development sectors'. The researchers classified the five top-priority fields as education, health, human rights and governance, women's issues (including women's rights) and agriculture and rural development.

Comprehensive, annual data on sources of international private giving to South Africa is not readily available. However, *The State of Social Giving* project investigated private foreign giving and concluded that there are more than 70 foreign-based private foundations and almost 60 faith-based and non-governmental organizations with a development/poverty focus currently active in South Africa. The authors of the Nonprofit Study linked to Johns Hopkins 'assumed on the basis of anecdotal evidence and received wisdom in the sector, that the US based foundations are the largest funders of South African NPOs' (Swilling and Russell 2002). This assumption may have been influenced by the fact that many bilateral donors shifted their funds from NGOs to government after 1994 and private foundations continued to fund civil society. However, funding civil society does not always translate to the promotion of equity. In fact, there are indications that it has been the smaller, community-based organizations that have lost funding as a result of shifts in donor funding trends.

Despite this trend, there are several examples that show that international private foundations have developed programmes focusing on advocacy for marginalized communities. Atlantic Philanthropies programme focuses on reconciliation and human-rights-funded refugees, farm workers and other marginalized communities. Atlantic has also provided significant support to the Treatment Action Campaign. The Ford Foundation supports programming focused on human rights, social and economic rights, and public-interest litigation. The Kaiser Family Foundation focuses on health and HIV/AIDS in South Africa, and the Kellogg Foundation used to have programmes focused on rural development. While these foundations have spent great deals of money on evaluations and assessments, there is no single repository that gathers and analyzes the work of private foundations and their impact on equity in South Africa.

Conclusion

Philanthropy is an important aspect of, but is not sufficient to ensure, a democratic and equitable society. Such societies do not rely merely on generous individuals and companies that give back a percentage of their profits to community needs. Democratic societies need democratic governance and just and accessible institutions – both public and private – that build a more equitable society. In South Africa, poverty and unemployment, as well as other forms of inequity, could continue as a reality for generations to come, especially given the pace at which these issues are being addressed. Those who benefit from South Africa's economy need to move more quickly to implement strategies that address South Africa's poverty. It is the role of the government to align incentives and guide big business in that direction. Government must promote redistributive justice that includes attention to assets such as land reform, as well as income transfer such as pensions, child support grants, and a basic income grant.

Traditional philanthropy has developed as the way that wealth accumulation by a small proportion of the population is used to address unmet basic needs for those who are lucky enough to be the beneficiaries. This model is not sustainable nor worth replicating. In South Africa, there is a need to explore an alternative vision of philanthropy.[21] Philanthropic resources can be targeted to address the rights offered to South Africans under the Constitution and provide for greater equity across gender, race and socioeconomic status. In order to achieve this vision, philanthropy will have to better address the structural issues of inequity. This can be done in a number of ways. One way in which the role of philanthropic giving can be enhanced to greater address inequity is by supporting non-governmental groups that represent those most affected by inequity so that they can voice their views and advocate for themselves. This approach involves support for civil society organizations that foster greater voice and participation for those who are marginalized; it also includes support to groups to demand accountability from state actors, influence public policy, and in other cases demand accountability from the private sector.

There is also a great need to advocate for public accountability in order for existing policies to be implemented and for rights under the law to be made more accessible. For example, access to justice in general and women's rights in particular is in need of greater support from the philanthropic sector. Local paralegal advice offices that operate in poor communities do not receive adequate support, often because their work does not provide grantmakers with short-term outcomes. Without a longer-term approach it is clear that funding efforts will continue to focus on service delivery for a few, without providing structural change. Another way to promote equity is to support existing forms of philanthropy and giving that have an explicit focus on equity, provide the opportunity for marginalized groups to control and allocate resources, and have a greater inclination to support groups calling for change. Philanthropy should build upon existing *local* South African institutions that already address inequities. It is possible to build on existing processes of giving such as *stokvels* and savings clubs. The WHEAT Trust, the Social Change Assistance Trust and the Foundation for Human Rights are examples of local grantmakers that make greater equity their focus. It is still to be determined if other local grantmakers such as community foundations will address inequity in any significant way. While some international private foundations have made a contribution towards equity issues and grantmaking for social change, they cannot be relied on to play that role in the long term. It is critical that local, South African institutions take on this approach. They will be better positioned to support such efforts in the long term, and to work at a more local and provincial level. A commensurate need is for philanthropy to build the capacity of local organizations focused on transformation and social justice. It is not only how much money can be summoned to a particular issue, but also the strategies used and the resources devoted to ensure institutional capacity and effective delivery.

In addition to providing advocacy and capacity-building support to groups that are addressing inequity, another area in which philanthropy can make a greater impact is in supporting a space for public dialogue on important social issues. Just a few examples of such issues in South Africa are the stigma surrounding HIV/ AIDS, violence against women, access to justice, and how to support a safety net for those living in poverty. In these cases, convening people to talk about an issue publicly could initiate needed public debate and could possibly influence public opinion. Creating public dialogue around social and economic inequalities can make a major contribution and give these issues greater legitimacy. Given the concern in South Africa for growing inequality, any philanthropic organization that adopted such an approach would likely receive significant public support.

As South Africa looks ahead to the twentieth anniversary of democracy in 2014, philanthropic resources can make a difference to whether there will be greater social and economic equity to celebrate or not. A scenario planning exercise in Cape Town put forward one scenario for 2020 in which:

> South Africa is considered a social and economic miracle. Not only did it reach all the millennium development goals, it has eliminated backlogs in social infrastructure, services and its education and skills deficit. The president, in her state of the nation address to parliament, proudly announces that for the first time not a single South African lives in destitution. A major black economic empowerment player has partnered with *stokvels* in Soweto to form a community bank providing finance at competitive rates to local business and for community development. Others have followed suit, giving many access to capital (Hooper-Box 2005).

With less than a decade to go before 2020, and given the current levels of poverty and inequality in South Africa, it is unlikely that this scenario will be achieved. It is possible, however, for South Africa's philanthropic actors to play an important role in contributing to this vision for the future. In order to do so, they will need to be bold, take on the root causes of inequality and promote a greater voice for equity.

Endnotes

1   This chapter is based on a paper originally commissioned by the Global Equity Initiative (GEI) at Harvard University and completed in 2005. I would like to thank Adele Simmons, Paula Johnson and Lincoln Chen for offering me the opportunity to write this paper. I owe a great debt of thanks to Barbara Merz for having the patience and persistence needed to convince me to finish it. Thank you to Peter Geithner for his critical editing assistance at the end. Outside the GEI fold, I'm indebted to Caroline Hartnell and Gerry Salole for taking time to read through an early draft and offer wise and useful advice, even though I didn't always take it, and to Malusi Mpumlwana for commenting on a later draft. I'd also like to thank all of my colleagues at the C.S. Mott Foundation, especially Bill White, for offering me the opportunity to open the Mott Foundation's South Africa office and run it for over a decade. I couldn't have asked for a more amazing life opportunity than that, and without that experience I wouldn't have had much to say in this paper. Lastly, I greatly appreciate the Ford Foundation's decision to include this paper as a chapter in this book. I'm grateful to Tade Akin Aina, Jenny Hodgson, and Bhekinkosi Moyo who saw the book to completion.

2   Interview with Nelson Mandela by Christa Kuljian, published in 'South Africa: Tapping Local Resources to Address Local Needs', *In Focus*, Charles Stewart Mott Foundation, October 2001.

3   Quoted from briefing session at the Synergos Global Senior Fellows Meeting, July 2004, Philippines.

4   For more information on this research, see http://www.ukzn.ac.za/ccs/ and click on 'Social Giving' under CCS Research.

5   I want to state my own uneasiness with the term 'philanthropy'. I feel that the term connotes a sense of misplaced nobility. In South Africa, or in any developing country context, I rarely use the term. I feel more comfortable discussing 'development funding' and how to 'encourage local giving', which implies the need to work with local organizations on local priorities to promote development that makes sense in the context of changing circumstances.

6   Offered by Bruce Shearer of Synergos at a GEI seminar in September 2002.

7   Government Communication and Information Service (GCIS) on behalf of the Presidency, *Toward a Ten Year Review*, October 2003, 24–5.

8   Seekings and Nattrass (2005:381) argue that an expansion of low-wage jobs must be accompanied by greater educational opportunities for poor children, redistribution of assets including land, and greater assistance to the unemployed poor.

9   Interview with Tim Modise on *Carte Blanche*, December 7, 2003.

10   Mbigi as quoted in Kellogg Foundation background paper on African philanthropy, 2002.

11   *Henry J. Kaiser Family Foundation Report 2002* as quoted in Kotze 2003.

12   This assumption is thoroughly investigated and deconstructed in 'Development and community participation: decoding the conceptual 'stock and trade' of the voluntary sector' by Edgar Pieterse in *Development Update* 1998. Pieterse asserts that 'the supposedly 'representative' community organizations and structures with which development NGOs choose to work are often not representative at all. They may be controlled by elites, rife with conflict and they may ignore the interests of women and other marginal social groups.'

13   I am grateful to Gerry Salole (1991) for raising this point in his paper on mutual support associations in Ethiopia, which has relevance for Southern Africa as well.

14   It is important to note that in South Africa, in the late 1960s and early 1970s, some of the first non-governmental organizations focused on poverty and economic development came out of the churches, including the Edendale Lay Ecumenical Centre, the Christian Institute and the South African Council of Churches. Thank you to Malusi Mpumlwana for helping me to clarify this point.

15   Author's conversation with Shelagh Gastrow of Inyathelo, Institute for Advancement, Cape Town.

16   For more information, see Inyathelo's website at www.inyathelo.co.za.

17   For more information on the Donald Gordon Foundation and the entire interview with Hylton Applebaum, see *Global Giving Matters*, Issue 8, October–November 2002, Edited by Synergos/World Economic Forum (2002).

18   See December 2006 article in *Engineering News* at www.engineeringnews.co.za/article.php?a_id=97733.

19   For a more detailed exploration of the reasons for Interfund's closing and its impact, see Kuljian (2005) at www.allavida.org/alliance/axdec05f.html.

20   These ten foundations, in descending order of magnitude in 1995, were W. K. Kellogg, Ford, Rockefeller, Open Society, Henry J. Kaiser Family Foundation, Andrew

M. Mellon, C.S. Mott, Genesis, Carnegie Corporation and the MacArthur Foundation. Kaiser, Mellon and Mott confined their grantmaking in the region to South Africa.

21 See interview with Kavita Ramdas (2004:26), for further comment on the need for a new model for philanthropy.

CHAPTER 8

CONCEPTUAL FRAMEWORKS INFLUENCING SOCIAL JUSTICE PHILANTHROPY: A STUDY OF INDEPENDENT FUNDERS IN SOUTH AFRICA[1]

HALIMA MAHOMED

Introduction

Social justice philanthropy is an increasingly common term with a multitude of interpretations. This chapter examines interpretations of social justice philanthropy, and puts forward a modified South African conceptualization of the terminology in relation to existing northern frameworks. Based on this vantage point, the chapter then outlines the conceptual ideas and motivations that influence whether and why Independent Funders in South Africa engage in philanthropy that addresses the symptoms and impacts of social injustice or its underlying causes.

Social justice philanthropy is often referred to as philanthropy which supports efforts to address the structural dynamics underlying social injustice. This practice, however, is not very common amongst South African funders. According to Kuljian (2005) and also in this volume, philanthropic funding efforts that seek to mitigate the impacts of poverty and inequality, referred to here as traditional[2] philanthropy, are preferred to funding for efforts that seek to address its structural foundations.

Given that philanthropic institutions are themselves rooted in various sectors of society,[3] a general sample of funders could not be used. Accordingly, this study sought to isolate a specific type of funder, that is, one that has the independence and flexibility to make its own decisions. Referred to here as South African Independent Funders (IFs), the term denotes organizations that (i) are indigenous to and with headquarters in South Africa and (ii) have independent boards whose grantmaking decisions and processes are autonomous from institutions or mandates that are external to the organization (thus, family foundations, corporate social investment agencies, faith-based foundations and state funding agencies are excluded from this study). Within this pool, a further classification was made: (i) educational bursary providers and disaster/emergency relief funders were omitted, as these have very specific mandates at the outset, (ii) only IFs whose grantmaking coverage is equivalent to or greater than a district[4] were included (thus small community or workers' trusts have been excluded) and (iii) only IFs who have engaged in at least two grantmaking cycles were included. Based on these criteria, a population of 24 IFs was identified. These 24 funders were identified with the recognition that a small number of additional organizations could be identified during the actual research process. One more organization was subsequently identified, bringing the total population to 25.

Utilising a qualitative methodology, the study combined documentary analysis as well as in-depth interviews with the leaders of IFs in South Africa. Employing a stratified purposeful sampling method, the population of IFs was first divided into two groups (i) those that appear to engage in social justice philanthropy (Group A, which comprises 41 per cent of the sample) and (ii) those who either appear to engage in traditional philanthropy or for whom information at hand was not adequate enough to make a determination (Group B, which comprises 59 per cent of the sample). These were then further categorized according to scale of operation (national vs. district/provincial) and geographic location. Excluding one interview cancellation on the last day of fieldwork, a total of 15 IFs across five provinces (the total population covered six provinces), representing both national and district/provincial level funders and representing both social justice and traditional philanthropy organizations were interviewed. The interview sample represented 60 per cent of the identified population.

In addition, in-depth interviews were also conducted with experts in the South African philanthropic arena. These experts represent a very small and specialized cluster of international private foundations, academic institutes, civil society organizations and independent consultants, each of which plays an important direct role in facilitating philanthropic activity and/or shaping theoretical thinking around philanthropy in South Africa. Through random selection, eight experts were interviewed.

Core questions

Academic research on South African philanthropy is still in its infancy and there is little baseline information on the South African context from which to begin this particular study. Key texts on South African philanthropy include Kuljian's (2005) paper on the role of philanthropy and equity in South Africa; Wilkinson-Maposa

(2005), who looks at vertical giving amongst the poor; Moyo (2004), who looks at the challenges and opportunities related to philanthropy in Southern Africa; Habib & Maharaj's (2007) compilation of papers on different resource flows for poverty alleviation and development in South Africa; [5] and Fig (2007), who looks at the issue of corporate social environmental responsibility. To date, however, there is no academic analysis of the conceptual framework and strategies of South African funders in general or of social justice philanthropy in South Africa.

Using Kuljian's (2005) paper 'Philanthropy and Equity' – which asserts that the majority of South African philanthropic entities do not engage on issues related to equity (a critical component of social justice) – as a baseline, this chapter reflects on the strategies and reasons for the engagement (or lack thereof). Cognisant of not taking the terminology of social justice philanthropy for granted, the research first explored a South African conceptualization of social justice philanthropy in relation to existing northern frameworks and the implications this has for local practice. This was followed by an exploration of IFs' understandings of the development challenges in the contexts within which they work; how they perceive their role in regards to these challenges; and how they perceive their role in relation to that of other development actors. Finally, the research investigated the ideas, visions and frameworks that motivate these organizations and shape their programmes.

Reflections on the literature

The issue of the variations in the use and understanding of terminology related to social justice philanthropy was central to this research. Before unpacking this, however, a brief discussion of the term social justice is necessary. Commonly used in relation to development initiatives and objectives, there is no common agreed-upon definition of social justice. The World Bank Institute's Development Education Programme states that social justice is linked to 'equality of opportunities for well-being, both within and among generations of people ... having at least three aspects: economic, social, and environmental'. The World Social Forum (WSF) Charter of Principles refers to 'social justice, equality and sovereignty' but there is no explicit WSF definition. Similarly, a review of United Nations Development Programme (UNDP) literature reflects use of the term as an important factor in their goals and strategies, yet there appears to be no UNDP definition. A multitude of other documents all use the terminology implicitly, without defining what it means. Moreover, there appears to be no consensus or discussion on whether the term refers to a strategy, a goal or a conceptual/ideological framework.

A review of literature relating to the theory of social justice also reflects fundamental differences.[6] To illuminate some of the contestation: Rawls advocates the notion of 'justice as fairness' and the way in which the social institutions distribute fundamental rights and duties (Craig 2005:1). Robert Nozick (Clayton and Williams 2004) focuses on justice of entitlements; Ronald Dworkin (ibid.) emphasizes the equality of resources; Amartya Sen (1999:18) posits the idea that the focus of a just society is in expanding the capabilities of people to lead the kinds of lives they have reason to value; Elizabeth Anderson looks at the elimination of oppression and the fostering of equal social relations, and Brian Barry (2005:17) looks at the interlinked patterns of injustice. Each of these theorists makes detailed philosophical arguments that have different implications for what constitutes a just society and different implications for the mechanisms that are required to attain a just society. Elements of these philosophical arguments, particularly those raised by Rawls, Sen, Anderson and Barry can be seen in the assumptions and ideals underlying the practice of social justice philanthropy.

A reflection on philanthropy literature, however, shows that only a few texts refer to these theorists. Moreover, these do not engage with the assumptions and implications of the theories on practice. The remaining literature includes the ideas raised by these theorists as implicitly accepted and, as in broader development practice, assumes a common understanding of social justice without explicit delineation. Instead, the literature reflects the general use of the term social justice in the philanthropic sector as related to notions of rights, equality, equity, freedom, fairness and levelling the playing field in relation to social, economic and political opportunities, resources and relations. The philanthropy literature is vague on the issue of the constituent elements of social justice and is unclear on whether it is seen as a strategy, a goal or a framework.

The use of the term social justice in this chapter draws on the ideas raised by Rawls, Sen, Anderson and Barry, as well as the way in which it is generally used in the philanthropic sector, but with some clarification. The first is that social justice is seen here as a framework, not a strategy. Secondly, drawing on Sen's argument that equal opportunities in the face of unequal capabilities is problematic, this research prefers to look at equitable opportunities (i.e. fair and just opportunities), which would take into consideration capabilities. Lastly, access to rights alone is not enough. Access to rights must lead to just outcomes. As such, this research refers to social justice as:

> An overarching framework for development wherein the existence of equal rights and equitable opportunities to access those rights result in the realization of just outcomes for those who bear the brunt of poverty, inequality, marginalization, vulnerability, oppression, and discrimination.

With regards to literature[7] on social justice philanthropy, also referred to by some as social change philanthropy or progressive philanthropy,[8] very little published academic work exists (see Kuljian 2005; Slim 2002 and Lawrence 2005). There are a number of smaller pieces, commissioned research and articles written by people who have long engaged with this practice and/or who hold senior academic qualifications,[9] as well as 'how to' manuals by practitioners. Within most of these, the term is discussed in contrast to traditional philanthropy, which is seen as focusing on the symptoms of poverty, injustice and inequality. This, however, is where the agreement ends. Discussions on the definitions and practice of the term are varied and highly contested, but three broad strands can be distinguished,

The first delineates social justice philanthropy by its explicit focus on addressing the structural foundations of societal problems (e.g. Lawrence 2005; Carson 2003; and National Committee for Responsible Philanthropy 2003). Within this strand of thought, there is a broad variance in practice relating to the choice and/or prioritization of strategies, the range of issues and priority areas that are deemed to constitute a structural change and the level at which social justice philanthropy is targeted (societal vs. individual/community level). Based on this primary focus of addressing structural issues, the second strand of thought emphasizes the process of inclusive, participatory grantmaking as a critical component of social justice philanthropy (e.g. Shaw 2002; Liberty Hill Foundation 2005; and Community Foundations of Canada 2004). Within this strand, there appears to be differentiation as to whether social justice philanthropy and traditional philanthropy are compatible or distinct strategies. The third strand appears to be very loose and, whilst defined as social justice philanthropy, there is not necessarily a particular focus on underlying causes but rather on using philanthropy as a *tool to address social justice*, without elucidating whether this refers to structural issues or impact mitigation. Reflected primarily by a group of community foundations from developing countries (see Synergos undated), the distinction between 'philanthropy as a tool for social justice' and 'social justice philanthropy' is an important one. This is because it raises questions around whether foundations in developing countries understand and practise social justice philanthropy differently from those in the north, or, whether the terminology itself is the root of the variation.

This requires elaboration: the term social justice philanthropy is somewhat of a misnomer and this appears to contribute significantly to the source of contestation. This chapter presents social justice as an overarching framework, with traditional philanthropy and social justice philanthropy as dual parts of a strategy directed at addressing social injustice, albeit in different ways (see Figure 8.1).

The literature reviewed does not address this differentiation and, in fact, often *social justice philanthropy* and *philanthropy aimed at social justice* are used interchangeably (e.g. Smith 2003; Synergos undated; NCRP 2003a and NCRP 2003b). The resultant impression created is that only social justice philanthropy is directed at social justice, whilst traditional philanthropy has other lesser aims. This study began

Figure 8.1: Social justice philanthropy vs. traditional philanthropy

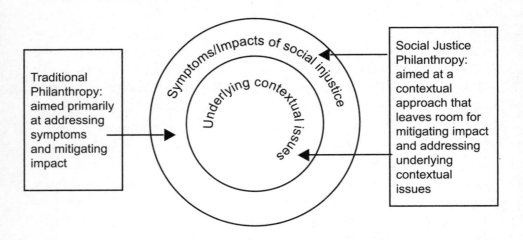

from the standpoint that addressing social justice requires interventions directed at both impact mitigation and at underlying causal issues and that the two are not mutually exclusive, but could be combined within a holistic approach.

Reflecting on the definition of social justice discussed earlier and the first two strands of thought derived from the literature, this research initially proceeded with the following *preliminary* definition of social justice philanthropy:

> Philanthropy aimed at addressing the structural issues and barriers that prevent (i) the recognition of equal rights for all, (ii) equitable opportunities to access those rights and (iii) the realization of those rights into just outcomes for those who bear the brunt of poverty, marginalization, vulnerability, oppression and discrimination.

The issue of imposed northern concepts is important to consider in any social science research. According to Everatt et al. (2005:276), much of the literature on philanthropy originates in the north, with the result that many existing definitions fail to reflect the rich traditions of giving in multicultural contexts. Everatt et al. (2005:277) and Kuljian (2005:5) also note the unease with which the terms philanthropy and charity are used, and the foreign connotations and assumptions that these bring with them; and Wilkinson-Maposa's 'Poor Philanthropist' (2006) and Everatt and Solanki (2005) radically challenge some of these assumptions. My research findings corroborate this. For instance, the term social justice is used by only a handful of IFs to articulate their work, and they use it in relation to notions of rights, equality, equity, freedom, fairness and justice. The larger proportion of organizations, however, prefer to talk about a *just society* or about *development,* referring to terms such as *equal rights, benefits to all, justice for all, a conducive environment, serving the public good* and *poverty alleviation.* Many IFs feel that the concept social justice is an imported one that does not have much resonance for them. The term social justice philanthropy is not used at all by the organizations in the study. Preferring to use language they feel is understandable both to them and to the communities they work with, some articulate their work as efforts aimed at *change, rights, justice, a just society* or *addressing root causes*.

With regards to the barriers to engaging with social justice philanthropy, there is a fair amount of practitioner literature on the challenges in the United States and Canadian contexts (e.g. Carson 2003; NCRP 2003; Shaw 2005; Heller and Winder 2002; and Lawrence et al. 2005). The literature provides lists of challenges and barriers, but no substantive interrogation of these. Analysis reveals that these lists can be demarcated according to factors that are internal or external to the organization. The external factors relate to (i) the possible inhibiting political or regulatory environment; (ii) the agendas and interests of larger donors and; (iii) the absence of a cohesive field of social justice philanthropy organizations. The internal factors relate to (i) the quality of leadership; (ii) limited understanding of underlying contexts; (ii) risk aversion; (iv) sustainability concerns; and (v) perceived limitations of philanthropy.

Key findings

Elements of a South African approach

The study reveals that a social justice philanthropy approach, from a South African perspective, has five critical components:

- It is premised on rights-based values: social justice philanthropy is as much about why funding is given as it is about the impact of the funding. Organizations engaging in social justice philanthropy place emphasis on the fact that they are not motivated by a desire to help or be charitable but that their existence is based on values that refer to every individual's right to justice, equality, equity and dignity in every sphere of life.

- It is contextual: the common thread running through the literature is the focus on structural change. The social justice philanthropy practitioners in the study talk about change, but not necessarily 'structural' change. Instead, reflecting that what is deemed structural is subjective and can be looked at from different levels, more often they speak about change in reference to underlying issues, root causes or contextual issues. Their approach takes account of the underlying contextual dynamics surrounding an issue or problem and then looks at how to address the problem through changing these contextual dynamics, at whichever level is appropriate.

- It is an overall funding approach: social justice philanthropy is not designated according to the types of activities supported or the strategies utilized, as is the case with much of the northern literature. Instead, it refers to an overall funding approach, which can include addressing the impacts of problems, but which is ultimately aimed at addressing the contextual issues that contribute to the problem. Rather than polarizing impact mitigation and underlying causes as two ends of the debate, this practice sees social justice and traditional philanthropy as complementary strategies, which often run parallel to each other within a broader approach. The literature does reveal a few organizations that see the two types of funding as complementary, but the difference is that these are two separate approaches coexisting, not as one approach with multiple strategies.

- Its processes are inclusive: social justice philanthropy is about both strategy and process. Interacting with the beneficiaries of support as equal partners, and adopting the principle that grantmaking decisions will be informed by the issues articulated by those most affected, is seen as a critical component. The idea that funding decisions cannot be taken in isolation of an in-depth engagement with those most affected is central.

- It can be directed at both individual and community/society-level interventions. All organizations canvassed expressed the opinion that, in a society with such a critical transformation imperative, individual-level support is just as crucial as societal-level change, and the development of individual leadership, competencies, assets and skills is seen as critical to bolstering social change and a just society. The literature tends to refer primarily to structural issues as relating to those that have a direct impact on the community or society level. Philanthropy that aims to benefit individuals directly does not receive significant attention. This is not at all to say that the practice in the north does not look at this, but rather that the literature does not engage this issue conceptually.

Based on the research, this chapter puts forward a definition of social justice philanthropy, from the perspective of South African IFs, as:

> An inclusive funding approach, premised on the notion of a just society, which seeks to ultimately address **the contextual issues** and barriers that prevent (i) the recognition of equal rights for all, (ii) equitable opportunities to access those rights, and (iii) the realization of those rights into just outcomes for those who bear the brunt of poverty, marginalization, vulnerability, oppression and discrimination.

Towards a typology of Independent Funders: Defining parameters

To engage with the factors that influence the grantmaking choices of independent funders it is important to first look at the distinguishing characteristics of the different types of IFs in the study. Table 8.1 illustrates the parameters of a basic typology of the IFs in the study. There is no academic study that provides a comparative analysis of social justice and traditional philanthropy organizations. This typology thus attempts to develop a framework within which the conceptual and operational differences between these two types of funders can be more easily differentiated and explained. Typologies are bound to be problematic; however, this tool is used not to present an ideal type, but rather to illustrate the key differences.

The research identifies IFs as falling into one of two broad groups, each of which is then divided into two sub-categories. On the vertical axes, there is a division between Group 1, which refers to social justice philanthropy funders, and Group 2, which refers to traditional funders. Determining whether an organization falls into Group 1 or Group 2 is related to two factors: (i) values and (ii) context. On the horizontal axis, a subdivision of Group 1 and 2 is illustrated. This subdivision distinguishes between (i) organizations that have a cohesive funding approach and focused programmatic strategies (referred to here as strategic funders) and (ii) organizations that have a fragmented funding approach and weakly developed programmatic strategies (referred to here as the less-focused funders).

Table 8.1: Basic typology of Independent Funders

	Group 1: Social Justice Philanthropy	Group 2: Traditional Philanthropy
	Values based on notion of rights Contextual, holistic approach	Values based on notion of assistance Singular, individualized approach
Cohesive funding approach and focused programmatic strategies	**Category A** Strategic social justice philanthropy funders	**Category B** Strategic traditional funders
Fragmented funding approach and weakly developed programmatic strategies	**Category C** Less-focused social justice philanthropy funders	**Category D** Less-focused traditional funders

Values: Social justice philanthropy funders see their work as being premised on rights-based values, i.e. values premised on the notion of the necessity of equal rights for all. They identify their strategies as being based on *rights, justice* or *development for social justice* and see the attainment of a just society as the primary motif for their work. Traditional funders see their work as being premised on values related to *charitable giving* and *assisting those in need*. They articulate their work in relation to providing help and improving people's standard of living. Assisting others to attain a better quality of life is articulated as the primary motif for their work.

Context: The social justice philanthropy funders adopt an approach that locates the problem within society and the broader contextual environment. Their funding approach is thus aimed at addressing the contextual issues underlying and perpetuating the problem. Traditional funders tend to locate the problem at the level of the individual. Consequently, their funding approach tends to focus primarily on mitigating the impacts of or alleviating the symptoms of the problem as they manifest at the individual level. The status quo underlying these crises is not the subject of attention. Where contextual factors are addressed, this is marginal.

Strategy: These two groups of organizations are not homogeneous, hence the second parameter of the typology, i.e. the cohesiveness and strength of the strategic approach adopted. Within the social justice philanthropy group, the strategic funders gave very serious consideration to underlying contextual issues and developed a framework that consists of targeted and focused strategies for how they will address problems contextually. They tend to take a proactive approach in addressing these issues. The less-focused social justice philanthropy funders are 'still working this out'. Whilst maintaining a contextual approach, they are still engaging in research and analysis of the problems and the underlying contextual factors in order to develop and refine strong proactive strategies. Within the traditional funders group, the strategic traditional funders gave serious consideration to the problems at hand and have developed focused and targeted strategies that primarily address and mitigate the impacts of these problems. The less-focused traditional funders do not articulate a detailed approach or strategy underlying their work. They have defined broad sectors of support and their grantmaking is framed as a reactive approach to needs that arise.

Some operational differences: Substantive vs. technical focus

Within this typology, three core operational differences need highlighting. These relate to (i) funding criteria, (ii) organizational development and (iii) monitoring and evaluation. The research reflects that, in relation to these, the social justice philanthropy and traditional philanthropy groups have different focus areas and that, within both the social justice philanthropy and traditional funder groups, the strategic funders have stronger operational systems and processes than their less-focused counterparts.

With each of the three operational functions, the social justice philanthropy funders adopt a two-pronged approach: (i) They look at the technical aspects related to competency, effectiveness, efficiency, governance and leadership etc. (ii) In addition, they accord equal priority towards engagement with substantive programmatic issues, which include questioning programmatic assumptions, merits and limitations, exploring the interaction of the programme with contextual dynamics and its ability to stimulate both short-term and long-term impacts. The trend of these IFs is to support and strengthen both strong programmes and strong institutions.

Conversely, the trend within the traditional funders group is to concentrate primarily on technical competencies, with some prioritizing broad community acceptance as an essential criterion.

The strengths, limitations and assumptions of the interventions are dealt with either within a service provision framework (i.e. they interrogate the value and impact of that service as a stand alone) or not at all; and questions around scope, process and duplication appear to be prioritized over engagement with substantive programmatic issues. The trend here is a focus on supporting and strengthening strong institutions.

Table 8.2: Operational differences between Independent Funders

	Group 1: Social Justice Philanthropy	Group 2: Traditional Philanthropy
	Focus on technical and substantive issues	Focus primarily on technical issues
Funding assessment criteria	• Technical competency • Relation to identified need • Merits and pitfalls of the outcome • Long-term impact on beneficiary and context	• Technical competency • Relation to identified need • Merits and pitfalls of the output/service • Immediate impact on beneficiary • Broad community acceptance
Organizational development / capacity building for grant beneficiaries	• Organizational effectiveness, efficiency, leadership, governance • Assessment of impact • Springboard to build strong institutions and strong programmes • Engagement with substantive programmatic issues • Advocacy and challenging unequal gender/power dynamics	• Organizational effectiveness, efficiency, leadership, governance • Assessment of outputs • Springboard to build strong institutions

Table 8.2: Operational differences between Independent Funders (Contd.)

Monitoring and evaluation (M&E)	• Appropriate use of the grant funds • Capacity to conduct activities • Assessment of impact • On-going M&E – feeds into programme	• Appropriate use of the grant funds • Capacity to conduct activities • Assessment of outputs • M&E at end of grant cycle – no feedback loop to programme

Conceptual factors influencing the funding choices of Independent Funders

As mentioned earlier, analysis of the literature reflects that engagement with social justice philanthropy is a factor of a set of internal and external challenges. The research reflects, however, that engaging with social justice philanthropy is not just about overcoming challenges or the mere absence or presence of factors; rather, the conceptual framework underlying philanthropic giving is *the* critical factor influencing the type of philanthropy a funder engages in. The findings show that the way in which funders conceptualize why, how and to what end they do the work they do reflects critical differences that influence their strategic programming. Moreover, the way in which they conceptualise their role as a funder, in relation to the roles of external actors, has critical implications for the nature and scope of their funding priorities and programmes.

Table 8.3: Conceptual differences between Independent Funders

	Group 1: Social Justice Philanthropy Funders	Group 2: Traditional Funders
Conceptual starting point	What is unjust?	What is the need?
Raison d'être	Agent of change	Intermediary/conduit
Neutrality	Partisan stance	Neutral role-player
Reflection and learning	Technical and substantive	Technical only
Leadership	Technical and programme expertise	Technical expertise and networked boards
Role of state	Donor involvement does not limit grantmaking	Donor involvement limits grantmaking
The role of beneficiaries	Beneficiaries should actively engage development programmes	Beneficiaries should fit into development programmes

Table 8.3 provides a summary of what this research identified as critical and inter-related conceptual differences that influence the programming priorities of the IFs in the study.

Conceptual starting points

What are the framing questions? Social justice philanthropy funders begin with the questions, what is it about the situation that is unjust? Why is it unjust? And what needs to be changed to make it just? Consequently, they address the dynamics underlying the injustice. The traditional funders begin with the question, what is the need? And how do we fill the gap? Consequently, they address the gaps that result from the injustice. The provision of basic services can itself reflect an implicit justice agenda, and this is enveloped in a view of social justice as an over-arching framework. The absence of a conceptual starting point that questions why the situation is this way, however, is still a differentiating factor.

What is the time frame of the issue? Social justice philanthropy funders tend to adopt a long-term view of the problem, emphasizing that the crises people face daily will continue to manifest unless the underlying causes are addressed. The traditional funders tend to adopt a shorter-term approach focusing on the immediate crises, and are of the view that that these must first be eradicated before a long-term approach can be taken.

What are the causes and the consequences? Social justice philanthropy funders begin by framing the problem in relation to underlying dynamics. Traditional funders begin framing the problem in relation to its manifestations. I use the problem of poverty to illustrate this. The social justice philanthropy funders tend to see poverty as a consequence of underlying dynamics and thus focus primarily on changing the factors that contribute towards poverty. The traditional funders see poverty as the reason why people are deprived of their basic needs (i.e. poverty is the cause), and hence focus on mitigating the symptoms and impacts of poverty.

What is the end goal? Traditional funders talk about development as the end goal of their interventions. What is meant by development, however, is not clear; though it appears to be centred on the notion of assisting people to move out of poverty. Moreover, some tend to talk about development and charity interchange-ably. The social justice philanthropy group emphasizes development as a process for reaching an end goal, asserting that development in and of itself is not adequate, and begs the question, 'development for what?' These organizations thus talk about *development for social justice*, *development for equality* and *development for equal rights*.

How are the issues articulated? The social justice philanthropy funders articulate the issues they address in relation to a rights-based discourse, which sees the interconnectedness and indivisibility of the various rights (civil, political, economic etc.). Their funding approach thus takes cognisance of the barriers to these rights as contextual issues that need to be addressed. Moreover, the various rights are viewed as equally important, and are not seen on a hierarchical level. Their funding approach thus does not necessarily prioritize immediate basic needs over rights that are deemed to require longer-term contextual changes. The traditional funders tend to articulate the issues they address in relation to tangible and measurable needs. As a result, an approach that addresses needs on a hierarchical basis is favoured and their funding prioritizes immediate and urgent basic needs over addressing longer-term or underlying contextual causes.

Raison d'être

What is the role of a funder? Some may argue that there is a very basic role, i.e. to distribute philanthropic resources. Beyond that, however, lies a more complex issue. The research reflects two strands of thought (i) those funders who identify their primary role as the mobilization and/or the distribution of resources and (ii) those which identify their primary role as being agents or facilitators of change. The two motivations are not mutually exclusive, but it is where the primary emphasis lies that is critical. This emphasis in turn influences their funding approaches and strategies.

The majority of the funders in the social justice philanthropy group were established with both reasons in mind, although the primary reason was to advance a cause or to correct inequalities in the status quo. There appears to be a shared emphasis that the distribution of resources is not the defining characteristic of the organization but rather a means that is used to facilitate an end. Achieving that end is the defining role. This sentiment was also shared by some expert respondents, one of whom refers to a paper by Joyce Malombe,[10] which says that the need in South Africa is not to have community foundations, but to have community *development* foundations. The first limits the role to resource distribution whilst the second indicates an active change-oriented role.

The traditional funders appear to emphasize their role of resource mobilization and/or distribution. With the exception of the endowed organizations in this group (who are not dependent on external funding), the other funders place significant emphasis on their primary role of grantmaking, that is, to effectively, efficiently and responsibly mobilize and/or distribute philanthropic resources. The role of being a grantmaker appears to be emphasized over the role of facilitating change, such that the two roles become separate issues. Consequently, a significant internal focus of many of these IFs is on the *process* of grantmaking, rather than the *impact* of the grants.

Neutrality

The role that IFs play cannot be viewed in isolation. How they see their role in relation to other relevant role-players (beneficiary groups/communities, larger funders and government) appears to be critical in influencing their frameworks and grantmaking. This relative role can be related to whether IFs see themselves as neutral entities or not.

The social justice philanthropy funders tend to take a deliberate stance that they exist to support and promote the issues they believe in and will do so on behalf of, or together with, those affected and whose voices are not heard. They take a strong partisan stance, be it in playing an intermediary role between various role-players, brokering funding with corporates or negotiating with local government. Moreover, they themselves proactively advocate on critical issues that affect their beneficiary groups. For these funders, there is no separation between being a grantmaker and being an activist. Instead, they see themselves as activist grantmakers who are there to facilitate change. This stance is shared by both the strategic and less-focused social justice philanthropy funders, though to differing degrees.

Traditional funders adopt a less activist approach, preferring to focus on their role of coordinating dialogue or brokering partnerships, such that they appear to be objective actors. None of the IFs in this group refer to themselves as activists, and where they talk about change, it is primarily focused on changing processes – how corporates give their funding; how communities can take initiative; how resources can be mobilized; and how beneficiary needs can be met. Some are committed to addressing the concerns of their beneficiaries and to creating opportunities to raise issues on their behalf, however, they experience a tension between doing this and simultaneously projecting themselves as an objective broker that provides a safe space for all. Consequently, many of these funders end up adopting a neutral stance.

The issue of neutrality has two facets. On the one hand, by conceptualizing their primary role as intermediaries, IFs position themselves as a bridge between external stakeholders and their beneficiary groups. This is valuable in providing an open and accessible space for a range of voices to be heard. The position of neutrality, however, can make it difficult to raise issues that challenge the unequal power dynamics between role-players and within the contexts that they work, as doing so removes the status of impartial broker. Consequently, the nature of issues these IFs raise with external stakeholders tends to revolve around processes, such as furthering collaboration and mobilizing resources.

On the other hand, cognisant of not imposing a donor-driven agenda, these funders place strong emphasis on inclusive processes and on responding to community-identified needs. Taking this stance can have the positive effect of recognizing that the voices of those most affected are critical and places some degree of control with beneficiaries. Applied narrowly, however, this stance can limit IFs from taking a more activist role and raising issues or strategies that go beyond those identified by beneficiaries. What does this mean? Whilst beneficiaries may understand the underlying issues, they may not know how best to address certain types of obstacles, which networks, mechanisms and role-players need to be targeted and/or how to access them, or may feel that the barriers to addressing them are too great. The role of the IFs in such cases can be a critical catalyst. The position of non-interference adopted by these IFs, however, constrains this catalyst role, resulting in the adoption of a neutral stance. For one respondent, this is related to IFs not being able to navigate between playing a leadership role without being leaders.

Within this group, there is further variation. The strategic traditional funders appear to deliberately position themselves as neutral entities. Philosophically, they recognize the existence of unequal power relations and underlying dynamics, but practically, the neutral position they adopt places a constraint on addressing these. The less-focused traditional funders appear to be neutral by default. It must, however, be recognized that many of the traditional funders are trying to maintain both credibility and sustainability; and challenging the status quo can have negative repercussions. Thus, a neutral position, whilst imposing limitations, may still be seen by them as positive in that funds are being transferred to critical services or initiatives. This neutrality, however, whether consciously or unconsciously, directly influences the strategic funding framework of the organization.

Reflection and learning

Reflecting on practice and learning from the findings of that reflection is critical in enabling organizations to stay relevant, adapt and enhance impact; thereby influencing funding strategies and priorities. There are two levels at which this is important. First, there is reflection and learning on the technical processes of the organizations, such as efficiency of the grantmaking process, effective fundraising, accountability in reporting, good governance, etc. The strategic social justice philanthropy and traditional funders appear to engage in very detailed reflection and learning around the technical issues and utilize this learning to improve and adapt where required. The less-focused social justice philanthropy funders are still developing these technical systems and are engaged in reflection and learning at a much more informal and less structured way. The less-focused traditional funders appear not to engage in any deliberate reflection and learning around processes or technical functioning of the organization.

Second, reflection and learning can also look at issues such as the relevance of a programmatic framework, impact on the contextual dynamics and the ability to build civil society institutions with strong programmes. Within the social justice philanthropy group, the strategic funders engage in reflection and learning that looks at these factors as an integral component of their functioning. They do so in a very substantive manner, devoting a fair amount of resources to this. For the less-focused social justice philanthropy funders, however, this is a challenge and they are still grappling with learning and reflection on substantive issues. Within the traditional funders group, the strategic funders reflect on the technical impact of programmes, such as how many people have been targeted, how many grants they make, how much funding has been disbursed, how many capacity building programmes were provided, how to broaden the reach of their programmes etc. Reflection on the relevance of the programmatic framework or the impact of their funding on building strong programmes on the ground does not feature as a priority. As a result, they may experience difficulties in reflecting on the appropriateness of their organizational strategies and priorities in the absence of data that reflects the impact of their work, not just the outputs. The less-focused traditional funders do not appear to engage in reflection and learning on impact at all, thus their ability to judge the relevance of their interventions or make changes in light of fluid social contexts can be questioned.

The extent to which organizations engage in learning and reflection can be further related to two aspects (i) the framework underlying the perceived role of the funder and (ii) the demands placed on leaders of IFs. The first relates to whether the funder sees itself as an intermediary for distributing resources or whether it sees itself as a catalyst for change. If the first, then the reflection and learning tend to revolve around technical aspects of being effective, efficient and responsive grantmakers. If the second, then reflection and learning also involve funders interrogating the issues of programmatic impacts, alternatives and changing contextual dynamics.

With regards to the issue of demands, there are some strategic traditional funders and less-focused social justice philanthropy funders that are keen to either begin or enhance the level of internal reflection on programmatic issues. Often, however, they feel there is very little space or time to do so. With younger organizations, the directors are simultaneously responsible for mobilizing resources, enhancing sustainability, institutionalizing effective and efficient systems, ensuring good governance, marketing, consulting with and coordinating between role-players and developing strategies. With minimal operational costs, and often minimal staff, they feel extremely overburdened and hard-pressed to devote enough time to learning and reflection on vision, strategy and impact. This acts as an indirect constraint that limits the scope of funding strategies.

The existence of peer support and networks also influences this issue. A number of IFs belong to a range of membership or umbrella initiatives (in South Africa and abroad) that look at learning and sharing within the sector. The networks in South Africa, however, are still young and the focus of these initiatives is primarily on issues related to technical organizational processes. Reflection on substantive issues and impact has not been addressed significantly. With regards to international networks, some respondents are of the opinion that these networks also focus on process, endowments and sustainability. Consequently, many of these IFs are focusing on the technical issues raised by these networks at the expense of a focus on substantive issues. Moreover, the use of northern concepts and frameworks that do not adequately reflect southern contexts has also been critiqued.

Leadership

All the cases in the study reflect that an organization is defined by its leadership. Strong leaders, who can understand the issues at hand, explore creative solutions, advocate their organization's mission and values and manage the complex sets of demands that accompany their positions, are vital. The strength, capacity and values of the head of an organization thus play an instrumental role in taking it forward. With the exception of two organizations in the less-focused traditional funders category (which are managed by field/programme staff), the remaining IFs are headed by strong dynamic leaders. What distinguishes the organizations in this arena, however, relates to (i) the conceptual framework of the leadership, (ii) the nature of the demands placed on the leaders of these organizations, and (iii) the nature and extent of opportunity to learn, reflect and strategize. These are dealt with elsewhere in the paper.

The leadership provided by the board of directors, however, also requires examination. The strategic social justice philanthropy and traditional funders are both groups led by strong and involved boards. What distinguishes them, however, is the kind of board expertise that the IFs seek out. The social justice philanthropy funders appear to focus on recruiting board members who have expertise in relation to both technical (e.g. management, legal and financial) and programmatic issues. They want boards that can go beyond technical and financial oversight, to hold the organization to account on the nature of its programmatic decisions and impact and stimulate the organization to think about the contextual relevance of their interventions.

The strategic traditional funders stress the need for boards that have technical expertise, thus it may be difficult for these board members to provide substantive input on programmatic decisions and impact or to question the assumptions and limitations of those decisions. Moreover, they place emphasis on getting board members that can facilitate access to resources and networks. Thus, considerable effort is put on finding board members who are *linked* – to corporates, to local government, to traditional authorities, to wealthy individuals – and who conse-quently provide access to these sectors. This can be seen as part of a proactive fundraising strategy, but the inadvertent result is that these types of board members are often overwhelmingly sought at the expense of people who have knowledge on the development issues at hand or who are able to understand community dynamics and articulate those within the broader societal challenges. A related factor is that these funders place strong emphasis on trying to build the organizational reputation through association. They thus aim to get boards that include high-profile members of society. Whilst this certainly assists in building their credibility and legitimacy, at times these high-profile board members are unable to give adequate time and energy to guiding, nurturing and developing young funding institutions. Whilst influential, they may not necessarily provide programmatic guidance and direc-tion. Poor programmatic board leadership in turn influences and/or constrains the framework and strategy of the organization.

The less-focused social justice philanthropy funders are young organizations with young boards that can perform basic due diligence requirements but do not appear to be engaged in the functioning of the organization. One explanation raised is that young organizations have very high expectations of their boards and make too many demands on them. Consequently, board members feel overburdened and reduce their participation. Another explanation is that young organizations may not have adequately worked out the delegation of responsibilities between the board and staff, resulting in tension and limited participation As a result, board involvement can become constraining. Finally, the challenge of seeking to enhance its reputation through association and emphasizing the necessity of board members who are linked to resources is also felt by some in this group. Consequently, the types of boards that these organizations have may not necessarily be the types of boards that they require.

The less-focused traditional funders appear to be characterized by over-involved boards. With one exception, these funders have board members whose terms of appointment have long expired, but who are loath to hand over control. These board members are able to conduct their technical due-diligence requirements, but substantive programmatic discussions do not appear to be prioritized. Where new board members are sought, the focus is on getting people who have influence and access to networks.

Independent Funders and the new democratic dispensation

The way in which IFs view their mandate in relation to the mandates and devel-opment prerogatives of the new democratic dispensation in South Africa, and the resultant interaction with the state, is an important factor influencing their funding choices. Exploration of the issue of engagement with the state, in the context of a relatively new democracy, reflects that in the social justice philanthropy group (SJP), the strategic IFs see the achievement of democracy as one part of the struggle for a just society. All the funders in this category appear to have engaged in serious reflection about the limitations of the existing democratic dispensation in addressing the structural issues and contextual dynamics that underlie societal problems. Consequently, they have taken a deliberate decision to address these dynamics and to play a role that engages the state – through partnership, advocacy and, particularly, through their grantmaking – on its limitations in addressing these issues. Each of these funders has made engaging with the state and holding it accountable to its constitutional mandates an active component of their funding strategies. The less-focused SJP funders share the acknowledgement of the limitations of the state in this regard but have not yet formulated strategies for how to engage the state on these. What engagement does take place is more ad hoc and fragmented, and prone to less contentious issues.

In the traditional funders group, the majority of IFs see the state as responsible for the broader development programmes and infrastructural issues, and hence define their own role as aligning with or fitting into these plans. There is no discussion about the possible limits of the state in addressing its development imperatives or what implications these limitations may have for the work that these funders support. These IFs appear to have demarcated their role such that (i) they themselves do not actively engage the state on contentious issues that are important to their beneficiaries (which links to the neutral role alluded to earlier), and (ii) the scope of activities they fund rarely include active engagement with the state, especially not on issues where the state is failing its mandate. What engagement does take place revolves around finding synergies with local government development plans or collaborating on initiatives and priorities that have already been defined by the state. These plans and priorities of the state, however, are not interrogated. The less-focused traditional funders, with the exception of one (which the organization feels has had too much state influence), do not engage with the state at all. They do their work in isolation of the state's development mandates and do not see a role for them to collaborate, engage or challenge state decisions and programmes.

What explains the nature of the state engagement in the traditional funders group? One possible argument is that this is not an issue limited to philanthropic organizations only. There is a broad consensus that post-apartheid civil society in general has become less challenging in its engagement with the state. Accordingly, philanthropic entities too may have moved in this direction. The research reflects, however, that, where philanthropic entities have moved, it has been in the opposite direction from broader civil society. Most of those in the strategic social justice philanthropy group initially began funding on a very general, reactive basis, with no clear strategy, and they did not overtly engage with the then-apartheid state. Over the years, these funders have evolved and today all of them engage with and challenge the post-apartheid state directly (through advocacy, research, initiating or participating in various fora) and indirectly (through funding for advocacy, research, community mobilization and civic engagement efforts). They do this based on the premise that it is their democratic right and obligation to do so.

Some in the strategic traditional funders' category have also evolved from their initial establishment as welfare funders to encompassing a broader developmental role, but they have not changed the nature of their engagement with the state. One way of analyzing this could be that, where the motivation of deploying resources to communities is conceptualized within a rights-based framework, engaging with the state is seen as necessary to that role; where the rationale is primarily about acting as intermediaries to devolve resources, then engagement with the state on its responsibilities may not be seen as essential to that role. Another is that some IFs may feel constrained by the authority of the state or that, on a number of fronts, the democratic dispensation itself has struggled to engage with structural changes. Within this context, these funders are unable to separate advocacy from opposition and so are grappling with how to engage, challenge and dialogue in ways that reflects active citizenship but not opposition to the state.

Some expert respondents argued that, with organizations that neither challenge the state nor hold it accountable, there is some element of belief that a democratically elected state will automatically be mindful of the interests of the poor and marginalized. Accordingly, the development priorities of the state do not need to be questioned. The research reflected that some IFs indeed adopted the position that communities need to take the initiative at the local level because the state is busy getting the broader fundamental issues right. These IFs thus see their role as supporting initiatives and efforts that allow people to play their part, but in so doing they inadvertently divorce the initiatives of communities from the development mandate of the state. Not only does this approach limit the nature, type and scope of the funding programmes of these IFs, it also shifts responsibility away from the state to communities. Finally, another opinion raised by a number of experts and IFs is that some of these funders equate the achievement of the democratic struggle with the achievement of a just society, i.e. the fundamental issues have all been addressed, and all that is left now is to implement and provide services.

The role of larger donors

The pool of independent funders included in this sample represent institutions that: (i) are fully endowed, (ii) are still building endowments and simultaneously fundraising from larger donors (either corporate, international funders or even the state) or (iii) have no endowment reserves at all and raise all their funds from external sources. Thus the issue of donor influence on the programme priorities and strategies of these IFs must be examined.

The issue of donor-driven programming is a significant cause of concern in the development arena, and this also applies to larger donors who provide smaller funders with money for re-granting. The power that larger donors bring to the table alongside their funds needs to be carefully navigated by smaller funders. The study reflects that none of the IFs that receive funding from larger donors feel that their donors impose a rigid agenda. Whilst some IFs reflect that a few donors want to prioritize certain issues or geographic locations, in general they feel there is room enough to accommodate for this within the existing scope of their work without it fundamentally altering their work.

What appears to be important, however, is not just the issue of explicit donor influence, but whether these donors or the potential pool of donors have an indirect constraining influence on the type of grantmaking that IFs engage in. In striving to be neutral entities and focusing on their role as conduits for donor resources, the potential backlash from donors could very well be a contributory factor that informs the decisions of IFs to deal with less controversial issues. For example, do IFs shy away from controversial issues that may challenge, embarrass or hold accountable corporates or state bodies that fund them or that could potentially fund them? Or do they keep a distance from specific types of interventions because they think that it may not be an activity that would attract funding?

The social justice philanthropy funders appear to have confronted and reflected on this issue internally, and the strategic funders in this group have developed clear strategies for how they respond to this dynamic. The less-focused social justice philanthropy funders are still grappling with how to strategically deal with it. With traditional funders the issue is not raised at all. Either it has not been reflected on internally or it suggests a deliberate decision not to take a partisan line. More than one organization talked about promoting the types of issues that attract funding and there appears to be a tension in that, whilst some IFs may recognise the need for alternative strategies, the necessity of raising resources leads them to emphasize the types of projects and programmes that they think will be appealing to their donor base.

On a related but different note, three remaining issues that relate to larger donors deserve some attention here. First, a number of expert respondents reflect that there is an increasing demand from large donors that their grant recipients show the impact of their work and do so within short timeframes.[11] There is some evidence that, whilst donors may not necessarily directly dictate a specific agenda, some organizations do experience a pressure to align the activities they support to donor demands for tangible impacts. This can result in prioritization of activities with short-term, visible outputs as opposed to the more complex and less tangible interventions that address contextual issues.

Second, a discussion about larger donors cannot ignore the issue of financial sustainability. Philanthropic entities that are not fully endowed feel the pressure to become less reliant on external funding sources, and this has seen an increase in the offering of services that generate an income stream. Thus the provision of re-granting, application assessment or evaluation services for large corporates or individual donors is on the increase within some IFs. This in itself can be positive as it contributes towards the IFs' financial sustainability.

There is, however, an almost unintended consequence of emphasizing a service provision role. Some organizations have placed a substantial focus on honing the grantmaking process and proving how effective, efficient and responsible they are. As a result, a significant amount of energy is spent on showing accountability to their donors, and less energy on being accountable to the communities they serve or to ensuring that they are fulfilling their mandate. With a number of strategic traditional funders, there appears to be a strong notion that they have to market a product – the product being the skill to invest the donor rand appropriately and accountably. This product, rather than the development issues that require attention, then becomes the leverage point for resource mobilization. In emphasizing their grantmaking skill and accountability as the focus, they concentrate less on why the issues are important and more on how they can provide a good service.

Finally, the issue of sustainability (or lack thereof) has been raised in the literature as a key factor that limits IFs from engaging in social justice philanthropy. This research reflects, however, that the availability of resources does not appear to be a critical issue influencing the type of philanthropy engaged in. This can be illustrated by looking at endowed organizations. Contrary to general opinion that endowed organizations are able to make more risky and challenging funding decisions, and hence easily engage in social justice philanthropy, the study reflects that this need not be the case, as endowed organizations were found in both the social justice philanthropy and traditional philanthropy groups. Moreover, both groups had organizations that varied considerably in their levels of financial sustainability. Accordingly, this research puts forward that it is not the extent of resources that influences the type of grantmaking an IF engages in, but rather that the conceptual framework of the organization plays a more important role in directing how those resources are spent.

Role of beneficiaries

An analysis of how IFs perceive the role that the beneficiaries of their funding play is also an important factor influencing the strategies they adopt. Almost all the IFs in the study place significant emphasis on beneficiaries driving their own development. The differences, however, lie in the scope of agency that they accord to beneficiaries. The scope of agency of beneficiaries can relate to four factors: (i) the power to make decisions on the nature of development initiatives they undertake, (ii) the power to influence the nature of development initiatives undertaken by others on their behalf (state, corporates, large NGOs etc), (iii) the power to hold these institutions accountable when initiatives are not in the interests of the beneficiaries, and (iv) the power to challenge existing inequalities and power dynamics in the status quo.

The strategic social justice philanthropy funders see the agency of beneficiaries as related to all four elements, and consequently fund initiatives related to all four respects. These IFs thus support the involvement of communities in engaging local governance processes, in demanding transparency and accountability of governance systems and officials, and of advocating, at local level to claim their rights and challenge the violation of rights. With regards to challenging unequal power relations, these IFs emphasize the active role of beneficiaries in initiating and spearheading such interventions. These types of activities all allow for the contextual and underlying issues of a problem to be looked at. The less-focused social justice philanthropy funders recognize that the target groups they work with have agency in all four respects; however, they have not yet given in-depth consideration to how to address issues around unequal power relations and intra-community inequalities.

The strategic traditional funders appear to relate the issue of agency primarily to the first factor, i.e. the power of beneficiaries to make decisions on the nature of development initiatives they undertake. As such, their funding strategies focus primarily on that type of intervention. They do not see beneficiaries as having a role to play in relation to active citizenship, advocacy or challenging power relations. Beneficiaries are encouraged to raise issues and discuss and debate solutions, but these involve primarily internal 'community-led' solutions and take place within a limited sphere of influence. Some funders in this category recognize some agency in relation to the second and third factor, evidenced by their support of a limited number of organizations that provide services relating to immediate needs as well as address underlying causes. The bulk of their funding, however, does not reflect this pattern. The less-focused traditional funders look only at agency in the first respect. They do not see any scope for the target groups they work with to influence broader issues or address broader inequalities except through the projects these groups initiate, nor do they see any need to work together with or engage local government.

In exploring this issue during the research, an element that was alluded to by a number of funders relates to the myth surrounding advocacy. Many funders appear to have the perception that advocacy is beyond their beneficiaries, i.e. advocacy cannot be supported because communities cannot access structures at the national level and because contextual issues are beyond communities' scope of influence. These IFs either do not recognize advocacy as relevant and practical at the grass-roots level or they do not acknowledge it as being their primary role to support.

With regards to challenging inequalities, traditional funders do not perceive this as a central role for beneficiaries. They recognize that inequalities exist, but see these as beyond the sphere of influence of the beneficiary groups. Moreover, with some traditional funders that act as conduits for corporate donors or have close affiliations with traditional leaders or the government, supporting initiatives that challenge the status quo can be difficult and could jeopardize these relationships.

Conclusion

This chapter has put forward a social justice philanthropy approach, in a South African context, that emphasizes five critical components: (i) social justice philanthropy is premised on rights-based values, (ii) social justice philanthropy emphasizes contextual issues, (iii) social justice philanthropy is an overall funding approach that can address both impact mitigation and underlying causes (iv) social justice philanthropy processes are inclusive, and (v) social justice philanthropy can be directed at both individual and community/society level interventions.

The findings of this research indicate that there are a number of differentiating factors influencing the choice of a social justice or traditional philanthropy approach and that these are both internal and external to the organization. The critical issue, however, is not the absence or presence of factors but the way in which these factors are conceptualized. Thus, the conceptual frameworks that underlie the rationale behind their work, their end goals and where they locate the source of the problems play a central role in defining the nature and scope of the strategies and approaches IFs adopt. Moreover, the way in which independent funders conceptualize their role as a funder in relation to the role of other external development actors such as the state, larger donors and their grant beneficiaries, has wide-ranging implications for the nature and scope of their funding priorities and programmes. Finally, the extent to which IFs conceptualize and engage with the substantive programmatic issues and the assumptions underlying their subsequent interventions are contributory factors influencing their funding approaches.

Traditional philanthropy plays a valuable role in South Africa but, on its own, it is constrained. Traditional funding approaches need to be supplemented by a social justice philanthropy perspective. External limitations to this approach exist, and these need to be addressed. This research, however, demonstrates that internal conceptual frameworks are the central factor in developing self-imposed boundaries that limit the type of philanthropic approach adopted. Only when these conceptual frameworks – the frameworks of the mind – are engaged with, can the ideas of social justice philanthropy take root and be built upon.

Endnotes

1 This chapter is based on a thesis submitted to the Faculty of Humanities, University of the Witwatersrand, Johannesburg, in fulfilment of the requirements for the degree of Master of Arts in Development Studies, 2008.

2 The word 'traditional' as used here, should not be confused to imply indigenous systems of giving. It is used in this paper to refer to the traditional way in which institutionalized giving has been carried out.

3 Private corporations, religious bodies, wealthy families, statutory and public bodies, which have a broad range of motivations and mandates.

4 In South African local government, a district is an administrative sub-division which consists of more than one municipality. No central data exists for organizations that may operate below this district level, thus inclusion of only some organizations in this category would not be representative.

5 Based on a research project produced by the Centre for Civil Society. This project included, amongst others, research on individual giving, corporate foundations, official development assistance, private foreign giving and religious giving.

6 These works are highly philosophical in nature, and a more substantive reflection of the philosophical differences can be found in the original research report. See Mahomed (2008).

7 At the time of writing this chapter in 2008, very little published literature existed. Although since then there have been several publications on the topic, this chapter does not engage with the post-2008 literature.

8 Also referred to by some as strategic philanthropy. This research takes the standpoint that social justice philanthropy and traditional philanthropy can both be strategic (as will be shown in the development of typologies later in this report) and does not use the term strategic philanthropy as the literature does.

9 Dr Emmet Carson, Barry Smith, Dr Peggy Dulaney, Collin Greer and Barry Knight, to name a few.

10 Prepared for the World Bank.

11 Impact in the general philanthropic sense refers to the effect of the intervention. Increasingly, with a number of donors, especially corporate donors, an emphasis on impact is used to mean an emphasis on tangible outputs. It is to these outputs that the expert respondents are referring.

CHAPTER 9

PHILANTHROPY IN EGYPT

MARWA EL DALY[1]

Introduction

Illiteracy, unemployment, poor health conditions, malnutrition, and general back-wardness are problems that threaten women, children and the young generation of the African continent – not excluding those Arab countries that find themselves with dual affiliation to Africa and the Arab World, to Christianity and to Islam, to traditional ethics and to western influences that have become inseparable from people's way of life. While studies reveal that the Arab world today has suffered a 20-year growth slowdown, nonetheless, poverty levels in the Arab world are not as bad as in countries with similar levels of income. One of the reasons for this given by the recent Arab World Competitiveness Report 2002–2003 is the 'cohesive system of private social responsibility' that distinguishes the Arab region, and within which families help their disadvantaged members through religious giving systems (24). This system is called *takaful* – mutual social assistance. With the failure of governments to respond to increasing needs, and the international aid organizations' misdirected assistance that has in many cases created a whole third sector profiting from aid money, it has become increasingly necessary to invest in and strengthen this system of *takaful* by mobilizing local resources, corporate social responsibility (CSR) as well as the diaspora to unite their efforts in meeting development benchmarks and directing giving towards achieving real change.

In this respect I am talking about philanthropy, where giving and volunteering are consciously directed towards achieving social change through organized and institutionalized mechanisms and not simply through ad hoc charity that is mostly scattered, occasional and for the most part not leading to real change in peoples' lives; charity often feeds the vicious circle of poverty by nourishing dependency and killing organized visionary attempts to invest in supporting people to help themselves. Although in some cases charity is essential, in most cases, if it is not accompanied by development and change-driven philanthropy, it leads to dependency, destruction of local self-help mechanisms and to a no-win situation where aid becomes a habit difficult to abandon. And the gap between the rich and the poor, the giver and the receiver becomes wider and wider.

Philanthropy in Egypt: A deeply-rooted social phenomenon

If the river Nile defines Egypt's antiquity then philanthropy is as old as the Nile – and, like the river, throughout history philanthropy has sustained Egyptians, especially the disadvantaged. Charity is practised by rich and poor people alike in Egypt, and charitable contributions are managed by secular and religious institutions. In a region where Judaism, Christianity, and Islam originated, perhaps it is not surprising that Egyptian culture is heavily influenced by religion. Philanthropy is no exception: many of the beliefs and practices that shape philanthropy in Egypt are founded in religion, even if their original meaning has been forgotten or distorted over time. Egyptian governments in recent history have played a role in the distortion or disappearance of certain faith-based philanthropic practices. For example, for centuries endowments, *waqf*, pl. *awqaf*, were the backbone of Egyptian philanthropy supporting all aspects of public life in Egypt, as well as in many other Muslim countries. These endowments began to seriously deteriorate starting in the nineteenth century. In the case of Egypt this was the beginning of what was called Modern Egypt governed by Mohamed Ali; however, the complete seizure and deterioration of civic endowments took place in the 1950s in Egypt and later in Syria.

At that time the government assumed control of all aspects of public life and became the provider of all services; it took over the properties of the civic endowments and changed the outlets and purposes that used to be supported by them according to the *shart al waqif* – the conditions set by the endowers. The income-generating endowments that the endowers had established to support long-respected causes were abolished, and *shart al waqif* was left to the choice of the Minister of Awqaf, or the new *nazir*/comptroller. This shift from civic to government management, together with the government's abolition of family *waqf* (*al waqf al ahly* that used to support the endower's offspring) brought a complete stop to this institutionalized form of philanthropic foundations.

Currently civic life is mostly represented by new forms of non-governmental organizations (NGOs), that are supervised by the Ministry of Social Solidarity; these are mostly Community Development Associations (CDAs), which are semi-government civic institutions concerned with local development, secular and religious associations, and newly emerging private foundations, together with a new model of a community foundation as seen in the establishment of the Maadi

Community Foundation, or Mu'ssasat Waqfeyat al Maadi al Ahleya. Most of these NGOs, except for very few established foundations, do not have an endowment and do not enjoy financial sustainability. Individual philanthropists give mostly to charity and rarely form any institutionalized structure, now that the old rooted system of *waqf* has been eradicated without any attempt to modernize and fit it within the new philanthropic structure.

The problem remains in the numbers. According to the UNDP Egypt Human Development Report 2005, over 20 per cent of the Egyptian population live below the poverty line and face harsh economic conditions as well as health problems. Strong positive correlation between poverty and illiteracy makes the situation difficult for development. Egypt is amongst the nine countries with the highest illiteracy rate in the world, reaching 40 per cent among men and around 60 per cent among women, with the highest rates among the rural communities. In addition, international aid influx has been in Egypt for over 30 years now, with no remarkable development benchmarks achieved nor poverty reduction measures succeeding. There are currently more than 20,000 NGOs working in Egypt, a growing third sector, but most of these organizations are small and ineffective or drained with meeting basic needs with no developmental agenda. *Takaful* is once again manifested in occasional giving, and a sense of as yet non-tangible local assistance circulating, but still not forming any considerable power in development.

Information on local philanthropy is still not adequate in terms of its quantity, nor its forms, trends, preferences, contributions, potentials or challenges. If collected systematically, it could provide a measure that would open the door for quality investments and valuable strategic interventions, instead of thousands of uncalculated development attempts. From this premise I led, together with some prominent researchers, a quantitative and qualitative comprehensive study on philanthropy, the first in Egypt to explore and estimate the impact of philanthropy and its institutions in development, and accordingly came up with recommendations for action based on the potentials and challenges revealed. Below is a description of the methodology and the findings.

Research methodology: A brief overview

The primary methodology for this study is based on both quantitative and qualitative components. The quantitative component consists of a general survey on trends of philanthropy in Egypt that was distributed in 10 Governorates (out of 22) in Egypt, to 1200 philanthropic institutions (almost 10 per cent of the total registered institutions at that time), and to 2000 Egyptian households representing the Egyptian public at large, with 95 per cent confidence interval and a permissible error of 5 per cent. This quantitative dimension was supplemented by a series of in-depth interviews aimed at deciphering general perceptions, attitudes and motives underlying philanthropic attitudes in Egypt. The list of interviewees included chairpersons and board members of philanthropic institutions, donors and beneficiaries in six Governorates.

The researchers involved with this study also conducted 120 in-depth interviews with leaders of the most prominent religious institutions (mosques and churches) engaged in social work, as well as the donors and beneficiaries of these institutions. These interviews were conducted using a random sample of board members, donors and recipients affiliated with around 60 institutions in six regions, or 5 per cent of all institutions included in the quantitative survey.

In order to grasp the general perceptions that influence philanthropic trends, the researchers investigated how Egyptians understand and imagine fundamental concepts and ideas such as philanthropy, social justice and other basic charity and development-related vocabularies. The word 'philanthropy' does not have a literal equivalent in Arabic; the closest term is *al `ata' al ijtima`i*, which means 'social giving.' The question posed to the respondents was therefore: what comes to your mind when the word 'philanthropy' is said? Their answers demonstrated that people understand philanthropy to mean charity, and make no connection between charity and development as a process to empower individuals. An overwhelming 90 per cent of those surveyed associated philanthropy with charity for the poor. Less than one per cent associated charity with donating for development projects. This staggering discrepancy clearly suggests that Egyptian people understand philanthropy as a form of charity to the poor and draw little or no correlation between charity and the socioeconomic processes of development.

Furthermore, both Muslims and Christian Egyptians alike associate philanthropy with faith-based giving, as 86 per cent of those surveyed defined philanthropy in terms of either Muslim almsgiving (*zakat*) or Christian tithes ('*ushur*). In addition to religion, perceptions of philanthropy in Egypt are also heavily influenced by the twin ideas of social solidarity and compassion (*takaful*). This conclusion is supported by the finding that 80 per cent of respondents explained philanthropy as an expression of social solidarity. When asked who were the most worthy to receive alms, a clear majority (87 per cent) of respondents indicated the poor and the needy were the most deserving. The other targets of philanthropy that respondents identified were people suffering from chronic diseases, regardless of religious affiliation.

The concept of social justice possibly revealed the most varied and ambivalent responses. Respondents interpreted the idea of social justice in a variety of ways. Moreover, these different modes of understanding social justice varied most strongly according to education levels and economic status. In general, those with higher levels of education understood the term 'social justice' as a political concept. Since social justice is frequently associated with images of political divisiveness, several respondents shied away from a discussion on the subject. For example, while responding to questions on social justice, one respondent categorically stated, 'I do not want to talk about politics, please!' Such hesitation clearly reveals that for some people it is problematic to discuss social justice with strangers as it relates to socialism and political systems (religious or secular) that oppose the trend of governance of the Hosni Mubarak regime. From this perspective, talking about social justice is talking opposition, an opposition to be avoided when talking publicly because it might bring problems with government authorities.

Social justice conceptually was also associated by several respondents with the idea of social solidarity (*takaful*). Here, an interesting trend observed is the commonality among both Muslims and Christians in the regular association of social justice with social solidarity. Moreover, respondents often drew on examples from the time of the Prophet and his companions to articulate their understanding of social solidarity and the role of the ruler in establishing a socially just political order. As one of the respondents stated, 'We must go back to the Islamic system, to apply the concept of *shura* (consultation), *muba'ya* (electoral politics) and the caliphate succession system, where no ruler remains in power for so long.' The last statement is an obvious reference to the long rule of President Mubarak, who was deposed in 2011 through the Arab uprisings. This gentleman continued, 'People always follow the religions of their rulers, which means people follow the principles that are adopted by the rulers. Hence we need a good role model, a role model like Umar Ibn Khattab (Second caliph in Sunni Islam, famous for his social justice).

Social justice was also understood in terms of addressing socioeconomic inequalities by several respondents. The top three reasons for the prevalence of socioeconomic inequalities in Egypt were identified as: the growing disparity between the rich and poor, an inequitable distribution of economic and natural resources between different sections of society, severe disparity in both the quantity and quality of social services available in central urban locations and the rural peripheries of the country.

There is a correlation between illiteracy and popular modes of predestination. Among individuals with high levels of illiteracy, the presence of social inequalities was often attributed to God's will and desire. According to such respondents, it is only God who possesses the power to distribute wealth among people, and it is only He who has the ability to cause any kind of social justice. However, here one should be cautious; this finding does not necessarily establish a causative relationship between lower income levels and a visible predilection for reliance on God's will on matters of social justice, rather, there can be a host of other factors at work. Moreover, this submissive attitude can be a product of both intense devotional piety and a mindset of resignation whereby the power of the Almighty is invoked as a pretext for escaping any form of personal responsibility. It could also be a product of an educational system and a cultural and political environment encouraging passive thinking. That said, these attitudes point to an image of philanthropy that is heavily infected with notions of divine beneficence. In an even more explicit reference to religious and theological underpinnings of philanthropy, respondents also explained social justice as 'the right of God' (*haqq Allah*). In financial terms, the right of God here refers to equitable notions of income distribution predicated on a system of giving whereby a regular exchange of resources from the rich to the poor is established. One respondent provided scriptural evidence for this kind of a system by referring to the Qur'anic verse: 'And in whose wealth there is a right acknowledged for the beggar and the destitute' (Qur'an 70; 24: 25). Obligatory Muslim almsgiving (*zakat*) is the key element in the religious idea that links philanthropy to social justice. As one of the five obligatory pillars of Islam, almsgiving clearly stipulates the centrality of philanthropy to any ethics of Muslim subjectivity. One *shaykh* (religious scholar) interviewed commented: 'If social justice starts with equality of all people in the eyes of God, then social justice is at the heart of Islam.'

One of the major findings of this study is that religious leaders in Egypt generally perceive economic development as a religious duty. Furthermore, they tend to believe that the public and clergy share a common commitment to facilitate economic development in the country. Several religious scholars referred to Prophet Muhammad's teachings while making their case in favour of structural development, which they believed is preferable according to Muslim teaching. According to one respondent, 'The Prophet, blessings and peace be upon him, said, "If the day of resurrection befalls and one of you has a seed in his hand, he should plant it."'

Religious scholars interviewed also advocated the proper application of labour and the exercise of restraint from begging. They argued that the Prophet forbade begging in many of his teachings, and called upon his followers to be proactive and industrious with their work. It is useful to note here that, while articulating their preference for socioeconomic development over independent charity, several respondents (especially religious scholars) copiously drew on prophetic narratives to propound their argument. For example, several religious scholars referred to the story of a beggar who once accosted the Prophet asking for charity (*ihsan*). The Prophet inquired whether the beggar owned any possessions, to which the beggar replied that he only owned a blanket and a drinking pot. Then, instead of providing the beggar with instant charity, the Prophet helped him organize an auction at which he sold the two items that the beggar owned. With the revenue generated by these sales, the beggar was able to buy an axe with which he could work and thus support his family. This story's regular rendition in the Egyptian public sphere clearly demonstrates the way social justice is associated with the prophetic spirit. Clearly, the mobilization of this prophetic spirit represents a key variable in the acceptance of a philanthropic culture that is based on social development as op-posed to individual giving. Invoking reports, stories and narratives that associate the Prophet with an entrepreneurial as opposed to a charity-driven attitude can serve as a highly effective rhetorical device for the promotion of a collective mindset that privileges economic development over individual giving. Fostering an attitude that will prefer development over individual charity will take considerable time, energy and some robust campaigning. However, the signs indicated in this study are quite encouraging. According to the results gathered in this study, most Egyptians agree that development represents a much more effective tool for sustainable social change than charity. As one respondent to our survey so trenchantly remarked, 'Charity is only for consumption and does not solve any problem in the long run.'

Charitable practices in Islam

The chief source of the institutionalization of benevolence and charity in Islam is almsgiving (*zakat*). Egyptian Muslims consider almsgiving a sacred duty. Although respondents displayed general familiarity with the concept of almsgiving in Islam, they were largely unaware of the different varieties of almsgiving that exist in the Islamic tradition. Moreover, they also seemed unfamiliar with the specific benefits associated with particular forms of almsgiving sanctioned by the Qur'an. The majority of respondents showed an awareness of *zakat al-fitr* (charity given at the end of the month of Ramadan), but they were much less informed of *zakat il-mal* (charity to be paid on possessions, a system that prevents the stagnation of capital). Both these types of charity are obligatory on Muslims. In Egypt, the stipulated minimum for *zakat al-fitr* is a relatively small sum, around US$1 per person. This amount must be paid by all Muslims regardless of age, gender, economic or social status as an expiatory tax at the completion of Ramadan, the month of fasting. Most Muslims, rich and poor, in Egypt are familiar with this requirement, can afford it, and pay it consistently. Even single mothers who support families of five members or more and earn a monthly income of less than US$17 fulfil this obligation of paying the minimum amount of US$1 for each of their direct family members every year. One of these women said, 'After Ramadan I give the *zakat al-fitr* for myself and for all my children to the *Shaykh*. This is God's money.' This woman donates almost a quarter of her monthly income at the end of Ramadan. She willingly donates because of her belief that the dispossessed in society have a claim over her wealth and because of her conviction that the donated money is the right of God. Therefore, the act of awarding a donation affirms her devotion and piety towards God.

Several well-educated respondents expressed their concern that the system of Islamic almsgiving is poorly understood by Egyptian Muslims. Respondents argued that if people understood the system of obligatory annual Islamic almsgiving in all its complexities and then accurately calculated and paid their share of it accordingly, then poverty in Egypt could be eliminated or radically decreased. Also, interestingly, nearly 40 per cent of Muslim respondents were willing to make people of other religions beneficiaries of their general charities. Some 34 per cent of Egyptian Christians reflected the same attitudes.

The concept of the 'endowments' (*waqf* pl. *awqaf*) is poorly understood by most Egyptians. *Waqf* in Arabic literally means 'to cease' or 'to stop'. In the context of charity, its definition is extended to mean 'to tie up' profit or income. Around 60 per cent of those surveyed could not identify any institutions that were endowments (*awqaf*) and 30 per cent did not understand what the term means at all, while the vast majority confused the meaning of *waqf* with government's possessions (as many of the *waqf* properties all over the country are known to be owned and managed by the Ministry of Awqaf). The few who were able to recognize the term *waqf* mainly understood it as part of an obsolete vocabulary with no relevance to the present. Some respondents complained that the Ministry of Awqaf is monopolizing the management of charitable and family endowments in Egypt, and defended the origin of *waqf* that stipulated the financial autonomy of endowed structures and emphasized the importance of private management that respects the conditions of the endower (*shart al waqif*).

Historically, endowments were the backbone of civil society in Egypt; they were independent and autonomous financially sustainable institutions that were initiated and funded by private individuals and families to support charity work, development projects (on the national and regional levels) and family heirs. The responses by some of the respondents indicate the massive transformation of the institution of endowments from its earlier practice. As previously indicated, over the years the Egyptian government nationalized all charitable and family endowments, and civil-managed *awqaf* foundations came under the supervision and management of the Ministry of Awqaf. Hence, the *waqf* structure lost its autonomy and independence, and became associated with a government body. This resulted in people losing faith in the institution, preferring other means of philanthropy. By all indications, knowledge about the proper application and characteristics of charitable and family endowments has evaporated in Egypt. However, the term *waqf* continues to resurface in the Egyptian public sphere in the articulation of certain proverbs and olds sayings. For example: 'She is left with no man, like the house of *waqf*' is a popular Egyptian saying that refers to a rented house whose income is used to fund social work.

The widespread ignorance about endowments is a major obstacle to the institutionalization of philanthropy in Egypt. The cultivation of a strategic culture of philanthropy in Egypt will not be possible without the awareness of the Egyptian public about the proper uses and applications of endowments. Here, a quick comparison with the case of Turkey is useful. In general, Turkey has been quite successful in protecting the autonomy of charitable endowments and in sustaining the growth of Islamic endowments. The Turkish example provides valuable lessons for Egypt and other Arab and African countries, like Sudan, where central governments have assumed an unhealthy degree of control over formerly autonomous private endowments. Government interventions have crippled or destroyed the endowments system in Egypt and other Arab countries while it continues to gather steam in Turkey. Undue government interference in the endowment sector in Egypt has resulted in highly undesirable economic consequences, such as discouraging entrepreneurs from investing their money and driving away social philanthropists desirous of aiding development in the country. Therefore, in order to ensure the autonomy of philanthropists and entrepreneurs, it is imperative that the interference of the Egyptian government in the endowment sector of the economy is minimized and properly managed.

Philanthropy and the government

Three governmental bodies monitor NGOs in Egypt: the Central Accounting Office, that audits financial operations, the Security Department, which investigates security concerns and, together with the Ministry of Social Solidarity, plays the role of official supervising authority. Many board members of NGOs stated that governmental regulations are not a concern as long as NGOs comply with the law. On the other hand, some organizations expressed their frustration with government oversight. They argued that censorship is often annoying and obstructs the organization's work, especially when the state's security apparatuses interfere.

The Egyptian government has a significant influence on the country's NGOs. The Ministry of Social Solidarity, the central supervising body, strictly monitors the work of NGOs in Egypt and must be informed of all external funding coming to the organizations. However, most representatives of NGOs reported a decent relationship between their organizations and the Ministry of Social Solidarity, which is a positive trend. Board members reported that the government has simplified the requirements for establishing a new organization, but some complained about the government-mandated security check on the founders of their organizations. Approval of NGOs can often be an arduous and tedious process, with frequent delays and red tape hampering the process.

Egyptian law permits NGOs to invest money in ways that guarantee a sustainable and secure income. However, NGOs are forbidden from engaging in risky ventures like investment in the stock market. This study found that only 30 per cent of NGOs took advantage of the opportunity to invest in savings accounts under their officially registered names. Some NGOs were unaware of the law, and believe it was illegal for them to invest their income.

Mosques and the government

The government also exercises control over mosques, through the Ministry of Endowment and through Nasser Bank, which supervises the activities of each mosque's almsgiving committee. Most religious scholars registered a strong sense of disapproval of government intervention in their affairs. As one religious scholar from northern Egypt said,

'The Ministry of Endowment appointed a government employee as our Imam, and he dutifully follows the instructions of the government on what to say in his sermons. How can we advocate a religious platform of our own when all the sermons in our mosques are dictated to us by the government?'

Another religious scholar registered his emphatic protest by saying, 'Men of religion have been turned into government employees. In the past, the Imam used to be highly respected for his religious education and knowledge. He used to preach for the sake of Allah, but now Imams are government employees. They have been chained.'

The Nasser Bank supervises every aspect of the *zakat* committee, from opening the collection boxes to checking receipts for expenditures. The government operates on a very narrow definition of charity. For example, government officials offer no leeway for the *zakat* committee to extend charity to development projects founded on micro-loans, according to many of the respondents from the *zakat* committees. In fact, the strict governmental control of almsgiving funds has forced several *zakat* committee members to establish their own NGOs so that they are able to escape the strings and invasive scrutiny of the government.

Monies collected in mosques through 'oath *(nuzur)* boxes' are another point of contention between the government and the religious sector. Devout Muslims who take an oath for religious purposes often accompany their pledges with a charitable contribution to the needy or as an act of expiation for breaking an oath. Mosque attendees often drop their donations into these designated boxes. These donation boxes are opened by the Ministry of Endowment, which is supposed to allocate these funds to mosques for the purpose of renovations and upgrading facilities. However, there is no public record of how and where these donations are spent. As one donor to these 'oath boxes' stated,

'The Ministry does not spend as much money on local mosques as it should, so the local mosques must pay for their own building maintenance and renovations. After 50 years of government neglect, we finally renovated our mosque's bathrooms at our own expense.'

Philanthropic motives

What motivates Egyptians to engage in philanthropy? What compels them to give? The central driving force behind philanthropic activity in Egypt is religion, or rather a strong commitment towards religious teachings that command the magnanimity towards the less privileged. Both Muslims and Christians share the perception that charity is a religious duty. Egyptian Muslims mostly associate the concept of charity with almsgiving. Muslim respondents explained that withholding alms is equivalent to snatching money from the poor. They also argued that the idea of God's claim (*haqq Allah*) forbids Muslims from hoarding wealth that belongs to the poor. As one respondent said when asked about his motives to donate, 'I donate to serve God. As verses from the Qur'an indicate, "what you do to any of my little ones you do to me".'

Social solidarity (*takaful*) is the principal motive that propels philanthropy in Egypt. Social solidarity rests on the twin notions of compassion and a sense of communal interdependence. The idea of social solidarity is deeply rooted in Egyptian culture, and people's commitment to it has resulted in widespread philanthropic activity. Moreover, most Egyptians consider the imperative of *takaful* as a religious obligation directly derived from the Qur'an and the sayings and teachings of the Prophet (*Sunna*). Other respondents declared that compassion is an innate natural-born imperative that cannot escape any human being. As one respondent said, 'Helping is an imperative that is found in the inner part of a human being. It is a psychological motive; it is the instinctive love for doing good things to others.'

Respondents indicated that their first obligation in charitable acts is towards needy relatives and neighbours. Interestingly, respondents also indicated a strong preference for distributing alms locally and within their own neighbourhoods rather than in remote and distant places. Again, several respondents drew on the prophetic example to support their preference for engaging in localized philanthropic activity. For example, many respondents made reference to the following prophetic saying: 'Gabriel kept advising me to treat my neighbour in a kind and polite manner to the extent that I thought that he would order (me) to make them (my) heirs.' In short, the tradition of social solidarity has ensured that philanthropy remains a vital part of Egyptian society even as awareness and knowledge of the specific requirements of almsgiving continues to dwindle.

Other major philanthropic motives vary from individual to individual. Retired people, for example, volunteer their free time in community outreach activities. Others donate wealth out of genuine compassion for the poor and because they fear that withholding alms equates to stealing from the needy. Some people donate as a means to receive divine blessings and in expectation that their generosity will result in the acceptance of their prayers and in the fulfilment of earthly needs.

Tax deductions and the enhancement of social prestige are the least common motivators for philanthropic activity in Egypt, as indicated by individual respondents. However, they remain one of the primary discouraging factors for institutionalized philanthropy, which would permit individuals to deduct their charities from their taxes. As tax exemption laws are not clear and not well articulated, people in general as well as the third sector personnel are ignorant about them. Reviews of these laws need to take place and the third sector needs to be engaged in providing its points of view with regard to the law. Social prestige is not a motive in a culture that values anonymous giving. However, in some cases, politicians may distribute funds as a means to secure votes in an upcoming election. This kind of political manoeuvring is not commonplace. However, because of the increasing number of businesspeople entering the Egyptian political scene, it is becoming increasingly common to engage in philanthropy as a pretext for the acquisition of political gains. Here, it should be noted that if these types of donations were directed at developmental projects, they would not only serve the interests of the community but would also service the political ambitions of politicians. In addition, a reform in the current tax law is a necessity as the current one does not play any role in encouraging philanthropy like in most of the advanced countries.

Philanthropy in Egypt today is oriented towards charity and service. People tend to give directly to individuals they know (40.2 per cent among Muslims and 21.7 per cent among Christians), or to charitable or service-oriented organizations (12 per cent) that serve the poor. Very few of the respondents would give to local NGOs engaged in development efforts such as granting small loans or creating job opportunities for the unemployed (1.2 per cent). Egyptians tend to give most generously to whom the Qur'an describes as *al-aqrabun*, those nearest in kin (78.6 per cent) or neighbourly proximity (36.3 per cent). Especially in small villages, this system of interdependence enables communities to survive on local initiatives. The widespread sense of responsibility towards one's community indicates good possibilities for establishing community foundations, especially if it simultaneously revives the community *waqf* tradition.

Nearly 80 per cent of respondents give to relatives and nearly 40 per cent give to neighbours. Even NGOs rely on local networks of relationships because their fundraisers usually end up developing close personal ties with donors. That Egyptian people feel more inclined to donate to their community members bodes well for the possibility of establishing a robust foundation of institutionalized philanthropy.

Difficulty in quantifying philanthropy in Egypt

There is a direct correlation between the state of the Egyptian economy and the intensity of philanthropic activity. For example, the economic crisis of 2008 has resulted in a sharp decline in charitable contributions to individuals, NGOs, mosques, and churches. However, even as general economic conditions worsened, voluntary services in the country continued to take place. This may be due to the fact that those who can no longer donate money contribute in the form of volunteering their time and skills. Voluntary activity may also be attributed to rising unemployment, which enables people to contribute more time to charitable causes. When respondents were asked why they did not give to charity, the vast majority of them explained that they did not have enough resources to do so. Some 70 per cent of those who make charitable contributions donate on an irregular basis. Less than 15 per cent of respondents make charitable contributions more than once per week, mostly by way of giving to beggars in the streets.

As this was the first attempt to quantify philanthropy in Egypt, it was very difficult to obtain information because of a philanthropic environment where privacy is highly valued and distrust is widespread. Respondents exhibited a constant fear of intervention from the government and other international organizations that they suspected might be harbouring hostile agendas against Arabs in general and Muslims in particular. People were also hesitant to break confidentiality about their giving practices, since in their view Islam and Christianity value anonymity when it comes to charity.

Nonetheless, from the data collected in this study, we are able to report some important quantifiers of Egyptian philanthropy. The total annual donations in Egypt in 2003–04 reached more than 5.5 billion Egyptian pounds (LE), or approximately US$1 billion. We also found that just over 6 per cent of Egyptians volunteered an average of 2.5 hours per month in 2004. Thus, an average of 2.3 million hours is volunteered per month, c.28 million hours per year. Volunteering adds approximately US$10 million annually to the Egyptian economy, if one hour of volunteering were roughly equal to LE2. Thus, the total annual philanthropic contribution in Egypt is over LE5.5 billion (c.US$1 billion).

The 2003 World Bank Report stated that the average per capita economic foreign aid to Egypt was US$13 annually, noting that the population at that time was 67.5 million. The average per capita philanthropic contribution from this study can be calculated by dividing the total philanthropic contribution annually by the total population. This brings the per capita philanthropic contribution to US$14, just more than the average per capita economic foreign aid. This comparison underscores the tremendous impact that Egyptian philanthropy can have on poverty alleviation and social justice in the country.

Most Egyptian NGOs rely on national resources rather than foreign funds. The philanthropic organizations we surveyed rely primarily on membership fees (95 per cent), local charitable donations (83 per cent) and almsgiving funds (45 per cent). To a lesser degree they also rely on service-related income (36 per cent). Only 8.5 per cent of organizations receive foreign funding, and less than 3 per cent receive funding from foreign Arab and Islamic sources. Therefore, there are several examples of successful national NGOs in Egypt that can serve as splendid role models of local funding and financial sustainability. However, Egyptian NGOs continue to face numerous challenges to their fundraising potential, including culturally-ingrained giving patterns, lack of trust, and other legal and economic constraints.

Nearly 70 per cent of the NGOs surveyed do not invest their resources to generate more income and to guarantee better rates of growth and sustainability. The organizations that do invest their resources primarily do so in fixed bank deposits (27 per cent). Fewer than five per cent invest in investment certificates, and none of the organizations invest in the stock exchange, as do grantmaking organizations in other countries, because they are forbidden from doing so according to Egyptian law.

This study also found that a strong culture of anonymous giving prevails in Egypt: 95 per cent of respondents maintain secrecy in their giving. Of this total, 66 per cent believe that secrecy in charitable activities is a religious duty. People give in secret primarily because they believe that if their gift were made public, they would lose heavenly credits for their charity. To a lesser degree, respondents maintain secrecy in their giving practices in order to preserve the dignity of their beneficiaries. Anonymous giving presents a central obstacle to development-oriented philanthropy, because people who give anonymously are also more likely to give directly to the needy rather than to organizations. In addition, public appeals for funds are less effective with donors who prefer to maintain anonymity.

Conclusion

The question remains: in light of these findings, is the region ready for a wave of change that could lead institutionalized philanthropy towards achieving more development and more social justice? The answer is yes. First, the deteriorating economic conditions in impoverished Arab and Islamic countries have compelled the governments to allow space for socially responsible citizens to intervene, giving up the idea of being the sole provider of care and services (like the social spirit of the 1950s, for example). There is an emerging class of businesspeople and rich

Gulf philanthropists who feel the drive to help their fellow Arab and Muslims and write their names in history books that have a page wide open inviting them to fill a present gap. An example of this is the rising number of NGOs registered in some North African countries such as Egypt and Morocco and the rise of a relative freedom of civic engagement in a country like Saudi Arabia, even allowing for women-led developmental initiatives to take place. The recent uprisings in the region are also a testimony to what citizens can do if they took initiatives to drive their own development.

The second reason inviting optimism is that non-traditional international donor agencies have become more conscious about their role in supporting social entrepreneurs and offer awards to innovative philanthropic interventions that are sustainable and by default institutionalized and organized. This has shifted people's attention towards local philanthropic models and rung a bell for learning, signalling a shift in direction that now entails concepts such as change, social justice, social mobility and a socially responsible sector, both in business and at individual level. One of the remarkable examples is Ashoka and the Prince Talal Award, two initiatives that are encouraging others like Synergos to adopt new programmes that invest in the social innovators of the region; not to forget TrustAfrica, with its model that attempts to explore and mobilize on local resources and look inwards to achieve change and development.

Third, the study on philanthropy in Egypt[2] which is presented in this document is another influential reason, as it has been the cornerstone for the emergence of a wide range of initiatives willing to explore philanthropy, and to work on means of organizing and institutionalizing giving to achieve development. This study is the first scientific attempt to explore philanthropy and forms of institutionalized philanthropy in Egypt as well as in six other Muslim and Muslim-inhabited countries. It followed a scientific methodology with a representative sample of the population and the civic sector, included case studies, and was published and disseminated widely, firstly at a major conference in Egypt. The conference was held under the auspices of the Minister of Social Solidarity and the Ministry of Endowment, with the sponsorship of a private sector philanthropist, and socially responsible cooperation with the participation of top-notch civil society representatives from all over Egypt, people of religion and the media sector.

Fourth, the private sector, and especially this young generation of private philanthropists and young people heading the CSR programmes, began to play a leading role in their quest for change. It has become evident that there is a win-win situation in enhancing the status of the society, and civic initiatives to influence their thinking have led to the emergence of three types of private interventions: i) private foundations like that of Sawiris Foundation for Development in Egypt,

Sheikh Mohamed Bin Rashid Al Maktoum in the United Arab Emirates and others across the region; ii) a type of NGOs supported by private-sector philanthropists like the Food Bank Initiative, Orman NGO-organized giving campaign, and others in Egypt and elsewhere in the Arab region; and iii) the secretive private-sector philanthropists who support developmental initiatives but on a personal, individual, yet sustainable basis.

It encourages philanthropists, CSR, and the diaspora to invest for social change through organizing their giving and reviving the *waqf* endowment model that aims at social mobility, starting with a specific geographical area. It was observed by this foundation, founded in 2007, that philanthropists in the Maadi area and beyond are eager to endow and bring sustainability to their giving but they lack the models and knowledge on the efficient use of their philanthropies.

Fifth is the emerging model of community foundations, a system to serve certain geographical areas to gradually achieve and monitor change. The Maadi Community Foundation – Waqfeyat al Maadi al Ahleya – was the first community foundation to be created in Egypt. The foundation is also a pioneer initiative of this type of foundation (*mu'assassat*), emerging with non-traditional missions seeking to revive institutionalized philanthropy in the form of *waqf* and standing as a facilitator for philanthropists, young and old, on the most strategic means to achieve change. They are monitored by the Maadi Community Foundation, the he first community foundation to be established in Egypt aimed at mobilizing institutionalized philanthropy.

Another community foundation from the region is the Dalia Foundation in Palestine; this foundation represents locally-driven initiatives that advocate for change on the policy and the social level. Finally there is also the Abu Dhabi Foundation, which is a foundation that works on serving the area of Abu Dhabi in the United Arab Emirates, yet it also extends its services regionally and internationally. National and regional links between foundations and especially local initiatives is a promising factor for organized and institutionalized philanthropy in the region.

Sixth, CSR is growing faster and faster, with multinational companies expanding their work in the Arab world and to a large extent in the Gulf; in countries like Saudi Arabia, the United Arab Emirates, Kuwait and others, CSR programmes have very impressive interventions that influences local initiatives of institutionalized philanthropy.

Seventh, technology, like the use of internet facilities and programmes such as MSN, Facebook, and others, allow the young Egyptian cultured generation to come together, share the causes they believe in and activate groups that mobilize efforts and resources to achieve certain objectives. These cyber tools are promising for attracting similar-minded people and in spreading messages.

Eighth, legal reform of the civic sector has been taking place since 1999 when the old NGO law No. 32 of year 1964 was finally revised and a new law, 153/99, was issued but soon proved to be unconstitutional. However, this left space and momentum for the formulation and inauguration of law 82/2002 that was a positive albeit incomplete revision of the older NGO law that had lasted unchanged for about 40 years. The new NGO law distinguished different forms of civic structures and gave shape and accordingly birth to private foundations. This was a significant step in encouraging institutionalized philanthropy in Egypt, as it allowed philanthropists to start an endowment and have a board of trustees to manage foundations, unlike the former model of semi-governmental structures referred to as Community Development Associations that lacked local initiation and had to involve government representatives on their board of directors.

Ninth, the major implication of the study is that philanthropy constitutes a considerable power that, if properly allocated, could contribute to development and change. This does not only apply to Egypt, but to the Arab and African region that has known civic movements that sustained living in spite of the harsh economic conditions and authoritarian governments. Indigenous mechanisms of local interdependence, if modernized and enhanced to fit the modern demands and structures, are the best means to combat challenges as they stem from within and are the results of generations of care for one's community.

To sum up, local giving in Egypt is a substantial force but it is rather wasted in a vicious circle of charity that is mostly personal and non-institutional. Even those local monies and efforts that go to support institutions tend to be channelled towards those working in charitable activities like orphanages, yet only around one per cent would support development associations. However, one positive aspect remains that most NGOs in Egypt operate by relying on membership fees and religious giving, whether Christian or Muslim. Hence the local NGOs that are found working in the field trying to meet people's needs are independent from international aid, yet are small and charity oriented. The few rather big NGOs that are mostly connected to international aid donors and work in the capital of the country are those that absorb most of the international aid, and work in cooperation with the government in the bi-governmental aid agreements to provide trainings, do workshops, etc. Those that do development are not financially sustainable, rely on aid money and often act as brokers between international organizations and small NGOs. On the other hand, NGOs that are locally driven and do represent the people are charity oriented and do not act as partners in the development process. This formula needs to shift. International aid needs to be invested well and in response to achieving concrete benchmarks. Broker NGOs that enjoy much more supervisory freedom than local ones should be engaged in a partnership relationship with local NGOs where financial sustainability of both is compulsory. And local NGOs need to learn how to mobilize philanthropies and gain the trust of people to envision together a plan for the future where collective efforts are geared to achieve.

If people are taught what *waqf* means and how important sustainable sources of financing like endowments are, local philanthropy would gradually rise to play an even more vital role than international aid. However, people need to see that their contributions could make a difference and that the system that they are invited to contribute to benefits this poor person knocking on their door, yet it would help in a decent discreet and organized way. As for philanthropic foundations, as seen from the study, only 30 per cent invest their resources to guarantee sustainability and money growth. The other 70 per cent must learn to accept the fact that international donations and charities are not a long-term solution and local philanthropy needs to invest in developing *waqf* or endowments. In addition, the third sector must advocate for laws that facilitate its efforts to invest and also for the inauguration of a more encouraging tax law. Even if the government does not take the initiative to consult the third sector on its development agenda, philanthropic organizations should come together and invite the government, socially responsible corporations and philanthropists, media and international organizations to collectively draw a development map, set benchmarks and assign responsibility.

Monitoring and evaluation techniques must be incorporated and followed up by committees. In addition, media should be the source of knowledge to the public and bridge the gap between philanthropic organizations and the people; it should be working closely with all stakeholders, not forgetting the third-sector researchers, field-workers, academia with related students clubs and activists. In addition, philanthropic foundations need to take the lead in making partnerships amongst themselves; as shown from the study, the majority of people do not know about the third sector's work, and hence refrain from actively engaging. Developing greater knowledge of third-sector work would make work in the field more sound and credible.

When the research team was undertaking the study on philanthropy all over the country, in the small villages, with givers, receivers, Muslims, Christians, secular, religious, etc., the researchers felt a wave of optimism and the interviewees, with their different backgrounds, began expressing their dreams. This enthusiasm manifested further in a successful conference attended by participants who came from all over, expecting no return except that they were heard and that there is a potential for change. This momentum must be created by philanthropic organizations, no matter how busy they are with their daily work.

Finally, the diaspora should be energized by philanthropic foundations in co-operation with student groups, chambers of commerce and upon invitations by international donor organizations. The diaspora must have a precise role to play, and trust measures like good governance of NGOs, transparency, as well as constant reporting are the best means to gain the support of the diaspora. However, above all the diaspora should feel part of the agenda setting and that it really contributes to change. Educating philanthropists and the diaspora about development remains the responsibility of philanthropic organizations.

And international development organizations should invest in local NGOs, by providing them with means to help themselves in order to allow them to help others. NGOs must put forward clear visions, develop business plans and investment tactics, manage endowments and revive the *waqf* system. Responsible CSR people within corporations should be development specialists before being marketing personnel. Roundtables involving them, NGO people and government officials must be a habitual event. The government's position in this relationship should be more of guidance than control in order to gain trust from this sector and from the masses at large. Transparency, along with trust, is absolutely a critical issue for the growth of philanthropy in Egypt. A lack of transparency undermines trust throughout the philanthropic sector. More than 80 per cent of Egyptians remain reluctant to donate to NGOs because they are suspicious of what these organizations will do with their money. More than 60 per cent of respondents expressed a lack of trust of NGOs, and more than half pointed out that there is a lack of transparency in the philanthropic sector. Therefore, programmes promoting trust are urgently needed. Programmes promoting education are vital; not only for NGOs, but for philanthropists, the diaspora, government officials concerned with social solidarity, and all the coming young generations that should know about their philanthropic history, their indigenous development mechanisms, their potential to achieve social solidarity and their power to change the world through passing on knowledge and good work.

Endnotes

1   Marwa El Daly was selected in 2007 by Ashoka as a Social Entrepreneur from the Arab region in recognition of her efforts in institutionalizing philanthropy and the revival of the *waqf* endowment system. The novelty of the model of the Waqfeyat al Maadi is its structure, mission, approach and the influence it has started to make on policy change, qualifying it to be a pioneer initiative in the domain of institutionalized philanthropy in Egypt and in the region at large.

2   Marwa El Daly. 'Philanthropy in Egypt: A Comprehensive Study on Local Philanthropy in Egypt and Potentials of Directing Giving and Volunteering towards Development'. Egypt, CDS 2007. This study was funded by the Ford Foundation and the research was led by Marwa El Daly, Program Manager of Philanthropy for Development Program at the Center for Development Services (CDS) at that time and founder

and current Chairperson of the Maadi Community Foundation, Waqfeyat al Maadi al Ahleya (MCF/WMA). This national study was part of an international study that involved six countries: Egypt, Indonesia, Turkey, the Muslim communities in India, Tanzania and the United Kingdom.

CHAPTER 10

PHILANTHROPY IN NIGERIA: STATE OF THE PRACTICE AND NEW FRONTIERS

KAYODE SAMUEL

Introduction

As with many societies, charitable giving has been an aspect of life in Nigeria, having its roots in both traditional beliefs and religious injunctions. The incipient variants of philanthropy that were prevalent in many parts of Nigeria assumed new and systematized forms with the onset of the economic crisis in the early 1980s. However, since the country's return to democratic rule at the turn of the century, wealth accumulation has concentrated mostly in the oil, banking, commodities and telecommunications sectors. This new wealth has fuelled the rise of business barons and big organizations that have in turn sought to impact charitable and philanthropic giving with a fresh verve.

This chapter examines the underlying traditions as well as current state of giving in Nigeria. It seeks to identify forms and variants of philanthropy and to propose ways to further systematize and institutionalize giving in Africa's largest nation. The approach adopted is to situate philanthropy as one of the many responses to the challenges of development and democratic consolidation in a country that is still undergoing a complex transition. The chapter presents the state-of-the-practice in the philanthropic sector and examines nascent and extant forms of giving. It also outlines aspects of Nigeria's multifaceted crisis of state, society and economy that could be amenable to philanthropic intervention, as a contribution to strengthening the basis of the country's young democracy. It further argues that a properly structured system of strategic philanthropy that gives due cognizance to local realities, could assure increased pools of local support for development initiatives and help to expand the civic space, thereby brightening prospects for social justice that had been constrained during Nigeria's years of economic down-turn and despotic military rule. The chapter concludes by identifying some of the most recent initiatives in the field of private and corporate philanthropy, noting that the development of philanthropy in Nigeria is still largely work-in-progress.

Political economy context and background

By the mid-1990s, Nigeria was counting the costs of a Structural Adjustment Programme (SAP) that was largely inspired by creditor nations and international financial institutions a decade earlier to address the country's economic difficulties and huge debt overhang. The social and economic consequences of the programme have been copiously documented and continue to generate much scholarly and policy interest if not recrimination in many circles. But in Nigeria the programme also had serious political consequences that may not have been as sufficiently ex-plored as the social and economic ones.

By the mid-1990s, Nigeria had entered a most delicate and volatile phase of the national crisis that erupted in the aftermath of the annulment of the June 12, 1993 presidential elections and the failed democratization project of the military regime. The crisis itself was a direct consequence of a debilitating culture of patronage politics that fuelled primitive accumulation and made the struggle for state power literally a matter of life and death amongst elite actors. Ethnicity, regionalism and religion were routinely deployed as weapons of warfare by the political elite. In Nigeria, access to state power, more so in a milieu in which accountability and transparency rules were still in their infancy, had been largely coterminous with access to wealth, thus making the struggle for power quite intense. The annulment crisis, however, went beyond anything that the country had ever witnessed, espe-cially because it erupted within an 'adjustment environment' where the disloca-tions wrought by SAP and the culture of repression that festered under prolonged military rule had dangerously radicalized dissent, constraining the efficacy and legitimacy of non-violent approaches to conflict resolution and crisis management.

The annulment crisis heralded the military regime of General Sani Abacha, which had by 1995 consolidated itself in power. The return of full-blown military rule, after feeble attempts at democratization, further compounded the multifaceted crisis of state and society in Nigeria. In less than four decades since independence, Nigeria witnessed in turn an astonishing regression from the euphoria of decolo-nization and independence; to the political turmoil of the mid-1960s and a brutal civil war (1967–70); prolonged military rule; a short-lived civilian interregnum in the Second Republic; the return of the military; and a convoluted transition programme that in the end delivered the still-born Third Republic and more crisis still. The latter half of all of this happened amidst economic chaos, the failure of Structural Adjustment and a precipitate fall in average standards of living.

Civil society organizations, especially of the left-leaning activist variant, had first emerged on the national scene as the SAP unfolded. In 1989 they were quite prominent, alongside the trade unions, in organizing the May anti-SAP demonstrations that were brutally suppressed by the military junta. They were subsequently to be very active in opposing the annulment and resisting the ensuing military dictatorship. Also, NGOs focusing on environmental advocacy, community development and poverty reduction had been quite visible since the onset of economic crisis in the early 1980s. Their interventions were largely solidarity based, with some focusing on financial intermediation for resource-poor groups. Many of these organizations were, however, largely dependent on external donor funds, with little or none of their funding coming from local sources. This fact was to assume great significance as the national crisis unfolded in the mid-1990s.

Meanwhile, the emergent cycle of resistance and repression that followed the return of full-blown military rule late in 1993 fuelled tension in the country, ultimately deepening Nigeria's isolation from the international community. Repression was to plumb new depths with the execution in November 1995 of the writer and environmentalist Ken Saro-Wiwa, alongside eight activists from the oil-rich Ogoni minority group, after a controversial trial and without the conclusion of the legal appeal process. The Ogoni Nine, as the victims came to be known, were protesting the impoverishment of their people, the denial of minority rights and the harmful environmental practices of multinational companies operating in the oil-rich Niger Delta. John Major, the British Prime Minister at the time, described the executions as 'judicial murder'. The massive wave of international condemnation that the execution of the Ogoni Nine occasioned had a debilitating effect on the climate of development in Nigeria. As many countries severed links with the repressive Abacha regime, donors took flight from a country that they perceived to have become both irresponsible and hostile. The ensuing isolation triggered a precipitous drop in the quantum of external support for development initiatives – multilateral, bilateral and private. This fact was compounded by the outlook of the military regime, which was seen by many to be leading Nigeria down the slippery slope of becoming a 'failed state' and therefore unlikely to promote people-oriented development.

Interestingly, the situation in Nigeria coincided with the end of apartheid and the inauguration of majority rule in South Africa. It also came fast on the heels of the emergence of Eastern Europe as a new target for development support, following the collapse of communism in the early 1990s and the coming of many ex-Soviet bloc countries into the arena of international development as competitors for donor assistance. The changes in these two regions made the Nigeria case doubly challenging. Nigeria's loss was South Africa's gain, as some of the vibrant local initiatives in development, such as microfinance institutions that had emerged in Nigeria in the 1980s in response to the difficulties of the 'adjustment environment', lost their sources of support as donor funds to Nigeria dried up.

Given this context, the need to expand local philanthropy by growing indigenous foundations assumed a new urgency. In essence, three factors were driving interest in the local philanthropic sector in Nigeria at that time. These were:

i.   The need to encourage the development of appropriate structures for corporate giving in Nigeria to scale up impact;

ii.   The need to foster partnerships between the private sector and the community, especially NGOs, community-based organizations (CBOs) and civic advocacy groups for poverty reduction and sustainable development; and

iii. The need to nurture a conducive fiscal and policy environment that could inspire the confidence of the private sector to support local NGOs or encourage them to float philanthropic initiatives of their own.

Overview of the Nigerian philanthropy landscape

Nigeria has historically presented a paradox both in its political economy and development outlook. This paradox has been accentuated by prolonged military rule and subsists in the context of an incomplete transition to democratic rule, despite the efforts of successive reformist administrations. The country's disturbingly grim statistics, though already trite from constant retelling, bear restating if only to underline this paradox: Africa's largest nation is notionally rich; yet it is largely populated by poor people, over 70 per cent of whom subsist on less than two dollars per day. Over US$550 billion earned from oil exports since the early 1970s have not translated into tangible positive impact in the life of the average Nigerian. The prevalence of poverty seemed to have heightened with the influx of oil money, as the character of successive regimes assumed more violent and corrupt forms.

Thus, on the country's return to democratic rule in 1999 after nearly two decades of military rule, the Nigerian condition was largely characterized by collapsed infrastructure, decaying public institutions, an unstable business environment and corrupted moral values. All of these negative tendencies were accentuated by an increasing recourse to violence by aggrieved sections of the country, especially in the oil-rich Niger Delta, raising justifiable concerns about the country's capacity for non-violent resolution of its multiple flashpoints. The capacity of government to address these issues appears to have been severely whittled and fears persist in knowledgeable circles that Nigeria could yet become a failed state. This has raised renewed interest on the areas of possible civil society intervention, imparting an added urgency to the need to grow the philanthropic sector.

There is an increasing realization of the need to grow the local philanthropic sector in Nigeria as a critical element in the development of a strong and vibrant civil society, and as a major contribution to expanding the space for citizen well-being that was shrunken by decades of despotic state-forms and citizen disempowerment. Twelve years after the return to democratic rule, there is a broad national and international consensus that difficulties persist, especially with regard to the ability of the new democratic state to process and address sometimes conflicting demands from an often fractious plural polity. In the specific context of the issues that could be amenable to philanthropic intervention, the key challenges are to:

i.   Strengthen the foundations of the country's young democracy to enable it carry through a complex transition;

ii. Promote viable strategies of poverty reduction, environmental stewardship and economic development;

iii. Rebuild social solidarity and expand local capacities for non-violent conflict resolution, especially in the light of fresh Islamic sect insurgency in some of the northern states and continuing violence in the Niger Delta;

iv. Extend the frontiers of social justice with particular reference to minority rights, disadvantaged/excluded groups, e.g. youth, the disabled, etc.;

v.   Create a conducive environment to address gender issues and concerns on women empowerment;

vi. Prosecute the war on corruption with added vigour.

Philanthropy in Nigeria: Origins and trends

Strong traditions of charitable giving exist in many parts of Nigeria, cutting across virtually all of the country's cultural groups, faiths and regions. Amongst largely republican groups in the south-east and the north-central, age grades, hometown unions, trades guilds and other associational forms have historically supported society's weak members, especially where income-earning ability is constrained by inclement conditions. In many Nigerian communities, chieftaincy and priestly roles have been devised specifically to provide for the poor, the old, the infirm and the otherwise vulnerable members of society. Across the country, the royal tradition of honouring society's affluent members who devote their wealth to supporting the have-nots persists to the present times.

These strong traditions have been reinforced by faith-based injunctions to help the poor and the needy. Adherents of the three major faiths in the country – Christianity, Islam and indigenous African religion – are united in their belief in the transcendental and redemptive efficacy of charitable giving. The injunction to *zakat* (almsgiving) is one of the five pillars of the Islamic faith, while the Biblical parable of the Good Samaritan is often cited in both secular and spiritual circles as a universal validation of the need to show generosity to the afflicted. At the turn of the twentieth century, when the first set of African business elite of the colonial era emerged in the major cities of Lagos, Port Harcourt and Kano, to be referred to as a philanthropist rated quite high on the social status scale, equal to if not higher than the appellation of 'Prince-Merchant' that was the high point of public adulation for the commercially successful in those days.

This status symbol survived till the early years of independence. At the corporate level, many business organizations showcased their social giving programmes even when many of such programmes rightly belonged more in the realm of marketing or public relations than in philanthropy. In all, there was a positive connotation to the word that made it a socially acceptable label.

Increasingly, however, initiatives in Nigeria (both in civil society and in business) have sought to move the conversation from the paradigm of giving as charity to enlist in the global drive towards strategic philanthropy that delivers large-scale impact in a sustainable context. To this end, there is an increasing recognition of the limitations of the traditional 'philanthropy' deployed by flamboyant 'moneybags'. Today, the focus is shifting from what development practitioners often refer to as 'retail charity' to strategic philanthropy, which properly focuses on social issues, is able to leverage broad-scale impact and develop appropriate structures and institutions to sustain it. Private and corporate foundations and trusts are the emerging institutional forms in this effort.

Nigeria has a largely nascent foundation sector. The Lambo Foundation, reputed to be the first indigenous initiative to have been legally incorporated, was established by Professor Thomas Adeoye Lambo, a former Deputy Director-General of the World Health Organization in 1982. Not surprisingly, many indigenous charitable organizations do not meet the strict definition of the foundation in the western sense. Issues of appropriate nomenclature persist vis-à-vis the identification and taxonomy of private foundations in Nigeria. These issues have been rendered more complex by the emergence on the scene of some initiatives of rather problematic classification.

Prominent amongst these are the so-called 'First Lady Foundations' set up by the wives of political office holders such as presidents, governors and local government chairmen as well as the wives of legislators. These 'foundations' have acquired some prominence and a large measure of resilience since Maryam Babangida, the wife of a former military president, Ibrahim Babangida, launched her Better Life Programme in the late 1980s.

A measure of controversy continues to surround the activities of first lady initiatives with particular regard to how they fit into the larger definition of local philanthropy. Generally, these initiatives mostly focus on poverty alleviation and provide various kinds of support to the target populace – mostly women, children and senior citizens. Their programmes have, however been criticized for being highly personalized and idiosyncratic, ad hoc in nature and largely lacking in continuity or transparency. Some of these initiatives have been described in some quarters as a distraction, while others have accused them of negatively affecting the growth of the sector they seek to impact. For example, the offer of free funds under politically motivated microcredit and business support schemes has been seen as distorting the market and negatively affecting the work of groups that had over the years sought to build a clientele based on business discipline and responsible use of credit. In the mid- to late-1990s, the Family Economic Advancement Programme (FEAP), championed by Mariam Abacha, wife of the military president, Sani Abacha, offered credit on terms that were much below the rate offered by established microcredit groups. This created distortions in the market and stunted the growth of micro-credit programmes being run by professionally sound microfinance institutions. FEAP did not outlive the collapse of the Abacha regime but the damage it inflicted on the microfinance sector has been long lasting.

For virtually all First Lady initiatives, each change of government saw a discontinuity in programme objectives, strategies, resources and management staff. In effect, the programmes were only relevant for the period of time the First Lady's spouse was in office. There is a need to further explore the possibility of using first lady foundations to create permanent and enduring structures. It has been argued that thinking of perpetuity is the beginning of philanthropy. The First Lady initiative, which has been described in some quarters as a variant of state feminism, has many of the attributes of the typical social investment initiative – a defined goal, a focus on issues, and an interest in seeking resources to tackle the issues. Like corporate entities, they focus on reputation management albeit for their spouses. The challenge could be to position them to see beyond the spouses' tenure. With the advent of democratic rule, these initiatives have mushroomed across the states, promoted by the wives of elected civilian governors, but the controversy that surrounds their operations persists.

While the foundation sector is relatively new in Nigeria, there have existed over a period of time private philanthropic initiatives that seek to address the issues of poverty and community development. Over the past decade or so, new landmark initiatives focusing on strategic giving have emerged on the Nigerian philanthropic landscape. These include:

- CLEEN (Centre for Law Enforcement Education in Nigeria) Foundation was established in 1998 'to promote public safety, security and accessible justice through empirical research, legislative advocacy, demonstration programmes and publications in partnership with government and civil society';

- Fate Foundation, which was established in 2000 by Fola Adeola, who was then the Chief Executive of Guaranty Trust Bank, one of Nigeria's most successful new generation banks. Its focus is to foster wealth creation through business and entrepreneurship development among Nigerian youth;

- New Nigeria Foundation, which was initially promoted by Citizens Energy, a company associated with the Kennedy family but which has now been fully indigenized. The Foundation focuses on promoting health and livelihood initiatives in the oil-rich Niger Delta region;

- MTN Nigeria Foundation, established by the giant telecommunications firm MTN in 2004, and funded from one per cent after tax profit of the firm. The Foundation focuses on health, access to education and economic empowerment;

- UBA Foundation, which was spun off by United Bank for Africa, one of the first generation banks in 2004 to focus on environment, education, economic empowerment and special projects (EEES);

- Shehu Musa Yar'Adua Centre, named after a former military Chief of Staff (1977–1979) and leading politician who died in prison during the Abacha regime. The centre focuses on promoting unity, good governance and a democratic society through meetings, a think tank and a programme that supports merit scholars;

- TY Danjuma Foundation, established in 2009 by a one-time chief of army staff and former defence minister, focuses on healthcare, education and income generation;

- Dangote Foundation, established in 2006 by Aliko Dangote, a merchandising and manufacturing mogul who is listed by Forbes as Africa's richest man. The Foundation focuses on improving living conditions through support for projects that tackle hunger, water supply problems, strengthens quality of healthcare and education and promotes economic empowerment at the community level;

- Mike Adenuga Foundation, established by telecommunications baron Michael Adenuga as an indigenous African grantmaking foundation focusing on entrepreneurship development, education, health and rural development;

- Tony Elumelu Foundation, founded in 2010 by one of the country's leading new generation bankers to generate action and capital that fosters competition in the African private sector through leadership development initiatives, policy work with government and other entities, investment in innovative African businesses, research and data initiatives on African private sector and a grants programme.

But the combination of a breakdown in the extended family system and the prevailing socioeconomic circumstances in the 1980s resulted in an increase in the numbers of the needy and destitute in various communities. Interventionist initiatives promoted by visionary founders emerged to serve as alternative safety nets for the needy. So did hometown unions and community associations which promoted a variant of diaspora philanthropy that was largely supported by remittances from Nigerians abroad. Community trusts, which were particularly active in the late colonial era (1945–60), have also played a large role in boosting community development. Infrastructure such as schools, clinics and town halls were part of their focus to encourage people to give back to their local communities. Scholarship awards for indigent students have also been a substantial part of development initiatives to reduce poverty. For example, the Ugborodo Trust was founded in the mid-1960s to support local development in the oil-rich Escravos area of the Western Niger Delta, where the American oil firm Chevron has much of its operations. Over the years, the Trust, despite some controversy that surrounds its leadership and operations, has sought to play a representative role as the community interface with the oil companies towards promoting local development. This has been a problematic role, but the model of the community trust and community development association persists in many parts of Nigeria.

Corporate philanthropy has in recent times also emerged as a major form of giving in Nigeria, as companies push development-oriented programmes to the top of their business agenda. Pharmaceutical firms and household products manufacturers pioneered corporate philanthropy with school donation programmes. Youth development initiatives, which had been the area of initial focus, have now given way to much more expanded development focuses such as education, health, and human development. Relatively new players in the field, such as banks and telecommunication firms, have centred their focus on education, literature and the arts. The LNG prizes, endowed by the Nigeria Liquefied Natural Gas Company, are an example of a corporate body promoting the arts and sciences as part of a larger corporate goal of advancing human achievement.

There is a continuing debate as to the driving force behind corporate philanthropy, not only in Nigeria. Is the ultimate goal market expansion and reputation management or does there exist a genuine regard for corporate responsibility and social investment? There is a need to shift the focus of corporate philanthropy from the heavy public relations slant to development-oriented programmes. There is also a need to determine whether what should be of concern is the motive or impact; or the objective or achievement of philanthropy. What is the strategic view of philanthropy from the perspective of the corporate sector? There should be an increasing focus on how to get businesses to see social investment as a critical input into social stability, which is good for business. The business case for corporate social investment needs to be further sharpened and there is a window of opportunity to creatively use imperatives of market expansion and market retention to drive real philanthropy. In all, it can be argued that the development of corporate philanthropy in Nigeria is still in its infancy and its impact relative to the needs of the populace remains low.

Emerging issues and new frontiers

Areas requiring further inquiry in order to grow the philanthropic sector in Nigeria to enable it promote social justice and human-centred development include the following:

i.   The pattern of spatial occurrence of foundations and philanthropic initiatives in Nigeria is similar to the observable patterns of existence of other civil society groups and non-governmental organizations. These organizations are heavily clustered in the southern part of the country, especially the Lagos-Southwest axis, and thinly spread in the northern states.

ii. Quasi-public voluntary agencies, mostly with a religious bias and largely devoted to evangelism, are present in the northern states, with some of them lately suspected to have links with global terrorism.

iii. Prevalent attitudes, customs and traditions that seem to celebrate the 'self-made' man and individual striving appear to be responsible for the relative paucity of foundation-type philanthropic initiatives in the southeast.

iv. The growth of private foundations in the oil-producing areas, where the factors of social need and resource availability seem to converge, seem to raise some issues that require further inquiry.

v.   In the communities where there are relatively few or no foundations, a variety of alternative social mechanisms exist to play the traditional role of the foundation. These include age grades, hometown unions, thrift and credit societies, cooperatives, etc.

vi. There is still some misconception both in the public mind and among operatives of foundations as to what foundations really do. People seem to associate charitable giving more with handouts than with programmed interventions.

vii. Legacies, such as a good name or an illustrious public service record, are emerging as the more common bases for forming foundations rather than the one-off monetary endowment. The approach seems to be that third-party actors rally round a name and use it to leverage public subscriptions that are then converted into endowments.

viii. Building up endowments through prudent portfolio management is the more common method of creating a capital base, rather than the big bequest. Foundations in Nigeria are, therefore, more the products of managerial acumen than of the big-time donation, although this now appears to be changing with the advent of big players from the banking, oil and gas, telecommunications and merchandising sectors.

ix. Executive capacity for setting up and managing foundations is gradually being built up in Nigeria. Identified skill gaps in areas such as board development, fundraising, programme design, advocacy and outreach as well as portfolio management are being addressed.

x. Charitable giving undertaken with a view to securing public relations advantage exists in abundance in the business world. The challenge is to shift the focus of corporate philanthropy to development-oriented initiatives that may not come with obvious PR mileage.

xi. Managers and spokespersons of private foundations are of the view that big business can and should be doing more, either by creating their own foundations or by supporting third-party entities to meet their philanthropic objectives.

xii. The models of intervention used by some local businesses such as the Leventis Group and Chanrai merit further examination by businesses that are interested in creating their own giving programmes.

xiii. There is a need to nurture a habit of public reporting by philanthropists. While the spirit of altruistic giving may not permit 'noisy' philanthropy, there should be ways of making the public and potential donors know who is doing what.

xiv. The sustainability of philanthropic initiatives beyond the visionary (founder) stage is a source of common and continuing concern. How the interest of scions of wealthy families in philanthropy can be sustained and how to get committed managers to take over from pioneer executives remains an area of concern.

xv. For many philanthropic initiatives in Nigeria, mission statements and programme focus are still evolving. The practice seems to be to raise the money first and then decide on the mission/focus later.

xvi. There is a continuing concern with how to address the issue of 'inappropriate' philanthropy, i.e. out-of-proportion endowments that have a limited focus. How can such endowments be redirected into addressing areas of greater need?

xvii. Categories overlap in the appreciation of philanthropy in the Nigerian context, as there is no strict boundary separating grantmaking foundations from operating foundations or advocacy groups.

xviii. There is still insufficient understanding of the difference between programmes and activities, as many foundations engage in many activities with no programmatic coherence, due to the continually evolving nature of their mission statements.

xix. Boards are often constituted before focus is established. This explains the observable discrepancy between the expectations of the foundation and the level of involvement of its board members.

xx. The legal/policy framework guiding the start-up and operations of philanthropic initiatives by individuals and corporate organizations needs to be firmed up to encourage people to give through tax exemptions and other incentives. The National Assembly has in the past few years sought to focus on the enunciation of legal and policy frameworks, but the results have been largely mixed. There is a need for increased legislative activism in this regard.

Conclusion

In Nigeria, there is an increasing realization of the need to 'make philanthropy more relevant to the enterprise of national development'. Scholars and development practitioners are of the view that this can be achieved by 'broadening the contemporary understanding of foundations and philanthropy in Nigeria'.

It has been observed that 'the experience of building foundation endowments in Nigeria is markedly different from what obtains in Europe and America, where funds are usually derived from a single source – either by an individual, family or corporation. In Nigeria, the endowments of foundations are often built around illustrious names which serve as instruments of mobilizing and attracting donations from the government and the public. These foundations invariably operate under the pressure of permanent fundraising drive to support their activities. The challenge here is that a foundation with such origins could easily lose sight of its goal, which is to address issues of poverty and social justice and become enmeshed in what has been described as 'high-decibel' giving and political charity.

For many Nigerian philanthropic organizations, institutional instability has been a bane of mandate implementation. There is an increasing realization of the fact that philanthropy could be an investment in social stability. There is thus a need to promote further understanding of the field by deconstructing philanthropy into its various elements from the perspectives of government, businesses, families and communities. Emergent forms and categories such as voluble philanthropists and faith-based organizations need to be further researched into. The potential of the Pentecostal movement as a new philanthropic window needs to be carefully assessed, given the size of funds held and its possibilities as a major source of resource mobilization.

Conceptual and operational questions need to be raised and answers found. Is every social investment to be categorized as philanthropy? Is there a tension between philanthropy for social stability and philanthropy for social justice? It has been argued that at the level of the have-nots (resource-seekers) it is the promotion of social justice that matters, while at the level of the haves (resource-givers) it is social stability that matters. It should be acknowledged that the promotion of social solidarity, which many civil society initiatives seek to achieve, may sometimes lead to demands for self-determination, which is a social justice issue. For example, does support for an organization such as the Oodua Peoples Congress (OPC), an ethnic solidarity group that organizes security and neighbourhood watch activities in Southwest Nigeria, qualify as philanthropy? In the context of Nigeria's largely unresolved nationalities question, how do we disaggregate the role of OPC as a civil defence initiative and its political objectives as a self-determination group? What is the permissible political content for philanthropy strictly defined? Where is all of this leading? What is the future? Is the role of philanthropy constricting or expanding? Is the nature of philanthropy going to change? What does that do for the field in terms of professionalization, new capacities, etc? What kinds of philanthropy would emerge? What kinds of values would they promote?

It is acknowledged that traditional forms of giving have a long history in Nigeria. However, beyond being romanticized and seen as objects of anthropological fascination, are the indigenous forms of philanthropy of strategic and socially transformational value on a scale that is large enough to make a difference towards the reduction of poverty and social injustice? Also, in its current forms, is local philanthropy largely service-delivery oriented (e.g. provision of water to the needy), advocacy oriented or change oriented? For example, how much of real change in the lives of the people have the social giving programmes of oil companies, which are largely service-delivery oriented, achieved? Is philanthropy in the Nigerian context 'giving to help' or 'helping to give'?

It is clear from the foregoing that a new field is emerging. There is a need to grow it into actual philanthropy that serves the needs of a society in transition from despotism to democracy and from rigid state control to economic liberalization. There is a need to stake a Nigerian claim to philanthropy in a modernist context. There is also a need to develop the internal systems and service-delivery capabilities of these organizations. A strong case needs to be made for the creation of a network of foundations in Nigeria to serve as a clearing-house for activities in the philanthropic sector. The establishment of this interfoundation auspices for the exchange of information and ideas should be accorded high priority in efforts to grow the philanthropic sector in Nigeria.

CHAPTER 11

INSTITUTIONAL FORMS OF PHILANTHROPY IN FRANCOPHONE WEST AFRICA

MOHAMADOU SY & IBRAHIMA HATHIE

Introduction

Although Africans have a rich culture of giving, sharing and mutual support, the field of philanthropy in Africa is not that well documented. Perhaps what are common are foundations – national or international – as structures that are set up so that funds can be made available to specific kinds of recipients generally as grants and sometimes as loans for underprivileged people. It is a fact that resource mobilization is a key issue not only for small not-for-profit organizations but also for African foundations. For these African foundations to impact positively on the development of the continent, they need to be financially supported by Africans and not just rely on foreign resources. As foundations, they have a variety of potential mechanisms to make use of in order to fulfil their mission. The political and socioeconomic context in which African foundations evolve determines to a large extent their ability to fulfil correctly their core mission. The state of democracy and freedom, decentralization and good governance are critical attributes of the socio-political environment. On the economic front, the financial constraints that most countries have to cope with certainly influence businesses and the private sector and undermine their willingness to invest in philanthropic activities.

The landscape of African foundations is one of a corpus of diverse institutional forms (individual, community-based, religious or corporate foundations) with their own internal dynamics. It would therefore be interesting to understand how these entities differ and on what assets they depend. How do African foundations mobilize monetary and non monetary resources (methods, strategies)? Who contributes to their budgets (individuals, organizations, businesses, members, boards) and to what extent (percentage of local resources versus foreign ones)? What limitations and obstacles do African foundations face in their resource mobilization strategies and practices (such as lack of information, lack of strategic planning, and lack of skills)? Are these foundations and philanthropic institutions financially sustainable?

To address those questions, we conducted a comparative analysis of actions that are still evolving in West Africa: the Fondation d'entreprise Sonatel, the Karanta Foundation, the Fondation pour le développement durable du Sahel – also called Fondation Sahel, the Fondation 2IE (Burkina Faso), and the Fondation Youssou Ndour – Youth network for development. The outcomes of the case studies shed light on some of the essential characteristics of West African foundations. They also contribute to a better understanding of the state of philanthropy in West Africa and subsequently feed into the knowledge gap in the field of philanthropy as it is practised in the African context.

The first section of this chapter presents the methodology of the study. It first introduces the rationale for the choice of the case studies. Then it explains the data collection methods and instruments. The second section describes the African context within which foundations develop, while the third discusses the institutional forms of philanthropy, with three subsections: i) forms of philanthropy; ii) African foundations and case studies; iii) the internal dynamics of foundations. The challenges and the emerging issues are presented in the final section.

Methodology

Five West African foundations were selected for the case studies. The research process included different phases, among which were literature reviews, design of a survey instrument, data collection and analysis and, finally, report writing. To address the issue of the institutional forms of philanthropy, we chose different models of foundations. The underlying hypothesis was that these institutional forms would greatly influence resource mobilization strategies and endowment sources. The first is Fondation d'Entreprise Sonatel, a corporate foundation. As is often the case, these foundations keep the name of the businesses primarily funding them. As a result, their philanthropic actions also contribute to the recognition of the company. The Fondation Sonatel[1] was created by Sonatel, a telecommunications company based in Dakar, Senegal, with its mobile branches present in Mali, Guinea and Senegal. This foundation provides funds primarily to support education, health and culture.

The second type or form of foundation is that initiated by a cluster of West African intergovernmental agencies (often ministries) to tackle specific issues that require sustainable resource mobilization strategies. In this category are the Karanta Foundation and the Fondation pour le développement durable du Sahel. The Karanta

Foundation,[2] dedicated to non-formal education, was created in 1999 by four West African countries (Burkina Faso, Mali, Niger and Senegal) under the auspices of the Ministries of Education. A core mission of this foundation is to mobilize resources to support initiatives for the development of non-formal education and training in Africa. The foundation has its headquarters in Mali and a focal point in each of its member states. Funding for the foundation comes from contributions of member states and other external donors. IDRC was a key financial and technical partner for the foundation (Ba et al. 2000:69).

The Fondation Sahel was created by the Head of States of the Comité permanent Inter-Etats de Lutte contre la Sécheresse dans le Sahel – Permanent inter-states committee for drought control in the Sahel (CILSS).[3] The foundation supports the CILSS to mobilize additional financial resources on a regular and sustainable basis so as to fulfil its mandate, which is to invest in research to secure food and fight desertification.

The third type of foundation studied here is that created by an individual. Here we chose the Fondation Youssou Ndour as a case study. In several aspects, individual initiatives of this nature are close to corporate foundations, partly because the initiator is often a recognized business entrepreneur. Ndour is no different. He is a leader and owner of a musical group, and possesses a diversified portfolio (musical industry, media, etc.) which allows him to dedicate some of his wealth towards philanthropy.

The last form of planthropic initiative that we studied is one that is designed specifically as an international public–private partnership. The Fondation 2IE was given responsibility to manage 2IE, a specialized institute for water and environmental engineering of the former EIER-ETSHER Group based in Ouagadougou, Burkina Faso.[4] This partnership is an innovative solution to help meet the challenge of decreasing governmental funding for universities and other institutions of higher learning. This is a very different model of institutional arrangement for resource mobilization. Some of these foundations have a regional scope, while others are just local institutions.

To conduct the case studies, several steps were followed, including thorough desk work and review of the literature, a questionnaire survey, and telephonic interviews as well as face-to-face discussions. Given the qualitative nature of the endeavour and the need to deepen our understanding of the issue at hand, face-to-face interviews were also conducted with beneficiaries, experts, other resource persons and officials in the ministries in charge of these foundations. The questionnaire that was sent to the managers of the foundations comprised of four subsections:

- Foundation identification: besides the name and the date of creation, this subsection outlined the mission, objectives, priority areas and target groups.

- Resources: human and financial resources were explored. The section stressed the roles of the board of administrators and its contribution to resource mobilization. It also looked at the use of volunteers.

- Resource mobilization strategies: in this subsection, questions sought to see whether there are strategic and resource mobilization plans, including resource mobilization strategies.

- Additional enquiries: this subsection examined three different issues: difficulties confronted by the foundations and the solutions recommended; support and other benefits received from the government; the foundation's achievements, and its priorities for the coming years.

The West Africa context

Is a new Africa emerging on the outset of the twenty-first century? The idea of African renaissance has regained attention in recent years both within and outside the continent. A powerful wave of Afro-optimism has been channelling various initiatives involving African policymakers, intellectuals and scholars alongside the international donor community. This new shift in Africa's development paradigm has begun to reshape the daily interactions between different partners and has evolved within a favourable political and socioeconomic environment.

The current political context is marked with increased pressure for democracy and good governance. The fight for effective popular participation in the political process has gained ground and the reign of dictators questioned, especially after the end of the ideological divide induced by the 'Cold War'. Promoting democracy and empowering people through decentralization have become major state objectives in most countries. Good governance is increasingly included in donors' conditions for resource allocation. A set of norms and principles (accountability, transparency, human rights, etc.) are spelt out to represent minimum standards to which policymakers are held accountable. In this context, civil society organizations have grown to challenge political leaders and offer alternative views.

West Africa's situation gives a good picture of the overall African scene. Until recently, political instability had troubled many states in the region and deprived millions of people of developmental potential. Throughout the 1980s and 1990s, the region suffered inter-state armed conflicts and civil wars with negative spill-over effects to neighbouring countries. As a consequence, many states became fragile and were hardly able to meet the basic demands of their citizens. The political and military involvement of ECOWAS in resolving some of the regional conflicts underscored the new engagement of West African leaders for an environment conducive to peace and prosperity.

Several countries in West Africa coped with this political turmoil while absorbing the painful recipes from the adjustment programmes of the 1980s and 1990s. Earlier, in the 1960s, most states assumed a central developmental role but failed to deliver and became increasingly oppressive and corrupt. A conjuncture of negative factors i.e. mismanagement, the deteriorating international environment with the first oil shock in the 1970s, and cyclical droughts contributed to a profound economic and financial crisis which precipitated the calls for IMF and World Bank intervention. These institutions prescribed painful remedies based on a market-oriented model of economic development which confined the state to limited functions. As a result, key sectors such as education and health were almost abandoned and the poorest populations left unassisted. In many areas, local solidarity and nongovernmental organizations' involvement and supply of services for potable water, sanitation, health and education alleviated the situations of many people and offered a way out for the most vulnerable. The fragile states of the 1980s and the 1990s were disqualified; they were often incapable of meeting the basic needs of their populations and failed to deliver essential social services.

The beginning of this new century has witnessed remarkable changes, e.g.:

- The development community is now convinced that states have to assume key functions, in contrast to the liberalization wave that tended to dispossess states from their major functions;

- The emergence of Poverty Reduction Strategy Papers (PRSPs) and the Millennium Development Goals set the stage for a focused state intervention in areas such as education and health, even though other actors' contributions are expected;

- The Paris declaration and the post-Busan agendas promote 'aid and development effectiveness', seek to fight against aid dispersion, and try to develop a mechanism based on country-led partnerships and co-responsibility.

On the regional front, there is increasing agreement among leaders for popular participation in the construction of the ECOWAS region. The erection of the ECOWAS Parliament and the involvement of civil society in the definition of core policy options and strategies clearly indicate the path towards the well-being of the West African people. The setting up of a common external tariff (CET), and the harmonization of the rules that govern the different member states, point to the collaborative strategies for economic integration. Likewise, within the franc zone, the West African Economic and Monetary Union (WAEMU) strives to facilitate economic and monetary integration through instruments such as the CET and the Common Agricultural Programme.

Although the overall picture depicted above displays contrasting results, philanthropy would find a suitable and enabling environment for development in the West Africa region. On the positive side, the need for support, i.e. the demand for giving, is overwhelming and induces many coping strategies. Among these, Africans have other ways of giving that may not always be considered under the classical domain of philanthropy. Besides, the ambiance of democracy that has prevailed and/or improved in recent years in the region favours the emergence of philanthropic institutions, foundations in particular. Foundations initiated by states or relying on public funds for the initial endowment will find the environment rather depressing. During the structural adjustment period, there was almost no probability of survival on the basis of public funds. Nowadays, state contributions may be secured, but one should not underestimate the financial constraints West African countries have to deal with.

Institutional forms of philanthropy

Nowadays, it is widely admitted, in terms of the political economy, that the modern economy is based on three key sectors – the state, private sector and civil society. The state's distinctive role is to work for the common good. The private sector's competence is market exchange, and the third sector's competence is to promote the private choices of citizens who share common values and who are willing to organize themselves for the achievement of common goals or to express their solidarity with underprivileged individuals, groups or communities. Most of the time philanthropic work is done using institutional forms, i.e. structures and mechanisms of social order and cooperation governing the behaviour of a set of individuals or groups. These institutional forms can be formal or non-formal.

Philanthropy is a broad concept that can be defined in different ways. The conventional definition, which is widely inspired by experiences of Americans, can be misleading in an African context. Therefore, there is a great need to address philanthropy as it is practised daily in Africa by Africans. The key elements of definition can be (1) the individual or collective effort or inclination to increase the well-being of a person, a group of people or humankind; (2) the sense of solidarity and sharing with people in need; (3) an activity or institution intended to promote human welfare. Philanthropy is ultimately a matter of context. As mentioned by Richard Holloway (2001): 'There are likely to be cultural traditions about giving. However few cultures remain static – they are changing and changing dramatically'.

Philanthropy goes beyond charity and altruism, as not only does it work for the dignity and fulfilment of all people, but it also seeks to root out the causes of poverty, suffering and inequality. Philanthropy inspires and promotes individual growth and community welfare. Philanthropy in West Africa is not generally supported by formal foundations but by individuals, groups and communities. However, corporate, individuals, religious and public foundations do exist and perform essential roles that serve society at large.

In Africa, specifically, philanthropy is shaped by community and social values. It is also true that philanthropy as a set of values and practices is a mirror of social values, visions and norms. There are diverse and dynamic traditional forms of philanthropy in Africa. In fact, like the great majority of donors, Africans give for various and sometimes for complex reasons. In general, people want to give to noble causes, if they are asked to, if they know where to give and if they think their donation is useful or can make a difference. Some people may give from the head, others from the heart, and sometimes from both.

The main form of African philanthropy is predominantly non-formal, in the sense that it is difficult to capture all the donations made because they are often done in secrecy. The African ethos of help and sharing can be described not just as a conventional form of philanthropy for community, but as philanthropy of community. The first form of philanthropy refers to vertical relationships between the rich and the poor and the second one implies horizontal relationships between the poor themselves, or, at least, people who are not wealthy, as is discussed by Fowler and Wilkinson-Maposa in this volume. The African form of philanthropy is not tied to times of boom or prosperity. It is practised daily. In hard times, people will probably give less in other societies. In Africa, hard times are also moments of sharing and togetherness. In Africa, philanthropic foundations as defined below are a new phenomenon: 'Structures that are set up so that funds can be accumulated and made available in perpetuity to specific kinds of recipients as grants and/or loans to be used for specified purposes'.

There are various forms of philanthropy in West Africa:

- *Individual philanthropy*: Many individuals are effective givers in both urban and rural areas, whether they are rich or poor. African philanthropy is directed more towards individuals than groups or organizations. People give more to the members of their families, friends and neighbours than to unknown organizations for projects such as the building of hospitals or schools, for example. Philanthropy is geographically and socially very limited in this instance. In general, individual philanthropy does not benefit unknown people.

- *Community-based philanthropy*: several associations, grassroots' organizations or community-based organizations work as private entities that pursue activities to relieve suffering, protect the environment, provide basic social services and undertake community development. These organizations are value based and not for profit. They may also be membership organizations made up of groups of individuals who have come together to further their own interests. These associations develop philanthropic activities and rely on their own resources to carry such activities. In general, they serve a specific population in a given area. Unlike local NGOs, they do not develop and implement development-related projects or advocacy activities.

The case of the African diaspora can be interesting because West Africans abroad have a lived sense of solidarity with their peoples. In almost all cities, whether in Africa or elsewhere, many solidarity associations exist and were created to assist their members in need but also other people at the village. In the north of Senegal, a lot of schools, wells and nurseries were built and continue to be funded by the diaspora. Many villages and towns rely on their financial support.

- *Religious philanthropy*: As in many countries, philanthropy for religious purposes is very developed in Africa. Religion is traditionally a powerful and driving force for generosity; it serves as a generous booster of philanthropic inclinations. For example, for religious purposes, Islamic believers are encouraged to make donations that are called *zakat*, used to buy food and clothes for the poor or the building of hospitals and orphanages. It may be argued that *zakat* contributions do not build self-reliance or fight poverty, but they are still valid mechanisms of solidarity. In Christianity, generosity is also another expression of philanthropic impulse, in particular in the fields of education, health and water. African churches also perform daily voluntary work to support the poor financially and morally.

- *Corporate philanthropy*: As the case studies reveal, the emergence of African corporate foundations is relatively new, especially in West Africa. In Senegal, the case of the Sonatel foundation is a good example of a thriving business that now invests in the social realm for the common good. Sonatel does not see philanthropy as a simple act of giving but as a means to fulfil a social purpose while pursuing financial profit.

Foundations

African philanthropy is also embodied by foundations that are created for various motives and purposes. Five types of foundations can be mentioned: individual foundations, corporate foundations, service-delivery foundations, university foundations and intergovernmental foundations. Modern forms of philanthropy as represented by foundations exist also in Africa. However, with the exception of Senegal, in almost all West Africa Francophone countries there is no specific legislation for foundations. All civil society organizations, such as associations and NGOs abide by one legislative instrument. For historical reasons, these countries do not have a tradition of foundations as is the case in English-speaking countries.

Many organizations named as foundations are not foundations in the proper sense and understanding of a foundation, and also if we use the definition given by the ministries in charge of foundations (finance, social development). For example, the West African Rural Foundation (WARF) in Senegal and the Community Development Foundation (CDF) of Burkina Faso are registered as associations. Where they exist, most of them are intermediary organizations; very few African foundations have endowments and provide grants to people in need.

Individual foundations are created by outstanding men or women for particular interests such as the protection of endangered species. In general, the founders are rich individuals (business people, successful politicians or scientists) who establish these as means of sharing their wealth or earning credit for the afterlife. In Senegal, there is the Fondation Léopold Sédar Senghor, dedicated towards education, science and culture, and in Mali the Fondation pour l'Enfance, for the protection and promotion of underprivileged children.

For businesses, having a foundation can be viewed as a way of being a good corporate citizen willing to share its profits with society and mindful of having a separate entity. More than ever, universities are also creating foundations for the sake of mobilizing resources from alumni and the business community for educational and research purposes. The cases of 2IE in Burkina Faso and Cheikh Anta Diop University of Dakar are good examples. Governments have also been known to set up non-political and independent foundations. Foundations like Karanta in Mali or Fondation Sahel in Burkina Faso are owned by several states and pursue community goals.

African foundations are created for various motives and purposes. More often these are established without any endowment fund, but simply as avenues for foreign funding. As noted by the Director of the Foundations Office at the Senegalese Ministry of Finance:

> Many people are interested in creating foundations but unfortunately either they do not know what foundations are and how they operate or they are motivated by the search for personal interest instead of common good. For a foundation to exist there must be an inalienable endowment fund representing the initial allocation of the foundation.[5]

Below are case studies of selected foundations in Francophone West Africa.

Case Studies

Fondation d'Entreprise Sonatel

Sonatel is the main telecommunications provider in Senegal. In 2002, it created the Fondation d'Entreprise Sonatel, governed by a council which comprises:

- The President of the board. The Director of Sonatel is the President of the Foundation's board according to its governing statute.
- A representative of Sonatel's staff, selected by its labour union;
- A representative of the State;
- Two external resource persons drawn from the Foundation's areas of work.

As early as 2002, Sonatel disbursed an initial endowment fund of 125,000,000 CFA (about €190,561) to endow the foundation. Revenues from this initial endowment, contributions from other institutions pursuing the same objectives and government subsidies constitute the main sources of financial resources for the foundation. The foundation's statutes promote partnership with other organizations to engage in philanthropic actions. The foundation's financial resources may also come from calls for public generosity and donations.

With the above resources, the Fondation d'Entreprise Sonatel seeks to support projects which value human development efforts, in particular in areas such as health, education and culture. Between 2002 and 2007, the foundation financed over 2 billion CFA (about €3,048,980) to improve the health conditions of the population, and participate in the development of the education and culture sectors. So far, 80 per cent of the expenditures have been devoted to the health sector and 10 per cent to education.

Funding has also been channelled to the health sector to support people with disabilities; fight malaria, diabetes and other debilitating diseases; and research. In the education sector, the focus has been mainly on giving scholarships to promote female schooling. Additional funding was devoted to students' educational tools. Finally, on the cultural front, financial resources went to support creative work and to enhance cultural events.

As a corporate foundation, the Fondation d'Entreprise Sonatel enjoys stability and a relative financial sustainability stemming from its founder's strength. The foundation offers Sonatel a unique opportunity to make a highly appreciated contribution to the needy and to polish the public image of the company.

Despite its relative success and the proven durability of the foundation (based on the existence of the endowment fund and the continuous support of the founder), there is still need for additional funds, which may require a resource mobilization plan if one expects a sustainable result. The administrative board which oversees the functioning of the foundation may want a dedicated body for resource mobilization. For now, even though public generosity is seen as a source of financial contributions, there are no mechanisms and human resources (volunteer) to tap on these potential resources.

Fondation Youssou Ndour – Youth network for development

In 2000, the Senegalese musician and entrepreneur Youssou Ndour launched the Youssou Ndour Foundation, a network for development committed to youth well-being and to the promotion of entrepreneurship in disadvantaged areas. The Foundation also fights poverty, ignorance and illiteracy. It is part of the coalition against child labour and it contributes to the promotion of children's rights. Education and civic duties are also important areas for the foundation.

The foundation is governed by a board whose 14 members are chosen by the founder based on their specific knowledge and their qualifications with regards to the foundation's areas of focus. The Foundation appoints a President among its members for a renewable three-year term. An administrator leads the operational team and may be chosen among the council's members.

At the outset, the founder made an initial endowment fund of 10,000,000 CFA (about €15,245). In addition to the initial endowment fund, the foundation's revenues are supposed to come mainly from public or private donations, subsidies, and the setting up of fundraising events.

This diversity of objectives and the wide spectrum of areas of interest are reflected in the activities of the foundation: they range from economic, social, educational, volunteering, art and culture. In the economic front, funding goes essentially to micro-projects and support for the youth. In the social field, funds are spent on vaccination campaigns, to subsidize hospitals, provide for treatment, drugs and health equipment and participate in sensitization campaigns. At the education level, the priority is scholarships to students from needy areas, especially women and girls. The foundation offers funding opportunities to civic duty training programmes, and training activities in arts and culture. Culture events are also eligible for funding.

The Youssou Ndour Foundation carries out its mission like a corporate foundation and in many aspects possesses the latter's strengths. It is, however, slightly different from the Sonatel model as it depends more on the goodwill of the founder, who is an entrepreneur and a musician. This model of philanthropy, which is based on an individual and autonomous African initiative, managed by an independent body and formally structured, is relatively new. Together with the Sonatel initiative, these types of foundations are making a great difference in areas where the demand for support is continuously growing.

The strength of the Foundation resides also on its ability to organize key fundraising events. It is taking advantage of the founder's visibility and his leadership activities in the musical arena.

If there is any weakness that may emerge from a diagnosis of the Youssou Ndour Foundation, it would be its lack of a guiding line which is often provided by a strategic plan. Instead of this forward-looking stand, interventions may be greatly influenced by the daily happenings, even if those events might not enter the main objectives of the foundation.

Karanta Foundation

The Karanta Foundation is a public body which supports non-formal education policies headquartered in Mali. Karanta was created in 1999 in Ouagadougou (Burkina Faso) by the ministries in charge of education of the founding member states (Burkina Faso, Mali, and Senegal, later joined by Niger) with the support of the International Development Research Centre (IDRC). The convention to create the foundation was signed in 2000 in Dakar, Senegal. The foundation is still open to new member states. Within each member state, the foundation is under the guidance of the ministry in charge of non-formal education.

The objectives of the Karanta Foundation are: 1) to assist the member states in the design and implementation of non-formal education policies; 2) to mobilize resources destined to support development initiatives, both qualitatively and quantitatively, in the area of non-formal education; 3) to provide backing to non-formal education projects presented by member states; 4) to facilitate networking among non-formal education practitioners. Karanta is funded by contributions from member states, financial partners and other private sources of funding.

The organs of the foundation are the Board of the Foundation (direction and control) and the Management of the Foundation, which implements policies defined by the Board. In addition, there is a national technical support committee in each member state.

It took more than five years for the three founding member states to ratify the Convention establishing it. Although Mali executed its duty as early as 2001, Senegal followed only in 2004 and Burkina Faso one year later in 2005. In spite of the benefit foreseen in this type of organization, along with its regional integration features, it is clear that long delays may lessen its potential impact. In addition, the reliance of the foundation on member states' financial support is a serious weakness, especially given the economic and financial constraints these countries face.

Fortunately, with the financial assistance of a few international organizations (e.g. UNESCO, the Agence de la Francophonie), Karanta has been able to display some milestones both in terms of designing teaching matērials, and backing research in multilanguage dictionaries. This support may not last, and it is urgent that the Board implements policies that would generate a flow of resources in a long-term basis.

Fondation 2IE

Fondation 2IE was created in January 2007 in Burkina Faso in order to manage the pedagogical, material and financial objectives of the International Institute for Water and Environment Engineering. Members of the foundation are from 14 African states, financial and technical partners, universities and the private sector. The foundation is governed by a General Assembly of five bodies (financial, state, scientific and business), an Administrative Board with seven committees, among which are areas of employment, strategy, ethics, student life, etc. The managing director is supported by a permanent staff of 41 permanent teachers, 12 associate teachers, 29 part-time teachers and support staff. With a professional planning and management system, the Foundation offers a large spectrum of services (vocational teaching, consultancy, distance learning, etc.). In each academic year, about 550 students from 20 African countries are trained.

The Foundation is an interesting case study for various reasons:

- The Foundation grew out of the former EIER-ETSHER Group that went through an organizational crisis. It is a kind of a rebirth as a community foundation. So far, this new shift can be considered as being successful. In fact, after a series of crises, the former school has managed to develop strategic thinking and work effectively to achieve its goals. With a good leadership, it is quite possible for foundations not only to survive in a difficult context but also to thrive.

- The membership is open and inclusive; it gives the opportunity for partners from different backgrounds to work for a common goal on a win-win basis. Not all foundations see the usefulness of developing partnerships to achieve common goals.

- The relationship with the Government of Burkina Faso is a good example of public support to a private initiative. In fact, many advantages are offered to the foundation in terms of immunities, land property, free entry and visa, tax incentives, etc. The government has succeeded in creating avenues for the foundation to operate easily to the benefit of the community. The foundation's achievements illustrate the key roles universities can play to support governments in their mission. It is always good to seek government–foundation complementarities where it is possible.

- Good and diversified resource mobilization strategies exist and, as a result, several grants were received and service contracts signed with the European Union up to €4.565 million by 2008. There is a widespread belief that resources cannot be mobilized in poor environments. The example of 2IE shows that if foundations are market driven and if they can respond to the demand, it is easier to raise funds. Using professionals to mobilize resources is also a key

factor, and this is well understood by the foundation, which has staff dedicated
to that purpose.

•   Unlike the Fondation Sahel, instead of relying on state financial contribution,
     2IE has mainly sought their political and institutional support. That support
     can help in building credibility and in the long run mobilize resources.

As the foundation is relatively new, its impact cannot be easily assessed yet.
However, its example can be interesting for newly born university foundations like
Cheikh Anta Diop University Foundation.

Fondation pour le Développement Durable du Sahel

The idea of creating the foundation was discussed for the first time in April 1994
in Praia (Cape Verde). But the convention creating the foundation was only signed
in 2001 by the nine heads of member states as a public-interest and not-for-profit
organization with the mission to assisting CILSS in mobilizing additional, regular
and sustainable financial resources necessary for the achievement of its general
mandate of sustainable management of natural resources (water, lands, forestry,
energy), intensification and diversification of agricultural, livestock and fish production, improvement and access to food and basic social services for vulnerable
groups, and intervention in the event of emergency situations resulting from
natural disaster. The membership is open to Sahelian states, development partners
and civil society. The organs of the foundation are the board and the management.

The resources of the foundation accrue particularly from an endowment fund
representing the initial allocation (made available in the form of cash subscriptions) and grants from the donor community. In 1998, 20 billions CFA (about
€30,500,000) were needed to start the endowment fund.

So far the Convention has been ratified by seven member states out of nine.
Senegal and Guinea Bissau have not ratified the convention yet, for unspecified
reasons. Political reasons and competition for leadership may be explanatory factors.

Several important lessons were learnt from this experience. Firstly, the establishment of an autonomous management structure such as a foundation is time-
consuming and bureaucratic because there are many governments involved, a lot
of paperwork, and frequent institutional change. Even though it is important to
develop community policies to fight desertification in the Sahel, putting in place
an intergovernmental organization remains difficult and challenging.

Secondly, participatory approaches, good communication and close coordination
between constituencies are crucial. The desire to promote such approaches should
not result in wasting years planning and evaluating. Sometimes, it is good to jump
in, and adjust plans if necessary. If action is not taken, opportunities are missed.

One positive aspect is the awareness of the constituencies to develop a true spirit of solidarity and active partnership to look for food security and combat the effects of drought and desertification. On the other hand, a negative aspect is to realize that, after 14 years, no concrete action has been undertaken to operationalize the foundation. It is also legitimate to question the political will of some member states.

Like the Karanta Foundation, the Fondation Sahel has, so far, little impact on the lives of West Africans. The quests for food security and access to basic social services for vulnerable groups are noble causes. Meanwhile, it is relevant to wonder if intergovernmental foundations are the solutions. Having entrepreneurial states is not an easy thing. Therefore, why not provide local foundations with an enabling environment and build on their autonomy, flexibility and cost-effectiveness?

The internal dynamics of foundations, challenges and emerging issues

Philanthropy has a long tradition in West Africa but foundations are relatively new. Because the nature and quality of West African foundations vary, from one country to another, depending on the life cycle, it is not easy to talk about the strengths of foundations in general. However, some key elements can be highlighted, such as:

- Long-term commitment and emphasis on specific issues – mainly social ones;
- Field-based development expertise, as several projects are conducted using participatory and gender approaches and tools;
- Flexibility, because of their small size and the way they operate.

Some of the main weaknesses of West African foundations are:

- Limited institutional capacity;
- Limited financial resources;
- Small-scale interventions;
- Lack of coordination and umbrella groups.

As a matter of fact, West African foundations are limited from an institutional viewpoint. Not all foundations have the skills to promote organizational development and achieve effective strategic planning and operational management, resource mobilization, networking, lobbying, communication and organizational evaluation. For example, for resource mobilization campaigns to be successful, it is important for the foundation to have very committed boards of administration that can play several key roles.

However, most West African foundations have relative good relationships with their governments. Governments tolerate even non-formally established foundations. Generally, foundations enjoy freedom of speech and association. However, the operational collaboration with foundations is weak. In the great majority of West African countries, foundations do not have a clear legal framework; they do not enjoy good taxation policies and duty exemptions. With the exception of 2IE in Burkina Faso, all the other foundations are not well supported by their governments.

The confusion over the status of foundations, the lack of coordination and communication among foundations themselves, and between foundations and their governments, are real obstacles. In countries like Burkina Faso, associations, NGOs, organizations for common good and foundations have the same legal status. There is no specific legislation for local foundations. But according to the coordinator of the NGO division, the government is looking for solutions:

> We are interested in developing local foundations, but we don't know how to do it. We have difficulties to make the difference between foundations and other types of organizations. At present, we encourage foreign foundations because unlike local foundations they have the financial resources to carry development programmes. It is not interesting for us to support local foundations if they rely on the government and the donor community to mobilize resources.[6]

So far, local giving adds very little value to African foundations. People are willing to give and share but they do not see foundations as adequate and effective means to channel their donations. Five main reasons can account for their reluctance:

- First, for cultural reasons, people are not used to making donations to foundations. Partly because foundations are relatively new in West Africa and also because it is easier to give to a close friend, a relative or a neighbour than to give to an institution;

- Second, foundations are perceived as being rich. For the great majority of people, they have good buildings and nice vehicles and their staff travel most of the time. Because of the psychological impact of international philanthropy, being a local foundation is regarded as an opportunity of mobilizing resources through international grants;

- Third, giving in poor countries can be very complicated. Cash donations are sometimes used for other purposes, mishandled or simply stolen. Because of poor management of donations, lack of accountability and communication, the act of giving is problematic.

- Fourth, it is often expected that foundations provide services free of charge. One common error is to believe that they should work as unpaid organizations, even though they face overhead costs. Most of the time, foundations find it difficult to ensure popular financial participation.

- Finally, local foundations themselves assume that local communities have nothing to offer. Those communities are not engaged in matters of resource mobilization and strategic planning but are just considered as passive benefactors.

And the communities are not prepared to value themselves and recognize their participation as a key ingredient in achieving effective and sustainable local development.

Wilson (2001) believes that:

> In the future, organizations will thrive financially only if they know themselves, if they plan carefully both for their programme and their fundraising, if they are credible to the community they serve, if they are governed and managed effectively, if they are financially responsible and if they communicate well.

As the case studies reveal, the emergence of modern and truly African foundations is relatively new. But still, some foundations do exist, like Youssou Ndour's foundation and the corporate foundation of Sonatel in Senegal, the university foundation of 2IE in Burkina Faso and the governmental foundations of Karanta in Mali and Fondation Sahel in Burkina Faso. But the question is how can they survive in a context of political, economic and social crisis? If the mission of foundations is praiseworthy and their role crucial in the socioeconomic development of Africa, the lack of qualified human resources, adequate funding or the reliance on foreign donors can be a real threat to their long-term development and sustainability. A good dialogue between foundations and governments can boost the development of philanthropy in West Africa. It is crucial to understand the importance of foundations. Foundations can contribute to the quality, effectiveness and sustainability of development projects. Working with credible foundations can be an opportunity to develop and experiment innovative strategies and extend projects impact beyond the micro level.

In order to reinforce the relationships between foundations and governments, what should be done in terms of responsibility and power sharing? Are both parties well prepared to work in partnership? Is it always appropriate to encourage government–foundations collaboration if foundations risk losing their autonomy and credibility by accepting government funds, for example? What kind of government policies in matters of legislation, registration, governance, capacity building, reporting requirements, taxation, incentives and funding should be promoted to ensure foundations' organizational development? What kind of friendly environments should be promoted by governments for rich individuals and families wanting to create private foundations and endowments? The issue of funding is of particular interest. Many organizations are in danger, as they lack money and have no tax incentives. Poor economic environments, inappropriate laws, lack of governmental support, and sometimes mistrust of the donor community can be considered as hostile elements for foundations' growth. Most African foundations do not have endowments (funds, land or property permanently invested to provide income), and this makes them really vulnerable. The great majority of African foundations behave like NGOs; they compete for the same resources and face almost the same financial problems. With the exception of corporate foundations, almost all the other foundations work as paid consultants or contractors.

Another constraint for foundations is the limited range of income-generating activities, the reliance on foreign donors, and the weakness of local philanthropy. In such circumstances, how can foundations fulfil their mission, if they lack financial resources? Acting as a contractor to deliver services can push a foundation to neglect its primary mission. At the same time, foundations need money to survive. Obviously, they will experience a tension between short-term project goals and long-term community goals. If local foundations cannot address local problems, what would be their contribution to the social and economic development of West African societies?

If directed towards productive investments for social good, religious philanthropy can be an interesting philanthropic alternative. Local foundations can explore practical ways of channelling the resources provided by individuals and religious groups. Instead of short-term actions, foundations can use the resources to contribute to long-term sustainable community development. Today, more than ever, there is a great need for local foundations to imagine innovative solutions for their survival as organizations that respond to local needs by mobilizing adequate financial resources. To achieve that goal, they may need to build their credibility, develop income-generating activities, have more committed boards of administration in resources mobilization, build staff capacity in organizational development, and promote local philanthropy. That kind of work can be easier if foundations are well structured and capable of voicing their cause through strong umbrella organizations.

Businesses may not be interested in creating foundations but willing to fulfil social purposes. This can be a good opportunity for local foundations to partner with businesses to mobilize resources.

We conclude this chapter by stating that the modern form of philanthropy as represented by foundations is gaining ground in West Africa in general and in Francophone countries in particular. The case studies above show early successes, even though most West African foundations, in particular in the French-speaking countries, are relatively new and thus are in the early stages of their development. To foster the actual trend, it is imperative that policymakers provide a supportive legal and fiscal environment. Foundations should also dedicate some time and resources towards building their capacity in organizational development.

Endnotes

1   http://www.fondationsonatel.sn/index.php?lang=french
2   The Karanta Foundation is a public institution under international law; for more information see http://www.fondationkaranta.org/index.php
3   The *Comité Permanent Inter États de lutte contre la Sécheresse dans le Sahel* – Permanent Interstate Committee for Drought Control in the Sahel (CILSS) is composed of the following countries: Burkina Faso, Cape Verde, Gambia, Guinea Bissau, Mali, Mauritania, Niger, Senegal, and Chad. For more on Fondation Sahel, see http://www.cilss.bf/htm/fondation.htm
4   http://www.2ie-edu.org
5   Interview with authors.
6   Interview with authors.

CHAPTER 12

DIASPORA PHILANTHROPY AND DEVELOPMENT: ZIMBABWEANS IN SOUTH AFRICA

JAMES MUZONDIDYA & BERTHA CHIRORO

Introduction

The impact of diaspora philanthropy on development in Zimbabwe, and Africa in general, is not well researched, as most of the 'diaspora-giving' on the continent is still under-documented. Yet, the emerging role of diasporas in national development should not be underestimated. For many countries such as China, Mexico, Ghana and Lesotho, the diaspora is becoming a major source of foreign direct investment, commercial contacts, political connections, advocacy and technological transfer (Johnson 2007; Higazi 2005). Diaspora philanthropy in these countries and others has become an agent of change and development. Rapid progress in communications technology is providing Africans with new opportunities for networking and enterprise and increasing numbers of Africans in the diaspora are reconnecting with their home countries in imaginative new ways involving creative development strategies. Africans in the diaspora from other countries frequently organize into associations based on home town, ethnic, alumni, or equivalent associations aimed at effecting positive change in their regions of origin (Chikezie 2005).

Since the beginning of the economic and governance crisis in Zimbabwe, around 2000, a large number of Zimbabweans have emigrated to Europe and North America as well as the relatively prosperous neighbouring countries of South Africa, Botswana and Namibia. Many of these Zimbabwean emigrants, forming an incipient Zimbabwean diaspora, have maintained strong ties with their home country through remittances to families and different forms of philanthropic giving. A study carried out on the development potential of Zimbabweans living abroad or in diaspora by the International Organization for Migration (IOM) in 2005 showed that at least 96 per cent of Zimbabweans in the United Kingdom and South Africa maintain regular social contact with family members (Bloch 2005). The diaspora-giving methods and channels have become diverse. Whilst remittances are sent to families, there is also an amount that is sent as charitable donations towards community development, i.e. to build and rebuild schools, churches and hospital (Bloch 2005; Maphosa 2004). A large proportion of diaspora giving is practised informally and privately through personal and kinship ties as well as through direct gifts. This philanthropic giving by Zimbabweans abroad has remained under-studied and under-appreciated.

This chapter explores the range, contours and characteristics of Zimbabwean diaspora philanthropy and its impact on development in Zimbabwe. It specifically focuses on Zimbabweans in South Africa (by far the most important destination for both unskilled and skilled Zimbabweans seeking economic survival outside Zimbabwe because of its proximity and relatively larger economic base in the region). An estimated one to two million Zimbabweans, including both legal and illegal immigrants, now live in South Africa (Goliber 2004; Polzer 2007: 5; Makina 2007). The chapter specifically focuses on the following:

- the context in which diaspora philanthropy takes place, including the historical, cultural and traditional factors influencing diaspora philanthropy;

- notions of philanthropy among Zimbabweans both living abroad and at home;

- political, social and economic factors promoting and impeding diaspora philanthropy;

- the forms and extent of philanthropy among Zimbabwean diasporas, including the amount of remittances used for philanthropic purposes (i.e. for the public good rather than just to help family and other dependants);

- limitations, challenges and opportunities for diaspora philanthropy on development in Zimbabwe.

Research for this chapter was based on both fieldwork and desktop research. Our desktop research focused on published primary and secondary sources, including newspapers, online sources, books and reports. Much of the evidence for the study is based on primary interviews with Zimbabwean migrants and participant observations. Some of the oral evidence is gleaned through informal conversations with Zimbabwean migrants in the provinces of Gauteng and the Western Cape, which host the largest numbers of Zimbabweans in the country. Our study adopts a transnational approach which tries to develop a broader understanding of diaspora philanthropy from the perspective of both diaspora Zimbabweans in their various locations abroad and their associates back home. This cross-border methodological approach, focusing on data collection in both Zimbabwe and its neighbours which now host many Zimbabwean nationals, not only enables the study to develop a broader perspective but also allows the researchers to develop a more informed view of the issue through fieldwork.

Contextual background: Notions of philanthropy among Zimbabweans

Philanthropy has been defined in mainstream literature as 'the private voluntary transfer of resources for the benefit of the public' (Johnson 2007:6). The conventional understanding of philanthropy is about volunteerism, charity and efforts to change the world through giving or social advocacy. Philanthropic giving could be money, goods, services, knowledge and skills given for the public benefit. Such money or material is often given for the building of schools, community centres and church renovations or to rehabilitate hospital equipment. Philanthropic investments have a lot to do with the public good rather than personal gain. In this strict sense, remittances sent to family could be regarded as an obligation. Only money sent to an organization or to assist the poor or to people one is not related to, could be regarded as philanthropy.

Diaspora philanthropy has many variations, which include homeland philanthropy, migrant philanthropy, and transnational giving. Migrant philanthropy refers to the act of giving by compatriots based outside to support development initiatives in the motherland. Migrant philanthropy sees citizens abroad sending back home cash and in-kind donations to benefit socioeconomic development causes in the home country. Such charitable giving from individuals who reside outside their homeland – but maintain a sense of identity and connection with the home country – usually occurs as a means for migrants to keep their ties with their country of birth, and with people in the motherland. Transnational relations between migrant donors and those in the country of birth (individuals, groups) are then built or maintained.

However, diaspora philanthropy, like any other form of giving, does not occur in a vacuum. It occurs within specific historical contexts and complex economic, political, religious, social and cultural influences which shape people's giving behaviour. Changing political environments and economic trends also continuously shape diaspora philanthropy.

The political and economic contexts influencing diaspora philanthropy, for instance, could be the political and economic situation in the home country, including government policies that might work against maintaining ties between the diaspora and the home country and make philanthropic investments difficult; the reasons for original migration; and the economic and political situation of the emigrants in the host country. The cultural context influencing diaspora philanthropy includes a community's traditional and cultural norms. In the case of the 1.8 million Filipino-Americans who collectively send about US$5 billion to the Philippines every year, for example, their philanthropy draws on Philippine social norms and cultural values. It builds on values of kinship ties, *bayanihan,* and the idea that blessings need to be shared (*www.filipinodiasporagiving.org/*). Equally, donations of modest gifts to home town institutions by older generations of Chinese-Americans are very much rooted in traditional Chinese culture. Scholars who have written on the question of overseas Chinese philanthropy locate it in a long tradition of reciprocity and giving that draws on the Confucian ideal of benevolence (*ren*), reinforced by Bhuddhism and Taoist teachings. These ideals engendered among the Chinese the idea of a corporate personality, not an isolated and insular self produced by the modern, Western capitalist system (Lee 1990; Deeney 2002). Against this background, as John Deeney explains:

> Chinese giving is essentially private, personal and informal (as opposed to public and professional), starting with family and gradually extending to institutions that support the family spirit such as schools and churches or temples. (Young and Shih 2003:17)

As shown below, Zimbabweans living in South Africa's notions of giving, as well as their philanthropic giving behaviour, are very much rooted in their complex histories, politics, cultures, traditions and societal values. For many Zimbabweans, as in the case of the overseas Chinese, the family and kin remain the primary targets of assistance before the wider community and society. According to anthropologists and other traditional institutionalists, the family is the biological, procreative and child-rearing structure. The emphasis is on the biological relationship among family members. But the twin concepts of family and kinship in both Ndebele and Shona societies, as in many other African communities, are broad. Family (*mhuri/imuli*) represents a deep-abiding kinship among both communities and is the basis for society. Family is understood to encompass much more than a nuclear family of the husband, wife, and children or immediate family members connected to each other by blood. The family unit includes members of the extended family and others who might not be connected to the unit by blood. Kinship, especially among migrants far away from home, does not only refer to distant relatives, connected by blood and social ties, but to multi-stranded social relations which often overlap with other types of relations, such as a common village of origin. The wider kin group of an extended family can thus be very extensive (Bourdillon 1987; Holleman 1952; Kaarsholm 1997; Andersson 2001:101–3).

In the absence of organized social welfare, Zimbabweans relied on traditional or informal social welfare systems based on kinship ties and cultural practices of solidarity for much of the colonial period. The extended family remained an important social welfare system, which provided material and non-material support to its members. Resources of the extended family were mobilized in support of the needy, and the system looked after its own destitute, sick, handicapped and elderly (Kaseke 2006:217).

The concept of family and kinship among Zimbabweans has indeed not been static but evolving. The pressures arising from urbanization, migration, growing economic hardships during the ESAP and the post-2000 crisis, as well as increasing economic demands on individuals, have all affected individual views towards family and kinship (Harrison et al. 1997; Munro 2003:6–7). The changing nature of the family has become even more important as more and more Zimbabweans disperse in search of economic livelihoods across the world. However, family and kinship ties have remained very important among many Zimbabweans. Those in the diaspora particularly value, and have often rekindled, family and kinship ties as they seek to survive the harshness of diaspora life. To help deal with the vagaries of life in South Africa, many migrants, especially the illegal and unskilled, rely heavily on extended family and kinship networks from Zimbabwe for accommodation, employment, savings and remittances to Zimbabwe as well as other forms of support in times of financial troubles, family disputes, sickness or bereavement. These networks are normally activated in times of need, such as periods of unemployment when the immigrant would need support in terms of both accommodation, food and transport money to go and look for a job. The networks are also relied on to help migrants to continue to support both their immediate and extended families left behind (Muzondidya 2008; Dzingirai 2007).

Unlike in most Western societies, many Zimbabweans have always viewed assisting members of the wider family, kinsman or fellow villagers, as is the case with many other African societies, as an obligation rather than an act of philanthropy. Historically, there has always been a sense of collective sharing of burdens and fortunes among most Zimbabwean ethnolinguistic groups. The principal historical determinant of Zimbabwean philanthropy is their communal upbringing that emphasizes the collective being rather than the individual. As Vupenyu Dzingirai (2001) has noted when writing about the rural southern district of Chivi, there is a positive value associated with giving and sharing, and people consider giving as a virtue. 'Better off' households are expected to give assistance, in the form of goods or services, to others less privileged. Giving is not an activity that is confined to the rich. The poor also give each other resources, and even assist the well-to-do households with goods and services.

Culturally, when a young Zimbabwean man or woman gets employed or becomes rich, there is a social obligation to help the other members of the family or kinship group. When a migrant says he is supporting his family from remittances or goods earned abroad that might mean much more than the nuclear family. For both the givers and recipients, especially among rural households, giving and sharing is a part of their everyday life experiences. In this regard, remittances sent to family members cannot be excluded from discussions about diaspora philanthropy, for the remittances are for both the immediate family and the public benefit. Both the giver and the recipient know that whatever they receive has got to be shared by the wider social group in one way or the other. The poverty, economic and social insecurities experienced under the current crisis have generated a greater need for patterns of mutual service benevolence among most Zimbabweans. As in the case of Chinese philanthropy, Zimbabwean diaspora-giving progresses from remitting money to relatives to social investment in communities of origin. The evolving notions of philanthropy among Zimbabweans are also significantly shaped by their experiences in terms of class, race, gender, ethnicity, generation and location, and the following discussion shows how all these differences intersect to inform emigrants' ideas about philanthropy and their involvement in it.

History, culture, tradition and diaspora philanthropy

Philanthropy is by and large a product of the interplay between culture, tradition and history. Custom and tradition obligate people to give. The Shona and Ndebele traditions play a part in shaping actors' notions of what is expected behaviour in times when kinsmen and women require help. The concept of help – *rubatsiro* in Shona and *uncedo* in Ndebele – is culturally specific with a broader resonance to humanity. Zimbabwean culture revolves around *ubuntu* – *hunhu* (common humanity) as mutual responsibility for others. This common humanity does not allow those who have to ignore those who are deprived. What has happened is that traditional forms of giving and receiving have persisted and adapted to wider socioeconomic changes brought about by colonialism and global forces. These forms are influenced by kinship, neighbourhood, friendship and associational ties. Philanthropy is regarded as giving or help. 'Help translates to giving one who is in need, one who does not have or lacks' (Mombeshora 2004:68). In Zimbabwean culture it is a moral obligation to give to relatives, neighbours, friends, orphans, the elderly, the disabled, the ill, strangers, the church, and the bereaved. Help is given to relatives – *hama*' in Shona and *izihlobo* in Ndebele. It is customary to help during happy times, such as when a baby is born – relatives would come to congratulate with gifts as a way of appreciating the growth of the family. Similarly, during times of sadness or illness relatives pay social visits in order to support each other emotionally and financially. At funerals, food and money are brought in to assist with the burial. The contribution is called *chema* in Shona and *zibuthe* in Ndebele – condolence money. Giving is driven by a sense of altruism, and the giver does not expect anything in return. One's social positioning in the kinship network comes with obligations that have a bearing on whether one has to receive help, and the choices in doing so. Cultural meanings define what is and is not help and who belongs to or is excluded from the community. Zimbabwean culture has a strong sense of community, in which wealthier members of the community can look after the poor. Resources are shared, including food, clothes, tools or ideas, and sharing becomes essential for the survival of the community.

During the colonial times remittances came from those who were working in the towns to the rural areas. Kinship ties were maintained. Philanthropic ties continued between the rural and urban areas. Kinship ties have largely guided this form of philanthropy. Within the new forms of diaspora philanthropy, kinship ties are at the core of giving and giving is not guided by the amount of resources available. Those who earn little can still pool resources together to send orphans to school, donate medicines, support grandparents back home. This compassionate culture exists regardless of the governance and political crisis in Zimbabwe

Composition of Zimbabweans in South Africa, and patterns of giving

Zimbabweans living in South Africa, like their compatriots in different parts of the globe, comprise both individuals who have chosen to migrate formally, especially professionals or those with skills or funds and old networks abroad, and others who have been compelled to move by their complex political or economic circumstances. The emerging Zimbabwean diaspora community in South Africa is complex and multifaceted, and this affects its attitude towards philanthropy as well its capacity to give. While a significant number of these Zimbabwean immigrants, especially the skilled professionals, have already settled permanently or semi-permanently in South Africa, most Zimbabweans, like their counterparts scattered all over Europe, the United States and other overseas countries, do not see their stay there as a permanent or semi-permanent one. Their presence abroad, like that of many other post-colonial African migrants before them, might turn out to be more permanent, but many still regard it as temporary and see themselves as economic exiles waiting to return to their country when conditions normalize (Chetsanga and Muchenje 2003; Muzondidya 2010:37–58).

The Zimbabwean community in South Africa comprises both voluntary and forced migrants. It is, in the main, made up of asylum seekers, political refugees, skilled expatriates, students, semi-skilled and unskilled labour migrants, undocumented/illegal migrants and others who have naturalized. The illegal, seasonal migrants who occasionally sneak in and out of South Africa, and fit into the category of economic refugees or exiles rather than diaspora, constitute the largest proportion of Zimbabweans in South Africa (Sisulu et al. 2007; Chetsanga and Muchenje 2003).

Zimbabweans in South Africa can be further categorized into earlier and recent immigrants, and the immigrants' philanthropic behaviour is also largely influenced by their migration history, social status and settlement patterns. Among the older immigrants are, for instance, Zimbabweans who, together with hundreds of thousands of other unskilled and semi-skilled contract labourers from Malawi, Zambia and Mozambique, moved to South Africa to service the labour needs of the growing South African mining industry during colonialism (Crush et al. 1991; Van Onselen 1976; Ranger 1989). Many of these older immigrants were either forced contract workers (*chibalo*) or labour migrants who voluntarily moved across the borders in search of employment and better wages in the mining, commercial agriculture and domestic service sectors. Some of these older migrants started families in South Africa as they married into local communities, and eventually settled permanently.

Older Zimbabwean immigrants in South Africa also include white emigrants who initially fled from the 1970s war of independence and later the introduction of black majority rule in 1980 (Selby 2006:117–8; Godwin 1984). But the larger group of post-independence emigrants consisted of political refugees from Matabeleland and parts of Midlands who came in the early 1980s, fleeing the state-inspired Gukurahundi violence and killings in Matabeleland of 1983–87. Some of the refugees eventually acquired South African citizenship, both lawfully and unlawfully, and settled permanently in South Africa (Sisulu et al. 2007:554; Solidarity Peace Trust 2004). Though alienated from the Zimbabwe state, which drove them into exile, many of these Zimbabwean immigrants continued to look at Zimbabwe as home and to support their home communities in various ways.[1] As one informant who left Zimbabwe in the 1980s explained:

> Many of us realised that the ZANU PF government was not interested in the development of Matabeleland and we needed to take the initiative to help our own communities. When we got here some of us decided to form self-help organizations and appeal to foreign donors to rebuild our neglected and destroyed schools and clinics.

Others decided to help their communities by sending material support directly to relatives and friends left behind, or helping them to come and settle in South Africa. Also involved in the philanthropic activities by these early post-independence refugees were labour migrants, especially from the drought-prone districts of Midlands and Matabeleland South, and others who mainly came in the late 1980s and 1990s when the Zimbabwean economy showed signs of trouble, and small numbers of Zimbabweans began to leave, searching for better-paying jobs in South

Africa, Botswana and Namibia (Mandava 2001; Tevera and Crush 2003). Many of these early immigrants managed to secure jobs in skilled positions or as general labourers and established themselves in South Africa. Having stable jobs and homes, some of these labour migrants, popularly termed *injiva* back home because of their perceived status of being wealthy, continued to help their extended families and communities of origin through regular remittances and occasional donations to schools, orphanages, and clinics.

Focusing his research on immigrants from the Matabeleland South districts of Bulilima, Mangwe, Gwanda, Beitbridge and Matobo, Frances Maphosa noted that remittances from migrant labourers working in South Africa are an important source of support for many families. Remittances contribute significantly to the improvement of the livelihoods of the receiving households through the purchase of food and clothing, and payment for health care and education, building and improving houses. Bicycles and scotch carts, major forms of transport in these rural areas, are some of the major investments made by migrants, while some of the earnings are invested in solar power and boreholes, used not just by the recipient households but by the community. Water, according to both Ndebele and Shona custom and tradition, is a communal resource even if it is privately funded. Scotch carts (usually donkey pulled) are used as private transport for daily needs such as fetching water and firewood. They are used as ambulances and hearses for the community (Maphosa 2004:14, 16–17).

Inside South Africa, the earlier immigrants' philanthropy towards their compatriots has been exercised through their help to the recent migrants who migrated from Zimbabwe in the post-2000 period, when political uncertainty and the economic 'meltdown' in the country drove hundreds of thousands of Zimbabweans into South Africa. Unlike the earlier immigrants, many of the post-2000 immigrants have struggled to settle down in the hostile and competitive environment of contemporary South Africa. Many have had to rely on the earlier immigrants, who provide them with accommodation and protection. Having been in the country for a much longer period and having been settled economically, the earlier immigrants are usually relied on to provide employment or access to employment networks to the recent arrivals.[2]

Clearly, the Zimbabwean community in South Africa is a complex social formation, in terms not only of its composition, cultural and class diversity, but also its migration history and settlement patterns, as well as its tendencies and practices.

Forms of giving and the extent of philanthropy

Some of the studies that have been done on Zimbabweans abroad suggest that Zimbabweans do not have a strong philanthropic culture of giving back to their communities, and that even for wealthy individuals who can afford to give some of their accumulated wealth, the family and kin remain the primary targets of assistance before the wider community and society. Seventy-four per cent of Zimbabweans interviewed by Alice Bloch in the UK and South Africa in 2005 pointed out that they sent remittances to support family members, while only 14 per cent contributed to charities (Bloch 2005). Maphosa (2004) also found that, while remittances from migrants working in South Africa are contributing much to alleviation of poverty and the development of households in Matabeleland South, there is very little investment at the community level and most of the giving is adhoc. Very few migrants have been involved in philanthropic giving at the level of either refurbishing a hospital, buying equipment for a school, or supporting sports events.

However, this study found out that, although philanthropic giving among Zimbabweans is not formalized or institutionalized, there is a significant level of giving to the communities through various less formalized channels. Because much of this giving is unrecorded, it is difficult to quantify it. In response to their complex socioeconomic circumstances, the hard-pressed communities of Zimbabwe in South Africa and abroad are reviving some indigenous traditions of collective action and self-help, and applying them to alleviate poverty and suffering in their communities and to forge development solutions appropriate to their needs.

Some of the wealthier Zimbabwean middle and upper class are involved in philanthropy not only through the traditional models of giving, that emphasize community giving through extended family and kinship networks, but also through formalized channels such as formal charitable institutions to facilitate their charitable support to development in their countries. These charitable organizations include professional philanthropic organizations that give grants to eradicate poverty and educate the less fortunate members of the society. For instance, the prominent Zimbabwean businessman who now lives in South Africa, Strive Masiyiwa, has been involved in community social investment programmes in Zimbabwe. Through his mobile telephone company, Econet Wireless, he has established the Joshua Nkomo Scholarship Fund (JNSF), a fund enabling academically gifted Zimbabweans to pursue their secondary and tertiary studies at local secondary schools and universities. The fund, in memory of the late nationalist and Vice President of Zimbabwe, Joshua Nkomo, gives grants to 100 students drawn proportionally from all the country's ten provinces annually. The scholarship, according to the trustees of the fund, 'has a unique vision of instilling ethics of community building and social responsiveness in each beneficiary'. Each recipient of the scholarship is expected to engage in a variety of community building activities as part of his/her active responsiveness to the numerous social challenges in various communities. Recipients are required to show selfless and patriotic service to community and nation.[3]

Masiyiwa is not the only Zimbabwean businessman in South Africa involved in philanthropic work in Zimbabwe. Some Zimbabwean entrepreneurs, such as Trevor Ncube (publisher of both the *Zimbabwe Independent* and South Africa's most popular weekly, *Mail and Guardian*) and Nigel Chanakira (the founder of Kingdom Bank), who have successfully set up businesses in South Africa, and others who have been appointed to positions of authority in the business and corporate worlds, have also been involved in diaspora philanthropy in one way or another. Some have been donating computers to schools, and this has helped to increase the information flow to fellow villagers, while others have provided satellite links in the form of digital satellite television to schools and townships with access to electricity, and this is providing communities with better links with the global world. Some of the giving has indeed been politically motivated. Zimbabwean post-independence politics has over the years been driven by a certain kind of materialism, which emphasizes bribery of the electorate through 'donations' ahead of every major election. Recently, a number of Zimbabweans who have established themselves in South Africa were accused by the Zimbabwe government of funding Simba Makoni, an independent presidential candidate in the 2008 election, in his bid to bring political and economic change to Zimbabwe through the presidency.[4]

Some of the giving occurring among Zimbabwean businessmen and professionals in South Africa has been taking place through formal bodies, such as the Batanai-Bambanani Zimbabwean Association, a social organization devoted to bringing Zimbabweans together and assisting each other in business and social affairs. In 2004, for example, the organization had over 200 members, mostly professionals occupying senior positions in South African businesses and institutions (Sisulu et al. 2007). However, the organization did not live that long, as it soon fizzled out after its inauguration. Unlike other African migrant communities with a much longer history of post-colonial migration, such as the Congolese and the Nigerians, Zimbabweans in South Africa have not been able to come together in sufficient numbers and establish social organizations representing their interests and others at home. As result, the few organizations that have tried to come up have not received mass support, especially among members of the professional and middle classes, who live in isolated spaces in suburbia.

The little organized social networking that has occurred among Zimbabweans has mainly taken place among the vulnerable unskilled migrants, who are developing their own social networks to help each other in times of trouble. These networks have taken the form of burial societies to assist each other in times of illness and bereavement. There are a sizeable number of burial societies formed by Zimbabwean immigrants in South Africa, including the Johannesburg-based Masasane Burial Society, one of the first burial societies to be formed by earlier immigrants who came to South Africa during the political upheavals of the 1980s, the Zvishavane Burial Society, which is also based in Johannesburg, and the Maranda and Mberengwa burial societies, both based in Pretoria. Members of societies meet once a month and pay monthly subscriptions, redeemable when there is bereavement in the family. The burial societies assist in covering funeral costs of their members and dependants, including transporting the body of the deceased back to Zimbabwe, where most immigrants are taken for burial. In cases where a member's relative based in Zimbabwe has died, the burial societies assist the member with burial costs or transport costs to attend the funeral.[5]

Some burial societies have moved beyond issues of death and bereavement and become agencies of development in Zimbabwe, by raising funds for the development of local communities inside Zimbabwe. In the south-western district of Tsholot-sho, for example, burial society money is being ploughed into the building of a library and a laboratory for a secondary school. As Mlamuli Nkomo, an official of Mthwakazi Forum, a Johannesburg-based, radical diaspora pressure group fighting for Matabeleland self-determination, explains, 'Burial societies have contributed hugely to their home communities by investing money they raise in exile into basic infrastructure.'[6]

Feeling marginalized from both the state and national development, immigrants from the drought-prone and underdeveloped western regions of Matabeleland and Midlands have since the 1980s established a number of organizations aimed at mobilizing both political and economic support for the development of the region. For instance, a group of Zimbabweans from Bulilima and Mangwe districts based in South Africa are reportedly building a motel and an office complex in the border town of Plumtree. The same group is also building a funeral parlour in the town and upgrading the long-distance bus terminus.[7]

Many other migrants originating from this region have made material contributions to Zimbabwean-based groups working towards the development of the region, either out of their own volition or in response to direct appeals from community and political leaders from the region. Some of the organizations formed by Zimbabwean migrants include Mthwakazi Action Group on Genocide, a political pressure group committed to compensation for, and helping, victims of the Gukurahundi violence of the 1980s; Mthwakazi Arts and Culture, a South African-based NGO that mainly assists Zimbabwean migrants, including artists in exile and vulnerable Zimbabwean migrants like those who are HIV positive; and Mthwakazi Foundation, a public charity organization registered in the USA and Canada but with branches in South Africa and Zimbabwe. The organization's primary objective is to offer assistance to the peoples and communities of Matabeleland North, Matabeleland South, Midlands and Bulawayo by improving their access to clean water, improving their access to healthcare by providing aid to hospitals, by rehabilitating existing hospitals, providing healthcare supplies, and improving their access to education by providing aid to schools for rehabilitating physical structures, providing benches, tables and classrooms and school supplies that include books, pens and pencils.[8]

Some of the Zimbabwean-based groups which have benefited from the support of Zimbabwean migrants in South Africa and beyond are the Community Foundation for the Western Region of Zimbabwe (CFWRZ), established in 1998; the Zambezi Water Project Trust, set up in 1993 to mobilize resources for the construction of a water pipeline to draw water from the Zambezi river to Bulawayo; and the Matabeleland/Midlands Gukurahundi Victims Development Association (MGVDA), established in 1998 and registered in both Zimbabwe and Britain as a charity organization.[9]

The CFWRZ was one of the most successful philanthropic groups focusing on Matabeleland which benefited from inputs from both local communities and Zimbabweans abroad. Utilizing the traditional Ndebele principles of *qogelela* (collective savings), *ziqoqe* (mobilize yourself) and *zenzele* (do it yourself), the grantmaking community organization mobilizes financial resources and technical assistance for local initiatives by serving as a co-financer, broker, and builder of partnerships between communities and the existing development actors in the region. The foundation concentrates on five programme areas – education, HIV/AIDS, women's economic empowerment, youth development, and water and agriculture. The Organization of Rural Associations for Progress (ORAP), founded in 1981 to mobilize villages to take charge of their own development, and the global philanthropic organization Synergos both played instrumental roles in founding the CFWRZ. But more than 50,000 community members drawn from the region contributed approximately US$8,000 as seed capital for the endowment of the foundation. The CFWRZ continues to rely on support from other local, regional and international donors, such as the Carnegie Corporation, which provided key funding for planning and start-up, the Ford Foundation, the Open Society Initiative for Southern Africa, the McKnight Foundation, W. K. Kellogg Foundation, the Netherlands' Bernard van Leer Foundation, and New Zealand AID. However, community members also match this support with their own resources.[10]

Broadly, Zimbabweans have been supporting their home communities as individuals in a number of ways. A number of Zimbabwean professionals interviewed for this study pointed out that they are quite aware of the numerous economic, health and educational challenges facing their communities at the moment and they try to help whenever they can. William, who works as a researcher in Johannesburg, points out that he knows that universities and research institutions in Zimbabwe are facing financial difficulties in acquiring reading resource material, and he always tries to take along books for his old university department whenever he goes home. William also adds that he knows of many other former colleagues now based in South Africa who occasionally donate books and other learning material to universities and schools. When he goes home on holidays, William also takes along all the old clothes that he and his wife are no longer using, for donation to members of the extended family and other relatives. In some cases, he further explains, he gives these clothes to village neighbours 'but to discourage them from developing a culture of dependency I will ask these neighbours to do a small job, like collecting firewood for my old mother'.[11]

A sizeable number of professionals interviewed who are working in the academic and research environments in South Africa talked about donations of books and other research material to their old schools and universities on an ad hoc basis. One of the librarians at the University of Zimbabwe interviewed in 2007 confirmed that the university was increasingly relying on former lecturers and students living abroad for books, because of the difficulty in procuring both funding and forex for the purchase of new books. The university has even introduced a scheme where it reimburses shipping costs to Zimbabweans willing to donate books in large quantities. Book donations are made not simply because books are readily accessible. The donations reflect the significance most Zimbabweans continue to attach to education.

Apart from book donations, Zimbabwean professionals in strategic positions are contributing to the skills training of young scholars and workers based in Zimbabwe, by recruiting or helping to place them in organizations and companies in South Africa and beyond. Others are helping to train them in Zimbabwe by getting them involved in collaborative projects that facilitate their skills training. Such collaborative research projects not only facilitate skills training but also greatly help with financial sustenance, as they enable them to get the much-required foreign currency. Even established professionals based in Zimbabwe have benefited from joint or collaborative projects initiated by their compatriots abroad.

The majority of parents are failing to feed and pay school fees for their children and most Zimbabweans can no longer afford hospital fees, while the schools and hospitals are also battling to provide normal services. Zimbabweans in South Africa, especially the middle and professional classes who have got the means, are also bringing up children who are not their own by paying for their education. Others are alleviating the suffering of the people in the country by adopting schools and hospitals and starting other programmes that help many vulnerable groups in Zimbabwe. Many of these Zimbabweans hardly talk about their services in giving. It is done quietly and in many discreet ways because it goes against Zimbabwean culture to go around telling people about your philanthropic contributions.[12]

The health of most Zimbabweans at home has increasingly come to depend on donations and provisions from those Zimbabweans based in South Africa. As Ruth explains, whenever she goes to Zimbabwe these days she always carries along some basic medicine like headache and malaria tablets because many hospitals and clinics in Zimbabwe currently do not have basic medicine. Some of the medicine she takes along, she explains further, is not just for her parents, who live in a rural village, but for use by her friends and relatives, who now know that she regularly brings those things and 'will ask my mother for pills when they fall ill.' Senior, a 33-year-old security guard in Pretoria, also knows that the vaccines and other medicine he buys for his cattle in Mwenezi are not just for his own use but for a number of his neighbours, who now rely on him and his fellow migrants to keep their cattle from dying from the rampant cattle diseases in this tropical hot district. He also knows that, if he refuses to share the vaccines and medicine with his village neighbours, his cattle will contract diseases from the untreated cattle in the common pasturelands. [13] Zimbabwean migrants are thus also assisting with the health and educational well-being of their fellow villagers and neighbours through the provision of basic supplies which are occasionally shared.

At the micro level, Zimbabweans living in South Africa are assisting with the social and economic welfare of their fellow countrymen at home through remittances to members of their extended families and kin – a practice as old as labour migrancy itself. In their research among farm workers in northern South Africa, Blair Rutherford and Lincoln Addison found out that most workers occasionally send money, food items and other consumer products to family members and dependants back in Zimbabwe (Rutherford and Addison 2007:628). The migrants have developed many formal and informal ways of saving their earnings, remitting part of these earnings back home and sending items too exorbitant or in short supply at home, such as clothes, cooking oil, soap, flour, sugar and salt (Bracking and Sachikonye 2006).

Remittances from Zimbabwean migrants have a direct poverty-mitigating effect in Zimbabwe and have helped to keep the country going. For instance, a survey carried out in Harare and Bulawayo in 2005 and 2006 showed that 50 per cent of urban households were surviving on migrant remittances for everyday consumables (Bracking and Sachikonye 2008:1). Remittances from migrant labourers working in South Africa are an important source of support for many families in the southern districts of Zimbabwe (Maphosa 2004:16), while most people in Malipati, one of the poorest and most remote settlements in southeastern Zimbabwe, survive on remittances sent by children and husbands working out of the country (IOM 2003). Many family households will be using their remittances not only for their immediate family, but also for their extended family, close family or neighbourhood friends (*sahwiras*). Zimbabweans, as noted above, have a great tradition of caring for the poor and those in distress, which goes back to traditional community set-ups.

Not every migrant sends remittances home (IOM 2003; Maphosa 2004:9). Remaining spouses and families interviewed in the rural district of Zaka complain that it is not uncommon for the men to forget about their families back home and stop sending money and food back home. Some immigrants interviewed in South Africa also conceded that the pressures of surviving in a foreign country on the meagre earnings that most undocumented migrants, especially the undocumented unskilled migrants, receive makes it difficult to save. At the same time, for most young men and women, the excitement of being away from home and the excitement of the 'bright lights of *egoli*' sometimes makes it easy for migrants to forget their extended family responsibilities. Even those who do receive remittances from their relatives in South Africa only get this money sporadically, and they can go without money for months.[14]

More importantly, there has been a lot of debate on the impact of remittances on the home country. Internationally, there has been concern that remittances are usually spent on consumption and prestige goods rather than on productive investment (Taylor 1999). However, the impact of remittances depends on their use. A study based on data from villages in northern Mexico shows that remittances from Mexican migrants in the United States are an equalizing factor in the villages' economies, while a study from El Salvador showed that the school drop-out rate is lower and the enrolment ratio higher in households that receive remittances (Ratha 2004; McCormick and Wahba 2003).

In the case of Zimbabwe, remitting behaviour differs according to households and class background. Some of the migrants interviewed in this study, especially the unskilled, are spending their earnings on consumption, mainly radios, television and other electronic gadgets. But, many are also acquiring capital, fixed assets and reinvesting back home. Bloch (2005) noted that a small sum is channelled into productive activities such as improvements in land productivity and setting up small businesses, while Maphosa (2004) found that some of the money is invested in rural businesses such as general dealer shops and grinding mills, that benefit the whole community. According to our findings, many of the skilled migrants use their remittances to invest in properties such as houses. Some of the utility goods being acquired by the unskilled migrants include wheelbarrows, bicycles, scotch carts, water pumps, grinding mill and motor engines, solar panels for the electrification of rural homes, and building material for the building of modern houses. A significant proportion of remittances from unskilled Zimbabweans in South Africa is also used to acquire cattle, a highly valued asset in most Zimbabwean rural economies. A vibrant market for cattle in rural areas has been created and a new class of young cattle owners is emerging (Muzondidya 2008).

Challenges and opportunities

There are a number of both historical and contemporary factors influencing philanthropic giving among Zimbabweans living in South Africa. Among some of the factors promoting philanthropy among Zimbabweans in South Africa are their historically and culturally inherited values of giving and sharing instilled among many Zimbabweans as they grow up. This cultural ethos instilled back home has continued to shape the behaviour of many migrants, and explains their greater willingness to share the fruits of their labour with their kin. At the same time, the challenges of being away from home and close members of the family have also made it possible for a revival of some of the collective ethos which was increasingly getting undermined by the rapid urbanization and pressures occurring in Zimbabwe after Independence. In coping with the social and economic pressures of living away from home, the extended family has become an important factor in social security for both migrants and those remaining at home.

For some Zimbabweans, being in South Africa, which is geographically close to Zimbabwe, has made it not only possible for them to stay in touch with developments at home but also relatively easier for them to continue playing a positive role in its economic and social development. Being in South Africa has also made it possible to effectively network and mobilize resources from international organizations and donors for their community development. South Africa is not just the hub of economic activity on the continent, but it is also the central nerve for most philanthropic and donor agencies. Living in South Africa has thus made it relatively easy for Zimbabweans to reach the relevant decisionmakers. Zimbabwean professionals employed in some of these organizations have also been able to use their influence to steer resources towards the funding of community development projects in their home country.

However, Zimbabwean diaspora philanthropy has also been hamstrung by other problems, such as the general logistical problems associated with mobilizing resources among widely dispersed communities. Zimbabweans in South Africa are spread all over the country, in the major cities of Johannesburg, Pretoria, Cape Town, Durban and Messina. The dispersal makes it difficult to organize Zimbabweans for organized philanthropy.

Another major difficulty is that most Zimbabwean migrants are faced with the day-to-day problems of survival outside, and have no time or little space in their lives for organized groups. In the specific case of South Africa, the majority of the migrants are illegal immigrants who are economically vulnerable, often have no fixed place of abode, and are on the run from law enforcement agents (Ranchod 2005:14; Chetsanga and Muchenje 2003). Besides, most Zimbabweans, especially blacks, have no strong history of involvement in the Western style kind of organized philanthropy which, in the developing world, as Ansilla Nyar (2004) explains when discussing philanthropy in South Africa, has connotations of elitism and paternalism.

The argument here is not to say that Zimbabweans have not been involved in organized philanthropy. Organized philanthropy has always been part of Zimbabweans since the pre-colonial era. Examples include the *Zunde raMambo* (Chief's Garden/Granary) – a traditional, village collective effort aimed at assisting orphans, widows and other needy people in the village. The *Zunde raMambo* in the traditional set-up would see a chief donate a field and members of the community (usually women) who would come together to tend the field. The produce was used to support the needy in the community or to be used by the whole community in an event of drought or famine (Kaseke 2006:1). During the colonial period, black Zimbabweans were involved in a number of philanthropic activities. The late Jairos Jiri was one of the greatest Zimbabwean philanthropists, who established the Jairos Jiri association in the 1950s to provide services to people living with disabilities. The funds for the association were raised from its own factories, as well as donations from Zimbabwean philanthropists at home and abroad.

The idea of giving help to communities through institutionalized bodies is, however, not very popular among many black Zimbabweans. Many of those interviewed pointed out that their contributions to their communities are either made directly to individuals in need, schools, clinics, hospitals and other institutions, or indirectly through their church contributions. In fact many interviewees pointed out that they mainly give donations to their local churches because they trusted that churches will use the donations for their intended benefits.

Zimbabweans are generally suspicious of organized philanthropic bodies, and many are afraid of donating funds to philanthropic organizations because some of these organizations have misused funds at the expense of the causes they are supposedly supporting. One of the main problems arising from the Zimbabwe crisis is the mushrooming of bogus political and social organizations, including charity organizations, falsely purporting to be concerned about resolving national problems such as human rights abuses, HIV/AIDS and growing poverty. Many of these organizations have turned out to be 'brief-case' organizations led by one person or a close clique of people interested in self-aggrandizement (Muzondidya 2006). Over time, some of these organizations have used and abused fundraising for selfish needs. In 2004, the BBC reported on how Zimbabweans in the UK lost their money to a fraudulent Zimbabwean community charity group, led by a certain Matapo. The 'Zimbabwean Community UK', created in 2003 with an initial £5,000 grant of lottery funding, raised funds among Zimbabweans ostensibly to help destitute Zimbabweans in the UK. Matapo reportedly spent the money on a luxury BMW vehicle and other personal items.[15]

Conclusion

The concepts and practice of giving and volunteerism is widespread among Zimbabweans living in South Africa. This giving from Zimbabweans abroad is what has helped to keep Zimbabwe going in its current political and economic challenges. Most of the households in Zimbabwe are surviving on remittances and goods sent by migrants based in South Africa. Migrants are also playing an important role in supplying Zimbabweans at home with some of the basic provisions like medicine. Others are paying fees for households which cannot afford to send their children to school. Much of the philanthropic giving that is discussed in this chapter is taking place through the traditional forms of giving, which emphasize giving through extended family and kinship ties rather than through organized philanthropic bodies. In line with tradition and culture, very little of the philanthropy taking place is widely publicized. Giving is usually done at the individual rather than group level.

Organized philanthropy seems to be more prevalent among Zimbabweans from the western regions of Matabeleland and Midlands. Most of these are people who have had a much longer history of living in the diaspora than their compatriots, whose migration to South Africa has been much more of a post-2000 phenomenon. Zimbabweans from the western parts of the country have had a much longer history of suffering from government neglect of developing their region, marginalization from both the economy and politics. As a result, they learnt to rely on themselves rather than on government earlier than the rest. Zimbabwean diaspora philanthropy has a developmental potential. Some of the investments made so far by migrants in their villages – such as solar energy, boreholes and water pumps – have the potential to lift the lives of whole communities. What remains to be done is greater coordination of some of the investment activities.

Endnotes

1   For more detailed discussion of feelings of injustice and marginality among the people of Matabeleland at home and abroad, see Ndlovu-Gatsheni (2003); Lindgren (2005) Ranger et al. (2000).

2   Interviews with Senior (pseudonym), 33-year-old security guard, Pretoria, 25 August 2007; Manuel Sango, 22-year-old assistant bricklayer, Pretoria, 25 August 2007 Kavelo, 26-year-old general handyman, Pretoria, 17 August 2007; Professor (pseudonym), security guard, Johannesburg, 26 February 2006.

3   See www.econet.co.zw/inside.aspx?pid=24

4   See 'Trevor Ncube Suspected of Funding Makoni' *The Herald*, 14 March 2008; 'British, SA firms 'fund' Makoni', http://www.news24.com/News24/Africa /Zimbabwe/0,,2-11-1662_2281699,00.html. See also 'Business under fire for supporting Makoni', Africa Report, No. 160, 14-Mar-08, http://www.iwpr. net/?p=acr&s=f&o=343394&apc_state=henpacr; 'A list of Simba Makoni endorse-ments to date', http://www.talkzimbabwe.com/pdf.php?a=1798.

5   Interviews with Bigman, entrepreneur and member of Mberengwa Burial Society, Pretoria, 19 August 2007; Professor (pseudonym), security guard, Johannesburg, 26 February 2006.

6   'Burial Societies' Influential Role in Zimbabwe', Institute for Peace and War Africa Report No. 92, 30 January 2007.

7   'Zimbabweans urged to shun bandwagons of doom', *Sunday News* (Bulawayo), 9 March 2008.

8   See http://www.mthwakazionline.org/ and http://www.mthwakazifoundation. org.

9   See http://www.synergos.org/africa/zimbabwe.htm and http://www.mgvda. com/2.html.

10 See http://www.synergos.org/africa/zimbabwe.htm and http://www.westfound. com/

11 Discussion with Wellington, Pretoria.

12 Discussion with Netsai, Zimbabwean professional who has been living and working in Cape Town since 2004, Cape Town, 2006.

13 Interviews with Senior (pseudonym), 33-year-old security guard, Pretoria, 25 Au-gust 2007; Ruth, 24-year-old shop assistant, 18 August, Pretoria.

14 Interview with Tinos Mupira and Magumise, Villagers, Zaka, Zimbabwe, 9 August 2006; Mutsai, 28-year-old housemaid, Pretoria, 17 August 2007.

15 Mugabe Coup Plot Mastermind Turns Out to Be Small Time Crook, *SW Radio Africa* (London),15 November 2007.

CHAPTER 13

DIASPORA REMITTANCES: MOTIVATIONS, ORGANIZATION AND CONTRIBUTION TO SOCIAL WELFARE IN CENTRAL AFRICA

GÉRARD TCHOUASSI
& FONDO SIKOD

Introduction

Social security is provided generally through savings when people are working and by the state for those who cannot provide for themselves. In the Central Africa region, and indeed, most of Africa, social security is provided mostly by the family and the ethnic group, or the clan through giving and sharing. A child belongs to the community. In this sense, altruism and charity are embedded into the culture of the people. Although with education and globalization, people are migrating from the geographical locations of their clans, they continue to live mostly according to the norms of the clans: clan leaders and norms continue to have a strong influence and impact on clan citizens wherever they may be. This influence and impact is passed on to children born in the diaspora. Thus, clan members that migrate, tend to repatriate funds to support various clan activities, besides continuing to support and provide for relatives.

Even though philanthropy is defined in many different ways by researchers and practitioners, its most simple definition is that it is the practice of giving, of sharing and helping the poor and those in need – a phenomenon that is embedded in the Central Africa cultures. It consists of the voluntary means that any culture, social group or individual uses to redistribute financial and other resources for the purposes of promoting some collective good and social well-being. The institutional, social and cultural mechanisms that surround these voluntary, altruistic and charitable practices vary across societies and their constituent communities (Copeland-Carson 2004). Philanthropy is the act of giving, or of donating money, goods, time, or effort to support a charitable cause, usually over an extended period of time and in regard to a defined objective. Charitable contributions made by individuals (Clotfelter 1992) and collectives constitute one of the main sources of finance for the vast non-profit sector in the world. In a more fundamental sense, philanthropy may encompass any altruistic activity which is intended to promote good or improve human quality of life.

Migration is a complex and dynamic process that changes the migrants' home and destination countries and, of course, the migrants themselves (Özden and Schiff 2006). By working in host countries, migrants typically provide, in addition to funds, business contacts and information about investment opportunities in source countries, laws and regulations, and differences in culture and ways of doing business. Thus, they end up serving as a bridge between the source countries and the countries of origin. We use the term diaspora to refer to all those who have migrated and settled in various countries or regions all over the world. The term diaspora, though, is of recent usage in the social sciences (Sheffer 1986; Bruneau 1995; Hovanessian 1998). Migrants can increase exchange between three sets of locations: i) between source and host countries; ii) between different host countries if people are from the same source country, source region, ethnic origin or religious group; and iii) between different regions of the same country in the case of internal migration (AFD 2006). The term diaspora has thus acquired a broad semantic meaning. It now encompasses an array of groups such as political refugees, alien residents, guest workers, immigrants, expellees, ethnic and racial minorities, and overseas communities. It is used increasingly by displaced persons who feel, maintain, invent or revive a connection with a prior home. Thus, the concept now includes history of dispersal, myths/memories of the homeland, alienation in the host country, desire for eventual return – which can be ambivalent or utopian, ongoing support of the homeland, and a collective identity defined by the above relationships.

Remittances sent by migrants or groups of migrants to their native country are a powerful economic and social force for socioeconomic development in most of Central Africa, providing financial resources that not only alleviate poverty by sustaining the basic needs of many families, but also support private-sector investment. In this chapter, we are interested in what motivates the migrants from the Central Africa region who are in the diaspora to remit part of their earnings to target development projects within their region of origin, to improve on the welfare of the local people. How are they organized to contribute to the development of their country of origin and family well-being? This approach views philanthropy as a social relation that may be manifested in different institutional guises (Schervish and Ostrander 1990). Besides contributing to the welfare of the poor in receiving environments, remittances are a form of showing the attachment migrants have with the country of origin (Sikod and Tchouassi 2007).

A considerable amount of research work has been conducted on the topic of diaspora remittances over the past few years (Mohan and Zack-Williams 2002; Mutume 2005; AFD 2006, Page and Plaza 2006), especially as the contributions have also become substantial – getting to over US$126 billion in 2004 (Sikod and Tchouassi 2007). Some of these studies assumed that migrants leave their countries, settle in a new country, start integrating in their new society, and abandon their ties with their country of origin. Today, however, globalization with its modern forms of communication makes it possible for those in the diaspora to remain connected with their native countries while residing abroad (Page and Plaza 2006). Given that the studies that have been done on diaspora remittances in Central Africa so far have looked at the contribution of these remittances to development (Tchouassi 2004; Sikod and Tchouassi 2007), this chapter is interested in venturing into the area of social and human sciences by examining the motivations of those remitting; whether these remittances are motivated by philanthropy or some other reason. Specifically, the chapter is interested in understanding and finding out how Central Africans in the diaspora are motivated to show their attachment with their country of origin. The chapter is also interested in how they organize remittances in their host countries. What are their contributions to social well-being in Central Africa? Are they, by remitting part of their incomes, bridging the poverty gap in their countries of origin?

We hypothesize that, in the Central Africa region, there is a long tradition of giving and sharing, which provides a good basis for the development of philanthropy. In order to stimulate and support effective development of basic social well-being, financial and non-financial resources have to be mobilized in the country and abroad.

This research is based on the hypothesis that the remittances of the migrants from the Central Africa region living abroad are organized and motivated by altruism to contribute towards improving the welfare of the local people.

This chapter is based on qualitative and descriptive methodologies. Because of the dearth of information on philanthropy in Central Africa, the study is fairly limited. It is based on mostly secondary data, and very limited primary data. The primary data is based on an informal random survey of households, individuals and groups carried out to determine how they receive remittances, what they use them for, and what they see as a motivation for someone far away, who may not know them, to contribute towards supporting them.

The chapter is structured as follows: location of Central Africans in the diaspora, organization of the Central African diaspora at home and abroad, motivations of Central African diaspora, and their contributions to Central African development and social welfare, conclusions and policy implications.

Location of Central Africans in the diaspora

Most of the sub-Saharan Africans (SSA) in the diaspora are found in Canada (206,425 immigrants born abroad and of SSA origin in 2001), in the US (881,300 in 2000), and in the European Union (1,042,897 in 2000). This does not include Ireland, Austria and Luxembourg. Disaggregating the immigrants in the European Union by countries gives 274,538 in France, 249,720 in the United Kingdom, 156,564 in Germany, 137,780 in Italy, 88,956 in Portugal, 39,336 in Spain, 23,806 in the Netherlands, and 18,900 in Belgium.

In the last few years, the number of people born in Africa and living in the US has grown considerably. A 2000 census in the US showed 881,300 Africans, representing 2.8 per cent of the total population born outside the country. By region, the Africans living in the US revealed the following figures: West Africa (326,507), North Africa (190,491), Central Africa (57,607), East Africa (213,299), Southern Africa (66,496) and 2,690 Africans unclassified.[1]

Central Africa in the larger sense refers to the Economic Community of Central African States (ECCAS), created in 1983, with its headquarters in Libreville – representing an enlargement of groups in Central Africa: Monetary and Economic Community of Central Africa (CEMAC) and the Economic Community of the Great Lakes Countries (CEPGL). ECCAS member states are made up of Angola, Burundi, Cameroon, Central African Republic, Chad, Congo, DR Congo, Equatorial Guinea, Gabon, and Sao Tomé and Principe. This makes the Congo Basin, Central Africa. In this region, migration is provoked mostly by political and economic instability, bad governance, interethnic and interstate conflicts, inequality and poverty. Those most affected by regional migrations are the most vulnerable groups in society, such as peasants and soldiers. And migrations to distant places like Europe and other rich countries are mostly by the average citizens, especially those with some means, from the political class, business class, and intellectuals.

The Central African diasporas have a human and sociocultural capital that is generally more developed than those that have remained back home. Although they migrate, they tend to be very sympathetic about the plight of those left behind. These migrants have international philanthropic networks that are located mostly in Europe and North America (Pourtier 2003). According to the 2002 United Nations report on international migration, of eleven African countries, only Equatorial Guinea experienced a negative migration during the 1995–2000 period. Eight other countries, including Cameroon, Central African Republic and Chad, experienced a positive migration (see Table 13.1). This represents a net loss in terms of the population each year.

Table 13.1: Net annual international migration: Selected Central Africa countries, 1995–2000 period

Country	Total Population (millions)	Net Annual Migration (thousands)	Rate per 1000 persons per year
Equatorial Guinea	0.5	-48	-6.2
Cameroon	14.8	1	0.1
Central African Rep.	3.7	2	0.5
Chad	7.9	20	2.7

Source: Authors' calculations, based on Tchouassi (2004).

The last three were those of the new category of migrants. People migrated because they were escaping from desertification, drought, and famine. There are also political migrants escaping from dictators and political instability, and economic migrants, who are victims of endemic unemployment, inequality and poverty. Migration of Central Africans to some Western countries has thus become an important international phenomenon of the twenty-first century. It is, therefore, not an exaggeration to use the concept diaspora to designate the Central African populations in voluntary or involuntary exile today, dispersed in the four corners of the earth. By Central African diaspora, we mean the communities of the different countries living and working in Europe, the US, Canada, the Antilles, and the Caribbean, among others. One can also include Central African communities living in countries of the sub-continent other than their country of origin (South Africa and Gabon, among others).

With these dynamics in the population, remittances become more and more important. Total remittances to Africa amounted to US$9 billion in 1990 and by 2003 had reached US$14 billion, and the continent receives about 15 per cent of flows to developing countries (Mutume 2005).

In Central Africa, the Republic of Congo is the largest recipient of remittances, constituting about 7.4 per cent of the gross domestic product. Though official figures are not readily available, economists believe that money sent home by the Central African diaspora, individual or collective, in various forms (among others, inside letters, from tourists, and relatives) and from different parts of the world (America, Europe, Asia and Africa) now exceeds those in Table 13.2.

Table 13.2: Remittances in selected Central Africa countries

Central Africa countries	US$ (million)	% GDP
Cameroon	267	1.5
Central African Rep.	73	4.9
Chad	137	2.1
Equatorial Guinea	77	5.7
Congo (Republic of)	423	7.4
Gabon	60	0.9

Source: Authors' calculation, based on IFAD (2007). www.ifad.org

Diaspora organizations

Today there is a critical mass of Central Africans in the diaspora with high skills and massive work experience. While many have completely integrated into the systems and cultures of their host countries and may have no desire to return to the continent, some still desire to return or be involved. This desire is being fuelled by the feeling of autochthony – a feeling of belonging to some group of people. Both groups, nevertheless, agree on one thing: that they have a positive and significant role to play in leveraging the socioeconomic development of the African region. For this reason, a significant number of Central Africans in the diaspora have maintained strong socioeconomic and sociocultural ties with the region.

Hometown associations, characterized by charitable and altruistic acts, have recently become the focus of attention because they have been identified as potential new development vehicles. These philanthropic associations aim to support migrants in their new location but, importantly, they also undertake collective efforts to support development in their home towns. Hometown associations,[2] the general appellation of the different types of philanthropic groups (Page 2007), bring together indigenes of a given place living away from home. They are a common means by which migrants in Central Africa maintain socioeconomic and sociocultural links with their place of origin, not necessarily a 'town' but sometimes a group of settlements, a district or a region. It can be their own place of birth, that of their parents, or an ancestral homeland. Although philanthropic hometown associations have tended to be more firmly established among the local diaspora (for example, in towns and cities of the home country), with growing international migration they are increasingly found in cities in Europe, North America, and various parts of the world.

Historically, the primary concern of philanthropic hometown associations was charitable and mutual support among migrants, particularly when one of their members or close kin died and altruist members would collectively contribute towards sending the body home for burial. Today, most philanthropic hometown association activities (charitable and mutual support or developmental) still rely on endogenous means, although more dynamic or well-connected philanthropic associations sometimes access resources from government, NGOs or international donors. Central Africa diaspora philanthropic organizations are characterized by considerable diversity in their form (individual and association), general objectives and focus (medical, education, arts and culture, tourism, environmental protection, refugee, etc.). A typology of Central Africa diaspora philanthropic groups is in Table 3.

Table 13.3: Typology of Central Africa philanthropic groups

• Individual	• Welfare/refugee group
• Hometown/country association	• Umbrella body
• Ethnic association	• Supplementary school
•Alumni association	• Virtual organization
• Religious association (foundation)	• Research/thinktank
• Professional association	• Tourism, arts and cultural group
• Development NGO	• Women's group (foundation)
• Investment group/business	• Development education centres
• Political group	• Service provider
• National development group	•Youth group (foundation)
• Medical foundation	• Educational foundation
• Peace foundation	• Social well-being association

Source: Authors' compilations, based on fieldwork.

The main objectives of these groups in Central Africa are to provide charitable funding, to support charitable, religious, educational, scientific, and health-related programmes and to help other organizations which are philanthropic in nature, and the community at large. A representative example of a philanthropic hometown association that has evolved over time is the Bali-Nyonga Development and Cultural Association (BANDECA), a constitutionally established, legally registered philanthropic association made up of both people living in the Bali-Nyonga fondom and also of people with an affinity to Bali-Nyonga who are living outside the fondom elsewhere in Cameroon (the 'domestic diaspora') (Page 2007), and outside Cameroon. It aims, first, to organize altruistic and charitable migrants so that they can give, share, help and support each other when they are away from home, and second, to foster social welfare and social development back in the 'home town'.

It is part of civil society – that sector of public life upon which such a burden of expectation has been placed in recent years.

Another hometown association is the Manyu Elements Cultural Association (MECA), which regroups the wider Manyu elements of the Southwest Province of Cameroon. It started in the 1970s with the Manyu elements in Yaoundé. Today there are sub-parts of it representing villages, and even large families. This development arises, of course, as those in the diaspora grow, and the larger philanthropic group becomes more and more difficult to handle. In reality, the sub-groups function as independent philanthropic associations.

The third association of Central Africans in the diaspora is the Association for Aid to Education and Development (AAED)[3] – a non-profit organization registered in Quebec, Canada with the aim to fight poverty in developing countries by promoting education and health, mainly in Africa. The AAED, besides making the Canadian public sensitive to the fight against poverty, supports projects in education and in health by collecting, acquiring and shipping drugs and pedagogic materials, as well as establishing partnerships between Canadian development organizations and their counterparts in the south.

In reality, philanthropic groups and associations are usually initiated by village elites, quite often because of chronic state neglect and the need to carry out various social development projects. These associations therefore become a channel through which village elites can solicit funds from village mates in the diaspora. Villages also emulate each other. By their very nature as dispersed peoples, the diaspora residents are experienced in the use of networking and building connections among their charitable and altruistic communities abroad as well as with their countries of origin.

In terms of organizing to send money back home, situations vary, depending on how each country views the diaspora remittances. Some African countries have adopted innovative approaches,[4] such as setting up transfer services among large migrant communities in industrial countries. These examples give an idea of how the population of Central African countries (Cameroon, Congo, Gabon, Chad, Equatorial Guinea, Central African Republic, DR Congo, Burundi, and Rwanda among others) in the diaspora and home are organized.

What motivates the diaspora?

Why do Central Africans give and share? In light of the apparent incongruity between giving, sharing and the kind of self-interested behaviour usually examined by economists, it is natural to wonder about the motives of Central African people to make charitable gifts in the first place. Indeed, members of philanthropic hometown associations in the diaspora are motivated to contribute by various factors: genuine altruism; economic self-interest; social or legal pressure; and, for some senior elites, the desire to nurture political capital at home. Underlying these activities is a sense of belonging, which connects a diaspora resident to his/her home place and fuses spatially dispersed indigenes into a community, variously described as 'translocal', 'multilocal' or 'extended' (de Jong 1999; Trager 1998; Lambert 2002). Also, somewhere on the cusp between sociocultural activities and economic roles comes pure philanthropy. The groups most able to demand peace are those that in some way enjoy a degree of 'protection', such as women and faith-healers. In the context of looking at diasporas, it appears that doing charitable work may be a way to provide a safe space for engagement with the home country whilst sidestepping some of the toxic politics of the period.

The Bali-Nyonga Development and Cultural Association (BANDECA) was launched in 1999, claiming a regrouping role to include the Bali Cultural Association of the United States of America, and the women's philanthropic association, Nkumu fed fed. This made it easier to handle resources sent to the village for various purposes by individuals and groups in the diaspora, who may or may not have had any direct ties with the village.

We see from the other African[5] diaspora situations that, even though the motivations are varied, sympathy and the desire to help are usually at the root of remittances. While a person who escapes the war in the DR Congo, Burundi, Rwanda, or Darfur may not want to go back there, the thought of those left behind who continue to suffer is a powerful motivation to support philanthropic activities in those areas. The most moving is usually a state of war or some natural catastrophe that leads to mass displacements of people, creating severe refugee situations either in some parts of the country, or in neighbouring or foreign countries. Central African countries are replete with such examples. Most such situations seem to be in Central Africa – including Darfur in the Sudan, which has led to mass movements into the Central African Republic and Chad; Rwanda and Burundi, the DR Congo, among others. Although some of these areas are now stable, providing for those who went through the shock and are back in these regions continues to pose major problems. Those from these regions who migrated and settled in other parts of the world look back with nostalgia, charity and sympathy, and feel morally obliged to contribute to the reconstruction of their homelands.

Contributions to development and social welfare

Migrant philanthropic associations in host countries are now playing an increasingly active role in financing projects to improve living conditions and promote development in their home communities in different regions of the world. In Central Africa, this has been part of a long tradition of community and ethnic solidarity. In recent years, the establishment of migrant associations in host countries has lent a new momentum to these efforts. For example, a significant proportion of Central African migrants' savings accumulated in France was channelled through migrant associations to finance community assets, including the construction of schools and health facilities, among others, in the village of origin. A striking feature of the new initiatives is that migrant philanthropic associations are mobilizing funds from external sources in the host country, leveraging their own, collectively pooled, remittances to support community-level development projects. These activities can range from the supply of consumer goods and purchase of farming equipment to income-generating business ventures. And sometimes, migrants from different neighbouring countries, but working in the same host country, join hands, forge interinstitutional links and plan collective action.

Female migrants from Central African countries have also been active in setting up philanthropic associations within the wider framework of Organisation de solidarité internationale issue de l'immigration (OSIM). In France, for example, there are several hundreds of Central Africa-oriented OSIMs. Initially focused on migrant integration and welfare in the host country, they are now more concerned with socioeconomic cooperation and development, and serve as valuable links between host and home countries. Their activities range from fundraising and canvassing for external aid, to hands-on participation in skills transfer to home countries. Central African female migrants have also been active in another philanthropic organization, the Initiatives des Femmes Africaines de France et d'Europe (IFAFE). Founded as an association in 1993, it was reconstituted as a federation in 1996, bringing together 23 member associations. Despite its limited resources, in recent years IFAFE has embarked on a variety of socioeconomic cooperation and development programmes, such as supply of medicine and school equipment, rural development – including building wells in the DR Congo, Gabon and Cameroon, vocational training for orphans, and provision of microcredit for women engaged in farming and business who lost their livelihood following natural disasters (IOM 2005).

The debate on the philanthropic role that the Central African diaspora can play in the development and social welfare of their country of origin has finally taken centre stage. Growing evidence shows that migration has positive effects on social and economic development in many Central African countries. Mohan and Zack-Williams (2002) argued that:

> We need to consider three inter-related aspects of diasporas' engagement with the world. The first is development in the diaspora, for example, the circumstances under which diaspora communities operate in the host country – jobs, housing, welfare, etc. The second is development through diaspora – the ways that globally dispersed diaspora networks support each other, engage in trade, etc. And the

third is home development by diaspora – the support that diaspora communities provide to ancestral home communities through, among others, remittances, lobbying, altruism and philanthropy.

Every day, thousands of Central Africans living abroad line up in money-transfer offices to wire home the odd dollar they are able to save. From the US, Saudi Arabia, Germany, Belgium, Switzerland and France – the top sources of remittances to Central African countries – some of the money finds its way deep into the rural areas of Central Africa. There, it may send a child to school, build a house, or buy food to sustain those remaining at home (Mutume 2005). Outside of those destined to individuals and households, remittances targeting village or other development generally go through philanthropic hometown associations. Philanthropic hometown associations (medical foundations, educational foundations, and other associations, among others: BANDECA, Bali Social and Cultural Development Association (BASCUDA), Association BINAM Canada, MECA and NUFI Cameroun), even if created in the diaspora, would tend to have a local or home-based branch that carries out activities as planned and financed by those in the diaspora. For example, MECA, whose early project was the construction of the Mamfe town hall, has recently supported improvements at Mamfe general hospital. MECA-US Branch continues to struggle with the construction and equipping of a mortuary in the hospital grounds in Mamfe. The benefits of a few other MECA projects are spread around the division, notably, medicines distributed to village health centres.

In terms of home area development, common Village Development Association (VDA) projects include construction of town halls, classrooms, health centres, places of worship, and farm access roads, and rehabilitation of pipe-borne water systems. It is the diaspora that supplies most of the cash and sometimes materials (such as cement) or expertise for VDA projects, either directly or indirectly. The effectiveness of VDAs as development actors thus depends partly on the size and dynamism of the village diaspora. For example, MECA membership comprises of 'Manyu citizens', a category that extends even to some people who have lived all their lives in urban centres outside Manyu but still express an attachment there.

Since 1999, BANDECA has raised tens of thousands of pounds (mostly from migrants within Cameroon) and has undertaken a number of projects. It has renovated a building in Bali-Nyonga for its own headquarters and it has also renovated the office of the government's principal official in town (the divisional officer) and equipped the offices of the new 'gendarmerie brigade' (the military police). BANDECA has provided bail for five Bali-Nyonga residents who were arrested after a violent land dispute with the people from a neighbouring subdivision. It has opened a public library with books provided by the Bali-Nyonga diaspora in the US and it has also organized a cancer-screening exercise. Its two largest projects to date are the reconstruction of the water supply and the equipping of the mortuary. The mortuary cost around 19.5 million CFA francs (around UK£20,000), which was raised through general development levies collected from the BANDECA, with huge support coming from the diaspora. The Bali Cultural Association (US Branch) also sent containers of medication and equipment to the Bali district hospital.

As for AAED, its resources are membership fees, fundraising activities, and generous donations. For example, its 2005 budget was approximately CAD$10,000 of which 99 per cent was spent on projects. Budget estimation for 2006 and 2007 were approximately CAD$40,000 and CAD$60,000 respectively. A quarter of this came from altruistic and charitable members, and the rest from external contributors. The main achievement during the past years has been the support to the Université des Montagnes (UdM), a community college founded in 2000 in Cameroon by the philanthropic non-profit organization named Association for Education and Development (AED). The development of this community college relies essentially on philanthropy and the mobilization civil society altruism, which made it a pioneering experience in the Central African context.

In terms of tourism, arts and culture, there are some interesting initiatives taking place on bringing charitable people from abroad to Central African countries. The charitable group that is being targeted as potential tourists are African-Americans – not recent diaspora, but those whose roots go back to the slave ships bringing their ancestors to the US several centuries ago. Johnson and Sedaca (2004) have identified other forms of diaspora involvement that bring economic benefits to the homeland. In addition to the widely-noted mechanism of remittances, they identify mechanisms such as business investments, investment instruments, and knowledge transfers. According to these authors, remittances are far from being the only vehicle for diaspora influence on the incidence of poverty in their home countries. But, for many Central African countries, the diaspora is a major source of foreign direct investment (FDI), market development (including outsourcing of production), and technology transfer. The quality of information, much less hard data, about diaspora influences in these dimensions is in general very poor, posing a serious challenge to policy development implications. An important function that diaspora investment can perform is to improve others' perceptions of the environment for business. In more stable environments, these types of business relations are possible. Here, we note that the motivation may not be only altruism or charitable, but profit, or a combination of the two.

Conclusions and policy implications

Central Africans, like everyone from elsewhere, face the same and sometimes even greater problems that oblige them to migrate. This phenomenon has intensified in the last two decades, with the sociopolitical problems in the Democratic Republic of the Congo, Rwanda and Burundi, The Central African Republic, and Chad. People forced by circumstances to leave their countries of origin continue to live under the nostalgia of one day returning to the same origin. Children born in the diaspora are taught about the home country of their parents, and so their attachment to the country grows, a phenomenon that gets passed down to the younger generations. This phenomenon is best exemplified by the US, where almost everybody identifies themselves in terms of some country of the origin of their forefathers: African-American, Irish-American, French-American, Jewish-American, etc. This means that, while remittances to individuals and families may be by recent migrants, those who remit to countries of the origin of their forefathers do so out of altruism. They know no particular person or family in those countries.

Generally, people in the diaspora belong to various types of philanthropic hometown associations that facilitate charitable and mutual help, raising funds for projects in the home countries of origin, and transferring various types of technologies, etc. While recent migrants are motivated by the need to support families back home, distant migrants are motivated largely by altruism and charity to sustain social welfare and, in today's globalizing world, they are motivated by the desire to bridge the development divide.

Central African governments and multilateral agencies have only recently begun to think systematically about the actual and potential philanthropic contributions of the diaspora to development and/or the reduction of poverty in their countries of origin. The dominant focus so far has been on remittance flows: how to increase them and direct them towards more 'developmental' and social welfare uses.

The most extensive set of policy implications with respect to the Central African diaspora has to do with increasing the gains not 'wastes' from remittances. These need to focus on four areas: (i) lowering transaction costs and increasing the security of individual and collective transfers; (ii) extending financial services to poor people, especially in rural areas, who are 'unbanked'; (iii) encouraging collective remittances from migrant philanthropic organizations, by offering them technical assistance, help with institutional development, matching funds, marketing assistance, and other business and financial services; and (iv) encouraging more 'productive' or 'developmental' uses of remittances for hometown populations' welfare.

Central African diaspora philanthropic groups may have difficulties agreeing on the uses of collective remittances, but these suggested interventions are designed to assist them in acquiring the organizational tools to make appropriate decisions and realize their chosen goals in philanthropic ways. By their very nature as dispersed peoples, Central African diaspora are experienced in the use of networking to build philanthropic connections among their communities abroad as well as with their countries of origin (Chikezie 2007). Central African diaspora networks have a strong developmental potential, such as those devoted to cooperation in business or information technology. Support to build and strengthen charitable networking should not be confined to the socioeconomic sphere, but should also extend to peace-building and reconciliation networks in the Central African diaspora.

By understanding Central African philanthropy, we have seen that diaspora remittances have a direct social impact on poverty, social well-being or its effects. Philanthropic support could take the form of technical and legal assistance to nascent charities or in some cases, where a solid track record has been established, co-funding of activities may be appropriate.

Endnotes

1   Source: United States Immigration and Naturalisation Services, Annual Statistics Report, 2003.
2   In all the Central African countries, foundations are the main hometown association working in health and education sectors. In some countries these associations are regional; depend on ethnicity, languages and religion. For example, in Cameroon and abroad, for example in the US, Canada, Germany, UK, France, Switzerland, and Belgium, we have identified some networking hometown associations: BANDECA, BASCUDA, AAED, Association BINAM Canada, NUFI Cameroon, MECA working in different areas. The members of these associations are living in America, Europe, Africa, and Asia.
3   AAED is a registered charitable organization based in Montreal, Quebec, with members residing across Canada and the US.
4   In Paris, France, for example, three banks – the Banque de l'Habitat du Sénégal (BHS), the Banque de l'Habitat du Mali and the Banque des Ivoiriens de France – offer special incentives to their nationals at rates lower than those charged by private agents to assist migrants to build houses in their countries of origin. As a result, the banks make about 400 transfers a day. In 1999, some US$24 million was transferred to Senegal through the scheme.
5   For example, in Britain in 1995, Action for Children (AfC) was formed by a group of British-based Sierra Leoneans. From early fundraising campaigns they moved to partner with an established international NGO working in Sierra Leone, Concern International, and this is now an important partnership. In the US there seem to be a number of philanthropic initiatives, including Grassroots Empowerment for Self Reliance (GEMS), and the Sierra Leone Fund begun by childhood friends in the US.

CHAPTER 14

FISH OR FISHING LINES?
MUSLIM WOMEN AND
PHILANTHROPY IN TANZANIA

SAÏDA YAHYA-OTHMAN

Introduction

Feminist discourse has long held that women constantly adopt strategies and choices that reflect a lot more power on their part than would be thought possible in strongly patriarchal societies (Rosaldo 1974:9). Such strategies are no less manifest in the philanthropic practices of Muslim women in Tanzania. However, in a world where change is one of the few things that are certain, it would be curious if these practices had not changed in both their nature and structure over the decades. Women have been forced to rethink their philanthropic initiatives, as they have others, by manifold pressures, including the fragmentation of their communities, their having to head households on their own, cost-sharing in the social services and the increase in the number of their dependants arising from the HIV/AIDS pandemic and other social upheavals. The question is whether Muslim women adopt new philanthropic strategies to enhance their power and status in society, to book themselves a better 'space' in the hereafter, or to advance the cause of social justice (Kingman and Ngondi-Houghton 2004). This question brings into sharp focus three facets: the 'Muslim', philanthropy, and social justice.

Let us begin with the 'Muslim'. For the purposes of this chapter, we do not take 'Muslim women' to be simply those who profess Islam, and who in addition undertake some philanthropic activities in their lives, in the same way that believers of other faiths, or even non-believers, do. That group alone would not justify the title of this chapter. Our interest is rather to examine those practices by women which are guided by 'a conscious application of the ... tenets of Islam, and by an incorporation of those tenets of Islam' (Asad 1985, quoted in Weiss 2002:9). In other words, those tenets have to be incorporated into the women's philanthropic endeavours. Thus, although below we will touch on forms of giving which do not conform to a 'conscious application', the main discussion will be of Islamic women's groups which are conformist.

'Philanthropy' and 'social justice' are more involved. Philanthropy, however defined, must involve giving (Kingman and Ngondi-Houghton, this volume) and, while Tanzanian women have been hugely generous in spite of their own poverty, they have at the same time been the ones who have been most needy. In spite of making up 50.2 per cent of the active labour force and 53.9 per cent of the agricultural labour force, only 24.7 per cent of women constitute the paid employment category (TGNP 2004: 31). Muslim women are harder hit because fewer of their numbers are educated (Yahya-Othman 2006). Two things are noteworthy in relation to philanthropy in Tanzania: first, as one of the least developed countries, Tanzanian philanthropy has never conformed to the commonly held conception of philanthropy as the preserve of the rich. Until the late 1980s, there were very few rich people in the country to have had any meaningful philanthropic impact. The massive mobilization of the people in the 1960s and 1970s through the Arusha Declaration and the philosophy of self-reliance demanded for philanthropic acts to be self-directed towards the people's own development efforts. Individual resources, though limited, were directed towards communal capacity, from which the individual in turn also benefited.

Secondly, the foundation tradition is in its infancy in Tanzania, at the national level. The Aga Khan Foundation can be placed in the class of other international foundations which have their roots and resources elsewhere, but which may have local representation. The Mwalimu Nyerere Foundation, apart from being non-religious, has had very little impact in the interventions it has made. The Foundation for Civil Society, though professing national credentials, is entirely funded by foreign donors, and cannot therefore attribute its considerable success to the efforts of Tanzanians. The Tanzania Social Action Fund (TASAF) is operated by the government and provides funding for self-help schemes run by communities. The only Foundation which is both national and expressly aimed at putting Islamic philanthropy on a new footing is the Muslim Development Foundation (MDF). Established in 2004, it has started with a major project of the Muslim University of Morogoro. However, its proclaimed objectives also include the provision of a better environment, sanitation, health services and other amenities in the improvement of the lives of Muslims, as well as the support and promotion of appropriate self-reliance projects for the benefit of Muslims, particularly those in need. The Sahiba Sisters discussed below, though registered as a foundation since 1997, have eschewed seeking funding from major donors, preferring instead to create their own wealth which they then use for social justice activities.

The MDF has yet to prove itself and clearly demonstrate its contribution to social justice. It may help to fill the gap left since 1968 by the popular East African Muslim Welfare Society, which directed efforts mostly to health and educational interventions (Liviga and Tumbo-Masabo 2006). None of the Muslim women's organizations qualify as foundations, in the sense of institutions working through others by providing grants (Porter and Kramer 1999:122). (In the language of organized philanthropy, they would be more likely to be categorized as 'grantseekers' rather than 'grantmakers'.)

I will discuss in more detail the development of philanthropic initiatives by Muslim women but, generally, their giving has been constrained in two ways: they can only give in small amounts, and they can only give in an irregular manner. However, unlike in western practice where one might make regular contributions to one or two charities, Tanzanian Muslim women give widely and variously, in diverse ways ranging from the more stipulated forms of giving including direct alms and *zakat*, to personal donations for weddings, funerals and orphans and the disabled. The latter type may be more frequent than the stipulated form of giving. This is far from being straightforward, given that in Islam it is not only the specified forms of giving – *zakat*, *sadaqat* and *waqf* – that constitute worship (Weiss 2002:177); rather, other forms, such as those discussed below, can also be viewed as forms of worship.

In the consideration of philanthropy, three parameters keep emerging: reciprocity, motivation, and obligation. In the context of Tanzanian Muslim women's 'philanthropy', the three parameters appear to be very closely interlinked. The spirit of reciprocity has been nurtured over centuries, a key aspect of a cultural practice that upholds the extended family and other social ties in which members lend their support to others who are faced with expensive communal undertakings or difficult times. It was upon this premise of mutual support that the Ujamaa policy was based. Feierman (1998) demonstrates how reciprocity provided a social 'safety net' to vulnerable and marginalized members of the community in different African societies in pre-colonial times. In Tanzania it continues to do so to the present day.

Connected to reciprocity is obligation, which is both social and religious. For the Muslim, giving is a religious requirement but, additionally, one's social standing is enhanced or otherwise through giving. Even the richest in the community still receive donations, not because they need them, but because giving and receiving constitute part of belonging, and part of the social norms by which members are expected to behave. In many Tanzanian communities, the deprivation of one member questions the sense of responsibility of all the others. Thus, the realization of one's obligation in turn can constitute one kind of motivation. But the latter also introduces an external objective towards which one works. One example is indirect profit, unconnected to the immediate undertaking (tax rebates, increase in customers); another is the long-term improvement of the quality of life of those being assisted (education, housing, water); a third is escape from damnation (*da'wa*).

If the donors are not wealthy, are they any less philanthropic? Given the specific Tanzanian context, we have to have a conception of philanthropy which includes the efforts made by individuals, including poor individuals, to improve their own and others' lives through communal action. Thus, I am going to adopt a targeted definition of philanthropy, which will address the specifics of the topic of this chapter, and which goes back to the traditional understanding of philanthropy, even in western terms. The predominant language in Tanzania, Kiswahili, has no equivalent term for philanthropy. People talk of *kusaidiana* (assisting each other), *kujitolea* (to volunteer or sacrifice), *kuchangia* (to contribute), *kufaana* (to be of help), all of which implicate a very personal interactive exchange. The reflexive forms (*-na*) further underline the aspect of reciprocity.

We have heard of people being philanthropists without even knowing it – they give without thinking of themselves as philanthropists. I believe that the element of intention is significant in Islamic philanthropy. The giver has to perform an act intentionally, and direct it to recipients who have indicated a need for what is given. Giving food to one's guests at a wedding is not philanthropic, but providing food relief to those affected by drought or floods is. So the givers may not think of themselves as philanthropists, but they certainly perceive themselves as givers, as do-gooders. Gregory (1992:1) notes that it is easier to share with those with whom one has some common denominator such as blood ties, regional affiliation, religion or nationality. The philanthropic drive is stronger the more tenuous the connection. Unfortunately, Muslim women's philanthropic efforts are still closely tied to the home turf. Women give to their community members, to institutions run by friends or relatives, to their local mosque or madrassa. There are no truly rich women among the Muslim women. There are a few who depend on the largesse of their husbands for their philanthropic activities. The vast majority are poor, but their strength lies in their ability to organize and pool resources for others less endowed. Consequently, the distinction made between charity and philanthropy by Kingman and Ngondi-Houghton in this volume, as one between the giving of a fish and the offer of a fishing line, is not only considerably blurred for this group, but is often invalid.

Following this discussion on the peculiar characteristics of women's giving in Tanzania, I would now offer a working definition of philanthropy as *a conscious, intentional, offer of material or non-material goods to others who are in need, as an attempt at improving their quality of life, for whatever period, for whatever reason, with whatever immediate or future benefits or gain to the giver, from the receiver or from some other source.* This may sound tortuous, but it is meant to take account of reciprocity, motivation and obligation, and also of the requirements for social justice and forms of giving that may on the surface not appear to be philanthropic, such as appeasing the spirits that trouble someone or nursing another's baby. The Islamic requirement would then call for a specification of the reasons, and an element of obligation, in the sense of An-Naim's rights-based approach (An-Na'im and Abdel Halim 2004). The issue of 'gain' is also important – entirely selfless philanthropy is rare, if not impossible. If the giver does not expect worldly recompense, then she would be doing it as a form of worship, or a purification of her wealth, and therefore hope to reap heavenly benefit. Countless are the times when one has heard devout Tanzanian Muslim women who have lost something, given something inadvertently away or been short-changed saying *'Ah, basi, ndo sadaka yake tena'* ('Oh well, never mind, it'll be his/her *sadaqat'*)

What about social justice? One of the women in the Ummu Aymana Islamic Centre had this to say: 'How can I expect my convert to pray if she does not even have the means of getting the proper attire for praying?'

In most of the discussion, social justice impliedly involves the big decision-makers, who can bring about policy changes and human rights protection, institute structural change, and address the root causes of social and economic inequalities. Muslim women's philanthropy in Tanzania may have the objectives to achieve such goals, but definitely they have neither the wherewithal nor the political muscle to do so. In such a situation, the social justice must lie in the 'improvement of the quality of life' included in the definition of philanthropy above. They do the best they can. And happily, Moyo (2004:38) characterizes social justice as 'the empowerment of communities to take charge of themselves and control their destinies'. Encouraging another to pursue further education, and providing them with the money to at least pay for the application forms; raising an orphan who would otherwise be on the streets; and waiving tuition fees for nursery school children, can, in my view, constitute such 'empowerment'. In making possible such small enabling provisions, including the prayer dress, Muslim women seem to be addressing social justice.

Women's philanthropic traditions: A historical perspective

As has been noted in several of the chapters in this volume, philanthropy is considered by many as an importation from the West. The traditions of giving have developed divergently, many in African societies placing great emphasis on reciprocity. While external innovations may now be encroaching, the aspect of reciprocity is still transcendent. Tanzanian women's giving has emerged from long-standing cultural traditions developed in close-knit societies in which sharing constituted an essential part of the survival of the community. Some things have changed now, but Tanzanians still set great value on family and community ties, and good neighbourliness. Islam also enjoins collective responsibility, in the idea of *fardh kifayah*, which are 'duties incumbent upon the community as a whole, … which every person is under the obligation to perform, until a sufficient number of persons have performed it, the rest being then absolved from the obligation' (Weiss 2002:170).

In the maintenance of these cultural traditions, and the Islamic requirements, women have for centuries offered both material and non-material assistance to others in need. They have done this as part of a network of sustenance and support in which the threat of victimhood could fall on any of them. First and foremost, given Islam's emphasis on education, particularly Muslim education, the role of women as Islamic teachers and spiritual mentors has been crucial. They have provided Islamic education to both girls and boys in the madrassas, with very little material gain. In the last century the network of women madrassa teachers spread all over the country, and some of the women gained considerable reputations as sheikhs in their communities, providing spiritual leadership and undertaking serious study and teaching of various branches of Islamic *ilm*, and passing these on to the young (Maoulidi, unpublished paper). While many had their public voices subdued, some conducted radio programmes on religion, and others held private *darsas* with other women to satisfy the quest for deeper knowledge of the Qur'an and the hadith. Some of the sufi orders, such as the Qadiriya, advocated for greater involvement of women in the central religious activities.

The Qadiriya became prominent in Tanganyika from the 1870s, and not only allowed the participation of women in mosque activities, but also endorsed their leadership (Dunbar 2000:404). Unfortunately, the women teachers' influence has waned, especially in the urban areas, thus depriving them not only of the meagre income accorded through their teaching, but also the influence they used to wield over young children (Maoulidi op. cit.).

But it was in the formal education sector that women came into their own. On the one hand, formal education marginalized the madrassa teachers as their role came to be taken up by male teachers in the schools, on the other hand, its introduction at the primary level enabled women to open frontiers in starting new schools where none had existed before, and thereby expanding the opportunities for children of the poor as well as their peers. In remote areas, with the minimum of facilities and with hardly any other teachers, these were hard times. But women made these sacrifices. One teacher in Zanzibar narrates how she started several schools in both Unguja and Pemba, sometimes against her husband's wish, sometimes abandoned by her teachers, and sometimes meeting parents' opposition

(Mohammed 2001). This was in the 1930s. But early secular education was introduced by a Muslim community, the Ismailis, in 1895, with the first girls' schools in
Zanzibar in 1905. The secular and the religious came together in the appointment
of teachers in the primary schools who taught only religion. Maoulidi (op. cit.)
notes that the British had to make these concessions in the largely Muslim areas in
order to assuage the fears of Muslim parents about western education

Other philanthropic contributions having to do directly with Islamic practice
involved the work of *da'awa* that women conducted in areas where Islam had not
made inroads. Although this practice is stronger now, with Islamic revivalism,
Muslim women have always seen it as part of their Islamic duty to spread the word
of God to non-Muslims. Those who were posted in non-Muslim areas with their
husbands made it their sacred business to convert their pupils, their workers and
their friends. Although Muslims would assert that Islam is not evangelical, individual
Muslims are enjoined to increase the number of the faithful. In addition to preaching
to the unconverted, a small group of women have also provided essential services
to the communities in which they live, their recompense often at the whim of the
recipients or their families. They conduct special readings and special prayers for
various needs; they cleanse the dead, and officiate at religious functions such as a
reading of the Prophet's eulogy, usually conducted within the month to celebrate
His birth. In a context where the washing of the dead in Islam is guided by strict
rites and calls for knowledge of the prayers and the *du'a* to be cited, some of these
women hold considerable though unenviable power. The female dead cannot be
buried without their intervention. But they can be called at any time of day or night
and they respond as part of their social and religious obligation.

Outside the strictly religious (keeping in mind that in Islam nothing is strictly
'outside'), all African women are familiar with the role of being multiple mothers
to the extended family. Wilkinson-Maposa and Alan Fowler in this volume note
that a significant giver of help among the poor is the family, both immediate and
extended. The service that Tanzanian women perform in their lifetime of nursing,
raising, nurturing and educating members of their extended family cannot be anything but philanthropic. With Muslim women there is the added complication of the
polygamous relationship, in which they are expected to also sometimes look after
the children of their co-wives, and even the co-wives themselves. As one woman
told me, if anything will open the doors of heaven for her, it is her tolerance of
the extended family. African women traditionally had no idea that rights that their
counterparts might expect, of privacy, of planning ahead, of 'quality time' with
their biological children, even existed. Lihamba et al. (2007) provide a text of a
woman from the Iraqw ethnic group who, having moved in with her in-laws, got
so involved in housework for the whole family that she had no time to mend her

waist beads. She says this with great shame, this for her being the height of neglect. Luckily or not, her modern middle-class sister is more likely to complain of missing the latest episode of her soap opera.

Other practices which may not be perceived as falling under the traditional, western philanthropic experience, but which provide an invaluable support system, include female initiation, dealing with spirit possession and traditional healing. The secrets of female initiation have for centuries been the preserve of a few. While the sheikhs insist that these have nothing to do with religion, men have fought to uphold them, including the evil of female genital mutilation (FGM), because they sustain their patriarchal hegemony over the bodies of women. For many women still, their daughters must be initiated into the secrets of adulthood, and this service can only be provided in secret ceremonies such as the *unyago*. Lihamba et al. (ibid.) provide a text of a bequest letter from a Ndegereko mother to her daughter, through which she leaves her most valuable possession, an initiation bag, containing her 'tools' of the trade.

Spirit possession is one means that women have developed of negotiating and interpreting their reality, both for themselves and their sisters. Much has been written on the explanation for spirit possession, including the suggestion that it constitutes a means for women to vent their frustrations in a socially sanctioned way, in ways that would not be available to them otherwise. Dunbar (2000:399) makes the point that women have used spirit possession to create networks 'that promote spiritual, psychological and material support'. Through such networks, Muslim women have exported these spirit possession services to as far as the Middle East and Europe, to sustain their sisters in their diaspora. Mirza (2005: 33) discusses in addition the export of spirit possession cults such as *zar* and *bori* from Zanzibar during slavery times to Iran (then Persia), when they were also used for the purpose of treating psychological disorders.

Apart from spirit possession, traditional women healers provide an invaluable service in the use of traditional herbs in curing the sick. From children's upset tummies, to broken bones, to the ravages of strokes, the society depended on women specialists, who could be trusted to provide services more dedicated than any modern doctor. They often inherited their skills from their parents or some other member of the extended family. Services were often provided free, although grateful healed patients usually showed their gratitude in ways that provided adequate subsistence to the healers.

Mutual aid associations, which might perhaps be viewed as self-help endeavours, would not have been possible if women did not get together to put up the schemes, which included both contributions towards a member's special or unexpected occasion, such as a wedding or funeral of a relative, but also rotating games such as *upatu* (from *upatu*, a round tray made from raffia), or some other. These were designed to assist women over difficult times, when they had need for substantial amounts, such as for repairs to their homes, paying school fees and marrying off their children. While all members were potential beneficiaries, most still had to make a great effort to put money aside each month. The *upatu* system was essentially a savings scheme without interest, since members received only what they had invested. In contrast, the recently exported pyramid schemes which were presented to Tanzanian women as forms of *upatu* have brought many women to grief. The *upatu* systems were linked to women's organizing into social, usually class-based groups to arrange dance and other performance activities. The competition between these was often fierce, but it honed their social skills and exposed them to the public light. The songs they wrote for these performances were sometimes biting social criticism, as has been noted of Siti binti Saad's songs (Lihamba et al. 2007).

Some of these social women's organizations were the precursors of political and nationalist associations. During the nationalist struggles for independence, Muslim women, particularly in Dar es Salaam, provided essential support services in hosting clandestine Tanganyika African National Union (TANU) meetings, cooking for those attending, putting up delegates from upcountry, hiding their men's party membership cards and most importantly, mobilizing other women to join the cause (Geiger 1997). While the lives of the likes of Bibi Titi Mohammed (a key figure in Tanzania's nationalist struggle for independence waged by TANU, and the founder of the party's women's wing, UWT), were driven more by the nationalist ideals than philanthropy, their sacrifices made it possible for other women to be emboldened to start major women's movements, and to participate in the political life of the nation.

After independence, women could rest easy that at least some of life's essentials, such as education, health and land, would be provided by the state. But the daily upkeep and sustenance of the household was still the responsibility of the family – the land had to be cultivated, the many dependants had to be fed and clothed. This 'burden' fell mostly on the women. In Tanzania, 70 per cent of food for domestic consumption is produced by women. In addition, most women are in agriculture, which contributes 50 per cent of the GDP. Nevertheless, they have very little control of what they produce. This may explain why women are so generous in giving, even when they themselves have so little – they know where their sisters 'come from'.

Now, post-Arusha Declaration, the basics are no longer free, they all have a price, and women have had to rethink the ways in which they can continue to sustain their communities.

The context of women in Tanzania

Women constitute half of Tanzania's population, but their marginalized position in the society has generally not reflected this proportion. They are the main producers in the agricultural sector, and yet have little control over what they produce. More women are illiterate than men, and consequently the proportion that attains higher education is very limited. In the December 2005 elections, national election monitors noted that as many as 75 per cent of women voters in some constituencies had to be assisted in voting because of illiteracy (TEMCO 2006). From the bottom up, girls face hurdles in their education, and there have been particularly serious problems in the sciences. Some parents have a preferential system of offering education to boys over girls, but in addition girls have more responsibility in household chores than boys.

Because of their lower education levels, women also have limited access to good jobs, and are most visible in low-paying jobs, which do not allow them to support their families. This problem is compounded by the fact that the number of female-headed households is increasing, from various factors, including divorce and HIV/AIDS-related deaths. It has often been noted that the legislative structure since independence has attempted to address a lot of the legal hurdles that were facing women, through such legislation as the Marriage Act, the Sexual Offences Special Provisions Act and the Employment Act. Although all this legislation can do with improvement, currently the problem lies in its implementation.

Muslim women in Tanzania have been doubly disadvantaged, first by being women, and secondly by being Muslim. Muslims in general have been deprived of important opportunities in education, government and generally in the economic sector (Chaligha 2006; Yahya-Othman 2006). But because women have also had restricted opportunities in these areas, they have been doubly marginalized. This is in marked contrast to the powerful coastal Muslim women of yore, who 'played prominent parts in the public affairs of late medieval and early modern towns; they helped oversee important events concerning their teen groups, participated in public celebrations like the 'New Year' ceremonies, attended mosques with their men, and were encouraged to become literate and to study the formal Islamic sciences' (Pouwels 1987:28). Dunbar (2000:409) also reports on Portuguese accounts and oral traditions that point to the high social status given to women before 1600, which allowed them to have a role in public affairs of coastal towns.

However, Muslim women have in the last century been forced to abdicate power to an authoritarian patriarchal hegemony perpetuated in the name of Islam. It is possible that the secularism of the Tanzanian state has helped women to resist this, although some women have used the very same cover of religion to launch new initiatives which help them deal with psychological and economic hardships.

Young Muslim women have decided to study the Qur'an and the hadith for themselves, in order to gain a firmer understanding of Islam and the place of women in it. Whereas previously deep piety was mostly identified with elderly women, who taught in the madrassas, conducted the *khitmas* and performed all the Islamic rituals, now it is common to find young women who are deeply versed in the Qur'an and have a high understanding of Islamic knowledge. This may be due partly to the changes in the way in which the Qur'an itself is taught, and the contribution of young faithfuls who have trained in Egypt, Saudi Arabia and Sudan. In this context, Muslim women view their philanthropic work as being part of the efforts of raising the status of women in the society, by empowering them and giving them the means to take control of their lives.

Philanthropy practices

The 'traditional' or cultural forms of philanthropy in Tanzania have been very varied and wide ranging, covering various ethnic and age groups and social formations. I will focus specifically on those that we can categorize as 'Muslim' or 'Islamic', in which the donor acts within Islamic parameters even while observing age-old cultural traditions.

While in the past Muslims have given in a quiet unplanned way, depending on contingencies that emerged, more recently there has been an increase in more deliberate and more organized philanthropic activity, for various reasons. First the increased poverty brought on by neoliberal policies has naturally prompted greater demand for assistance. Women have been most hard hit by retrenchments and unemployment, due to deteriorating economic conditions in the region, con-tributed to partly by the Structural Adjustment Programmes (SAPs) sponsored by the international financial institutions (Chachage and Mbilinyi 2003:5). While SAPs were introduced to correct what was perceived to be the failure of Ujamaa policies, their effect has been to marginalize large sections of Tanzanian society.

Second, the withdrawal of government support from social services has reduced previously independent women to begging for essentials such as medicine and their children's school fees. Third, the eruption of problems such as HIV/AIDS has constituted an unprecedented assault on the normal health delivery provisions, and community initiatives have had to be called in. And fourth, the failure of the neoliberal agenda in benefiting the majority has had two opposing consequences, one a blessing, the other less so. On the one hand, communities have used their commonality to mobilize resources to meet the challenges that face them: women and youth have formed self-help or economic groups, parents have contributed to the construction of schools, the whole nation has responded to some emergen-cies that the government cannot deal with on its own, such as the 2005 campaign for women's breast cancer and the 2006 famine relief fund. But on the negative side, the collapse of the provision of social services by the government has also awakened allegiances that Tanzanians had thought were, if not dead, then certainly on the wane. Communities are now also mobilizing along ethnic lines – numerous ethnic societies have emerged in schools, colleges, even nationally, to pool resources to educate children, build schools and hospitals or 'develop' particular districts. While this can be welcomed as just another well-intentioned path in this struggle, its development is unpredictable and undesirable, given the gains in unity and cohesion that Tanzania had made so far.

Islamic philanthropy

We have seen that Muslim women's philanthropy in Tanzania is largely ad hoc and unplanned. The practice of regular donations to some charity or foundation is unknown. Most philanthropic acts are response based to special requests, rather than people having regular philanthropic causes that they support. Muslim women have always made ample use of the *waqf* services. Where the woman was survived by family, the *waqf* was usually of the *waqf ahli* type (family endowment), the beneficiaries being children and grandchildren. Where there was no family, the woman usually bequeathed her property to her community, in terms usually of ethnic affiliation or to a Waqf Commission, where one exists, as in Zanzibar (*waqf khayri*). In all cases, there has been marked neglect of such property, families bickering among themselves on its maintenance, and communities often ill-equipped both financially and legally to take care of it. However, the community *waqf* has been better qualified to achieve the social justice objective than the family one. Many properties have been used as social or sports clubs, or as schools and health clinics, the profits accruing to the community.

Other endowments have been made in the form of land and mosques. For instance, Zubeir (2003) notes that, of 51 mosques in Zanzibar Stone Town, seven were built by women devotees. These are now administered by the mosque committees under trusts, or as informal arrangements. Possi (2003) reports of a plot donated by a female nurse in Arusha.

The situation described above has given rise to the formation of many Muslim women's groups, intended to alleviate both the members' and others' economic hardships, but also to offer spiritual solace to a beleaguered society. However, considering the rapid growth of civil society organizations in Tanzania, which has been phenomenal since the era of liberalization began, the rise in the number of Muslim women's organizations has been quite slow.

Muslim women's groups

For purposes of the research, 18 women's groups were interviewed in Dar es Salaam, Tanga and Zanzibar. Tracing their location was difficult because most had non-functioning offices, or ran their organization from a member's house. Secondly, most of the women were reluctant to answer questions, partly because of their organizational set-up, which prevented one person making a decision, but partly also because of the suspicion they held about any attempts to probe into Muslim organizations and Muslim activity. Some declared that it was against their organization's interests to answer the questions. Others declined after holding meetings within the organizations and studying the questions in detail. In some cases it was possible to have discussion with some of the groups' leaders, and they declared that, post 9/11, they have been under such sharp and hostile scrutiny that they could not trust anyone. They felt that the information they would provide could have been used to undermine their activities. The level of mistrust engendered by the recent 'war on terror' was at its highest.

Most of the Muslim women's groups tended to be membership organizations, their membership varying from a few to a few hundreds. These numbers do not always refer to individuals, though some of the organizations, such as Sahiba Sisters Foundation, discussed below, have both individual and group membership. So their overall membership would be much higher. All the women's groups have the same general aims, i.e. the furtherance and welfare of the Muslim community. This general aim is not stated as such, but it is manifest in the specific objectives listed by respondents. By far the most frequent objective was the provision of social services, both in a general sense but also in a specific sense. The majority of the groups interviewed aimed at providing education, either to children or to their own members. Some wanted to build their own schools; others were less ambitious, and aimed at facilitating the education of others. In the provision of social services there were also groups which were concerned with establishing hospitals, assisting orphans and increasing women's capacity in matters of governance and management.

The next most frequent objective was that of advancing Islamic knowledge and *da'waa*. This was followed by the need to increase contacts between Muslim women, to establish networks and to share information. A few of the women mentioned 'raising the status of women' as one of their objectives. It was not specified what this is likely to entail, and it raises interesting questions of whether these groups perceive their members or Muslim women as having a lower status in society, or they aim to fight against the general social and economic subordination that faces all women in Tanzanian society.

There was also concern about the upbringing of children, and the general decline of morals that seems to be a frequently-voiced concern among many Tanzanians. Some of the women see this as a significant part of their groups' roles.

All the objectives discussed above are clearly philanthropic, and are aimed at improving both the material and spiritual condition of the society generally, and women in particular. Few groups mentioned their own economic advancement as an objective. While most women's groups in Tanzania are set up with the major aim of improving the economic welfare of their members, through setting up various income-generation projects, it would appear that this is not the concern of Muslim women's groups, although it is a fact that most of their members are economically disadvantaged. An important question that has dogged Muslim organizations is the degree of accountability and transparency within them. Many Muslim projects, including mosques, have been accused of lack of transparency and accountability. Too often, leaders have too much power, and they do not involve other members in making decisions relating to the running of the organizations.

If this was a problem in the past, it is even bigger now. In most of the groups, there seemed to be quite strict control over information concerning the organizations. Individuals were generally very reluctant to speak without the blessing of the leaders. One of the reasons they gave for this was the threat that faced Muslim organizations since 9/11. They had to be sure how the information they gave was going to be used. The second reason was they had a policy of only particular people acting as spokespersons for the organization, a common practice of Tanzanian organizations these days.

Other means of transparency and accountability that were looked at were the presentation of financial reports, internal and external auditing, management meetings and general meetings. The majority of those who responded stated that there was appropriate accountability through financial reports. Most of the organizations had instituted a system of internal auditing, but around the same proportion had no external auditing. On meetings, the record was good in relation to both management meetings and general meetings (at least two-thirds of the organizations surveyed held these regularly).

Generally, however, it would seem that the organization of Muslim women groups is far from satisfactory. Apart from the responses that appeared in the questionnaires, there are indications that many did not have appropriate and permanent offices, and that they had very limited administrative staff and hardly any equipment. Most of them appeared to conduct their activities from their own homes. For those who did have offices, these remained closed most of the time.

Most of the groups were established as informal neighbourhood or friends groups, which later began to think about registering. They therefore tended to have very clear structures, because the law would require this should the groups seek registration. One example of the structure is that of the women's wing of, the Muslim Students' Association of the University of Dar es Salaam (MSAUD) (see Figure 14.1). This example illustrates an elaborate top-heavy structure, clearly a burden to an organization of only 200 members.

The women's organizations surveyed were run mostly by 'working-class' women, who themselves were not highly educated (many of them were not currently employed, depending on husbands and parents for their own needs). Over half of the organizations did not have a board of directors or a patron. Of those who did have a board, the size varied from two to fifteen, and all worked on a voluntary basis. Surprisingly, the incidence of male board members was higher than that of female board members – four groups indicated male members, but only two had only female members. An explanation for this could be that the groups often seek to tap expertise among the board of directors that they may not have among their members, such expertise being more readily available among the men. However, two-thirds of those who commented on board meetings stated that no meetings were held, which would suggest that boards are often nominal – visible on paper but not really functioning.

In all these groups, it would seem that enormous power was wielded by single individuals, usually the chair, director or *amirah*. While there was no indication among the groups interviewed that this power was abused in any way, there is

Figure 14.1: Women's wing of the Muslim organization
of the University of Dar es Salaam

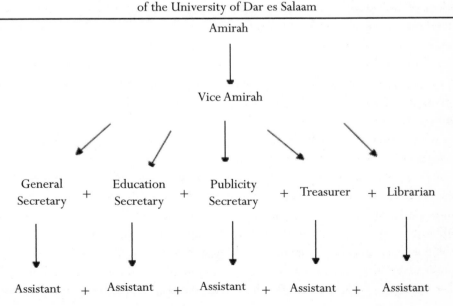

nonetheless clearly great potential for abuse of authority by unscrupulous individuals. This potential exists because most of the groups were unregistered, and therefore do not have any constitutions, and no mechanisms for limiting the powers of the leaders, making them accountable, or removing them from power. As mentioned above, the women's groups surveyed expressed concern that they faced difficulties in recruiting educated women. Within the leadership who talked to us, less than a fifth had university education. These included those who were still undertaking their undergraduate studies. Around half had only secondary education. But information that emerged from those either employed or volunteering in the organizations indicated that they have very restricted knowledge or skills. Only one out of the 18 organizations had a professional accountant, a woman. The same was true of an administrator. No organization had a marketing officer. Even secretaries were scarce, with only one organization having one. Sahiba Sisters Foundation was exceptional in having both an administrator and an executive director.

These figures clearly indicate that the organizations were very weak in their administrative resources, although there may have been organizations with employees who possess skills other than those enquired about. The area of funding and utilization of funds was very sensitive and was difficult to get information on. Respondents were generally reluctant to answer questions relating to funds, and between three-quarters and all of the questions relating to funding were left unanswered. There may be several reasons for this. One may have been distrust, not knowing how the information would be used. Another reason may have been a lack of records of accounts, especially among the unregistered organizations. A third may be an attempt to hide information because of mismanagement of the funds. And finally, it may simply have been that many of those organizations surveyed simply had no funds to speak of. Of the few organizations which indicated the allocation of funds to various activities, they could not state the percentage of this spending in relation to their total budget. This would suggest that they were either ignorant of the budget, or did not have any.

The researcher was interested in knowing the amount of funds that organizations used in relation to various activities. The area in which the heaviest spending was made was that of religious activities, although there was no mention of the specific areas in which the funds were used. This was followed by social services and health. All the remaining areas, such as education, trade, the environment, advocacy, etc. received little or nothing. In some cases, respondents indicated the percentage spent on certain areas, without indicating the amount.

What are the sources of funds for these women's groups? Again the responses were extremely limited but, for those who did respond, it is obvious that they received little or nothing from the likely sources in Tanzania, such as private companies, national and foreign governments, and national and foreign NGOs. Among the potential sources of funding that provided no funds whatsoever were private companies, the governments, both local and foreign and foreign individual donors. Surprisingly, even membership dues were not forthcoming, even for those organizations for which dues were part of the membership conditions. Only one organization out of the 18 mentioned receiving membership dues. If the organizations failed to mobilize funds even from their own members, it would be very difficult for them to do so from external agencies. Admittedly, as has been stated previously, most members were not themselves well off. But even in those organizations whose members were mostly middle-class and high-powered women, membership contributions were still negligible.

The donations received by the organizations were mostly in kind, in the form of secondhand clothes, food, copies of the Qur'an for use in madrassas (*juzuu*) and sewing machines. Individuals donated small amounts of money, and the sale of services and goods also contributed something for at least one organization. Another organization had received a building plot through *waqf*.

In relation to funds, there was also the question of the means of mobilization. Different groups had different preferences. Unsurprisingly, the most popular means was face-to-face interaction. This was also the cheapest means. Two-thirds of the respondents stated that they had used this method very often. A half prefers to use celebrities to help them raise funds. The use of letters, appeals at mosques and special events (such as Maulids, *khitmas*, etc.) are the third most popular means, while the TV and email attract about one-fifth of respondents. One new means mentioned by several respondents was texting, where members text people to request donations.

The next section will examine three different women's groups which have been carrying out philanthropic work of various kinds. The groups vary widely in the type of work they do, their target beneficiaries, and their motivations. The conclusion will examine how these variations relate to the parameters of obligation and reciprocity, which would give us an indication of the extent to which these organizations are now constructing new methods of philanthropic work, instead of perpetuating the traditional ways discussed above.

Philanthropic practice among Tanzanian Muslim women

A place in heaven: The Ummu Aymana Islamic Centre

The Ummu Aymana Islamic Centre operates in Tanga city, with six members. The group was established in 2002, but got registered only recently. All the women are of very modest means: only one has a job as a teacher, while some of the others depend on their husbands. The organization has no offices, but runs its activities from the house of one of its members, who is their leader. The latter, a retired civil servant, has also offered a part of her compound for building a nursery school, which has been operating for three years. They charge a small fee for the nursery school, just to cover running costs, such as salaries for the teachers. All of the administrative costs have to be paid for from their own personal funds. The members are all keenly aware of the implications of building a school on someone else's plot, especially considering that the plot owner has children, who would be her natural inheritors.

In seeking registration, the group faced several hurdles. Their write-up for the nursery centre was rejected by the relevant ministry, but the women did not have the resources to pay someone who could do a more acceptable job.

The main activities of the group, apart from the nursery school, are visits to villages and conducting Muslim lectures, teaching women to pray and conduct other Islamic imperatives, and spreading the teachings of the Qur'an. They state that one way of attracting poor women to come and listen to the lectures is to provide food. For this they have to canvas support from Muslim folk in Tanga, often going from door to door in search of sympathetic respondents. They also distribute used clothing that they collect from other Muslims, and if they get cash donations they buy mats for the village mosques.

The activities of the group are ad hoc and entirely dependent on the assistance they receive. For the few activities, such as Maulid al Naby and the lectures planned for the year, they have to conduct vigorous fundraising campaigns. But the other *da'awa* activities take place depending on what is available. According to the women, the overriding motivation for their efforts is the gain in God's blessings. They have no expectation of personal gain whatsoever. In discussion, they explain and justify all their activities with respect to very specific reference to the Qur'an, particularly in relation to the recompense they expect.

The group is now looking for a plot of land to put up their office and expand the school to secondary level. The premises, if obtained, would also allow them space to conduct their Islamic lectures. They are also thinking of starting an orphanage, to take care of the many children who are homeless.

Community responsibilities: CHAKUAMA orphanage

This centre is located in the Sinza area of Dar es Salaam, within a large compound with a spacious house and several outhouses, housing 90 children and 14 staff. The orphanage was registered in 1998, but its director has been raising children since 1982. She herself had ten children of her own, three of whom passed away. The children of the centre range from 9 months to 17 years. At least two were born at the centre, their mothers having come to the centre while pregnant.

The centre appears to have some resources. The house, donated by another woman philanthropist, is fairly well furnished, with solid furniture and freezers and a TV. There is a well in the compound which meets all the water needs of the centre. All the children were clean and properly dressed, and extremely well be-haved. The salaries of five of the workers are paid for by donors; the rest by funds raised by the centre itself.

The funding comes from various sources. Apart from those who pay the salaries mentioned above, there a few other donors who regularly contribute to the centre. Visitors to the centre almost always contribute something, others bring clothing and food. The children receive free medical treatment at several volunteer clin-ics, and some companies have offered doctors for house visits. More importantly, the centre itself produces handicrafts which it sells to visitors and at handicraft exhibitions. There are plans to set up a shop in front of the centre to display and sell these goods.

The children receive all services at the centre, as they would in their parents' homes. They have toys and books and they play games, watch TV, and have madrassa classes in the compound. The centre welcomes all children brought to it, as long as there is room. Some come from Christian backgrounds, others Muslim. But it is ob-vious that all the children are brought up as Muslims, and they are all demonstrably well read in the Qur'an and in various prayers. Those who reach 18, or when they leave the centre, are informed of their former Christian affiliation, and are then left to decide which religion to follow. All the children of the appropriate age go to school, some in government and others in private schools, including vocational centres. All their fees are covered by various donors, and this undoubtedly lifts a great financial burden off the centre. At the time of the interviews, five children had completed secondary school, but had no support for further education. The director talked of several of her former 'children' now holding important positions in government and the private sector. One of these donated a van to the centre, which partly addressed their transport problems.

The director stated that they have never received any official assistance from the government, although they have requested it several times. This is different from the occasional donations made by ministers and other civil servants when they visit the centre, or during Eid or Christmas holidays, when the President makes donations of food to such institutions.

The administrative functions of the centre, such as accounting and management, are carried out by professionals who volunteer their services. These also constitute the advisory group for the centre's outreach work. When this chapter was written, plans to move to two bigger premises on the outskirts of Dar es Salaam were underway. Some buildings have already been constructed on one of the plots, and the plan is to build hostels for other orphans as well. The building is conducted on a piecemeal basis, as and when the centre gets some surplus funds.

The above would all seem to suggest that the centre is relatively comfortable compared to other centres of that nature, or those which accommodate so-called 'street' children. But the lack of certainty is obviously a problem: the centre is never absolutely certain if it will have enough funds to sustain it even over the next month. The director's greatest concerns are transport and electricity. The latter is very expensive and gobbles up a lot of their funds, and the one car they have is not enough for sending the children to school and running other errands.

While the centre's activities and existence are made possible by the philanthropy of many, it is the work and commitment of Mama Khadija, the director, which hold the centre together. Defining the centre as her life's work, she says she had resolved all those years ago to serve God through bringing up children who had no parents. She wanted to reduce their sadness and oppression. She also aimed to please God by doing something for her parents, although they were already dead. She had not been able to do anything for her parents when they were alive, she said, so now she wanted to dedicate her life's work to them. But at the same time, she is not interested in simply providing the immediate needs of the children, such as food and shelter. She wants her children to be able to do as much as other children, to be good citizens, to make something sustainable for themselves, and to contribute to Tanzania's development. She says that her greatest hope is that her children will always remember where they came from and be moved to help others less fortunate than themselves. Mama Khadija's vision is thus one of a ripple effect from her centre to the rest of the world. The community will be enriched by the work of her children, and this is what the centre is about.

Social justice: Sahiba Sisters Foundation

Sahiba Sisters Foundation is registered as a trusteeship, with a board of trustees and members. Launched in 1997, it is not a single organization, but a network of several groups in Dar es Salaam and 12 other regions in Tanzania. Their main constituents are rural women and the youth of both sexes. They have various groups in their network, but very limited resources. They have a home office headquarters from where all business is conducted. Members communicate mainly through phone messages. The main thrust of the network is the introduction of change through education. They stress the training of teachers and advocate for changes in the school syllabi to incorporate religious education. They question the continued traditional education provided in the madrassas, which does not provide literacy in the Latin script and basic arithmetic and other skills. Resistance from teachers in the madrassas, especially the men, is considerable. This group is headed by highly educated women, who argue that their work has been misconstrued as seeking to challenge the position of women as presented in the Qur'an. They are thus treated with caution and sometimes direct animosity from the male leadership in the regions.

Interestingly, SSF themselves declare philanthropy as one of their concerns; but in their Kiswahili translation of this word, they talk of *kutoa*, which is giving, thus pointing to the problem of integrating this term within the Tanzanian context. SSF combine both educated middle-class women and poor provincial women, the latter constituting the majority. A major aim is to 'build the leadership and organizational capacities of women and youth so as to promote their civic engagement'. They claim to have enabled dozens of women to initiate community-based projects such as schools, legal aid clinics, orphanages, reproductive health programmes and economic projects. Unlike many of the other Muslim women's organizations, SSF clearly has a political and feminist agenda. Its constitution begins with reference to the Fourth World Conference on Women and the Beijing Platform for Action.

SSF business is funded from members' monthly contributions, *zakat* and *sadaqat* and donations from sympathizers. They regularly submit project proposals to various kinds of donors, including international ones, for consultancy, capacity building, research and travel grants, with some limited success.

SSF's feminist outlook has, as expected, placed them at loggerheads with other women's groups which have accepted to operate within the existing patriarchal structures, and also with Muslim men. Thus a major challenge facing the Foundation is how to adapt their feminist goals to the Islamic perspective. They achieve this through building very intensive formal networks with both government and non-government organizations, to explain the work they do and their objectives. This includes educating Muslim women on their rights and responsibilities under Sharia law.

Table 14.1: Focus areas, motivation and beneficiaries of groups

	Work type	Beneficiaries	Motivation	Obligation	Reciprocity
Ummu Aymana	Saving souls	Poor	Serving God	Religious	None
Sahiba Sisters Foundation	Education and information	Poor/educated women and youth	Social justice	Social	Some
CHAKUAMA	Raising children	Orphan children	Serving God + social justice	Religious	None

Table 14.1 presents a summary of the three groups' focus areas, motivation and beneficiaries.

Conclusion

The stories of these women's groups are a reflection of the peculiar ways in which philanthropy is practised and realized in Tanzania. The efforts of individuals with vision and commitment, assisted by friends, relatives and colleagues are beginning to make a difference in the provision of the basic services that the government has abandoned. The three groups are driven by different motives, but at least two of them can be viewed as models of community foundations in the Tanzanian context. They operate within close-knit networks, with limited resources, are strongly committed to what they do, and have no ambition of personal gain.

The three groups vary considerably in relation to several variables that are relevant within the philanthropic agenda. Their motivation determines the type of work they do, which in turn delimits their beneficiaries. But the variable of reciprocity seems to be less relevant in their work, since the services are provided by those who are better endowed, with knowledge, competence and capability, to those who are less so endowed. In this respect, there is still a sense in which the philanthropists are the 'richer' in having more than their beneficiaries although, in terms of socioeconomic indicators, they are still poor.

There are vast untapped resources within the Muslim community, and even within the women's community. Unfortunately, these groups and others like them have not yet succeeded in drawing upon these resources. The lack of qualified personnel and, more and more, of trust, is presenting major challenges to the women's philanthropic efforts. The Muslim community in Tanzania has yet to develop public organizations which can mobilize the potential resources and administer them for the benefit of the Muslims through the continued use of the traditional approaches to philanthropy, but also incorporating the rapidly developing paths such as foundations.

CHAPTER 15

ISLAMIC PHILANTHROPY IN TANZANIA: UNEXPLOITED TREASURE[1]

MOHAMMED A. BAKARI

Introduction

Tanzania has the largest Muslim community in Eastern and Southern Africa.[2] It has a long tradition of Islamic philanthropic activities dating back to the introduction of Islam in the ninth century. However, Islamic philanthropic institutions and activities are not well developed, particularly among the indigenous Muslim communities, where philanthropy is still organized largely in traditional forms and the volume of resources mobilized is still very low. In recent years, however, there has been an upsurge in the number of new Muslim philanthropic institutions in the country, and there have been some attempts to transform such institutions from their traditional perspective of a narrow religious focus (of spiritualism, piety, and charity giving to alleviate immediate hardships) into more modern forms that could pursue broad and long-term development-oriented programmes, including the provision of basic services to the Muslim community and the nation at large.

This chapter attempts to review the historical evolution of Islamic philanthropy in the country from the early twentieth century to the present, but the main focus will be on the post-liberalization era from the late 1980s. The chapter examines both formal and informal forms of Islamic philanthropy. It also examines the types of activities to which resources are channelled, and the extent to which such activities can promote social justice within the Muslim community and the nation at large. In assessing the potential of Islamic philanthropy for promoting social justice, this study investigates the management of philanthropic resources in terms of institutional/individual accountability and transparency as well as the kinds of programmes into which such resources are channelled. Since the establishment, development and sustainability of Islamic philanthropic institutions and activities depend on the political and legal environment, the chapter also examines the relationship of Islamic philanthropic institutions with the state.

Much of the data used in this chapter is extracted from a study on 'Islamic Philanthropy for Social Justice in Tanzania' conducted in 2004.[3] The research used both qualitative and quantitative methods and techniques. The methods used could be classified into five categories. The first two required quantitative analysis whereas the remaining three used qualitative analysis. These are:

- Survey research on both individual Muslims and prominent business people, using structured questionnaires;

- Survey research on Islamic institutions using structured questionnaires;

- Focus-group discussions;

- In-depth interviews; and

- Semi-structured interviews with government officials.

In total, over 450 individuals (432 individual Muslims and 22 prominent business people) and 134 religious institutions (national and international) were surveyed and 24 focus groups discussions were conducted.

The political and legal contexts

The creation, growth and structure of Islamic organizations in Tanzania are, among other factors, determined by the political and legal contexts. Constitutionally, the current state of Muslims and Islamic philanthropic organizations starts with Article 19(2) of the 1977 Constitution of the United Republic of Tanzania declaring the profession, practice, worship and propagation of religion to be the free and a private affair of an individual in which the secular state cannot interfere. However, this constitutional guarantee is subject to several limitations in relation to the actual application of Islamic law. Legally and politically, the emergence and operation of Muslim philanthropic institutions in Tanzania have been influenced by, inter alia, the status of Islamic law in the Tanzanian legal system, the failure to codify Islamic law applicable in Tanzania, and the law and practice regulating the right to organize and associate.

The Tanzanian legal system is described to be secular, setting strict legal parameters within which Islamic law may be applied. Today, Islamic law in Tanzania is confined to questions of marriage, divorce, legitimacy of children, guardianship, maintenance, bequests, inheritance, *waqf*, and gifts. Understanding the operation of Islamic philanthropic groups in Tanzania requires a full appreciation of the legal framework within which these organizations operate.

Right to organize and incorporate

To realize the ideals enshrined in Article 19(2), individuals need the right to organize and associate in matters of religion without state interference. This right is crucial because Islamic organizations are usually supposed to perform multiple functions, including the provision of educational, health, cultural and economic services for the well-being of the Muslim community and the general population. The right to organize and associate in Tanzania is closely regulated by written laws, with several legal frameworks being used to bring Islamic philanthropic organizations into being. Islamic philanthropic groups may seek registration as community-based organizations (CBOs), whose registration is determined by the nature of their activities. CBOs can be registered as: companies (under Companies Ordinance); cooperative societies (under Cooperative Societies Act, 1991); trusts (under Trustees Incorporation Ordinance); associations (under Societies Ordinance), or they may fall under a special piece of legislation (and therefore be exempted from registration as a society under Societies Ordinance).

The Trustees' Incorporation Ordinance and the Waqf Commission Ordinance of 1953 are two pieces of legislation that regulate the activities of philanthropic organizations. They ideally provide parameters within which Muslims in Tanzania may exercise their rights to organize and associate in entities beneficial to their welfare and well-being as a distinct community. But the right to organize and associate must not be assumed to exist by merely looking at the prevailing pieces of legislation. The political, economic and social environment constricted the ability of association in trusts and *waqf*.

Available research suggests that the restriction on the right to organize and associate in Tanzania is one of the major reasons for the slow and unsystematic growth of philanthropic groups in Tanzania as a whole. Many societies and associations in Tanzania are still governed by the Societies Ordinance of 1954. This is a good example of old legislation which has not undergone any change compatible with the emergence of multi-party democracy, and it has been used to suppress political and religious activities.[4] The Nyalali Report on Multi-Party Democracy (1991) had these views on the Societies Ordinance, 1954:

- Societies Ordinance, 1954 Cap. 337, gives the Registrar of Societies unnecessarily wide powers to register or to refuse to register;
- The President of the United Republic of Tanzania can also under the Societies Ordinance declare any society duly registered unlawful; and;
- The decision of the President or Minister cannot be challenged in court.

Again in October 2001 the Zanzibar House of Representatives passed a law affecting Muslims, under which the secular government is empowered to supervise and coordinate all Muslim activities, including the mobilization of Muslim resources. All mosques are now under the direct control and supervision of an avowedly secular government. As the chief government agent, the Mufti is duty bound to execute anything directed by the secular government. In 2003, for example, Muslims in Zanzibar were beaten up and taken to court by police officers for praying Eid al Haj prayers without government permission. The objective of the law has clearly been stated –'to control Muslim activities'. However, the control is discrimina-tory because it is only exercised over Muslims and their organizations. No similar control has been placed on other religions.

And in 2002, the Tanzanian Government enacted the Prevention of Terrorism Act. This Act, like the other legal instruments, also constrains the functioning of Islamic philanthropic institutions, particularly those deriving their resources from external sources.

Dissolution of Islamic philanthropic organizations

The right to organize in general, associate specifically in philanthropic trusts and congregate around *waqf* properties must be viewed within this general political environment where the right to organize was constrained. Registration of trusts is a small feat compared to the feat of actually operating for the benefit of the expected beneficiaries. Muslims in Tanzania have long had good reason to want to organize and associate themselves in philanthropic groups that can assist them to attain educational and health facilities, because such services had frequently been denied them. This desire to associate for philanthropic purposes saw the registration of the East African Muslim Welfare Society (EAMWS) on 27 October 1945.[5] The advancement and welfare of Muslims in East Africa was one of the stated objectives of this regional philanthropic body. Perhaps this society best illustrates how the enshrined right to organize can be used as a means through which the wealthier members of a community can reach out and assist the indigent members. The EAMWS had the massive responsibility of opening, building and running health centres and dispensaries, social centres, hospitals, schools and other charitable and benevolent institutions.

One of the major and most longstanding grievances of Muslims in Tanzania has been the denial of their right to self-organization at different levels – local, intra- and inter-denominational, national and regional (East Africa). Up to 1968, Muslims organized their religious affairs under the EAMWS, which was also championed by the Aga Khan (the spiritual leader of Ismaili Muslims), in collaboration with other Asians of Shiva and Sunni sects, as well as African Muslim groups.

The abolition of the EAMWS by the government in 1968, therefore, raised a lot of controversy, particularly surrounding the underlying motive. The government and BAKWATA, the newly created National Muslim Council of Tanzania, defended the decision by claiming that the organization was characterized by internal disputes centred on religious, cultural, economic and political issues. Those opposed to the decision, however, saw it as a deliberate move to ban an autonomous Muslim institution and replace it with a puppet institution (the BAKWATA) that could exercise surveillance and control over Muslims and their organizations so as to maintain the status quo, i.e. the Christian hegemony.[6]

The present disorganization and lack of unity among Muslims in Tanzania can therefore be partly associated with the demise of the EAMWS. Many Muslims believe that the EAMWS had quite successfully integrated Muslims of different sects and races during the period of its existence.[7] Today, however, there now seems to be a serious distrust between Muslim Asian communities and indigenous Muslims in Tanzania. Claims are made, for example, by businessmen from the Asian Muslim community that when they have been singled out for harsh treatment by the state, indigenous Muslims have been less than supportive. The Asian Muslim community occupies a strategic and potentially important position for the development of the Muslim community as a whole in Tanzania, given the volume of economic resources at their disposal (the commercial sector in Tanzania, particularly big business, is predominantly owned by the Asian community). This is evidently one of the few areas in which Muslims have a clear comparative advantage over their Christian counterparts. But due to the lack of solidarity between the indigenous and Asian Muslim communities, the development of Islamic philanthropic institutions continues to lag behind.

Mwaikusa (1995:280) has argued that the state in Tanzania has had good reason to concern itself with either appeasing or containing Muslim communities. He contends that

> Until independence Muslims lagged behind in secular education and for that reason they were the only community to form a political party based on religious identity: the All Muslim National Union of Tanganyika (AMNUT) was formed in 1959 and sought to challenge the main political party, the Tanganyika African National Union (TANU) by demanding that independence be delayed until more Muslims were educated.

After independence in 1961, the TANU government, unable to educate more Muslims overnight, had to be concerned about the possible Muslim dissatisfaction developing into mass grievances of an entire religious community. It suited the government to have an all-embracing Muslim Council through which their impatience could be assuaged. Accordingly, BAKWATA was formed in 1968 with active government encouragement. And from its inception, 'the organization and administrative set up of BAKWATA has been remarkably similar to that of the party' (ibid.).

One of the resolutions at the BAKWATA founding conference held in Iringa was for all Muslims to dissolve their then existing congregations and make them regional and district organs of BAKWATA. Most congregations dissolved themselves accordingly. The state assisted in implementing the resolution against the few con-gregations which were unwilling to dissolve themselves voluntarily. Thus, through the Government Notice Number 434 and 435 of 1968, the East African Muslim Welfare Society, along with the Tanzania Council of that society, were dissolved and ordered to wind up by the government. The Government Notice Number 169 of 1969 then vested their assets in BAKWATA. Similarly, the Al Jummiyatul Islamiyya of Tanganyika 'was declared an unlawful society, and its assets were subsequently vested in BAKWATA through the Government Notices Numbers 97, 98 and 312 of 1970' (ibid:282). Some Muslim groups tried to organize themselves indepen-dently of BAKWATA but most have failed to secure registration. One exception was the Baraza la Kusoma Kur'an Tanzania (BALUKTA) (Council for the Recitation of Qur'an) – which was established in 1991 and gained some prominence. But in 1993, BALUKTA was given notice of intention to cancel its registration (ibid:283).

Quite obviously, BAKWATA does not enjoy the support of the majority of Muslims in the country, particularly the urban-based intellectuals. The survival of BAKWATA is attributed much more to state protection than to legitimacy granted by Muslims. There have been a number of initiatives to create other independent organizations to promote the interests of Muslims and counter the influence of BAKWATA or even replace it. The first objective of reducing its influence has been partly successful, as exemplified by the existence of other organizations such as the BALUKTA mentioned above. BAKWATA's overthrow almost succeeded when their headquarters in Kinondoni were occupied for a week by Muslim youth organized under the Supreme Council of Muslim Institutions (BARAZA KUU). However, the government later intervened and aborted the takeover attempt. Other organizations which have emerged to counter the influence of BAKWATA include the Council of Imams (*Shura ya Maimamu*), and the Dar es Salaam Islamic Club (DIC), founded in 1997.

A striking example to illustrate the extent to which the government protects its own creation, BAKWATA, was when in 1994, the then Deputy Prime Minister and Minister for Home Affairs, Hon. Augustine Mrema, called upon the churches to raise funds for the General Meeting of BAKWATA. Quite a large amount of money was raised and Mr Mrema himself supervised the election of Muslim na-tional leaders. In his doctoral dissertation, Yusuf (1990:189) says: 'It is noteworthy that, in comparison to other religions of Tanzania, it is only the Muslims who were formally and officially connected to the State'. And according to Westerlund (1980), Muslims are brought under state control because they are perceived as politically dangerous.

Many Muslim philanthropic organizations in Tanzania have been registered under the Trustees' Incorporation Ordinance of 1956, which does not seek to interfere with Islamic philanthropic principles as long as the incorporation conditions are followed. The scope of Trustees' Incorporation Ordinance covers two types of trustees – those who hold property for charitable purposes, and those who hold it for social or sporting purposes.

Table 15.1: Sample of religious societies declared unlawful, 1965–95

Government Notice No. 287 of 1965	• Watch Tower Bible and Tract Society • Jehovah's Witnesses • International Bible Students Association • Millennial Dawnists • Standfasters • Russelites
Government Notice No. 434 & 435 of 1968	• The East African Muslim Welfare Society • The Tanzania Council of East African Muslim Welfare Society • All properties movable and immovable of the EAMWS Branch, and the Tanzania Council of the East African Muslim Welfare Society were from 2.30 p.m. on 19th December 1968 vested in the Administrator General.
Government Notice No. 169 of 1969	• Vested all property held or owned by East African Muslim Welfare Society in BAKWATA
Government Notice No. 97 & 98 of 1970	• Al Jummiyatul Islamiyya Bi Tanganyika
Government Notice No. 312 of 1970	• Vested in BAKWATA all property held or owned by Al Jummiyatul Islamiyya Bi Tanganyika.
Government Notice No. 154 of 1974	• Dini ya Imani ya Mitume
Government Notice No. 203 and 204 of 1975	• United Cutchi Sunni Muslim Jamaat
Government Notice No. 207 & 208 of 1975	• Jumuiya ya Waislam Madhehebu ya Shaffi R.A. Ijumaa na Adhuhuri Bukoba, West Lake Region.
Government Notice No. 162 of 1977	• (Revoking and Handing over of Interests) Jumuiya ya Waislamu Madhehebu ya Shaff (R.A.) Ijumaa na Adhuhuri Bukoba) Order, 1977.
Government Notice No. 148 & 149 of 1977	• Kristo Mwanga wa Ulimwengu

Table 15.1: Sample of religious societies declared unlawful, 1965–95 (Contd.)

Government Notice No. 166 of 1980	• Revoked GN 203 and 204, which had declared to be unlawful the United Cutchi Sunni Muslim Jamaat Dar es Salaam. Revocation came into effect on 22 October 1980. Properties handed over to the office of Regional Commissioner (Dar es Salaam) were returned to the trustees of the United Cutchi Sunni Muslim Jamaat Dar es Salaam.
Government Notice No. 415 of 1991	• Dini ya Mashahidi wa Jehova
Government Notice No. 301 of 1994	• Uamsho wa Wakristo Tanzania (UWATA). NB: Declaration of UWATA was revoked by Societies (Declaration of Unlawful Society) Order, 1994, GN 53 of 1998.

Legal framework on waqf property in Tanzania

A *waqf* can be defined as 'an action of a member of a Muslim society motivated by an element of the Islamic culture to transform some or all of his personal assets into pious foundations which will serve the public'.[8] The *waqf* is not mentioned in the Qur'an, but derives its legitimacy from various hadiths (the words and teachings of the Prophet Mohammed) or mainly one related to the acquisition of land in Khaybar by Umar ibn Al-Khattab (the second caliph), who sought the advice of the Prophet on ways to preserve his very valuable property. It is reported that the Prophet told him to make the land inalienable and give its yields away as alms.

Daniela Modonesi writes that in Muslim countries, the establishment of a *waqf* was the historical common practice to provide religious, charitable or social services or dedicate resources to other purposes, such as family support. Modern legislation distinguishes between *waqf khayri* (charitable trust) and *waqf ahli* (family endowment; the beneficiaries in this case being the donor's children and grandchildren). There are also cases of mixed *awqaf*. Sometimes the ultimate aim of the *waqf* was to avoid disintegration through Sharia succession. In Muslim societies, regulations on inheritance considered property as belonging to the owner and not his or her descendants, which caused the transfer of properties to the ruler at the owner's death. Rich families have established *awqaf* in order to allow their children become a part of the fortune as trustees.[9] In Tanzania, both types of *waqf* are common.

The Waqf Commission Ordinance was enacted in 1953 to control and protect *waqf* properties using the agency of a Waqf Commission (Tanganyika 1953:206–7). This law was made applicable to Muslims of all races. The membership of the Waqf Commission is designated as being not less than eight, of whom not less than five must be Muslims. The Waqf Commission Ordinance was amended in 1956[10] because it proved difficult to find a suitable person to undertake the duties required by the Ordinance, including the compilation of the register of *Waqf* properties. Following the 1956 amendment, it was decided to compile the register gradually, dealing with small portions of the country at a time.

So far, however, the law establishing the Waqf Commission has not been implemented on Mainland Tanzania. Many *Waqf* properties are not registered and therefore it is quite difficult to check their misuse.

Muslims in Mainland Tanzania have not realized the potential benefits of *waqf* properties, because the Waqf Commission Ordinance and its amendment of 1956 were not extended to the implementation level of the law. No commission was established after the 1956 amendment. This means that the management of property endowed by Muslims for such public utilities as schools, mosques, hospitals has not been accompanied with a working regulatory legal framework expected of Waqf Commission Ordinance. Tanzania Mainland is quite different from Tanzania Zanzibar, where the Waqf Commission is in actual operation to register and oversee property dedicated to trust.

The Waqf Institution in Zanzibar

Due to the paucity of records relating to *waqf* in Tanzania Mainland, much of our discussion on the subject is on Zanzibar, where some information is available covering the colonial times to the present. *Waqf* is one of the oldest Islamic institutions in Zanzibar and the entire coast of East Africa. There is, however, little documentary evidence of its existence and operation before the nineteenth century (Sheriff 2001:30–31).[11] Before 1905, the supervision and management of *waqf* properties was under the grand Sheikh of Unguja and Pemba, who acted with the blessing of His Highness, the Sultan of Zanzibar (NGO Resource Centre 1998:6).

The first initiative to formalize the *waqf* in Zanzibar was in 1905, when a decree was published for the establishment of a Waqf Commission for each of the two islands of Unguja and Pemba, charged with the duty of protecting *waqf* property and ensuring its proper management (Sheriff 2001:31). The Commission had three members – a British Officer, a Sunni Kadhi and an Ibadhi Kadhi, all appointees of His Highness the Sultan in consultation with the British Resident (Abdalla and Salim 1996:6). These three Commissioners were vested with the power to appoint up to three more Commissioners. Under this decree, all the *waqf* properties lacking properly constituted trustees were put under the administration of the Commission. Likewise, every trustee was obliged to register his/her *waqf* with the Commission. In practice, however, most of the *waqf* properties, particularly those based in the rural areas, remained unregistered. Besides, the Commission was vested with the wide powers not only of oversight and control but also of replacing trustees who mismanaged and misused *waqf* properties. In the latter case, the Commission was empowered to vest in themselves the right to administer *waqf* properties.

In both structure and functions, the Waqf Commission has undergone changes with time. Under the Waqf Property Decree of 1916, for instance, the two units of the Waqf Commission of Unguja and Pemba were merged, and the number of Commissioners was raised to eight. Four of them were ex-officio members, namely the Treasurer, the Provincial Commissioner and an Assistant Administrator General. The remaining four were appointees of His Highness the Sultan. These were a Sunni Kadhi, an Ibadhi Kadhi, a Sunni Arab and an Ibadhi Arab (NGO Resource Centre 1998:6).

In the early twentieth century, control of *waqf* properties was quite effective. According to the *waqf* legal framework, sale, lease, contract or other disposition of *waqf* property could only be effected with the authorization of the Commission. It was incumbent upon the Commission to ensure that the *waqf* properties were in accordance with the instructions of the founders – but it had also wide discretionary powers to divert the properties to other charitable purposes in case the original instructions could not be fulfilled, or in cases where there was any surplus revenue from the properties. Under the original decree such actions had to be approved by the First Minister but, following the revision of the decree in 1907, these powers were transferred to the Courts (Sheriff 2001:31).[12]

The Waqf Commission in Zanzibar, created in the early twentieth century, with its elaborate legal framework, is credited with great achievements, including the generation and preservation of important documents which constitute 'a very rich source for the study of social history and religious practice of Muslims in Zanzibar' (ibid.:32). *Waqf* played a crucial role, not only in religious development in its narrow sense (building of mosques, madrassa and provision of Islamic knowledge), but also in a wide range of purposes such as payment of religious teachers and students to buy books for distribution among poor Muslims students, accommodation of visiting Muslims, etc (ibid.: 34).

Generally, the development of *waqf* in Zanzibar was quite impressive. There were cases, for example, of transnational outreach of the institution. 'Several of the founders of *waqf* endowments dedicated part of their properties to the poor in Oman belonging to their tribes, and other for the poor in the holy cities of Mecca and Medina' (ibid.:38).[13] In 1949, it was reported that the Waqf Commission had a total of 165 houses, 110 shambas (farms) and various lands in Zanzibar vested in it (ibid.:33; National Archives of Zanzibar, NAZ, AB 22/8). In 1944, out of 2469 houses in the Zanzibar's Stone Town 158 (6.4 per cent) were under the Commission. In 1961, there were 175 *waqf* properties dedicated to specific purposes. Out of these, 39 were dedicated to mosques, and generated an income of about TShs.

270,000 (Sheriff 2001: 33). There were also 23 *waqf* properties, including ten shambas, eight plots and two houses, whose dedication was unknown. This income was used for the upkeep and management of the properties, payment of officials of various mosques, etc. (ibid.).

The construction of mosques in Stone Town reflected the denominational differences and their relative economic status. For example, the Sunni sect, in spite of its large proportion of followers, had fewer endowments than the Ibadhi sect, for the majority of the big landowners belonged to the latter. As a result, there was a marked variation between the Sunni and Ibadhi mosques, the latter generally conspicuously more endowed than the former. Quite interestingly, however, 'many prosperous Ibadhi landowners, including women endowed mosques for their Sunni brethren' (ibid.:34). By 1904, for example, there were 52 mosques in Zanzibar Town and six of them were founded by women (Zubeir 2003).

The drastic destruction of the *waqf* institution in Zanzibar occurred in the aftermath of the 1964 Revolution.[14] After the revolution, many of the *waqf* properties, including houses and plantations, were nationalized. Some of the *waqf* houses worth millions of Tanzanian shillings were sold for only TShs.15,000 (NGO Resource Centre 1998:11). Some of the *waqf* lands were distributed as three-acre plots and others were simply taken over by individuals (ibid.:43). After the 1964 Revolution, the Commission was dissolved and its duties transferred to the Registrar of Documents and Deaths. Whereas before the Revolution the appointment of *waqf* officials was strictly on merit, i.e. knowledge and piety, after the Revolution it was extensively based on political considerations.

The current Waqf Commission was founded under Act No. 5 of 1980. Its chairman is the Chief Kadhi. According to this Act, the Commission should consist of not more than six members, who are appointed by the President of Zanzibar. The question that arises is, whose institution is it? Is it a Muslim institution or an institution of a secular government? Relatedly, to whom is such an institution accountable? Is it accountable to the Muslim community or to the secular government? Is it appropriate for a secular government to completely own and manage religious institutions like *waqf*? These are some of the puzzling questions which Muslims ask themselves.

Since its establishment, there have been serious accusations by stakeholders and the Muslim community in general that the Commission is not effective in either supervision or management of the *waqf* properties in Zanzibar. The registration of houses and lands with the Commission has been on the decline. Whereas the major explanation is the confiscation of private properties including lands and buildings after the 1964 Revolution, the other contributing factor is inefficiency of the Commission and resultant people's loss of trust in it. Consequently, several people have applied to have their *waqf* properties returned so that they can manage them themselves (Zanzibar Government 2001:3)

When this chapter was being produced, it was observed that *waqf* properties, including houses, were not maintained; some of them are in ruins and others have been mysteriously sold without the approval of the board. Besides, the renting system is highly inefficient and corrupt. The Commission currently collects only about TShs.4 million out of the expected TShs.6.5 million for the 385 houses on Unguja and eight on Pemba which are under its care. The rent charged has for years been incredibly low and many tenants do not pay on a regular basis. But even if the entire expected amount is collected, it would not suffice to maintain the houses in good condition. In fact, the tenants who illegally rent the houses to others earn by far larger sums of money (kilemba) than the total revenue collected by the Commission. Recently, the Commission increased the rent rates for some houses but this has been haphazardly done without any expert advice.

Regarding the lands and farms, the situation is even more distressing. The farms (shambas) are not taken care of – some of them have been distributed to people as three-acre plots and others have become forests.

Generally, like the other religious institutions created by the state, e.g. Kadhi, Mufti, etc., the Waqf Commission is not Muslim-owned and managed but is in essence a religio-political institution accountable to the state and not to Muslims. Muslims, particularly those that are educated, question the integrity and functioning of such institutions. The image that the Waqf Commission has in the eyes of much of the public is that of a corrupt, ineffective, non-accountable and non-transparent institution.

Perceptions and practices of Islamic philanthropy in Tanzania

Charity giving for whatever purpose is a function of multiple factors, including ability, understanding/knowledge base, cultural traditions, religious beliefs, and organizational set-up (of philanthropic institutions), among others. These myriad factors help to shape people's attitudes to charity: to give or not to give, to whom to give, what and how much to give and for what purposes. They also partly determine the preferred modality – whether through formal or informal institutions or through individuals. Before we present the pattern of philanthropic practices in Tanzania we need to start with the knowledge base of Muslims, particularly their understanding of Islamic philanthropy and the role it can play for spiritual and social development.

In the research process, individual respondents were asked what they understood by social justice. Just over a quarter said social justice meant equity in society, another quarter said that it meant justice in accordance with Islamic law, a fifth said that it meant the right to get what one legally deserves, over a tenth said that it meant the performance of one's responsibility in society, and less than a tenth said that they did not know what it means. These perceptions indicate quite an interesting grasp of the concept of social justice – that it is not divorced from one's religious obligation. The fact that less than a tenth did not know what it means is quite impressive.

Likewise, respondents seemed to have an impressive understanding of *waqf*. About two-fifths said that *waqf* was property donated for projects to serve the purpose of Allah; one-fifth said that it is what was given for the donor to reap the benefits on earth and in the hereafter. A third of the respondents said that *waqf* was property given to help people without any payment. A sixth of the respondents said that they did not know what *waqf* was.

As for *zakat-l-mal*, half of the respondents clearly demonstrated that they knew what it meant, i.e. a portion of excess property given by a Muslim, usually on an annual basis, as a religious obligation. A quarter of the respondents said that it is property given to the poor by the rich. A sixth of the respondents either said they did not know or did not give any response. Table 15.2 shows the understanding of rates to be given for each kind of property liable for zakat. The kinds of property whose *zakat* rates are fairly known are livestock, money savings and deposits, and the least-known rates are those of farming products (apart from staple foods) and animal products (e.g. milk and honey) as well as rates for salaries, with the latter being the least known.

Table 15.2: Knowledge of the rates of *zakat-l-mal*

Kind of Property	Know % (N = 432)	Don't Know %
Money saving and deposit	10.4	
Gold	7.9	92.1
Silver	8.6	91.4
Discovered treasures	5.2	94.8
Crops		
Farming products (apart from staple foods)	4.1	95.9
Livestock	11.7	88.3
Animal products, e.g. milk, honey	3.6	96.4
Trading and industries	7.4	92.6
Remuneration (salaries)	2.8	97.2
Zakat Fitr	26.7	73.3

In the case of *sadaqat-jaariya*, two-thirds of the respondents knew what it meant, i.e. property dedicated to the cause of Allah, whose benefits continue even after the death of the donor.

Regarding Muslim views on altruism in society, the general perception among respondents was that altruistic attitudes seemed to be rather on the wane, with over three-quarters of the respondents saying that people were usually out for their own good. Similarly, the sense of overall trustworthiness in society was deemed to be very low, with three-quarters of the respondents saying that most people would rather lie to have their own way. Also, almost half of the respondents said that if a job or task was entrusted to somebody it would not be done properly.

Interestingly, although respondents were so negative about the motivations of others in society, they were generally optimistic about life in general. Four-fifths believed that poverty would be almost entirely eradicated if certain basic changes were made in the social and economic system. This is quite an interesting result, given the dire poverty situation in Tanzania. One would have expected people to lose hope but, on the contrary, a large majority still believe that, if fundamental changes are effected, there is a possibility of improving their well-being. This overall sense of optimism suggests a high level of social capital, which can serve as a potentially important and useful resource for the instigation of change and the promotion of social justice in society.

On humanitarianism, there is generally a high degree of humanitarian tendencies. About 74.7 per cent supported the idea that one should always strive to find ways to help others, particularly those who are less fortunate, while 71 per cent said that one should always be concerned with the well-being of others.

On the question of egalitarianism, four-fifths of the respondents thought that one of the biggest problems in Tanzania was that people are not given equal opportunities. Two-thirds thought that more equality in incomes would improve the well-being of their families. About the same number thought this would help reduce conflicts between people at different levels. At the same time, however, four-fifths of respondents believed that income equality would never be achieved because human beings are endowed with different capacities. Although people generally cherished some level of equality of incomes, there were reservations when it came to applying the same principle to women, with two-fifths saying that income equality between the sexes was not important, and a third of those surveyed did not agree with the idea of removing hindrances preventing women from getting into prominent positions in the public and private sectors

Institutional attributes

This study surveyed 134 philanthropic organizations across Tanzania, of which 84 were registered. The establishment patterns of these institutions indicate that while some were more than a century old, the larger proportion were established much more recently (almost three-quarters were established between 1991 and 2004).

This is consistent with the general emergence in Tanzania of non-governmental and private organizations focusing on social and community needs in the mid-1980s and early-1990s against the backdrop of economic and political reforms. However, it is noteworthy that outside the 1990s the second largest growth of institutions was between 1951 and 1970, the period just before and immediately after independence.

The unregistered institutions included in the survey were informal organizations that had achieved high visibility because of the services they provide to communities. In a number of cases, some of these were often more visible and relevant to communities than formally registered institutions. Of those institutions that were formally constituted, almost half of them were registered as trusts and a third described themselves as either NGOs or community-based organizations (CBOs). In terms of accountability and transparency the leading forms of registration were NGOs and trusts. Similarly, in terms of participatory decision-making, trusts and NGOs were also reported to be leading. A sizeable proportion of the institutions (47 per cent) operate a branch network. Table 15.3 indicates the numbers for each form of registration status.

Table 15.3: Form of institutional organization

Response	Number	Percentage
Non-governmental organization	21	24
Community-based organization	9	10
Trust	41	48
Cooperative	2	2
Government	3	3
Government permitted	10	12
Total	86	100

Managerial characteristics

Capacity to attract skilled staff

It is evident from the study that staffing is a significant problem among Muslim philanthropic organizations, with over half of respondent institutions viewing the ability to attract qualified staff as a big or a very big problem. The problem of qualified personnel is not only confined to associations whose membership is predominantly semiliterate, but it is equally pronounced among the organizations which have a highly educated membership. For example, The Tanzania Muslim Professionals' Association (TAMPRO) has a fully professional membership which is specialized in various disciplines. The same is true of the Dar es Salaam University Muslim

Figure 15.1: Trend of institutional establishment

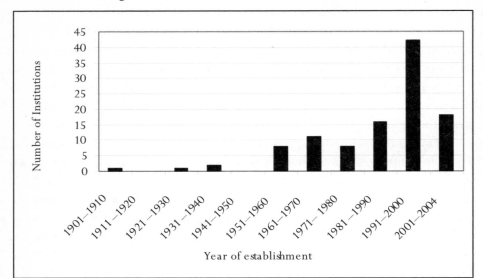

Trusteeship, whose members are mostly academics and administrators. Neither of these institutions have a full-time staff, mainly because they cannot afford the kind of remuneration necessary to attract qualified individuals. Others observed that morale was often low among their paid staff, because of their low remuneration.

Volunteer staff offer one solution to the problem of staff shortages, although well over half of the institutions surveyed also had difficulty in attracting qualified volunteers. In fact, excessive reliance on volunteers to manage an organization effectively can also present its own problems, because of constraints around time, commitment and motivation.

Institutional accountability

Views were sought on institutional accountability in terms of managerial and financial accountability and participatory involvement of interested stakeholders. Responses here were equally divided between those who saw no managerial problems within their organizations and those that did. Given the earlier views that attracting qualified staff was a major problem and that staff remuneration is not competitive relative to other NGOs, it is more plausible that managerial problems exist to a significant scale.

Three-quarters of respondent institutions prepared financial reports and most (three-quarters) felt that these adequately fulfilled their accountability obligations. Only one-third had their accounts audited by an external party, no doubt because of the high costs involved.

There was a marked difference in terms of accountability mechanisms between registered and unregistered institutions. About 70 per cent of the registered institutions reported that their institutions are duly accountable through internal auditing, only 55 per cent of the unregistered institutions reported to have some degree of accountability through internal auditing. Likewise, 90.6 per cent of the registered institutions reported to be accountable through external auditing whereas only 55.4 per cent of the unregistered ones reported to have some degree of accountability through external auditing.

As far as participatory involvement of stakeholders is concerned, the majority (four-fifths) of respondents indicated their satisfaction with democratic practices within their institutions, especially at operational levels. At the board of trustees/directors levels there was a less positive response: over half expressed dissatisfaction with governance practices within their organizations and, of these, two-thirds reported that board meetings were rarely held. This is consistent with the short-term orientation of many of the institutions, in which boards do not have a critical role except for the regulatory reason for their existence. Almost all board members in all respondent organizations serve on a voluntary basis and receive no compensation whatsoever. For further details on accountability, see the section on volunteerism on the degree of members' participation in decision-making processes in their organizations.

Institutional finances

Volume of philanthropic contributions

Of the 117 institutions that responded to the question on philanthropic contributions, more than three-quarters thought that low levels of contributions presented their organizations with a significant problem.

Several reasons were given for the low level of philanthropic contributions to these organizations: one was a lack of fundraising skills within the organization (over half of the respondents believed this to be the case) and another obstacle was the perception that only limited resources were available (the view of three-quarters of respondents). Another barrier to fundraising that was cited by half the respondents was the low level of community awareness towards Muslim philanthropic institutions.

Both local and foreign donations are avenues that institutions can potentially target to increase philanthropic contributions, and it was interesting that a large proportion of respondent institutions attached more reliance to local donations than foreign donations. Over 88 per cent agree completely and 8 per cent agree somewhat to preference for local resources, while 61 per cent, while 61 per cent per cent agree completely and 28 per cent agree somewhat to preference for external resources.

Financial improprieties

Concerns over the misuse of resources are often expressed in relation to civil society organizations, and the survey produced some very interesting responses in this regard. Three quarters of the 100 organizations that responded to the question around embezzlement of resources did not consider it to be a significant issue. Only 14 per cent regard it either as a very big problem (6 per cent) or a big problem (8 per cent). Perhaps this was because of the religious nature of organizations which engender trust and accountability not only in this world but in the hereafter as well.

Methods used for mobilization of resources: zakat and charity giving

The methods used for mobilization of resources, especially *zakat-l-mal*, can be categorized into traditional, modern and a combination of the two. Traditional methods are widely used, with the rate of *zakat* giving in Tanzania generally low for *zakat-l-mal* and high for *zakat-fitr*. Over a quarter of the individual non-business respondents (INBR) said that they contributed to *zakat-l-mal*, if not frequently, and two-thirds said that did not give at all. However, 63.6 per cent of the prominent business persons (PBP) said that they give *zakat-l-mal* very regularly, while 9.1 per cent said that they give sometimes but not all the time, 4.5 per cent said that they give very few times, 18.2 per cent said that they did not give and 4.5 per cent did not respond at all to the question. But among those who actually responded, only 40.9 per cent of PBP said that they gave *zakat-l-mal*, while 4.5 per cent did not give due to poor economic conditions and 22.7 per cent said that they did not give, while 31.8 per cent did not respond at all to this question.

When it came to people's ability to give *zakat-l-mal*, a surprisingly high number of respondents said that they were able to give, whereas those who actually offered are very few. In terms of the occupational distribution of those who were able to give *zakat*, businessmen and public workers came first, followed by private-sector employees, peasants and the self-employed.

Overall, almost two-thirds of respondents said that they had given *zakat-fitr* the previous year (almost all the prominent business people surveyed had given); the remainder generally cited poor economic circumstances as the reason for their non-payment.

The calculation of how much *zakat* is owed can be done by individuals themselves or with assistance from another person.

On the question of how *zakat* was given, respondents identified a variety of different preferences. Well over half of individual non-business respondents surveyed said that they preferred to give *zakat* personally to specific individuals if they had anything to give, while a quarter would choose to give through the mosques. What was noticeable was that very few would choose to give through the modern *zakat* institutions, and even fewer to other related (NGOs). The *waqf* institutions do not seem to be popular in Tanzania and they generally were rated lower than giving through trusted individuals. The government was the least preferred institution: this is most likely due to the sour relationship between Tanzanian Muslims and the government.

Most of the donors of *zakat-fitr* distribute it directly to deserving people. When intermediary institutions are used, the mosque is strongly favoured over all other kinds of institutions. See Table 15.4.

Table 15.4: *Zakat* distribution pattern to various institutions

Institution where zakat was given	Number of Individual Non-Business Respondents				Number of Prominent Business Persons only			
	Mal		Fitr		Mal		Fitr	
Mosques	21	4.9%	68	15.7%	1	4.5%	4	18.2%
Hospitals	3	0.7%	3	0.7%	1	4.5%	0	0.0%
Philanthropic institute	0	0.0%	0	0.0%	1	4.5%	1	4.5%
Religious organization	2	0.5%	7	1.6%	0	0.0%	2	9.1%
Government during disaster	0	0.0%	0	0.0%	0	0.0%	1	4.5%
Community development associations	0	0.0%	1	0.2%	1	4.5%	1	4.5%
Individuals	37	8.6%	160	37.0%	6	27.3%	11	50.0%
Islamic education institutions	4	0.9%	3	0.7%	0	0.0%	1	4.5%
National philanthropic projects	0	0.0%	1	0.2%	1	4.5%	1	4.5%
Missing	365	85.4%	189	43.8%	11	50%	0	0.0%
Total (approximate %)	432	100%	432	100%	22	100%	22	100%

Respondents were requested to state the means/institutions through which they would prefer to give the charitable contributions. The overwhelming majority of the 371 who responded (83 missing), 62.3 per cent, stated giving directly to the needy as their first preference while 11.8 per cent and 9.3 per cent chose that means as the second and third preference respectively. The second preference was the religious institutions. About 19 per cent of the 351 respondents (103 missing) chose religious institutions as their first preference, and 16.5 per cent and 23.3 per cent as their second and third preference respectively. The *waqf* institutions do not seem to be popular in Tanzania: only 6.3 per cent of the 333 respondents (121 missing) chose *waqf* institutions as their first preference and 20.1 per cent and 25.2 per cent selected that category as their second and third preference. In fact, giving through *waqf* institutions falls far below giving through trusted individuals, for which 7.4 per cent of the 351 respondents selected that channel as their first preference and 41.9 per cent and 21.9 per cent selected it as their second and third preference.

Among those who give *zakat-l-mal*, about 50 per cent offer amounts ranging from TShs.800 to TShs.26,000. The maximum amount given is TShs.22,000,000. If only INBRs are considered, then 50 per cent of them offer very small amounts ranging from TShs.800 to TShs.20,000, with a maximum of TShs.300,000. For PBP about 50 per cent of them offer amounts ranging from TShs.40,000 to TShs.417,000 and the maximum amount given is Tshs.22,000,000. *Zakat-fitr* ranged from TShs.500 to TShs.50,000 and from TShs.10,000 to TShs.35,000 for INBR and PBP respectively. The distribution of the sampled respondents is summarized in Table 15.5.

Table 15.5: Amount of *Zakat* distribution to various institutions

Amount Given (in TShs.)	INBR Only		Percentages		PBP Only		Percentages	
	Mal	Fitr	Mal	Fitr	Mal	Fitr	Mal	Fitr
500–8,000	13	56	3.0	13.0	0	0	0.0	0.0
8,000–80,000	22	27	5.1	6.3	2	7	9.1	31.8
80,000–200,000	3	0	0.7	0.0	0	0	0.0	0.0
200,000–500,000	4	0	0.9	0.0	3	0	13.6	0.0
500,000–3,000,000	0	0	0.0	0.0	3	0	13.6	0.0
3,000,000 –10,000,000	0	0	0.0	0.0	0	0	0.0	0.0
10,000,000 and above	0	0	0.0	0.0	1	0	4.5	0.0
Missing	390	349	90.3	80.7	13	15	59.1	68.2
Total	432	432	100	100	22	22	100	100

There is not much that is collected from zakat, be it *zakat-l-mal* or *zakat-fitr*, in spite of a bigger percentage of the latter. Only 1.6 per cent of INBR out of the 9.7 per cent who give *zakat-l-mal* contribute between Tshs. 80,000 and TShs. 500,000, while 27.2 per cent of PBP out of 40.9 per cent who give *zakat-l-mal* contribute between TShs. 200,000 and TShs. 3,000,000.

When it came to preferences concerning the religion or sex of *zakat* beneficiaries, only a third of respondents responded. Of these, a slightly greater number of respondents said that they cared very much about the religious affiliation of the recipients than those who did not. The sex of the beneficiaries was less of an issue among respondents, with only a small minority saying that it mattered to them.

Overall, the research findings suggest that charitable giving by Muslims in Tanzania is still heavily dominated by traditional and non-institutionalized forms. Alms and charity are not collected and distributed by the formal established institutions but rather they are given directly to the needy through personal contacts and an uncoordinated system.

Charity giving: *sadaqat*/donations

Respondents to the individual questionnaire were asked why they give to charity. The overwhelming majority (over three-quarters) cited religious obligation as their first choice, while much smaller numbers mentioned culture and customs, poverty reduction, personal interest and the rights of the poor to receive. Poverty reduction was most frequently cited as a secondary reason for giving.

When the individual respondents were asked whether they had made any form of charitable contribution in the last three years, over three-quarters had done so and, of these, the majority cited religious grounds for their charity giving and cited a sense of social responsibility as their second most important reason.

Whereas giving in material and financial terms was greater in urban areas because of the relatively better economic situation, rural households reported a marginally higher degree of volunteerism.

Only a small number of respondents said that they had ever established or helped to establish *waqf* institutions, some contributing to buildings, providing livestock or providing books and equipment.

About 3.2 per cent of the respondents who have either established or donated to *waqf* have contributed to buildings. This is followed by dominant firms and agriculture, to which about 2.3 per cent have contributed. On livestock, *waqf* accounts for only 0.9 per cent, the same proportion as that of industry and commerce. The other substantial areas of *waqf* are books and equipment, which accounts for 1.9 per cent.

As to cash contributions to *waqf*, only a handful of respondents replied at all to agree with the statement that cash was easy to handle, could be invested and was easy to contribute in small amounts. Of the small number of respondents who had contributed to *waqf* (less than one in ten of the total number of respondents), there were some confusion and disagreement as to whether cash could be contributed to *waqf*, and a number expressed the view that existing *waqf* institutions could be trusted to handle cash. Among those that had given to *waqf*, the main reason for giving was that its benefits were long lasting and that the benefits of their gift could be reaped long after the donor's death.

There were some very interesting responses to the question of why respondents had not been involved in the establishment of *waqf*. Nearly everyone surveyed responded to this question. Reasons given included a lack of understanding of the *waqf* and the laws governing it, but well over half said that they did not have the capacity to act or contribute. The *waqf* institution is generally very weak in Tanzania but in the case of Zanzibar there is quite a lot of documentation on the development of the institution, which will be reviewed below.

Volunteerism

Volunteerism is a crucial aspect of Islamic philanthropy. Although it is very difficult to quantify in monetary terms, its contribution may be more significant than all other monetary and other material donations. The survey conducted did not attempt to assess the monetary value of volunteerism but it focused on the propensity of people towards donating their time and skills (labour) for philanthropic activities.

Well over half of the individual respondents said that they volunteered. The most frequently cited reason given was as a religious obligation, although other reasons included deriving personal satisfaction from helping others and learning new skills. One striking example of the spirit of volunteerism is in the running of madrasas. Although in some areas parents may pay a token amount of money, in most rural areas most madrasas are run on the basis of volunteerism. Sometimes Quranic teachers make use of pupils' labour as a way of economic compensation for the time and training they provide, but this does not usually equal commensurate pay to their labour.

Volunteerism and charitable giving among Muslims depends partly on the extent to which people organize themselves into various forms of associations. Almost a quarter of those surveyed said they were members of religious organizations, and smaller numbers belonged to political parties, or to school development, women's, or village associations etc. Membership in charitable organizations was also listed but only by one in twenty respondents.

The spirit of volunteerism and giving appeared to be related to the degree to which members took part in decision-making processes in the organizations: in general, this was perceived to be rather low. Although a third of respondents said that they participated in decision-making within their organization several times a week, a fifth said that they almost never did.

Muslim Development Foundation: New attempts to consolidate Islamic philanthropy?

The creation of a Muslim university in Tanzania has long been the dream of many Muslims ever since the creation of the East African Muslim Welfare Society (EAM-WS) in 1945. Under the auspices of the Muslim Development Foundation (MDF), the successful mobilization of local donations for the University has demonstrated that there is a great potential for raising domestic resources for a specifically Islamic philanthropic institution in Tanzania.

Prior to the inauguration day of the university project in May 2004, ten wealthy Muslim businessmen had already contributed TShs.100 million. A further TShs.1 billion was raised on the day itself, with senior government officials pledging large sums of money, including the then President, Benjamin Mkapa, the President of Zanzibar, the Prime Minister and the Vice President. Fundraising on this scale and in such a short space of time is unprecedented in Tanzania.

What could account for this immense enthusiasm and willingness of Muslims to give for charity on this occasion? There are a number of different possible reasons. First, Muslims with their long-held sense of marginalization in Tanzania had been looking forward to the day when they would have their own university, ever since the days of the much respected EAMWS, which was banned in 1968. (The site of the university had even been proposed years before.) Secondly, there was a belief that the founders of the MDF, a trust organization, were credible Muslims with integrity and organizational and professional skills needed to run such a landmark project. Thirdly, the goodwill displayed by the Tanzanian President cleared the doubts and fears of many potential contributors, particularly at a time when many Muslim donors were apprehensive of philanthropic giving due to the on-going US-led 'war on terror'. And finally, the inauguration ceremony was well planned and organized – it attracted a lot of interest nationwide. Representatives of Muslims from all mainland regions and Zanzibar flocked to Dar es Salaam to provide both moral and material support to the project.

This unique undertaking provided incontestable evidence that the Muslim community enjoys a striking comparative advantage in the business community within the existing inequalities and structural imbalances in the political, educational and economic areas. If this comparative advantage is thoroughly exploited it could contribute immensely to the Muslims' struggle for equity and social justice.[15]

Relationship of Islamic philanthropic institutions with the government

One of the main research objectives was to examine the relationship between Islamic philanthropic institutions and the state in terms of the behavioural pattern and the legal regime that controls, regulates, restricts or facilitates the functioning of Islamic philanthropic institutions.

Institutions gave a mixed response to questions around the impact of the legal environment and government policies on their activities. Ambiguity of laws was cited by almost half the respondents as a problem and a similar number said that existing laws restricted the functioning of their organizations.

Similarly, over half the respondents (again, institutions) thought that potential donors were prevented from giving because they were scared by government. One of the areas in which Islamic philanthropic institutions come into contact with the government is that of taxation. Two out of five of the respondents thought that inadequate or nonexistent tax incentives presented institutions such as their own as a big or very big problem, although a similar number disagreed (most likely because a large number of Islamic philanthropic institutions are not formally registered and therefore not eligible for tax incentives or tax exemption granted to other religious philanthropic institutions). One third of those institutions surveyed had tax-exempt status.

Not many Islamic philanthropic institutions receive assistance from government and well over half of those surveyed said that this presented them with a big problem. On the question of whether there is a clear public policy environment for philanthropic institutions to thrive, half of the respondents said that lack of a policy guide is a big or very big problem.

These are some of the responses relating to policy and laws that are perceived to hinder the emergence and functioning of Islamic philanthropic institutions. Besides these, however, there are additional behavioural patterns of the government that are considered unfavourable to the success of Islamic philanthropy.

Table 15.6 shows that 61.7 per cent of the institutional respondents characterized their relationship with the government as generally cooperative and cordial, while 38.3 per cent characterize it as either hostile or one with mutual suspicion. Interestingly, there was no noticeable difference of opinion between the registered and unregistered institutions on this matter: the ratio of registered and unregistered institutions that regarded their relationship with government as hostile was one in three.

Table 15.6: Organizations' relationship with the government

	Frequency	Percentage
Cooperative (partnership)	8	6.7
Cordial (friendly)	66	55
Hostile	4	3.3
Organization suspicious of government	8	6.7
Government suspicious of organization	12	10
Mutual suspicion	22	18.3
Total	120	100
Missing	14	
Total	134	

Asked whether their relationship with the government facilitated or hindered their operations, a quarter of respondents said it was facilitative of their operations while a third said that it hindered their operations (while the remainder was indifferent on the issue). More registered institutions claimed that the government hindered their operations than did unregistered institutions. This difference suggests that the registered institutions are more negatively affected by the government than the unregistered ones, probably because the government is more likely to exercise strict control over the registered institutions than the unregistered.

When asked whether organizations received just and fair treatment when it came to competition for government resources with Christian organizations and CBOs, almost half of the respondents said that they did not, while a quarter of the respondents said that they did. When asked why other organizations might be favoured over Muslim organizations, two-fifths of the institutions surveyed cited poor government–Muslim relations, while a much smaller number (one in ten) suggested that good organization and leadership was a key reason.

The relationship between the government and Islamic philanthropic institutions in Tanzania appears to have further deteriorated as a result of changes in the international environment, particularly following the September 11 attacks in New York in 2001. Some of the Islamic philanthropic institutions surveyed seem to have been negatively affected by the on-going US-led war on terror. Asked whether revenues for their organizations had declined or would decline as a result of the 9/11 events, two-fifths of the institutional respondents answered in the affirmative and almost half said that the on-going global war on terror had negatively affected or was likely to affect their relationship with the government.

In the aftermath of 9/11 and against the backdrop of the passing of the Prevention of Terrorism Act in Tanzania in 2002, the environment for the functioning of Islamic philanthropic institutions seems to have worsened. Some Islamic philanthropic institutions have been banned, e.g. Alharamain Foundation based in Saudi Arabia and its branches all over the world. Some of the foreign officers who run Islamic philanthropic institutions have been declared persona non grata in Tanzania, e.g. Sheikh Abu Hudhaifa, Country Director of the Alharamain Foundation, Tanzania. Sheikh Said Abry, Director of the Dhinurayn Foundation, based in Iringa, was also arrested and placed in custody for about two weeks on suspicion of linkage with terrorism. Sheikh Al Assad, a Yemeni national and businessman, based in Dar es Salaam, was also arrested by the government.

Conclusions, prospects, challenges and recommendations

Although Tanzania is a poverty-stricken country with over 50 per cent of its population living below the poverty line, there is a great potential for the development of Islamic philanthropic activities aiming at the promotion of social justice. This study has demonstrated that there are considerable constraints when it comes to harnessing financial, material and human resources to improve the lot of Muslims in Tanzania. These constraints, however, are not constants – they are variable, subject to behavioural change that could be induced by, among other things, education/knowledge, organizational arrangements as well as the political and legal environment within which Islamic philanthropic activities are located. The study also revealed a strong sense of social obligation underpinned by Islamic religious beliefs, as well as social capital in the participation of Tanzanian Muslims in organized religion.

The state in Tanzania is increasingly withdrawing from direct provision of education, health, guardianship and protection of the homeless. Ideally, philanthropic organizations should grow and take the place of and in some cases supplement the efforts of state institutions. Space for the right to organize and associate is crucial for the systematic growth of philanthropic organizations. At present, Muslims in Tanzania do not have a viable national philanthropic organization, statutory or otherwise, that could manage *waqf* property or collect, distribute and account for the *zakat* from the well endowed to those less endowed. As a result, collection of *zakat* is an ad hoc, uncoordinated and highly informal mechanism through individuals rather than established institutions.

Islamic philanthropic associations and groups have not yet recovered from the impact of the one-party political system of governance, which muzzled all organizations operating outside the ruling political party. While other religious philanthropic groups have recovered to generate sources of funding within the country, many Islamic philanthropic groups have continued to rely on outside donations, making them even more vulnerable to volatile global events and changing policies of donors. The vulnerability of Islamic groups seems to have been increased with the enactment of anti-terrorism laws and financial regulations that saw massive reduction of funds flowing to philanthropic groups in Tanzania.

The organization of Islamic philanthropic activities in Tanzania is characterized by two broad contrasting features. Generally speaking, philanthropic institutions owned and run by the Asian Muslim minorities are well organized with a central authority, much better endowed, and they are quite effective in serving more or less exclusively their respective communities. On the other hand, Islamic institutions owned and run by indigenous Tanzanians are generally weak, disorganized, uncoordinated and less resourceful. The puzzling question is why institutions operating within the same environment have such remarkably different structures and performance.

To begin with, in terms of resources it is quite obvious that members of the Asian Muslim communities are much better endowed due to their comparative advantage in the commercial sector. They have more resources and smaller constituencies to serve. This, however, provides just part of the explanation and, apparently, not the most important one. In terms of aggregate wealth the indigenous Muslim community should, in theory, have access to a much greater resource base (human, financial and material) because of its broad membership. The second explanation is that, whereas the Asian Muslim communities usually employ modern forms and skills of organization, most of the indigenous Muslim institutions are still organized in a traditional way by people lacking organizational and professional competencies. The third factor relates to the varying degrees of the impact of political and legal constraints on Islamic philanthropic institutions.

It also seems that the relationship between the state and Asian Muslim institutions is cordial, whereas that of the state and indigenous Muslim institutions is in many cases either antagonistic or one characterized by mutual suspicion. The varying attitudes of the state in dealing with indigenous Muslim institutions is apparently shaped by the government assumption that indigenous Muslim organizations may constitute threatening power centres that could be utilized to challenge the authority and legitimacy of what might be described as a Christian-dominated state. Since the Asian communities have historically disassociated themselves from active national politics, and particularly opposition politics,[16] they are usually not subjected to excessive interference and control by the state. In contrast, since indigenous Muslim institutions are likely to be exploited as avenues for political mobilization and expression they are usually kept under a tight grip by the state. What is to be noted here is that the problem is in essence not the involvement of religious institutions in politics per se, but which side it is that they support. This is why some of the church institutions, although involved in politics to a considerable degree, have been able to maintain their cordial relations with the state.

Apart from the differences in organizational patterns presented above, it has been observed that the problems of Islamic philanthropic institutions in Tanzania are multifaceted and there is therefore a need for multiple solutions. There are problems at the micro-level, i.e. at the institutional level (individual organizations themselves), for example, an organization lacking internal mechanisms of control and accountability. There are also problems relating to the immediate context within which an organization operates, e.g. at a village or district level, in terms of awareness and support by the members as well as their skills and resources. The third dimension of the problem relates to the broader political and legal environment. In the case of Tanzania, it has been observed that the political and legal environments are not very friendly to the operation of Islamic philanthropic activities, particularly for the indigenous Muslim communities. The last dimension relates to the influence of the international environment within which philanthropic institutions operate. Tanzania more than Kenya and all other countries in the Southern African region has been much more pressured by the United States (since 1998, following the twin bombing of the American embassies in Dar es Salaam and Nairobi) to curb Islamic influence, which is now almost indiscriminately associated with terrorism.

The following are some of the major problems discovered by the study:

- There are no credible institutions both at national and lower levels to organize and supervise Islamic philanthropic activities. Muslims do not have trust in the philanthropic organizations and their leaders.

- The study has demonstrated the weakness of Islamic institutions in terms of their human, financial, and material resources. Many of them are organized in a traditional way without structures and rules of accountability.

- There is no unity among Tanzanian Muslims – intra-religious conflicts due to different perspectives or simply due to struggles for power and resources between different factions are very common – intra-religious conflicts were reported in both urban and rural areas.

In recent years some Muslims, particularly those involved in business, have grown apprehensive of making charitable donations. They fear being investigated or harassed by tax collectors or being suspected of having terrorist connections. This is probably one of the reasons why some Muslim donors prefer to donate in secret.

Historically, the policy environment has not been friendly for the operation of *waqf*. The sanctity of *waqf* properties in Tanzania is not well respected, for example, and the governments (of the Union and Zanzibar) have on several occasions taken over *waqf* properties or transferred them to unintended custodians, as was the case with the properties owned by the EAMWS which were transferred to BAKWATA.

The study also discovered that there is a problem of databases of useful information. There are no statistics, for example, of the needy and where they are. Even at the level of mosques, it is not easy to get reliable data relating to people frequenting those mosques, orphans, widows, destitute, and the elderly, who need assistance. Relatedly, there are no statistics on people who are capable of providing *zakat* and *sadaqat*.

The knowledge base of Muslims in Tanzania is generally very weak (both religious and secular). Many people identify themselves as Muslims but do not know even the basic tenets of Islam including that of *zakat* as a religious obligation.

Related to the above, most Muslims do not recognize the potential of Islamic philanthropy as an institution that could promote not only spiritual development but also socioeconomic development imbued with social justice. That is why many Muslims are much more inclined to donate for sports and cultural activities rather than for spiritual (pious) or socioeconomic development purposes.

However, despite all the aforementioned constraints and challenges, the future of Islamic philanthropy is not without hope. First, it is at least quite unlikely that the existing political and legal environment will worsen any further to obstruct the functioning of Islamic philanthropy. Second, the recent emergence of institutional forms of Islamic philanthropy provides important avenues and opportunities for organizational learning and generation of expert knowledge, as well as future models for managing philanthropic activities for social justice. Increased educational and professional achievements for the managers of Islamic philanthropic institutions are likely to improve their organizational skills and lead to increased accountability in the management of material and human resources for the realization of spiritual and social justice goals.

Under the existing arrangement, the domain of operation for Islamic philanthropic institutions is relatively constrained. They are supposed to be apolitical or, if political, then they should be pro the regime in power. If among their objectives is that of promoting social justice, Islamic philanthropic institutions should focus not only on social and economic activities but also on political activities, including information dissemination and advocacy on issues of politics, human rights, freedom of worship and association, just like other non-state institutions including the church. Some philanthropic institutions own newspapers, which do not only write about spiritual, economic and social issues, but also actively engage in the political discourse of the country. However partial and dogmatic they may be, they represent an image of a vibrant civil society institution that could check the excesses and hegemony of the state. Islamic philanthropic institutions are an integral part of civil society. They ought to be more than service providers and perform an advocacy role as well – identifying unaddressed problems and bringing them to public attention – economic, social, religious and even political concerns. If Islamic philanthropy can expand its remit to include a broad range of functions, then it will better placed to promote social justice, even if it means that at times it might be at loggerheads with the state.

Recommendations

- The existing political and legal environments be changed to make them non-hostile to Muslims so that Islamic philanthropic institutions can play a crucial role in society, not only for a limited constituency of Muslim beneficiaries in the country but for the well-being of the whole nation.

- The knowledge base of the Muslim community in Tanzania be strengthened. Muslims need to be educated and sensitized to engage themselves in philanthropic activities with the purpose of not only helping the poor but also establishing and managing productive projects that could help in the promotion of Muslim interests and social justice in society.

- Special schemes be initiated for the provision of loans and know-how to Muslims so that they can get involved in income-generating activities and in the course of doing so increase their capacity to engage in philanthropic activities.

- Basic education be provided to Muslims on the meaning and significance of Islamic philanthropy.

- Muslims of different denominations/sects and factions bury their differences and work together for the development of their community and the nation. Serious efforts have to be made to link the indigenous Muslim community with the Asian Muslim community, for they ultimately constitute one religious identity that could be strengthened for their collective well-being.

- Muslim leaders should not just stay in head offices. They need to visit Muslims in villages and learn their problems. Rural areas, in which the majority of Muslims live, ought to be organically integrated into Islamic philanthropic activities.

Endnotes

1   The author would like to acknowledge the precious inputs of several contributors, including a team of researchers on Islamic Philanthropy for Social Justice in Tanzania, the Ford Foundation, for funding the research project, Tade Akin Aina, a representative of Ford Foundation, Nairobi, whose facilitation was beyond his bureaucratic responsibility as it included academic input as well; and the University Consultancy Bureau (UCB), which coordinated research. The research report from which much of the data for this chapter is extracted was jointly prepared by a team of researchers headed by the author.

2 There are no up-to-date reliable figures, but it is estimated that about two-thirds of East African Muslims reside in Tanzania. In Zanzibar, they constitute almost 98 of the total population (Nimtz 1980). According to the 1957 pre-independence census, Muslims in Tanzania outnumbered Christians at a ratio of 3 to 2. However, in the first and the last post-independence census (1967) to include a religious category it was indicated that Muslims constituted only 30 per cent of the total population, against 32 per cent Christians and 37 per cent believers of African Traditional Religion (ATR) or non-believers. Thus, ever since 1957, the relative size of the religious communities and denominations has been a point of contestation. Some of the current sources estimate the current percentage of Muslims on the mainland at 35 per cent, Christians 30 per cent, and ATR 35 per cent (See e.g., Catholic Hierarchy.org, watchtower. org – 2002, Report of Jehovah's Witnesses Worldwide); CIA, December, 2003, US Department of State, Bureau of African Affairs (Nov. 2003) estimates the percentage of Muslims in Tanzania at 45 per cent, Christians 45 per cent and ATR 10 per cent. Geographically, most of the Muslims in mainland Tanzania are concentrated along the coastal areas, with some pockets in the hinterland particularly in urban areas and trading centres.

3 The research was funded by the Ford Foundation: comparative studies were conducted in five other countries, namely Indonesia, Egypt, Turkey, India, and the UK.

4 GN No. 198/1958: Societies Ordinance (Cap. 337) Societies (prohibition of Specified Acts (Geita District) Order, 1958. It was used to suppress the Tanganyika African National Union Geita District Branch, a local society that had been refused registration under the Ordinance. According to the Societies Ordinance, every unregistered organization of more than ten people which is not constituted for purposes of trade or political activity is an unlawful entity. Registration is mandatory if the group of ten or more wants any semblance of legality.

5 East African Muslim Welfare Society was registered as a regional body in Mombasa, Kenya.

6 Some prominent officials of the ruling party (TANU) were positioned to take charge of the newly created 'Muslim-state' body.

7 Interview with one of the leaders of Shia Muslims in Tanzania.

8 Daniela Modonesi quoting Yedýyildiz, Bahaeddin, 'Place of the Waqf in Turkish Cultural System', p.2, www.history.hacettepe.edu.tr

9 www.lexicorient.com

10 Waqf Commission (Amendment) Ordinance, 1956.

11 In 1891, there is a record of a *waqf* belonging to the 'Ali wa Dadi (or Al-Wadaad) mosques being leased with the consent of the Sultan to an Indian Bohora for 30 years, who undertook to maintain the mosques and render account to the then Sunni Qadhi, Sayyid Ahmad b. Sumayt (Sheriff 2001: 31).

12 See also Decree of 26/8/1905 and Decree 2/1907) in the *Zanzibar Gazette*, 30/8/1905), pp. 3, 6, and 1/5/1907).

13 See also Zanzibar National Archives, ZAN:HD 10/5, Waqf Properties dedicated for the use of Poor of Mecca and Medina'.

14 Sultan Jamshid bin Abdullah was overthrown by a band of several hundred men and Zanzibar was proclaimed a republic. Three months later, Zanzibar united with Tanganyika to form Tanzania.

15 The first batch of 165 students was admitted in October 22, 2005 and the university was officially inaugurated by His Excellency President Benjamin William Mkapa (who also donated TShs10 million in addition to the TShs10 million. he had donated earlier) as a farewell gesture to the Muslim community before he finished his presidential term.

16 A number of prominent Asian businessmen provide financial and material support to the ruling party presumably not necessarily because of their loyalty to the party but as a way of securing political favours in various forms including tax exemption and, in some cases, avoiding unfair treatment that could undermine their business undertakings.

CHAPTER 16

ROOTS NOT SEEDS: A CASE STUDY OF THE ORIGINS OF TWO SUCCESSFUL AFRICAN PHILANTHROPIC INSTITUTIONS[1,2]

JENNY HODGSON

A strong tree shall always grow from the roots and not the seeds.

(African proverb)

Introduction

Much has been written about how and why the outside world should help Africa. The continent's own traditions of giving – strong and deeply rooted in culture and social norms – have often been shamefully overlooked. This chapter charts the emergence and early days of two important African philanthropic institutions which have sought to offer an alternative model of development that is African led and which draws on African resources. Traditions of giving in Africa have always been strong, deeply rooted in culture and social norms. In poor communities in particular, local systems of giving and mutual support have often served to provide the kinds of social safety nets which many African states have failed to offer their citizens. Despite the long and rich traditions of *stokvels*, burial societies and merry-go-rounds, these systems of solidarity and support have remained largely invisible to economists and development institutions alike.

In recent years, however, more attention has been paid to documenting and understanding African cultures of giving as assets to be acknowledged and built upon in the broader processes of social and economic development (and other chapters in this publication are further evidence of this). Another significant development that has taken place over the last decade or so has been the emergence of modern, institutionalized forms of African philanthropy. Although the blueprints for this new generation of foundations and funds may draw both inspiration and elements of practice from philanthropic models developed in other parts of the world, they are deeply rooted in the local African context and are driven by visionary African leadership, drawing on local traditions and cultures while at the same time pursuing progressive agendas that embrace the values of social and economic justice.

As the stories of the establishment and early days of the Kenya Community Development Foundation (KCDF) and the African Women's Development Fund (AWDF) – told in this chapter – demonstrate, both institutions emerged out of deep, thoughtful and extensive processes, driven by the dreams of individuals but consistently shaped within the context of institutions by leaders who believed that sound, well-governed, well-managed foundations could offer new and effective models of institutional governance and accountability, foster a modern culture of African philanthropy as a driver of development and add value to external donor aid.

Kenya Community Development Foundation

'Culture of aid' vs. 'culture of giving'

The origins of the KCDF can be traced back to a process of critical reflection as to what was – or rather, was not – happening at the level of the community from a developmental standpoint in Kenya in the mid-1990s. Within many poor communities, low expectations of the state's ability to provide basic services, a lack of access to the formal financial services sector which might permit borrowing, and a prevailing climate of distrust brought on by the corruption that had become entrenched at so many levels of Kenyan society, had all contributed to a reliance on smaller, relationship-based forms of mutual support. However, while rotating savings and credit groups ('merry-go-rounds') or local fundraisers (*harambee*) to cover the costs of funerals, weddings or school fees were widespread and provided an essential social safety net to the very poor all over Kenya, they were rarely harnessed – or even acknowledged – in the formulation and delivery of development programmes.

Much of the vast amount of international donor aid that had been poured into Kenya following its independence in 1963 had been channelled through NGOs, and often the size and scale of these programmes had meant that locally-based and indigenous self-help initiatives were overlooked. In short, the booming 'culture of aid' that had emerged in Kenya with its signature four-wheel drive cars, competitive employment opportunities and its often inaccessible 'NGO-speak' language and terminology had served to crowd out Kenya's own, quieter 'culture of giving' from the development arena. Underlying this prevailing paradigm was the implicit assumption that Kenya's social and economic development would be funded largely with external resources. And yet, by the late 1990s, almost 30 years after independence, and despite the considerable scale of international development efforts in Kenya, 50 per cent of Kenyans continued to live below the poverty line (Kenya National HDR 1999:16).

The roots of KCDF

When a group of Kenyan development practitioners first came together in 1992 as part of an initiative of the Ford Foundation to explore new and more sustainable models to support community development in Kenya, the idea of establishing a foundation was not uppermost in their minds. They were more interested in examining the challenges faced by communities and grassroots institutions in addressing issues of poverty and deprivation in meaningful and lasting ways. As they saw it, communities were frequently excluded from their own development processes, the passive recipients of aid whose views and priorities were often neither sought nor heard. And although they were invariably best placed to articulate the concerns of their communities, local grassroots organizations were also often excluded from the development loop when it came to accessing funding, because they were institutionally weak and did not have the same kind of access to information as larger, urban-based NGOs. Instead, development projects tended to be implemented by these larger NGOs, whose links into the community were weak and whose systems and processes were designed to respond to the requirements of international donors rather than the communities that they were meant to be serving. Often the lack of local ownership and buy-in meant that development projects would fizzle out once donor funding had come to an end. One of KCDF's founders, Monica Mutuku, would illustrate this lack of ownership with the story of an international volunteer who installed a water pump in a community so that everyone would have clean drinking water. On a return visit to the village some years later he found that the water pump no longer worked. 'Oh poor thing!' said the community members, 'His water pump broke' (Mutuku in Criss 2006).

A key concern articulated by the initiative group at that time was around how to strengthen and channel more resources to grassroots organizations which were close to their communities so that they could play a greater and more proactive role in determining development priorities and devising solutions. Among the ideas that emerged in early discussions was the creation of district resource centres or of a national training establishment where grassroots groups could receive training.

It is important to point out that, at this early stage, the key objectives of the initiative group were very clear: *to strengthen capacities at the community level as a way to address issues of sustainability and increase community participation in local development processes.* Not only did the idea of creating a foundation not feature, but there was also no explicit focus on the role that local resources might play in the process. Despite the vast amounts of informal giving by Kenyans in their daily lives for social causes, the word 'donor' was still widely understood to describe only the faceless formal financial assistance that came from outside the country in the form of development aid. At that time, Kenya's own formal philanthropic sector consisted largely of a handful of family trusts and educational foundations, most of which operated in quiet isolation, disconnected from each other and off the radar of mainstream development agencies. However, it was not just the low profile of the philanthropy sector which made conversations about the role of local resources in driving development problematic. Previous nationwide efforts to institutionalize existing traditions of giving had had a mixed history which had left many Kenyans wary and sceptical.

The role of harambee in Kenya

Following independence in 1963, Kenya's first President, Jomo Kenyatta, had invoked Kenyans' spirit of *harambee*, or 'pulling together' in the new and ambitious project of nation-building that the country was embarking upon. *Harambee* became an integral part of the post-colonial government's development strategy. It was essentially a system of cost-sharing between the government and beneficiary communities, in which community members would contribute communal labour and/ or funds for capital infrastructure projects, roads and schools, in the expectation that the government would provide on-going funds to maintain them. During the immediate post-independence period, the practice of *harambee* drew heavily upon a culture and tradition of giving that had a social, as well as a financial aspect (Transparency International 2001). However, increasingly, the social and cultural aspects of this practice began to diminish and *harambee* became less a system of community resource mobilization and more 'a theatre of political contest'.[3] By the late 1980s and 1990s, as Kenya's political scene became increasingly turbulent, *harambee* had become progressively more corrupted, a tool through which members of parliament and local government officers would seek political influence and promotion. It was common practice for politicians to make contributions that far exceeded the financial realities of their salaries. While extra funds were often made available by central government for such purposes, it was not uncommon for cheques, lavishly and loudly presented in public, to bounce when it came to cashing them. In addition, a further element of coercion crept in during this time, with pressure exerted on all members of the community to 'show their support' for a particular cause by contributing to the *harambee,* and its success would be measured by the amount of money raised. There were virtually no controls or reporting mechanisms when it came to how and where the money was spent.

It is perhaps unsurprising, therefore, that a consequence of the murky practices associated with *harambee* during this period was that the concept lost much of its value as a tool for community development and, although *harambee* continued to play an important role for private purposes (such as weddings, school fees etc), Kenyans became increasingly sceptical of big public fundraising efforts.

In 2002, the new National Rainbow Coalition (NARC) government assumed office under the banner of a vigorous anti-corruption drive, which included efforts to clean up the practice of *harambee*. Although the anti-corruption credentials of the new government proved to be somewhat short lived, the reopening of a public discussion on *harambee* would present the by then fully operational KCDF with an important opportunity to demonstrate, by its own example, ways that public giving could be managed in transparent and accountable ways.

The birth of Kenya's first public foundation

The idea of creating a Kenyan public foundation was not born overnight. It followed a two-year period of discussion, consultation and exposure to existing community development models elsewhere in Africa and further afield.[4] In fact, it was during a visit from representatives of two US organizations, the Ford Foundation and the East Tennessee Foundation, to Kenya in 1995 that the idea of creating a community foundation in Kenya was first discussed. With its emphasis on the accumulation of permanent financial resources – big and small – for the long-term benefit of communities, the community foundation model offered a way into an entirely different way of thinking about development, giving prominence to the act of giving as a form of participation and moving beyond the 'project mentality' that was so prevalent in Kenya at the time.

In 1997, when it seemed that a broad consensus had been arrived at among the key partners as to the overall direction of the new institution, an agreement was signed between a five-person Kenyan advisory committee, the Ford Foundation and the Aga Khan Foundation (which had by then come on board as a partner) to take things forward. For a three-year pilot period, the KCDF would be a semi-autonomous project of the Aga Khan Foundation, which would act as its fiscal agent and provide it with separate office space in the Pangani district of Nairobi.

Community Development Foundation or Community Foundation

It is perhaps worth reflecting on the name of the new foundation, Kenya Community Development Foundation, as different groupings of the words can – and arguably, did – lead to somewhat divergent perceptions of its function and niche. Indeed, in the early years of the foundation's existence, different perceptions among its founders of the role and function of the organization certainly served to ensure an on-going and dynamic debate about what lay at KCDF's core. There was full agreement from the start that this new organization would not be the simple replication of any single model, community foundation or other. Rather, the process would and should be firmly rooted in the Kenyan context. At the same time, however, although there may have been a united view when it came to what the final outcomes of KCDF's work should be, the particular 'lenses' that different protagonists brought to the new institution resulted in tensions around priorities, methodologies and entry points which in many ways threatened to pull the new organization in different directions.[5]

For Monica Mutuku, the newly appointed project director, for example, it was a focus on community development that lay at the heart of the new foundation, with a particular emphasis on participation, local ownership and sustainability. For her, therefore, the natural starting-point for KCDF was in its programmes, which had a strong emphasis on capacity building for community-based organizations from the very start. Yet another reading of KCDF's name presents a different set of variables, i.e. the new institution as *community foundation,* which would imply a greater emphasis on grantmaking and building up of a local donor base.

Community foundations had started to appear in many different parts of the world in the mid-1990s, offering new ways of addressing local development issues. The community foundation had its roots in the United States in the early years of the twentieth century, but in the mid-1990s the changed nature of the post-Soviet, post-apartheid world had led to a renewed focus on civil society in a number of countries, including Russia and South Africa. The proliferation of community foundations at this time was supported by a handful of private US foundations (the Ford and C.S. Mott Foundations were particularly active), both in institutional support and endowment grants, and it was further facilitated by the new possibilities for informational exchange afforded by increased access to the Internet globally. Much has been written in recent years about the relative merits of the community foundation model as a universal tool for building local philanthropy, and how different economic, cultural and political contexts may necessitate different approaches and produce different versions of the 'original' US model. In the case of KCDF, the community foundation model undoubtedly offered new insights and possibilities that were at that time altogether missing from the development landscape in Kenya. It is also fair to say that, as time passed and KCDF's identity as a foundation began to mature, any initial resistance or scepticism towards the 'complete package' of the community foundation as grantmaker and donor service provider gave way to a new appreciation of the value of both elements as important cornerstones of KCDF's on-going development.

When it came to whether KCDF would in fact be a grantmaker or not, there were some reservations at first. Not only was the idea of a Kenyan grantmaker something of an oxymoron (in the Kenyan context, all 'donor' organizations were, by definition, foreign), but the hands-off nature of grantmaking seemed antithetical to the kind of direct engagement in community capacity building that KCDF's founders had in mind. Furthermore, a grantmaking approach necessarily required the existence of community-based organizations strong enough to be able to apply for and administer grant funding. Such an assumption could not be easily made in Kenya at a time when weak institutions were a large part of the problem. When KCDF came to develop its grantmaking strategy, therefore, it was closely linked to a parallel process of capacity building for local groups and organizations.

Another aspect of the US community foundation, which was hard to reconcile with KCDF's focus on bottom-up community empowerment, was the emphasis on services to donors. After all, it had been concerns over the influence of donor agendas on community development processes that had been a driving factor in the search for a new approach in the first place. And finally, there was the meaning of the word 'community' in the new foundation's name. In the context of the conventional community foundation model, community is normally taken to imply a geographic area, i.e. a group of people living in a common place. In the Kenyan context, however, the word has a more nuanced meaning: it can be used to describe many different types of groupings, based not only on geography but also ethnicity, as well as religion and social class. For example, individuals who have moved to urban areas will often continue to maintain strong links with their rural home areas and play an important role in channelling resources back to their community. In the context of local community-based philanthropy, therefore, it was likely that a significant donor base would most likely be located outside the geographically defined community.

Furthermore, in Africa the word 'community' often carries additional nuances and assumptions – both negative and positive – which are perhaps missing from other, particularly Western, contexts. For example, communities are often understood to be 'poor', 'traditional', inherently less developed, and therefore, by implication, in need of external help. At the same time, the word 'community' can imply extremely cohesive social units, far richer in social capital and interpersonal networks than the more disparate and disconnected kinds of human groupings more commonly found in many developed countries. As a national public foundation, KCDF would inevitably have to occupy quite a different position from the conventional (Western) community foundation, engaging from the outside with multiple communities, rather than situating itself within a single one, while at the same time seeking to embrace the most inclusive notion of a national, Kenyan community, an assumption that could not always be taken for granted in a country with a long history of ethnic rivalries and divisions. In addition, as an urban-based development organization, run by middle class professionals. it would have to grapple with very different power dynamics and seek different entry points in its work.[6]

In the early days, then, the capacity-building and grantmaking programme formed the core of KCDF's work. The grantmaking process was thorough and intensive from the start: it required the involvement of four key members of staff working with each grant partner in a nine-step process over a twelve-month period on all aspects of institutional development (financial management, programme development, administration and personnel and governance). Between 1998 and 2003 KCDF made 53 grants totalling KShs118 million (approximately US$1.5 million). The number of grants made in the early years was rather modest, and certainly if KCDF's main priority during this period had been to promote a range of grantmaking services among a potential local donor base, then this painstaking and costly approach towards grantmaking may not have been the most effective way of going about it. Grant funds represented only around 30–35 per cent of the annual budget, with the rest made up of capacity building, administration and other non-grantmaking costs. For local donors seeking cost efficiency in their giving, this ratio may well have appeared to be on the high side.

This approach was, however, completely consistent with the emphasis KCDF placed on developing the capacities of communities and on the need to invest in those communities if the injection of grant funding was to bring about any real and lasting change. Although it may have been less effective as a means of building a profile among local donors in the short term, it was important from the point of view of building a strong track record as a responsible and thorough grantmaker, which would have the credentials to attract new – and local – donors further down the line.

From sugar to seed: building an endowment message

Clearly, the development of KCDF should not only be considered in terms of how it did or did not conform to the conventional community foundation model. Of much greater importance would be its ability, over the long term, to establish itself as an authoritative and credible Kenyan philanthropic institution that would attract the support of a diverse range of domestic donors. As discussed above, the environment for organized philanthropy in Kenya was a difficult one. Scandals over the misuse of public funds were all too common and the *harambee* had lost much of its credibility. Terms like 'philanthropy' and 'endowments' were not in common parlance, and the concept of grantmaking was poorly understood outside the non-profit sector. It was clear that KCDF would need to articulate an argument that would resonate among Kenyans, and that marked a departure from the usual 'development culture', which rarely required any kind of philanthropic contribution from ordinary Kenyans. Kenya's well-established traditions of giving were an obvious starting-point upon which to build. As it was, most Kenyans were already 'donors' in their day-to-day lives, whether it was by paying school fees for members of the extended family, contributing to the building of a new school or one of the myriad of other ways in which Kenyans gave on a daily basis. Selling the concept of endowments, however, was potentially more difficult. In times of dire poverty, how could it be justifiable to lock money up in perpetuity, spending only the income it earned; and in an environment of distrust of institutions, and how could people be convinced to place their faith not only in the current leadership of an institution but that of the future too?

'From sugar to seed' was one of the messages that KCDF developed as a way to describe the shift from a 'harambee' way of thinking to an 'endowment' way of thinking. Many Kenyans were only too familiar with the metaphor of the 'bag of

---

Box 16.1: The Evolving Mission

The different development stages that KCDF underwent in its early years are reflected vividly in the evolution of its mission statement. In 1996, at the start of the process, the mission statement focused almost entirely on community development, with no mention of assets or endowments, or indeed of grantmaking. Its mission was *'To increase the participation of people in their own development, to build support for development from a diverse range of Kenyan funding sources and to build the strength of a cross-section of Kenyan organizations involved in community development'*.

Although it had already been agreed that KCDF would build an endowment fund, at this stage it was not regarded as central to the foundation's mission so much as a means of ensuring KCDF's own institutional sustainability. By 1999, the mission statement was expanded to acknowledge the central role of permanent assets, while maintaining its emphasis on community (although with no mention of grantmaking): *'To build permanent community resources (funds, capacities and assets) that increase the extent, equity, effectiveness and efficiency by which Kenyans take responsibility for the development of their communities.'*

In 2002 the mission statement was further revised to give equal weight to grantmaking, assets, and communities: *'To effectively mobilize resources for building permanent funds for grantmaking towards the development of communities'*, and that equal emphasis on a set of core activities to build communities continues to stand in its mission today: *'KCDF promotes sustainable development of communities through social investment, resource mobilization, endowment building and grantmaking.'*

sugar' which eventually gets used up. In development terms, there were endless examples of when the 'sugar had run out', whether it was funds, or skills to mend the broken water pump, or the frequent severe droughts that hit Northern Kenya every few years and which seemed to meet the country unprepared every time. In contrast, the 'seed' was like an endowment fund: if carefully used, it could be eaten today or planted (invested) to produce food in the future.

The NARC government's election in 2002 and its early, if short-lived, enthusiasm for rooting out corruption created one set of new opportunities for KCDF to make its case for endowment-building and asset development against a background of new demands from government and the public for greater transparency and accountability. It was also possible to make the case for endowments in the context of existing traditions: after all, the pooling of funds for community purposes had deep roots in Kenya. In April 2003, the government appointed a Task Force on Public Collections to review the *harambee*, with KCDF's Monica Mutuku as its vice-chair. The final report, which received widespread attention in the media, recommended the introduction of laws that would require audits of proceeds from public collections. It also highlighted the need to restore faith in philanthropy and promote a culture of accountability in Kenya. The report also served to increase the profile of KCDF as an authority on matters relating to philanthropy and giving.

Resource mobilization

The work to build the capacities of local organizations which KCDF undertook in its early years required a significant investment of time and effort, but it was embarked upon with the confidence and sense of excitement of a team eager to test a new approach to community development. The processes around local fundraising and endowment building, however, presented more of a challenge: as a pioneer in the newly-emerging philanthropic sector in Kenya there were few existing experiences that could be drawn upon from peers in the region.[7] The culture of Kenya's NGO sector and its heavy dependence on international funding meant that local resource mobilization was still relatively underdeveloped. Certainly, fundraising for grantmaking was more or less unheard of, and what local giving that did take place was targeted more towards 'feel good' issues such as children's health or education than to the rather more abstract concept of 'capacity building' in which KCDF was engaged.

It was clear that, for the purposes of financial sustainability as well as its institutional independence, KCDF would need to begin to expand its funding base, to engage with new types of donors and to start to get pledges towards the endowment. The immediate challenge that KCDF faced was that of identifying donors that would fund the three central axes of its work, namely grantmaking, capacity building and the endowment. Unsurprisingly, with the notable exception of the founder donors, the Ford and Aga Khan Foundations, there were few others who were inclined to buy into all three elements. KCDF's expertise in grantmaking, however, was certainly of interest to a number of international institutional donors because it could offer a unique opportunity to get smaller amounts of money to many organizations in a way that would otherwise be costly and logistically difficult. As a fundraising, grantmaking foundation with its own rather specific mission but without yet its own independent sources of funding, KCDF needed to consider its position in regard to those donors interested in its grantmaking competencies (but who were perhaps less interested in its focus on community development and its more specific focus on the role of local community development associations).

Part of the Ford Foundation's commitment to the new institution had been a commitment towards the endowment: grant funds would be awarded on a matching basis over a specific period. The endowment grant challenge issued by Ford offered great possibilities for KCDF; the bigger the endowment, the greater its long-term sustainability and the independence of its mission. It also lent a degree of credibility when it came to approaching other donors (although it may also have served as a disincentive among local donors, who may have sensed that it was rich enough already or in a different league altogether). The more unrestricted funding KCDF could raise, the more it could focus on its core mission of strengthening capacities of communities.

From 2002 onwards, once the programme side of the foundation was more established, KCDF began to focus more on a strategy for asset development and, in doing so, to adopt more of the strategies and language of the broader community foundation field, with the introduction of 'donor advised', 'field of interest' and 'non-endowed' or 'pass-through' grant funds. As much as it was able, KCDF stuck to its capacity-building approach, in which its role was as a mission-oriented changemaker, but it also began to talk of its capacities as a pass-through grantmaker.

With its track record as an effective grantmaker established, KCDF provided a mechanism through which larger institutional donors could direct financial resources to communities. Such donors often came with their own sets of conditions and reporting formats and they would be unlikely to make contributions to an endowment. The World Bank, NOVIB, Ford Foundation, Bernard van Leer Foundation and Allavida all used KCDF for pass-through grantmaking programmes at various points, although the degree to which KCDF's own mission and approaches were incorporated into the programmes varied.

KCDF began also to experience some success in attracting the interests of individuals who were drawn to the new model for philanthropy that KCDF offered. In one case, a group of young Kenyan professionals wanted to engage in philanthropic work but without establishing their own organization. The Hope Trust continues to exist as a donor-advised fund within KCDF, making grants to community-based projects on a regular basis.

It was in the development of community funds, however, that KCDF appeared to have found the ideal combination of asset development and capacity building that brought it closest to achieving its mission. The idea was simple: communities (normally represented by community development associations) would identify an issue or a set of issues that they wished to address. Each member of the immediate community would contribute a token amount (KShs50–100 or US$0.75–1.00) towards a pooled fund, and contributions would also be sought from community members based in urban centres such as Nairobi or Mombasa. The money raised would be used to establish a community fund within KCDF, which would act as the fund's steward and would also provide capacity-building support, particularly in the area of governance. Once the fund started to generate interest, KCDF would make this money available to the community organization, which would, through a participatory process involving the entire community, decide on its allocation. Small grants, or often school bursaries, would be awarded and part of the overall amount would also be used to cover the costs of the community development association.

The community fund model contained many of the key elements that KCDF had been striving to promote. Firstly, it had a local resource mobilization component reminiscent of the *harambee* tradition, which underlined the combined power of many small contributions and which was now managed in a more transparent way (the capacity-building process that the community development association was required to undergo was meant to ensure that it had the necessary management skills to ensure this). Secondly, community funds promoted local participatory development processes, with community members brought together to discuss priorities and concerns. And thirdly, by placing the fund within the larger endowment pool of KCDF, the mechanism provided poor communities with access to financial services markets from which they were normally excluded.

The idea generated a lot of interest, and communities across Kenya approached KCDF wanting to establish their own funds, particularly once it had been decided that, as an extra incentive (and as a way of expanding their own endowment pool rapidly), each community fund would receive a match from Ford's endowment challenge grant. The development of the community funds was consistent with KCDF's long-standing commitment to community development and empowerment. The harnessing and long-term deployment of community-based assets was quite distinct from the more conventional 'donor service-driven' community foundation model, and introduced a new and potentially exciting dynamic into the development landscape in Kenya.

As a new type of philanthropic institution that was seeking to find its niche, KCDF tested a number of different approaches in its early years. It had also proved itself to be a dynamic and flexible organization that was open to learning under the leadership of Monica Mutuku; involved in its inception from the very start, she had brought KCDF through its registration as an independent organization as well as the creation of the KCDF Trust, which is the legal steward of the Foundation's endowment.

In 2003–4, two factors came to dominate the affairs of KCDF and introduced a climate of uncertainty and of urgency: one was the leadership transition brought on by the impending retirement of Monica Mutuku, and the second concerned the challenge grant from the Ford Foundation. The process of recruitment was long and drawn out – it was a challenge to find an individual who could match the vision, creativity and energy of Mutuku – and it also hindered KCDF's endowment-building efforts. Mutuku was the figurehead and public face of the foundation and it proved a challenge to convince people to commit resources in perpetuity to an institution with an as yet unknown new leader.

Similarly, the promise of an endowment grant from the Ford Foundation, which would provide KCDF with its much-needed sustainability and autonomy, and the promise of which had served as critical catalyst in the early years, may also have had the less desired result of distorting a more organic process of development. The truth was that, over the seven or so years that KCDF had been in existence, it had proved very difficult to engage with local donors. While KCDF had developed an excellent track record among international donors through its pass-through grants programmes, the very time-consuming nature of the work had not brought money into the endowment fund. Grantmaking – and capacity building in particular – had proved difficult to sell to local donors. In an environment of concerns over accountability and trust, the logic of grantmaking, with its exhaustive procedures and checks, had a lot of potential appeal among Kenyans wanting to make their first steps in local philanthropy via a mechanism that was transparent and well managed. However, the resistance towards an all-out strategy to market the foundation's 'donor services' had served as an obstacle to engagement with a broader range of donors. As time passed, and the need to meet the target set for the matching grant grew, the community funds provided a quick and effective means of mobilizing resources, particularly with the added incentive of a matching contribution from the Ford Foundation grant. This strategy obviously had the effect of directing new resources to communities, but at the cost of reducing the size of KCDF's own unrestricted endowment (the funds belonged, after all, to the communities).

In 2004, Janet Mawiyoo, an experienced development practitioner (most recently with Action Aid Tanzania), became the second CEO of KCDF. Since the change in leadership, there has been a new direction and focus, partly the result of a steady accumulation of institutional experience but also due to the individual perspective and background that Mawiyoo has brought to KCDF.

Concerns that the Ford match was providing the wrong kind of incentive for communities to organize themselves and to create their own community funds led KCDF to shift away from proactively marketing the model as aggressively as it had previously. In a number of cases it seemed to be the more organized and politically well-connected communities, with resources more readily at their disposal, that had benefited from the opportunity to create their own fund. There were also increasing doubts about KCDF's ability to exert its influence at the level of governance and allocation of grantmaking funds (KCDF's 'grant' was the disbursement of interest earned on the community fund to a single community-based development associa-tion or organization, which was then responsible for the actual allocation within the community). In one or two cases the foundation had been forced to withhold the payout of interest because of such concerns.

At the time of writing, KCDF has largely renegotiated its position in relation to communities. Arguably, it has become less of a 'lone player' in the development field, by attempting to forge new alliances with a broader range of more mainstream development organizations, particularly with Kenyan NGOs that operate at a level that is one step removed from the grassroots. It now also involves itself less deeply in capacity-building processes, for example, by providing grants for such activities but outsourcing its implementation to other service providers in the field.

In the area of asset development there has also been a shift: notions of nurtur-ing or reinvigorating indigenous forms of philanthropy at the most grassroots level have arguably been joined by a more hard-headed analysis of the state of the Kenyan NGO sector as a whole. The idea of creating reserves or endowments has been expanded beyond the level of individual communities, and KCDF now seeks to offer a long-term solution to the stark funding reality facing many NGOs who are almost entirely reliant on international donor support for their work. For those more established NGOs that are prepared to engage seriously on the issue of sustainability, and that are have already reached a level of maturity in their govern-ance and accountability, KCDF is offering the opportunity to establish their own endowment fund. For the time being, the most significant sources of funding for such endowments remain grants from international partners and surpluses from project funding rather than a particular focus on domestic resource mobilization. In effect, the provision of such a service for NGOs casts KCDF in a new light – as a financial service provider to the non-profit sector, a responsible and involved sav-ings bank, more along the lines of an organization like the Charities Aid Foundation (a UK charity with offices in Russia, India and South Africa).[8]

In terms of grantmaking, KCDF has expanded its programmes along thematic lines (most recently, a fund for the girl child was launched, for example), and it makes grants on behalf of a range of international and local donor institutions. As a grantmaker it remains committed to the provision of institutional support grants, and relies on its own restricted funding from its endowment to ensure funding for this key element of its work.

Over ten years since it was founded, KCDF has established itself as a unique and leading philanthropic institution in East Africa. It has experimented with a vision to promote the value of local philanthropy at the most grassroots level, by facilitating the pooling and public allocation of small but significant amounts of money and encouraging the involvement of ordinary Kenyans in their own development processes. More recently, it has sought to instil a culture of sustainability and financial responsibility among more established Kenyan NGOs which have operated on a project-to-project basis for many years, with few ideas as to how to plan for their futures. Throughout, KCDF has proved itself to be a responsible and effective grantmaker, able to manage funds on behalf of a wide variety of donors but also responsive to the needs of organizations on the ground.

As a facilitator, convenor, grantmaker and independent voice of authority on philanthropy in Kenya, there are still many areas to explore, models to test and relationships to broker, and KCDF is still unique in its field as Kenya's only national public foundation. KCDF may not be community foundation in the mould of those found in the global north. However, as it seeks to develop its programmes and activities further, there is still a lot of useful learning to be derived from the simple logic of the community foundation model that dictates that a foundation's ability to raise resources locally depends on the effectiveness and perceived relevance of its programmes among local donors. International funding support for its programmes has been important in getting the new foundation established and funding more development-oriented issues, but it cannot and should not be expected to last far into the future. The next challenge that it faces will be a true test of its sustainability. It is one that it has hitherto shied away from and will require an enormous investment of energy and conviction: that of convincing Kenyans of all walks to life to contribute to the work of the foundation.

African Women's Development Fund

AWDF was officially launched in 2000. As an idea, however, it had been conceived some years earlier, the vision of three African feminists. Through their experiences of working in women's rights in Africa and further afield, Bisi Adeleye-Fayemi, Hilda Tadria and Joana Foster had each entertained thoughts of developing a way to add more muscle to an African women's movement, which, although sizeable and active across the continent, faced serious challenges of capacity and leadership, access to resources, fragmentation and political interference.

The global context

The 1990s was an exciting and important decade for women's rights around the world. Three UN conferences – the World Conference on Human Rights in Vienna in 1993, the International Conference on Population and Development in Cairo in 1994 and, finally, the Fourth United Nations World Conference on Women in 1995 in Beijing had created new momentum around women's rights, placing them at the centre of the mainstream development agenda. The Beijing Conference, in particular, provided a specific focus for the political work of women's organizations from across the world on a global stage, and it brought women together from every corner of the globe. These high-level conferences signified new international commitments to gender equality and women's empowerment at a governmental level. At the same time, they fuelled a sense of interconnectedness among women's organizations across the globe and led to the emergence of new networks across borders and continents. Women's rights activists increasingly began to locate their work in the context of the universal norms and standards espoused in the language of UN declarations, thus introducing new levels of accountability into the human rights discourse in their own countries and regions.

A women's fund for Africa

It was at the African Regional Preparatory Conference for Beijing that was held in Dakar in 1995 that Ghanaian, Joana Foster and Ugandan, Hilda Tadria first met. Both women had been involved in the women's movement in Africa for many years and they quickly understood that they shared many of the same concerns over the lack of funding available for women's organizations in Africa. The two women were attending a workshop organized by the Global Fund for Women as part of the conference. Hearing the story of the Global Fund – started by three women who had been concerned by the lack of funding available to women's activists around the world – and seeing how effective the fund had been in raising and distributing money to women's organizations around the world, Foster and Tadria were struck by the thought that a similar kind of fund for Africa could make a significant contribution towards building the effectiveness of the women's movement in Africa.

Africa has a strong tradition of women's groups and organizations, operating at many different levels. They range from informal self-help groups that serve as social and economic safety nets within individual communities, to more formally constituted organizations, associations, and coalitions that provide legal, educational and health services to women or that campaign and raise awareness on women's rights issues. For those more organized groups, it was an on-going struggle to secure the kinds of resources which would allow them to grow as organizations: frequently, the absence of regular income left them institutionally weak and low on capacity.

The energy and enthusiasm generated by global processes like Beijing presented important opportunities for the women's rights movement, but how could African women's organizations capitalize on this momentum if they consistently lacked the skills and resources that would enable them to bring about change? Smaller, locally-based organizations, meanwhile, have often suffered from a lack of visibility, their relatively modest financial requirements putting them beyond the funding interests of international donors who, for reasons of costs and efficiency, often prefer to make larger grants to a handful of partners.

Over the years, and prompted by a succession of United Nations conferences (during the 1970s, 1980s and the 1990s), international donors and agencies had allocated significant amounts of funding for women's issues. However, their priorities were frequently influenced by their own agendas and interests, which did not always necessarily coincide with those that African women might have defined by themselves. Some women's organizations, therefore, allowed their missions to drift towards the interests of international donors in order to secure funding. At the same time, others were being co-opted by governments: in many African countries, the success of women's organizations often depended on their proximity to the ruling party – or to the wives of senior politicians, who often became figureheads of the women's movement. Access to resources and to international forums was limited to such groups, and the voices of independent women's organizations were not being heard.

First steps

Following the Dakar conference, the two women set about developing their idea further. They received support in the form of modest grants from the Global Fund for Women and Mama Cash (based in the Netherlands) to conduct some feasibility work. However, new professional commitments (Foster joined Women in Law and Development in Africa as regional director) meant that the plans were temporarily put on hold.

At about the same time, in London, Bisi Adeleye-Fayemi, a British-born Nigerian, was having similar thoughts about the role a fund could play in reducing the high level of donor dependency in the African women's movement, both in terms of financial resources and in the setting of priorities. Adeleye-Fayemi was then the director of the UK-based Akina Mama wa Afrika (AMwA), an international development organization working on leadership development for African women in Europe and Africa. Through her own experiences as an African woman living and working in Europe, and her work at AMwA, Adeleye-Fayemi had a keen under-standing of the kind of marginalization and discrimination many African women faced both at home and abroad. She recognized the importance of creating spaces for women where their voices could be heard, and where they could determine their own needs. The African Women's Leadership Institute in Uganda, which was established by AMwA in 1999 as part of its contribution to the post-Beijing process, was created to tackle the question of leadership head-on: African women could receive training in critical thinking on gender issues, feminist theory and practice, organizational building and resource development. But the institute was only part of the solution: the question of getting resources to women's organizations working at the grassroots level across Africa remained a major concern.

At around this time, Foster and Adeleye-Fayemi met and, recognising that they shared a common dream, decided to join forces (together with Tadria) and renew their efforts to create a new fund. Initially, the fund was incubated as a project within AMwA, which provided it with a strong and credible institutional base in the short term. For two years, from 1998–2000, the three founders quietly discussed their plans for an African women's fund with a variety of partners – private foun-dations and other women's funds, in particular – who were sympathetic to their cause and excited by their idea. During that period they received several grants for institutional support, planning and networking.

Launch and start-up strategies

In June 2000, the Beijing Plus 5 Conference in New York presented the perfect opportunity to launch the new fund. The official launch of the African Women's Development Fund on June 8, 2000 attracted over 200 people, many of them Af-rican women in New York for the conference, and US$13,000 was raised towards the new fund. The high turnout and modest fundraising success represented an important and symbolic show of support from African women for the new fund. The objective of a second, smaller meeting also held at that time was to secure significant financial support from a core set of donors to see the fund through its first few years of operations. With the assistance of the Carnegie Corporation, AWDF brought together the Ford, Rockefeller and MacArthur Foundations and the Global Fund for Women who, between them, made pledges amounting to US$2 million towards the new fund. (Again, timing was in AWDF's favour: the Carnegie Corporation had recently changed its grantmaking themes in Africa and was looking to make a lasting investment in women's health and development as part of its exit strategy.)

The African Women's Development Fund finally opened its offices as a fully independent organization in Ghana in May 2001, with Adeleye-Fayemi as executive director and Joana Foster as board chair. During the period leading up to the launch of the new fund, the co-founders had made some astute calculations when it came to leveraging support for and interest in their new idea. Their starting-point for any discussion was an absolute belief in the cause of the new fund and its necessity. Success would come, according to Hilda Tadria, 'because the cause was and continues to be right'. The idea that they presented was already fully developed: the new institution would be an autonomous grantmaking fund, which would respond to the needs of African women as they were articulated and defined by themselves. It would seek out grassroots women's organizations and give small to medium-sized grants, and would also give modest, institutional development-type grants to larger organizations seeking to undertake a specific piece of work or invest in their own institutions. Grantmaking would be a function but not the *defining* function of the fund. The fund would be defined, rather, by its commitment to the promotion and protection of the rights of women. During the first few years of operations, the fund's focus would be on developing a grantmaking track record and demonstrating its overall viability and credibility. Developing an African donor base would be extremely important over the long term and would require a significant investment of time and resources, which might detract from the business of building a strong grantmaking institution. As such, it would not be a central activity for the fund in the first few years.

The key priority for the co-founders at this point had been to secure support and resources from partners who understood and were sympathetic to the idea of a new fund, who were attuned to the specifics of creating a philanthropic institution, and who shared similar values and a commitment to social justice. The Global Fund for Women continued to be an important partner at this time, providing financial support and acting as mentor to the new fund. Private foundations, such as Ford and MacArthur were another important group of potential partners: their support was sufficiently flexible to allow the new fund to grow organically and independently.

Finally, the co-founders demonstrated a judicious sense of timing in their planning. The Carnegie Corporation's changing programme priorities in Africa made them well disposed towards an enduring final investment in women's development issues in Africa, while the Beijing Plus 5 Conference in New York had brought the spotlight back once again, if only temporarily, on to women's rights at the top of the development agenda. Furthermore, the New York launch also brought the discussion right to the front door of some of its US-based partners, such as the Ford Foundation.

Building up track record and profile

It was clear to the co-founders from the start that the transition from AWDF as a bold and ambitious idea to AWDF as an effective and professionally-run grantmaking organization would need to be as smooth and efficient as possible. They were acutely aware that the fund needed to start demonstrating success immediately, and were extremely sensitive to the potential negative effects that any early glitches might have on the reputation of the fund: this was not to go down in the history of international funding as another 'failed African adventure'.[9]

The size of the task facing the new fund was not small: it had a small staff working from a single office serving the entire continent; it had no track record as a grantmaker, and a limited record as a fund receiver; it was promoting a potentially 'difficult' social justice agenda, elements of which might not necessarily attract broad popular support, while demand for its services among women's organizations across the continent far exceeded any amount of funding that it could either make available or process. In the first few months of operations, a balance would have to be struck between the need to manage expectations by producing some instant results, while at the same time ensuring that sufficient investments were made in the development of the new institution. Although a number of multi-year grants had been secured to see the fund through its start-up, it was also going to be important to bring in new donors in order to ensure the new fund's sustainability and to underpin the independence of its agenda. At the same time, the fund needed to begin to develop an identity as an African grantmaking foundation which was neither a local NGO nor merely the intermediary tool of foreign donor institutions.

Autonomous grantmaking

In launching a new programme, an operating organization can exercise a level of control over inputs and outcomes. For a grantmaker, however, no matter how much it invests in its processes (its theory of change, its selection criteria, etc), responsibility for the final outcome is delegated to its grantee. Grantmaking always comes with risks attached: one risk that all grantmakers take involves the assumption that, once the grant funds have been transferred, the recipient organization will spend it in accordance with the agreement. Social justice grantmakers anywhere often entertain higher levels of risk or uncertainty in their grantmaking, because outcomes may be more difficult to measure or cannot always be predicted, or because they are supporting broad processes which involve multiple players in complex environments and where change may happen over longer periods of time than that of a traditional grant-funded project. Grantmakers in Africa, as in other parts of the developing world, face additional levels of risk associated with operating in an environment where NGOs are often weak and unregulated. Where NGOs are weak, grants can be misused because of a grantee's poor management skills or lack of experience in administering funding (which is one reason why local grantmakers often make significant investments in capacity-building programmes). In other situations, where poverty is great and corruption endemic, even small grants can provide sufficient incentives for dishonesty, such as the phenomenon of the 'briefcase NGO', which exists only on paper. In its first round of grants, therefore, it was critical that AWDF make safe grants to a variety of well-respected women's organizations, accessed through existing contacts and reputable networks across the continent, to demonstrate that the basic mechanisms for effective grantmaking were in place and that their grants generated good results.

By taking the name of the African Women's Development Fund, the fund set itself an ambitious task. It was important to demonstrate from the start that it was committed to women's rights across the continent, not just in West Africa, where it was based, nor only in Anglophone Africa.[10] Within its five main programme areas of Women's Human Rights, Political Participation, Peace Building, Health Reproductive Rights and Economic Empowerment, the fund pursued a strategy of 'scattering' grants across the continent, with the aim of having at least one grantee in each African country. There was a strong feeling within the organization that without a grant in each country it could not make any claim to being an 'African fund' which spoke with authority on behalf of Africa's women.

It is arguable that spreading many, quite small grants to small women's organizations over such a huge region may not have been the most strategic approach in terms of impact, particularly for a fund interested in fundamental social change. At the same time, however, it is important not to overlook the context in which the new fund was operating. As a grantmaking public foundation, AWDF represented a new and unfamiliar type of philanthropic institution in Africa, in a funding landscape where grantmakers are usually foreign (or foreign-appointed intermediaries), and where grants are usually large and therefore only available to a handful of strong women's organizations. In reality, of course, AWDF was at this stage funded almost entirely by international donors, but by investing heavily in building contacts in individual countries, and reaching out to grassroots as well as more established organizations, it was marking a departure from the traditional funding habits of international donors, and carving out its own grantmaking identity. Scattering grants was an important first step in creating awareness of the new fund among women's organizations in many countries and recognition of the work that they did, often quietly and in relative isolation in their local context. It also sent a powerful message about the nature of the African women's movement, the heart of which was not only with articulate, middle-class activists but also down on the ground at the grassroots level, in the work that women's organizations were engaged in in individual communities across the continent. Making grants to women's organizations in many places in Africa was an important first step in the process of movement building and raising awareness, in creating and strengthening national and international networks, and in encouraging women to locate their work within a much broader context which lay beyond their own immediate sets of circumstances.

No doubt, over time AWDF will increasingly deploy more of the strategies associated with 'change-making' grantmakers in certain areas of its work, such as proactively seeking grantees rather than making calls for applications, making fewer, larger and more strategic grants and funding 'clusters' of grants, as well as funding new, untested, initiatives.[11] Indeed, evidence of this new direction can already be seen in some of its more recent grants, such as seed funding to the Society for Women and AIDS in Africa to establish a new regional office.

However, for a number of reasons it seems unlikely that AWDF would entirely move away from its more mainstream grantmaking portfolio, particularly the grants that provide economic opportunities for African women and which constitute approximately one third of AWDF's total grants.[12] Firstly, as is discussed below, grants that provide economic opportunities for women (usually in a very tangible way, such as through the purchase of equipment or materials) have a particular appeal to certain types of individual and corporate donors who want to see the physical results of their contributions and therefore have an important role to play in the development of a culture of organized philanthropy in Africa. Secondly, although such grants might not perhaps conform to notions of social justice grantmaking in the United States or Europe, which tend to focus on specific strategies and outcomes and are quite distinct from the broader field of charitable giving, they are not without a change-making role altogether.[13] In the African context, the field of local grantmakers and philanthropic institutions is sparsely populated and there are in fact few alternatives – traditional or strategic – to the kind of funding that AWDF is able to make available to women's organizations through its economic empowerment programme. Grants that provide economic opportunities for women are consistent with AWDF's theory of change: they represent an important first step in consciousness-raising by empowering women to take their 'destinies into their own hands'.

Administering a grants programme within Africa can present logistical problems. In many countries banks are weak, methods of communication are poor, distances are far and travel can be difficult. Accessing women's organizations in remote areas, monitoring and evaluating grants and even transferring funds can all pose major challenges to a grantmaker working across the continent.[14] In its relationships with grantees, AWDF casts itself very much as a partner in the women's movement, 'sisters' in the struggle, when it comes to its relationships with grantees. The

culture of trust and of collegiality that AWDF has sought to promote in its dealing with grantees – and which, it must be pointed out, has so far resulted in very
few 'bad grants' – has meant that AWDF has put less emphasis on monitoring the
work of its grantees. Twice, AWDF staff have conducted ambitious and exhaust-
ing monitoring trips across entire regions of the continent, with visits organized
to every grantee: with few grants exceeding US$25,000, and most around the
US$8,000–$10,000 mark, the in-depth monitoring of each grant would not be
cost-effective. Getting out to visit grantees is important from the point of view of
maintaining and developing AWDF's profile within Africa, building relationships
with grantees and gathering information on trends, developments and activities
at the local level which can be fed into its own programming and policy development. This kind of information-gathering exercise is also important from a resource
mobilization perspective: knowledge of the issues and stories of individual grants
are AWDF's main resource when it comes to fundraising. A network of regional
advisers also plays an important role in feeding back information to AWDF by
identifying potential grantees and also acting as mentors to them.

Power dynamics inevitably come into play between any grantmaker and grantee:
as a 'partner' in the African women's movement, AWDF has endeavoured to cast
the funding relationship on a more equal footing in its dealings with its grantees,
and partners' forums, capacity-building workshops and guides to basic project
management, governance and accountability all contribute to a sense of a shared
agenda. It would appear that grantees often feel more comfortable in their dealings
with AWDF than with other funders, seeing them as approachable and accessible,
although this comfort has occasionally bordered on complacency, with grantees
defaulting on their reporting requirements or producing poor quality reports.

Expanding the institutional donor base

As has been discussed above, AWDF was launched with the support of seven key
donor institutions, which provided the necessary start-up funds for it to run its first
rounds of grants and to invest in its own development as an institution. Maintaining independence of mission and its position as an activist grantmaker have been
central pillars of AWDF's philosophy, and so it has always been important to bring
in new donors, both to expand its funding base and to reduce its reliance on any
one particular donor. For donors interested in funding projects in Africa but constrained by financial, logistical – or even informational – constraints, AWDF was
offering a new and easy 'way in' to Africa and access to hundreds of organizations
across the continent. However, reaching out to new donor institutions presented
other challenges: as an institution, AWDF has always avoided the label 'intermediary grantmaker' or 're-granter', and Adeleye-Fayemi has been particularly

vocal on this issue. In her view, re-granting or 'acting as intermediary' describes a function which could be performed by any number of institutions (non-profit or for-profit), charging a management fee for their service. It implies that the agenda (and therefore the power) remains only in the hands of the original donor, who uses the grantmaking 'services' of the intermediary. Although this approach may provide many benefits to donors, and sometimes a healthy management fee to the intermediary grantmaker, it negates the real and fundamental value that African grantmaking institutions can add to the development process, including their depth of knowledge, a greater understanding of context, a permanent rather than project-length institutional presence and, over time, more likelihood of a culture of peer accountability.

In this regard, although AWDF has been aggressively proactive in pursuing new funding opportunities, it has also sought to ensure that its own vision and values provide the framework within which to engage with new donors.

Looking to African donors

Building relationships with donors in Africa has been a much slower process, and it is one in which AWDF will have to make a significant investment if it is to reap the rewards. Local resource mobilization, especially among individuals and local businesses, requires different messages and tools from those used in fundraising from institutions, as well as a significant investment of time and resources. AWDF's small staff and the rapid rate of growth of its grantmaking programmes over a relatively short period have meant that connecting with local donors has not yet been a priority, particularly because, in the short term, it has proved easier and more strategic to access larger amounts of funding from institutional donors.

There are many challenges to building a local donor constituency in Africa, particularly for an organization that works across many countries. The legal and regulatory environment for giving is not favourable in many countries, philanthropic giving to institutions remains relatively undeveloped, and banking systems are weak. And, for the time being at least, despite its continent-wide mandate, AWDF is somewhat limited in its ability to fundraise in other countries apart from Ghana without any local representation. Although institutional donors might be attracted by the idea of a fund that serves an entire continent, the same idea might not resonate instinctively among many potential domestic donors, who may prefer to see the results of their philanthropy in their own countries and communities.

AWDF associates itself strongly with a social justice agenda in its work: in this regard, it is not 'mission neutral'. However, because it is also a public foundation, without its own independent sources of income, AWDF must sometimes walk a tightrope between pursuing a sometimes controversial social justice agenda, and seeking to engage with a broader range of new or would-be supporters. Progressive private international foundations clearly have a role to play in supporting organizations such as AWDF, but there is also a wider question about the degree to which AWDF needs to mobilize support – and resources – from within Africa as a way of legitimizing itself as a truly African foundation.

As a grantmaking foundation, AWDF need not associate itself directly with controversy if it proves more strategic not to (for political reasons, or to avoid alienating new donors who might be sympathetic to certain, if not all, aspects of AWDF's work). As a grantmaker, it can give grants to others that work closer to the ground to engage directly on issues, rather than engage directly and itself. Secondly, it can use other, non-grantmaking tools such as convening different actors around particular issues, or creating funding alliances with international donor partners to add legitimacy to grassroots movements.

The creation of an endowment fund, a campaign for which was launched in 2005 and is still underway, is one way that AWDF will be able to secure its autonomy and both sustainability and flexibility in its programmes. Central to AWDF's long-term strategy for resource mobilization will be its ability to create spaces for diverse groups of donors, while ensuring that its programmes hang together in a coherent and consistent way and that its mission remains uncompromised. Within its programmes, a broad distinction can be made between those that address economic rights, and those that focus on civil and political rights. The small grants programme and economic empowerment grants programmes, for example, tend to focus on developing vocational and management skills and the purchase of equipment and materials for income-generation projects (such as agricultural machinery, vanilla vines). These represent an easier 'sell' to certain kinds of donors drawn to the idea of lives improved through economic change. A number of the grants made through other programmes, however, such as the Political Participation, Women's Human Rights and the Solidarity Fund, address issues for which it might be more difficult to mobilize broad-based support, either because they might be potentially controversial, such as female genital mutilation and other harmful traditional practices, lesbianism etc., or because they do not have tangible outputs (institutional support grants consisting of salaries and rent, or training etc).

There are clearly resources to be tapped in Africa, among the wealthy and middle classes, and for those who have lived, travelled or been educated abroad and had exposure to more organized forms of giving. The sizeable African diaspora, which has represented a largely untapped resource in terms of *organized* or *institutionalized* philanthropic giving (remittances and informal giving aside), constitutes another potentially important donor constituency for an institution like AWDF. Ties that link individuals to individual communities, villages, or ethnic alliances may well have loosened through the experience of living overseas, particularly among second-generation African diaspora, and given way to a broader sense of national or even continental identity.

Looking forward

At the time of writing, AWDF's institutional donor base has expanded to almost 30 institutions, including a grant of US$1 million from a major African donor, the Nelson Mandela Foundation. It has given grants to 400 women's organizations in 41 countries, totalling US$4.2 million.[15] As an institution, AWDF has invested heavily in networking and communications and has been successful in creating a strong profile, particularly at the level of international philanthropy. Its executive director, Bisi Adeleye-Fayemi, has been tireless in her efforts to promote the work of the fund and fundraise for it at international conferences and convenings around the world.

AWDF has come a long way as an organization in a relatively short period, establishing itself as a new and significant kind of player – the African grantmaking fund – on a continent too long dominated by the influence of external funders. Since its creation other African foundations have emerged, such as the Urgent Action Fund for Women and, most recently, TrustAfrica, both of which engage in social justice issues. The arrival of additional players is a healthy development, providing AWDF with important partners and peers on the continent. In the future, AWDF will no doubt continue to change and grow. It is already confronting the issue of regional expansion, and will face an even greater test when it comes to any transition in leadership. But as an established grantmaker, on its way to having its own endowment, the organization is well placed to help raise the voice, and develop the practices of African philanthropy.

Endnotes

1 Time moves on and institutions continue to evolve and, perhaps more significantly in these two cases, grow. The bulk of research and writing of this chapter was conducted in 2004–06 and its main focus is on the origins of both organizations. However, it is worth noting that between 2004 and 2008, KCDF had disbursed over US$4 million to local communities for capacity building and support and, by December 2011, the African Women's Development Fund had awarded over US$19 million to 800 women's rights organisations in 42 African countries and had appointed an Interim Executive Director, Theo Sowa, to lead the organization.

2 The author would like to thank the staff and board (past and present) of KCDF and AWDF for their time and openness in describing and reflecting on the work of their organizations.

3 Transparency International (2001:8).

4 This work was supported by the Ford Foundation Office for East Africa.

5 The Ford Foundation representative in East Africa at the time, Katharine Pearson, was another supportive force behind the creation of KCDF: previously she had been the President of the East Tennessee Foundation in the United States.

6 Despite this ambivalence towards the conventional community foundation model, KCDF certainly benefited from exposure to and involvement in emerging international community philanthropy networks, which tended to promote the community foundation model, including the East Africa Philanthropy Initiative, the African Philanthropy Initiative, Worldwide Initiative on Grantmaker Support (WINGS).

7 The Ford Foundation's Africa Philanthropy Initiative and East Africa Philanthropy Initiative had done much to strengthen a sense of a philanthropic sector in East Africa, bringing together previously disparate types of organizations around issues of local grantmaking and asset development.

8 A role that KCDF has not yet embraced, still preferring to describe the relationship between KCDF and fund-builder as that of grantmaker and grantee (with annual interest release as a 'grant' rather than as income), which suggests some ambiguity over actual ownership of assets in question.

9 Bisi Adeleye-Fayemi, interview, March 2006.

10 AWDF has one French-speaking member of staff and has made a number of grants to French-speaking Africa.

11 Such a strategy is not uncommon among grantmaking institutions in their early stages of development. Before it revised its grantmaking strategy to give fewer, more strategic grants in 2000, the Nelson Mandela Children's Fund in South Africa would give many small grants to hundreds of organizations.

12 Most grants are these.

13 'Social justice philanthropy is the practice of making contributions to non-profit organizations that work for structural change and increase the opportunity of those who are less well-off politically, economically and socially.' (National Committee for Responsible Philanthropy, 2003:6).

14 At the time of writing, project staff were about to set off on a monitoring and evaluation exercise to visit grantees in East and Southern Africa.

15 Information from Bisi Adeleye-Fayemi, March 2007.

REFERENCES

Abdalla, A. and Salim, K., 1996, 'Historia Fupi ya Uislamu Zanzibar' Unpublished paper.

AFD, 2006, 'Migrations and Development: Mutual Benefits? Proceedings of the Fourth AFD-EUDN Conference', Research Department, Paris.

Afigbo, A.E., 1972, *The Warrant Chiefs: Indirect Rule in Southeastern Nigeria, 1891–1929*, Ibadan History Series. New York: Humanities Press.

Africa Progress Panel, 2011, *The Transformative Power of Partnerships: Africa Progress Report*, Geneva.

Aina, T.A., 1993, 'Development Theory and Africa's Lost Decade: Critical Reflections on Africa's Crisis and Current Trends in Development Thinking and Practice' in Von Troll, M. (ed.) *Changing Paradigms in Development – South, East and West: A Meeting of Minds in Africa*, Uppsala: Scandinavian Institute of African Studies.

Aina, T.A., 1997, 'The State and Civil Society: Politics, Government and Social Organization in African Cities' in Rakodi, C. (ed.) *The Urban Challenge in Africa*, Tokyo: United Nations University Press.

Aina, T.A., Chachage, C.S.L., and Annan-Yao, E., 2004, *Globalization and Social Policy in Africa*, Dakar: CODESRIA.

Ake, C., 1988, 'Sustaining Development on the Indigenous'. Paper prepared for the Long-Term Perspectives Study, World Bank, Special Economic Office, Africa Region, SEO AFRCE 0390, Washington, D.C., December, mimeo.

Alexander, J., McGregor, J. and Ranger, T.O., 2000, *Violence and Memory: One Hundred Years in the 'Dark Forests' of Matabeleland*, Oxford, Portsmouth, NH: Heinemann and James Currey.

Alikhan, F., Kyei, P., Mawdsley, E., Porter, G., Townsend, J., Raju, S. and Va, R., 2006, *NGOs and the State in the Twenty-First Century: Ghana and India*, Oxford: International NGO Training and Research Centre.

Allavida, 2005, *East Africa Directory of Grantmakers and Grants Programmes*, Nairobi: Allavida.

Allen, T. and Thomas, A., 2000, *Poverty and Development into the 21st Century*, Revised Ed. Oxford, New York: Open University in association with Oxford University Press.

Alperson, M., 1995, *Foundations for a New Democracy: Corporate Social Investment in South Africa*, Johannesburg: Ravan Press.

Altman, M., 2003, 'The State of Employment and Unemployment in South Africa', in Daniel J., Habib A., and Southall, R. (eds), *The State of the Nation: South Africa 2003–2004,* Cape Town: HSRC Press.

Amoretti, B. S. (ed.), 2001, *Islam in East Africa – New Sources: Archives, manuscripts and written historical sources, oral history, archaeology: International colloquium, Rome, 2–4 December 1999,* Roma: Herder.

An-Na'im, A.A. and Abdel Halim, A.M., 2004, 'Rights-Based Approach to Philanthropy for Social Justice in Islamic Societies'. Paper presented at the Conference on Islamic Philanthropy and Social Justice, Istanbul, September.

Anand, P., 2004, 'Hindu Diaspora and Religious Philanthropy in the United States'. Paper presented at the Sixth International Society for Third Sector Research, Toronto, July.

Anderson, D., 2005, *Histories of the Hanged: The Dirty War in Kenya and the End of Empire,* New York: W.W. Norton.

Anderson, E.S., 1999, 'What Is the Point of Equality?', *Ethics* 109/2.

Andersson, J.A., 2001, 'Mobile Workers, Urban Employment and 'Rural' Identities: Rural–urban networks of Buhera migrants, Zimbabwe' in M. de Bruijn, R. Dijk, D. Foeken, *Mobile Africa: Changing Patterns of Movement in Africa and Beyond,* pp. 89–106.

Andreoni, J., 1990, 'Impure Altruism and Donations to Public Goods: A Theory of Warm-Glow Giving' in *The Economic Journal,* Oxford: Wiley-Blackwell.

Anheier, H., Glasius, M. and Kaldor, M. (eds.), 2004, *Global Civil Society 2004/5,* London: Sage.

Anheier, H. and Toepler, S., 2009, *International Encyclopedia of Civil Society* [online] http://www.springerlink.com/content/j62k806410114239/fulltext.html

Anyang' Nyong'o, P., 1989, 'State and Society in Kenya: The Disintegration of the Nationalist Coalitions and the Rise of Presidential Authoritarianism 1963–1978', *African Affairs* 88/351, 229–51.

Arizpe, L. (ed.), 1998, *UNESCO World Culture Report, 1998: Culture, Creativity, and Markets,* Paris: UNESCO Publications.

Asad, M., 1961, *The Principles of State and Government in Islam,* Berkeley: University of California Press.

Assaa, R.A. and Shaaban, B., 1996, 'Problems of Application of Islamic Law in Tanzania Mainland Courts'. Research paper for the LLB Degree Course, University of Dar es Salaam.

Axelrod, R.M., 1984, *The Evolution of Cooperation,* New York: Basic Books.

Ba, B., V. Dahany, V. Doulou, V., Kassoum, S. and Tapsoba, S., 2000, *La philanthropie, sources de financement alternatives de la recherche en Afrique de l'Ouest et de Centre,* Dakar: IDRC.

Bakari, M.A. and Musa, A., 2004, 'Islamic Philanthropy for Social Justice in Tanzania' Paper presented at the International Conference on Islamic Philanthropy and Social Justice, Istanbul, Turkey, September.

Baraza Kuu, 1993, 'Report by the Supreme Council of Islamic Organizations and Institutions of Tanzania'. Dar es Salaam: Baraza Kuu.

Barry, B., 2005, *Why Social Justice Matters. Themes for the 21st Century,* Oxford: Polity.

Barry, J.W. and Manno, B.V. (eds.), 1997, *Giving Better, Giving Smarter,* Washington, DC: National Commission on Philanthropy and Civic Renewal.

Bauer, P.T., 1981, *Equality, the Third World, and Economic Delusion* Cambridge, Mass: Harvard University Press.

Bebbington, A., 2006, *The Search for Empowerment: Social Capital as Idea and Practice at the World Bank*, Bloomfield, CT: Kumarian Press.

Berking, H., and Camiller, P., 1999, *Sociology of Giving. Theory, Culture and Society,* London, Thousand Oaks, CA: Sage.

Berresford, S., 2003, 'Social Justice Philanthropy and U.S. Political Traditions Remarks at the Woodrow Wilson international Centre for Scholars', Washington DC, June 19.

Bloch, A., 2005, 'The Development Potential of Zimbabweans in the Diaspora' No. 17 IOM Migration Research Series.

Bocock, R.J., 1971, 'The Ismailis in Tanzania: A Weberian Analysis', *British Journal of Sociology* 22/412.

Bonbright, D., 1992, 'An Overview of the Sources of Giving in South Africa', Johannesburg, Development Resources Centre.

Bourdieu, P., 2000, *Les Structures sociales de l'économie.* Collection 'liber'. Paris: Seuil.

Bourdillon, M.F.C., 1987, *The Shona Peoples: An Ethnography of the Contemporary Shona, with Special Reference to Their Religion.* Shona Heritage Series Third Revised Ed. Vol. 1, Gweru Zimbabwe: Mambo Press.

Bowers, A., 1971, 'Towards an Understanding of Islam', *African Ecclesiastical Review* 13/4.

Bracking, S. and Sachikonye, L., 2008, 'Remittances, Poverty Reduction and the Informalisation of Household Wellbeing in Zimbabwe'. Paper presented at Living on the Margins Conference, Stellenbosch, South Africa.

Bradley, T., 2005, 'Does Compassion Bring Results? A Critical Perspective on Faith and Development', *Culture and Religion* 6/3.

Braverman, M.T., Constantine, N. and Slater, J.K., 2004, *Foundations and Evaluation: Contexts and Practices for Effective Philanthropy,* San Francisco: Jossey-Bass.

Brighouse, H., 2004, *Justice. Key Concepts,* Cambridge, Malden, MA: Polity.

Broch-Due, V., 2005, *Violence and Belonging: The Quest for Identity in Post-Colonial Africa,* London, New York: Routledge.

Brown, R.M., 1993, *Liberation Theology: An Introductory Guide* , Westminister: John Knox Press.

Bruneau, M. (ed.), 1995, *Les Diasporas,* Montpellier: Reclus.

Buchanan, R. and Booker, J., 2007, *Making a Difference in Africa: Advice from Experienced Grant makers* New York: Council of Foundations and Africa Grant makers' Affinity Group.

Burkeman, S., 1999, 'An Unsatisfactory Company?' Transcript of the Allen Lane Lecture www.allenlane.org.uk/lecturesregform/1999.htm

Burkeman, S., 2004, 'Foundations, the State and Social Justice'. Paper presented at Synergos 2004 Global Senior Fellows Meeting, Building Assets for Social Justice, Manila, Philippines.

Cannon, L., 1999, *Life Beyond Aid: Twenty Strategies to Help Make NGOs Sustainable,* Johannesburg: Initiative for Participatory Development, Development Resources Centre and INTERFUND.

Carmichael, W.D., 1996, 'Transforming Southern Africa: An Overview of American Support for Southern Africa's Development'. A report to the Southern Africa Grantmakers Affinity Group.

Carson, E., 2002, 'Community Foundations at the Crossroads: Social Agents or Charitable Bankers?'. Keynote Address at the Community Foundations of Canada 2002 National Conference.

Carson, E., 2003, 'Reflections on Foundations and Social Justice'. Presented at the Synergos 2003 Global Senior Fellows Meeting, Foundations and Social Justice, Oaxaca City, Mexico. Available: www.synergos.org/knowledge/philanthropyissues [25 March 2007].

Center for Global Prosperity, 2011, *The Index of Global Philanthropy and Remittances,* Washington DC: The Hudson Institute.

Chachage, C.S.L. and Mbilinyi, M.(eds.), 2003, *Against Neo Liberalism: Gender, Democracy and Development,* Dar es Salaam: TGNP and E&D Ltd.

Chaligha, A.E., 2006, 'Perceptions of Public Servants on the Provision of Employment in Tanzania' in Mukandala, R., Yahya-Othman, S., Mushi, S.S. and Ndumbaro, J. (eds.), 2006, *Justice, Rights and Worship: Religion and Politics in Tanzania,* Dar es Salaam: E&D Publishers.

Chandhoke, N., 2007, 'Civil Society', *Development in Practice* 17/4/5.

Cheal, D.J., 1988, *The Gift Economy,* London, New York: Routledge.

Cheng, W. and Mohamed, S., 2010, *The World That Changes the World,* Hoboken: John Wiley & Sons.

Chetty, I. and Maharaj, B., 2011, 'Christian Social Giving in South Africa', *Man in India* 91/1.

Chetsanga, C.J. & Muchenje, T.B., 2003, *An Analysis of the Cause and Effect of Brain Drain in Zimbabwe.* Harare: Scientific and Industrial Research and Development Centre.

Chikezie, C.E., 2005, 'Accountability, Africa and her Diaspora' *openDemocracy,* www.opendemocracy.net/globalization-accountability/africa_2869.jsp

Chikezie, C.E., 2007, 'Strategies for Building Diaspora/Migrant Organization Capacity for Development'. Paper presented at the Global Forum on Migration and Development, Civil Society Day, Brussels, Belgium.

Christopher, R.C., 1983, *The Japanese Mind,* Ballantine Books. New York: Fawcett Columbine.

Clark, D.A., 2005, 'Sen's Capability Approach and the Many Spaces of Human Well-Being', *Journal of Development Studies* 41/8.

Clark, J., 1992, 'Democratising Development: NGOs and the State', *Development in Practice* 2/3.

Clarke, P.B., 1976, 'The Ismailis: A Study of Community', *British Journal of Sociology* 27/4.

Clayton, M. and Williams, A., 2004, *Social Justice. Blackwell Readings in Philosophy Vol. 14,* Malden, MA: Blackwell.

Clotfelter, C.T., 1992, *Who Benefits from the Nonprofit Sector?*, Chicago: Univ. of Chicago Press.

Cohen, J.L. and Arato, A., 1994, *Civil Society and Political Theory. Studies in Contemporary German Social Thought*, Cambridge, Mass.: MIT Press.

Cohen, R., 1997, *Global Diasporas: An Introduction. Global Diasporas. Vol. 1*, Seattle: University of Washington Press.

Coleman, J.S. with Court, D., 1993, *University Development in the Third World, The Rockefeller Foundation Experience*, Oxford: Pergamon Press.

Community Foundations of Canada, 2004, The Social Justice Spectrum. Seeing our work through a social justice lens: A perspective for community foundations. http://www.cfc-fcc.ca/link_docs/SpectrumNov2004 [22 April 2007].

Copeland-Carson, J., 2004, *Creating Africa in America: Translocal Identity in an Emerging World City. Contemporary Ethnography* Philadelphia: University of Pennsylvania Press.

Corbin, J.M. and Strauss, A.L., 2008, *Basics of Qualitative Research Techniques and Procedures for Developing Grounded Theory.* Third Edition. Thousand Oaks, CA: Sage Publications.

Cowen, M. and Shenton, R.W., 1996, *Doctrines of Development,* London, New York: Routledge.

Craig, G., 2005, 'Delivering Social Justice Through Philanthropy', *Alliance,* London: Alliance.

Criss, K.P., 2006, *Donors Ourselves: Rural Development Philanthropy from East Tennessee to East Africa and Beyond* Whitesburg, Kentucky: The Center for Rural Strategies.

Crowder, M., 1968, *West Africa, Under Colonial Rule,* Evanston Ill.: Northwestern Univ. Press.

Crush, J.S., Jeeves, A. and Yudelman, D., 1991, *South Africa's Labor Empire: A History of Black Migrancy to the Gold Mines*. African Modernization and Development Series Boulder: Westview Press.

CSI Handbook (various editions) Cape Town, Johannesburg: Trialogue.

Cunnan, P. and Maharaj, B., 2000, 'Against the Odds: Health Care in an Informal Settlement in Durban', *Development Southern Africa* 17/5.

Dalberg Global Development Advisers, 2011, *Impact Investing in West Africa,* Dalberg: New York.

Dangarembga, T., 1988, *Nervous Conditions,* London: Women's Press.

Dangarembga, T., 2006, *The Book of Not,* Oxford: Ayebia Clarke.

Daniel J., Habib, A. and Southall, R., 2004, *State of the Nation: South Africa 2003–2004,* Cape Town: Human Sciences Research Council Press.

Davidson, B., 1964, *Which Way Africa? The Search for a New Society. Penguin African Library,* Harmondsworth: Penguin.

Davis, D. and Mokgatle, D., 1993, 'Tax Status of NGOs'. Part of the Independent Study into an Enabling Environment for NGOs. Johannesburg: Development Resources Centre.

De Bruijn, M., van Dijk, R. and. Foeken, D., 2001, *Mobile Africa: Changing Patterns of Movement in Africa and Beyond African Dynamics. Vol. 1,* Leiden, Boston: Brill.

De Jong, F., 1999, 'Trajectories of a Mask Performance: The Case of the Senegalese Kumpo (itinéraires des spectacles de masques. À propos des masques kumpo sénégalais)', *Cahiers d'Études Africaines* 39/153.

Deeney, J., 2002. 'A Neglected Minority in a Neglected Field: The emerging role of Chinese-American philanthropy in US-China relations' in M.E. Sharpe, *The Expanding Roles of Chinese Americans in US–China Relations*, New York: Armonk.

Defourny, J., Develtere, P. and Fonteneau, B. (eds.), 1999, *Sociale Economie in Noord and Zuid: Realiteit en Beleid*. [*Social Economy in North and South: Reality and Policy*] Leuven: Garant.

Dekker, P. and Halman, L., 2003, *The Values of Volunteering: Cross-Cultural Perspectives. Nonprofit and Civil Society Studies*, New York: Kluwer Academic/Plenum Publishers.

Deneulin, S. and McGregor, J.A., 2010, 'The Capability Approach and the Politics of a Social Conception of Wellbeing', *European Journal of Social Theory* 13/4.

Desai, A., 2002, *We Are the Poors: Community Struggles in Post-Apartheid South Africa,* New York: Monthly Review Press.

Desai V. and Potter R. (eds.), 2008, *The Companion to Development Studies,* London: Arnold.

Dixon, J. and Scheurell, R.P., 2002, *The State of Social Welfare: The Twentieth Century in Cross-National Review,* Westport, Conn.: Praeger.

Donati, P., 2003, 'Giving and Social Relations: The Culture of Free Giving and its Differentiation Today', *International Review of Sociology* 13/2.

Dunbar, Roberta Ann, 2000, 'Muslim Women in African History' in Nehemia Levtzion and Randall Pouwels (eds.) *The History of Islam in Africa,* Athens: Ohio university Press; Oxford: James Currey; Cape Town: David Philip.

Dundes, A., 1965, *The Study of Folklore,* Englewood Cliffs, N.J.: Prentice-Hall.

Dzingirai, V., 2000, 'Saving to Death: A Study of Group Based and Other Saving Arrangements in Rural Chivi District, Zimbabwe'. A report prepared for the Food and Agriculture Organization, August 2000 http://www.fao.org/sd/PPdirect/PPre0071g.htm.

Dzingirai, V., 2007, 'The Role of Kinship in Displacement'. Paper prepared for the Lives for Transformation and Development Workshop, Nordiska Afrika Institute and Centre for Rural Development, Wild Geese Lodge, Harare, 28–29 June 2007.

Eade, D. (ed.), 2002, *Development and Culture,* Oxford: Oxfam.

Edwards, M., 2008, *Just Another Emperor? The Myths and Realities of Philanthrocapitalism,* London: Young Foundation. www.justanotheremporer.org

Edwards, M., 2011, 'The Role and Limitations of Philanthropy.' Paper Commissioned for the Bellagio Initiative on the Future of Philanthropy and Development in Pursuit of Human Wellbeing. Copyright Institute of Development Studies (IDS), the Resource Alliance and Rockefeller Foundation, New York.

Eilinghoff, D. (ed.), 2005, *Rethinking Philanthropic Effectiveness : Lessons from an International Network of Foundation Experts,* Gütersloh: Verlag Bertelsmann Stiftung.

Ekeh, P.P., 1975, 'Colonialism and the Two Publics in Africa: A Theoretical Statement', *Comparative Studies in Society and History* 17/1.

Ekeh, P., 1994, 'The Public Realm and Public Finance in Africa' in Himmelstrand, U., Kiyanjui, Kand Mburugu, E.(eds.) *African Perspectives on Development,* London, James Currey.

Elkins, C., 2005, *Britain's Gulag: The Brutal End of Empire in Kenya,* London, Jonathan Cape.

Emdon, E., Mgoqi W. and Rosenthal R., 1993, 'Establishment, Registration and Administration of NGOs' (part of the Independent Study into an Enabling Environment for NGOs), Johannesburg: Development Resources Center.

Emmerij, L., Jolly, R. and Weiss, T. G., 2001, *Ahead of the Curve? UN Ideas and Global Challenges* Bloomington, Indiana University Press.

Everatt, D. and Solanki, G.A., 2004, *A Nation of Givers? Social Giving Among South Africans,* Strategy and Tactics. The full survey report and supporting data is available on the Centre for Civil Society website at www.ukzn/ccs.

Everatt, D., Habib, A., Maharaj, B. and Nyar, A., 2005, 'Patterns of Giving in South Africa', *Voluntas: International Journal of Voluntary and Nonprofit Organizations* 16/3.

Everatt, D. and Solanki, G.A., 2005, 'A Nation of Givers? Social Giving Among South Africans'. The State of Social Giving in South Africa Series No. 1. Natal: Centre for Civil Society, University of KwaZulu Natal.

Evers, A. and Laville, J-L., 2004, *The Third Sector in Europe,* Cheltenham, UK; Northampton, MA: Edward Elgar.

Ewing, D., 2006, 'Understanding Private Foreign Giving in South Africa', *The State of Social Giving in South Africa Report Series, No. 6.* Natal: Centre for Civil Society, University of KwaZulu Natal.

Farouk, F. and Prytz, M., 2003, 'The Pulse of Online Fundraising in South Africa: Lessons and Challenges'. Paper prepared for the Charities Aid Foundation – Southern Africa and the Southern African NGO Network (SANGONetT) Thusanang Project.

Favis, M., 2005, 'The State of Giving in the South African Jewish Community', Natal: Centre for Civil Society, University of KwaZulu Natal.

Fehr, E., Fischbacher, U. and Gächter, S., 2002, 'Strong Reciprocity, Human Cooperation, and the Enforcement of Social Norms', *Human Nature: An Interdisciplinary Biosocial Perspective* 131 Michigan: Population Studies Center.

Feierman, S., 1998, 'Reciprocity and Assistance in Pre-Colonial Africa' in Ilchman, W.F., Katz, S.N. and Queen E.L. (eds), *Philanthropy in the World's Traditions* Bloomington: Indiana University Press.

Feurt, S. 2000. *Building a New South Africa Through Community Philanthropy and Community Development.* Brussels, Belgium: Charles Stewart Mott Foundation.

Fig, D., 2007, *Staking Their Claims: Corporate Social and Environmental Responsibility in South Africa* Natal: University of Natal Press.

Finnegan, R.H., 1977, *Oral Poetry: Its Nature, Significance and Social Context,* London: Cambridge University Press.

Finnegan, R.H., 1976, 1970, 1994, *Oral Literature in Africa. Oxford Library of African Literature,* Nairobi, Dar es Salaam: Oxford University Press.

Fleishman, J.L., 2007, *The Foundation: A Great American Secret: How Private Wealth Is Changing the World* New York: The Perseus Books Group.

Fortes, M. and Evans-Pritchard, E.E., 1970, *African Political Systems,* London, New York: Published for the International African Institute by Oxford University Press.

Fowler, A., 2001, 'Social Economy in the South: A Civil Society Perspective' *Proceedings of a Seminar on Social Economy in the South,* University of Leuven.

Friedman, S., Hudson, J. and Mackay, S., 2005, 'The Colour of Giving: Racial Identity and Corporate Social Investment', Natal: Centre for Civil Society, Univ. of KwaZulu Natal.

Fukuda-Parr, S., 2004, 'The Millennium Development Goals: The Pledge of World Leaders to End Poverty Will Not Be Met with Business as Usual', *Journal of International Development* Oxford: Wiley-Blackwell.

Fyfe, N.R. and Milligan, C., 2003, 'Out of the Shadows: Exploring Contemporary Geographies of Voluntarism', *Progress in Human Geography* 27/4.

Fynn, J.K., 1971, *Asante and Its Neighbours, 1700–1807. Legon History Series,* Evanston, IL, Harlow: Longman.

Galvin, M., 2000, 'Nothing to Lose But Our Chains', *OD Debate* 7/5.

Gariyo, Z., 1996, 'NGOs and Development in East Africa: A View from Below' in Edwards, M. and Hulme, D. (eds.) *Beyond the Magic Bullet* West Hartford, CT: Kumarian Press.

Geiger, S., 1997, *TANU Women: Gender and Culture in the Making of Tanganyikan Nationalism, 1955–1965. Social History of Africa Series* Portsmouth, NH, Oxford: Heinemann.

Geldenhuys, H., 2006, 'Church Slams Door On Women Leaders' *Sunday Times*, 15 January.

Gemelli, G. (ed), 2007, *Religions and Philanthropy: Global Issues in Historical Perspective. Part of the Master in International Studies in Philanthropy and Social Entrepreneurship Series.* Bologna, Italy: Baskerville Publishers Collana UniPress.

Ghai, D., 2008, 'UN Contributions to Development Thinking and Practice', *Development In Practice* 18/6 London: Routledge.

Ghai, D. P. and Ghai, Y.P., 1970, *Portrait of a Minority: Asians in East Africa.* Revised Ed. Nairobi: Oxford University Press.

Ghai, Y.P. and Ghai, D.P., 1971, *The Asian Minorities of East and Central* Africa. Minority Rights Group Report. Vol. 4 London: Minority Rights Group.

Gibbon, P., 1995, *Markets, Civil Society and Democracy in Kenya,* Uppsala: Nordiska Afrikainstitutet.

Gimode, E., 2004, 'Globalization, Islam and Social Policy in Kenya' in Aina, T. A., Chachage, S.L.C. and Annan-Yao, E. (eds.) *Globalization and Social Policy in Africa,* Dakar: CODESRIA.

Girard, L.F., B. Forte, B., Cerreta, M., De Toro, P. and Forte F. (eds.), 2003, *The Human Sustainable City: Challenges and Perspectives from the Habitat Agenda,* Hants, England: Ashgate.

Global Giving Matters, Issue 8, 2002, edited by Synergos/World Economic Forum.

Godwin, P., 1984, 'Whose Kith and Kin Now' *London Sunday Times Magazine*, 25 March.

Goldberg, A., 2003, 'Social Change Philanthropy and How to Do It' in *Trust and Foundation News*.

Goliber, T., 2004, 'Zimbabwe's Political and Economic Problems Hinder Effective Response to AIDS' Population Research Bureau website.

Gordon, A., 1993, 'Draft Report of the Bellagio Seminar on Strengthening Local Philanthropy, 20–22 April 1993', Prepared for Rockefeller Foundation, New York.

Gready, P. and Ensor, J. (eds.), 2005, *Reinventing Development? Translating Rights-Based Approaches From Theory Into Practice* London, New York: Zed Books.

Greer, C. and Knight, B., 2005, 'Social Justice Philanthropy: Introducing the Series' *Alliance Extra*, December, London: Alliance Publishing Trust.

Greer, C. and Knight, B., 2006, 'Social Justice Philanthropy: Roots and Prospects' *Alliance Extra* March London: Alliance Publishing Trust.

Gregory, R.G., 1992, *The Rise and Fall of Philanthropy in East Africa: The Asian Contribution.* New Brunswick, NJ: Transaction Publishers.

Groenewald, Y., 2004, 'A Little Goes a Long Way', *Weekly Mail and Guardian*, Investing in Life Insert, 6–12 August.

Grubb, E., 1917, In Hastings, J. (ed.) *Encyclopedia of Religious Ethics Volume IX – Munda – Phrygians* New York: Charles Scribner's Sons.

Guillot, H., 1980, *Ce qu'il ne faut pas oublier – Des grands écrivains des XVIIIe et XIXe siècles* Paris: Foucher.

Gumede, W.M., 2005, *Thabo Mbeki and the Battle for the Soul of the ANC,* London, Cape Town: Zebra Press.

Habib, A. and Kotze, H., 2003, 'Civil Society, Governance and Development in an Era of Globalisation', Natal: Centre for Civil Society, University of KwaZulu Natal.

Habib, A. and Maharaj, B. (eds.), 2008, *Giving and Solidarity: Resource Flows for Poverty Alleviation and Development in South Africa,* Cape Town: HSRC.

Hall, P.D., 2006, 'A Historical Overview of Philanthropy, Voluntary Associations and Nonprofit Organizations in the United States, 1600–2000' in Powell, W. W. and Steinberg, R. (eds.) *The Non-Profit Sector: A Research Handbook* New Haven, Yale University Press.

Haniff, G., 1992, 'Muslim Development at Risk – the Crisis of Human Resources', *American Journal of Islamic Social Sciences* 9/4.

Harbison, F.H., 1973, *Human Resources as the Wealth of Nations. Economic Development Series,* New York: Oxford University Press.

Harris, C., 2003, 'The Social Justice Gap', Ford Foundation Report.

Harrison, A.O., Stewart, R., Myambo, K., and Teveraishe, C., 1997, 'Social Networks Among Early Adolescent Zimbabweans in Extended Families', *Journal of Research on Adolescence* 7/2.

Hasan, S., 2007, *Philanthropy and Social Justice in Islam: Principles, Potentials and Practices,* Kuala Lumpur: A.S. Noordeen.

Haysom, N., Cachalia, F. and Molahlehi, E., 1993, 'Civil society and Fundamental Freedoms', Part of the *Independent Study into an Enabling Environment for NGOs,* Johannesburg: Development Resources Centre.

Heller, J., 2003, 'Is there a will?' *Alliance* 8/3 London: Alliance Publishing Trust.

Heller, J. and Winder, D., 2002, 'Pathways Towards Justice: International Working Group Report on Social Justice Philanthropy Meeting Report and Proceedings' http://www.synergos.org/knowledge/philanthropyissues [22 April 2007].

Henrich, J., Boyd, R., Bowles, S., Camerer, C., Fehr, E., Gintis, H., McElreath, R., et al., 2005, '"Economic Man" in Cross-Cultural Perspective: Behavioral Experiments in 15 Small-Scale Societies', *Behavioral and Brain Sciences* 28/6.

Herriot, P., 1970, *An Introduction to the Psychology of Language. Methuen's Manuals of Modern Psychology,* London: Methuen.

Higazi, A., 2005, *Ghana Country Study: A part of the Report on informal Remittance Systems in Africa, Caribbean and Pacific (ACP) Countries,* Oxford: ESRC Centre on Migration, Policy and Society.

Himmelstrand, U., Kinyanjui, K. and Mburugu, E.K., 1994, *African Perspectives on Development: Controversies, Dilemmas and Openings,* Nairobi, Dar Es Salaam: East African Publishing House.

Hochschild, A., 1998, *King Leopold's Ghost: A Story of Greed, Terror, and Heroism in Colonial Africa,* Boston: Houghton Mifflin.

Holleman, J.F. and University of Zambia, 1969, 1952, *Shona Customary Law, with Reference to Kinship, Marriage, the Family and the Estate.* Manchester: published on behalf of the Institute of Social Research, University of Zambia by Manchester University Press.

Hollingsworth, L.W., 1960, *The Asians of East Africa,* London, New York: Macmillan.

Holloway, R., 2001, *Towards Financial Self-reliance: A Handbook on Resource Mobilization for Civil Society Organizations in the South* London: Earthscan Publications.

Honey M., 2000, 'New Tax Law for South African NPOs'. Unpublished paper prepared for the NPO Legal Support Project of the Legal Resources Centre, Johannesburg.

Hooper-Box, C., 2005, 'Throwing the Bones at Mont Fleur', *The Sunday Independent* 15 May.

Horton, M., 1987, 'The Swahili Corridor', *Scientific American* 257/3.

Hovanessian M., 1998, 'La notion de diaspora. Usage et champ sémantique', *Le Journal des Anthropologues,* 72/3 Paris: l'Assocation Française des Anthropologues.

Hudson Institute, 2007, *The Index of Global Philanthropy,* Washington DC: The Center for Global Prosperity, The Hudson Institute. www.global-prosperity.org.

Hudson Institute, 2008, *The Index of Global Philanthropy,* Washington DC: The Center for Global Prosperity, The Hudson Institute www.global-prosperity.org.

Howell, J. and Pearce, J., 2001, *Civil Society and Development: A Critical Exploration* Boulder, Colo.: Lynne Rienner Publishers.

Hulme, D. and Edwards, M., 1997, *NGOs, States and Donors: Too Close for Comfort?* International Political Economy Series, New York: St. Martin's Press and Save the Children.

Hyden, Goran, 1983, *No Shortcuts to Progress.* London, Heinemann Educational.

Ilchman, W.F., Katz, S.N. and Queen, E.L., 1998, *Philanthropy in the World's Traditions. Philanthropic Studies,* Bloomington: Indiana University Press.

Iliffe, J., 1987, *The African Poor: A History. African Studies Series. Vol. 58,* Cambridge, New York: Cambridge University Press.

Iliffe, J. and American Council of Learned Societies, 1979, *A Modern History of Tanganyika. African Studies Series. Vol. 25,* Cambridge, New York: Cambridge University Press.

Index of Global Philanthropy and Remittances, 2011, http://rmportal.net/library/content/2011-index-of-global-philanthropy-and-remittances-may-2011/at_download/file

International Organisation for Migration, 2003, *Mobility and HIV/AIDS in Southern Africa: A field study in South Africa, Zimbabwe and Mozambique.* www.iom.org.za/Reports/MobilityHIVAIDSReport.pdf

International Organization for Migration, 2005, *World Migration Report* Geneva: IOM.

Iqbal, M. (ed.), 1986, *Distributive Justice and Need Fulfillment in an Islamic Economy*. Islamic Economic Series, Islamabad: IIIE.

Isaacman, A. and Isaacman, B., 1977, 'Resistance and Collaboration in Southern and Central Africa', *International Journal of African Historical Studies 10/1* Boston: African Studies Centre.

Jefferson Murphy, E., 1976, *Creative Philanthropy, Carnegie Corporation and Africa 1953–1973*, New York: Teachers College Press, Columbia University.

Johnson, B. and Sedaca, S., 2004, 'Diasporas, Emigrants and Development: Economic Linkages and Programmatic Responses'. Study conducted for the US Agency for International Development (USAID) Trade Enhancement for the Services Sector (TESS) project.

Johnson, P.D. , Johnson, S.P., and Kingman, A., 2005, 'Promoting Philanthropy: Global Challenges and Approaches' in Eilinghoff, D. (ed.), *Rethinking Philanthropic Effectiveness : Lessons from an International Network of Foundation Experts*, Gütersloh: Verlag Bertelsmann Stiftung.

Johnson, P.D., 2007, *'Diaspora Philanthropy: Influences, Initiatives and Issues' Research Report* sponsored by The Philanthropic Initiative, Inc and The Global Equity Initiative, Harvard University.

Jumah, M., 1999, 'The National UNV Scheme: A Little But Good Solution to Employment Crisis in Kenya' in *UNV Kenya News Bulletin* Issue 2.

Jumbe, A., 1994, *The Partnership: Tanganyika – Zanzibar Union, 30 Turbulent Years*, Dar es Salaam: Amana Publishers.

Kaarsholm, P., 1997, 'Inventions, Imaginings, Codifications: Authorising Versions of Ndebele Cultural Tradition', *Journal of Southern African Studies 23/2*.

Kaldor, M., 2003, *Global Civil Society: An Answer to War*, Cambridge, Malden, MA: Polity Press.

Kanyinga, K., 1995, 'The Changing Development Space in Kenya: Socio-Political Change and Voluntary Development Activities' in Gibbon, P. (ed.) *Markets, Civil Society and Democracy in Kenya*, Uppsala: Nordic Africa Institute.

Kanyinga, K., 1999, *Kenya Component of the Johns Hopkins Comparative NonProfit Sector Project: Historical Background*, Nairobi: University of Nairobi Institute of Development Studies.

Kaseke, E., 2006, 'The Revival of Zunde raMambo in Zimbabwe', *Focus 2/1* Emmarentia: VOSESA South Africa.

Kauffman, K.D. and Lindauer. D.L., 2004, *AIDS and South Africa: The Social Expression of a Pandemic*, Basingstoke, New York: Palgrave Macmillan.

Kay, A., 2006, 'Social Capital, the Social Economy and Community Development', *Community Development Journal* 41/2.

Kenya Community Development Foundation, 2001, *Report of the Pilot Phase of a Survey on Corporate Philanthropy in Kenya*.

Khan, S., 2005, 'The State of Social Giving Amongst Muslims in South Africa', Natal: Centre for Civil Society, University of KwaZulu Natal.

Kihato, C., 2001, *Shifting Sands: the Relationship Between Foreign Donors and South African Civil Society During and After Apartheid. Social Policy* Series Report No. 86, Johannesburg: Centre for Policy Studies.

Kingman, A. and Ngondi-Houghton, C., 2004, 'The Challenge of Philanthropy in East Africa'. Paper prepared for a Ford Foundation Retreat, Jinja, Uganda.

Kingman, A. and Edwards, J., 2006, 'Who's Afraid of Mutual Aid?', *Alliance* 11/1 London: Alliance Publishing Trust.

Kiondo, A.S.Z. and Nyang'oro, J.E., 2006, *Civil Society and Democratic Development in Tanzania,* Harare: MWENGO/ Prestige Books.

Koehn, P.H. and Yin, X-H., 2002, *The Expanding Roles of Chinese Americans in U.S.–China Relations: Transnational Networks and Trans-Pacific Interactions,* Armonk, NY: M.E. Sharpe.

Komter, A.E., 2005, *Social Solidarity and the Gift,* Cambridge, New York: Cambridge University Press.

Kotze, H., 2003, 'Responding to the Growing Socio-Economic Crisis? A Review of Civil Society in South Africa', *Development Update: an Annual Review* 4/4 INTERFUND.

Kraak, G., 2000, 'Tracking Trends in Donor Funding', *OD Debate* 7/5.

Krishna, A., 2002, *Active Social Capital: Tracing the Roots of Development and Democracy,* New York: Columbia University Press.

Kritzeck, J., Lewis, W.H. and Spencer Trimingham, J., 1969, *Islam in Africa,* New York: Van Nostrand-Reinhold.

Kuhlase, F., 2004, 'Industrial Development Corporation: Foundation Fund'.

Kuljian, C., 2001, 'Tax Incentives and Individual Giving' Paper presented at the Conference on Tax and the Nonprofit Sector, The Non-Profit Partnership.

Kuljian, C., 2003, 'Global Models, Local Realities: The Community Foundation Model in South Africa'. Paper presented at the Kellogg Conference on Community Mobilization'.

Kuljian, C., 2005, 'Social Justice Not High on the Agenda: Corporate Social Investment in South Africa' *Alliance* 10/2 London: Alliance Publishing Trust.

Kuljian, C., 2005, 'Why Did Interfund Close?' *Alliance Extra,* London: Alliance Publishing Trust.

Kuljian, C., 2005, 'Philanthropy and Equity: the Case of South Africa'. Paper commissioned by the Harvard University Global Equity Initiative.

Kumar, S., 2003, 'Development and Religion: Cultivating a Sense of the Sacred', *Development* 46/4.

Kuperus, T., 1999, 'Building Democracy: An Examination of Religious Associations in South Africa and Zimbabwe *Journal of Modern African Studies* 37/4.

Lambert, M.C., 2002, *Longing for Exile: Migration and the Making of a Translocal Community in Senegal, West Africa,* Oxford, Portsmouth, NH: Heinemann.

Landau, L., 2007, 'Drowning in numbers'. Paper presented at Workshop on Migration from Zimbabwe. Johannesburg: Centre for Development Enterprise.

Lawrence, S. (ed.), 2005, *Social Justice Grantmaking: A Report on Foundation Trend,* New York: The Foundation Center.

Lee, R., 1990, *Guide to Chinese American Philanthropy and Charitable Giving Patterns,* California: Pathway Press.

Levtzion, N. and Pouwels, R.L., 2000, *The History of Islam in Africa,* Athens OH, Oxford: Ohio University Press.

Liberty Hill Foundation, 2005, 'Insights & Lessons from 30 years of Building Social Justice Philanthropy in Los Angeles'. http://www.libertyhill.org/common [22 April 2007].

Lihamba, A., 2007, *Women Writing Africa.* The Women Writing Africa Project. Vol. 3, New York: The Feminist Press at the City University of New York.

Lin, N., 1999, 'Social networks and Status Attainment' *Annual Review of Sociology* 25 Palo Alto CA: Annual Reviews.

Lin, N., 2001, *Social Capital: A Theory of Social Structure and Action. Structural Analysis in the Social Sciences,* 19 London, New York: Cambridge University Press.

Little, K.L., 1965, *West African Urbanization: A Study of Voluntary Associations in Social Change,* Cambridge: Cambridge University Press.

Liviga, Athumani and Zubeda Tumbo-Masabo, 2006, 'Muslims in Tanzania: Quest for an Equal Footing' in Mukandala, R., Yahya-Othman, S., Mushi, S.S. and Ndumbaro, J. (eds.), 2006, *Justice, Rights and Worship: Religion and Politics in Tanzania,* Dar es Salaam: E&D Publishers.

Lodhi, A. Y. and Westerlund, D., 1997, 'Islam in Tanzania', http://www.islamtz.org/articles/islam2.htm.

Lodhi, A. Y. and Westerlund, D., 2003, 'African Islam in Tanzania' http://www.islamtz.org.articles/islam2.htm

Louw, D., 1999, 'Ubuntu: An African assessment of the religious other', http:/www.bu.edu/wcp/Papers/Afri/AfriLouw.htm.

Lukalo-Owino, R., 2008a, *One Woman at a Time: The Kianda Foundation,* Nairobi: Allavida East Africa.

Lukalo-Owino, R., 2008b, *A Legacy of Giving: The Story of Mohamedaly and Maniben Rattansi Educational Trust,* Nairobi: Allavida East Africa.

Lukalo-Owino, R., 2008c, *In Trust for Tomorrow: Kenya Community Development Foundation,* Nairobi: Allavida East Africa.

Mabogunje, A.L. 2000, 'Institutional Radicalization, the State and the Development Process in Africa'. *Proceedings of the National Academy of Sciences of the United States of America,* Washington DC: PNAS.

MacDonald, N. and De Borms, L.T., 2010, *Global Philanthropy,* London: MF Publishing.

Maharaj, B., 2002, 'Economic Refugees in Post-Apartheid South Africa – Assets or Liabilities? Implications for Progressive Migration Policies', *GeoJournal* 56/1.

Mahomed, H., 2008, 'Philanthropy and Social Justice in South Africa: Addressing Underlying Causes or Mitigating Impact?' MA thesis, University of the Witwatersrand.

Makina, D., 2007, 'Profile of Migrant Zimbabweans in South Africa: A Pilot Study', Pretoria: University of South Africa.

Maliyamkono, T.L. and Bagachwa, M.S.D., 1990, *The Second Economy in Tanzania,* London: James Currey.

Malombe, J., 2000, *Community Development Foundations: Emerging Partnerships,* Washington DC, The World Bank.

Mamdani, M., 1996, *Citizen and Subject: Contemporary Africa and the Legacy of Late Colonialism,* Princeton, NJ: Princeton University Press.

Manji, F., 1998, 'The Depoliticization of Poverty', *in Development and Rights,* Oxford: Oxfam Publications.

Maoulidi, S., (undated), 'Women and Religious Education in Colonial Zanzibar', Unpublished paper.

Maphosa, F., 2004, 'The Impact of Remittances from Zimbabweans Working in South Africa on Rural Livelihoods in the Southern Districts of Zimbabwe'. Paper prepared for CODESRIA.

Marais, H., 1998, *South Africa, Limits to Change : The Political Economy of Transition,* London, New York, Cape Town: Zed Books.

Marechera, D., 1978, *House of Hunger: Short Stories*. African Writers Series 207, London: Heinemann Educational.

Margolis, H., 1982, *Selfishness, Altruism, and Rationality: A Theory of Social Choice,* Cambridge, New York: Cambridge University Press.

Marshall, K., 2001, 'Development and Religion: A Different Lens on Development Debates', *Peabody Journal of Education* 76/3–4.

Martin, R. L. and Osberg, S., 2007, 'Social Entrepreneurship: The Case for Definition' *Stanford Social Innovation Review,* Stanford CA: Stanford Center on Philanthropy and Civil Society.

Marx, C., 2002, 'Ubu and Ubuntu: On the Dialectics of Apartheid and Nation Building' in *Politikon: South African Journal of Political Studies* 29/1.

Masamba Ma Mpolo, J., 1985, 'African Symbols and Stories in Pastoral Care', *Journal of Pastoral Care* 39/4.

Mathe, R., 2005, *Making Ends Meet at the Margins: Grappling with Economic Crisis and Belonging in Beitbridge, Zimbabwe,* Dakar: CODESRIA.

Mauss, M., trs. Cunnison, I., 1954, *The Gift: The Form and Reason for Exchange in Archaic Societies,* London: Cohen and West.

Mauss, M., Cunnison, I.G. and Evans-Pritchard, E.E., 1967, *The Gift: Forms and Functions of Exchange in Archaic Societies,* New York: Norton.

Maxwell, S., 1999, 'The Meaning and Measurement of Poverty', *Poverty Briefing* 3 London: Overseas Development Institute.

May, J. (ed.), 1998, 'Poverty and Inequality in South Africa: Meeting the Challenge'. Report prepared for the Office of the Executive Deputy President and the Inter-Ministerial Committee for Poverty and Inequality, Pretoria.

Mbiti, J.S., 1991, *Introduction to African Religion*. Second Revised Edition, Oxford, Portsmouth NH: Heinemann Educational.

McCaskie, T.C., 1995, *State and Society in Pre-Colonial Asante,* Cambridge: Cambridge University Press.

McCormick, B. and Wahba, J., 2003, 'Return International Migration and Geographic Inequality: The Case of Egypt', *Journal of African Economies* 12/4.

McLeod, M.D., 1981, *The Asante*, London: British Museum Publications.

McOsano, P. 'Youth and Volunteer Effort: Volunteerism and Youth Involvement in Kenya'

Meintjies, F., 2004, 'Black Economic Empowerment: Elite Enrichment or Real Transformation?' Isandla Development Communiqué. Cape Town: Islanda Institute.

Menkhoff, T., 2010, 'Powering Philanthropic Passions' in Cheng, W. and Mohamed S. (eds.) *The World that Changes the World: How Philanthropy, Innovation and Entrepreneurship are Transforming the Social Ecosystem*, San Francisco: Wiley.

Micou, A.M., 1993, *The Donor Community in South Africa: A Directory*, South African Information Exchange (SAIE) Working Paper 26.

Middleton, J., Tait, D. and Bohannan, L., 1958, *Tribes Without Rulers; Studies in African Segmentary Systems*, London: Routledge & Paul.

Milner, A., 2003, 'Change or Charity?' *Alliance* 8/3 London: Alliance Publishing Trust.

Milner, A. and Hartnell, C., 2006, 'Community Foundations: Silver Bullet or Just Part of the Answer?', *Alliance* 11/1 London: Alliance Publishing Trust.

Mirza, B.A., 2005, 'The Slave Trade and the African Diaspora in Iran' *ZIFF Journal: Monsoons and Migrations* 2 Swahili Web: Zanzibar International Film Festival.

Mitchell, J.C., 1969, *Social Networks in Urban Situations: Analyses of Personal Relationships in Central African Towns* Manchester: published for the Institute for Social Research, University of Zambia by Manchester University Press.

Moe, H.A., 1961, 'Notes on the Origin of Philanthropy in Christendom' *ZIFF Journal: Monsoons and Migrations* 105 Swahili Web: Zanzibar International Film Festival.

Mohammed, Z.H., 2001, *Hadithi Fupi ya Maisha Yangu* Unpublished manuscript.

Mohan G. and Zack-Williams, A.B., 2002, 'Globalization from Below: Conceptualizing the Role of the African Diasporas in Africa's Development', *Review of African Political Economy* 92.

Mokopanele, T., 2006, 'New Churches Eye Bottom Line of Black Middle Class', *Business Report* 19 March 2006.

Moloi, D., 2001, 'Pooling Pennies to Provide Housing for the Poor,' in *Focus, South Africa: Tapping Local Resources to Address Local Needs*, Flint, Michigan: C. S. Mott Foundation.

Mombeshora, S. 2004. 'Philanthropy of Community in Zimbabwe: Past, Present and Future'. (Discussion Paper for the Building Community Philanthropy Project, Centre for Leadership and Public Values, University of Cape Town).

Morris, S., 1956, 'Indians in East Africa: A Study of Plural Society', *British Journal of Sociology* 7/3.

Moyo, B., 2003, 'Community Foundations, Social Capital and Development in South Africa'. Paper prepared during residence at the Center for the Study of Philanthropy, Graduate School and University Center, City University of New York.

Moyo, B., 2004, 'Philanthropy in the 21st Century: Challenges and Opportunities, a Study of Southern Africa'. Paper Presented at the Ford Foundation Retreat, Uganda, March 28–April 2.

Moyo, B., 2009, 'Establishing the African Grant-Makers Network'. A discussion document prepared for the launch of the African Grantmakers Network, Accra.

Moyo, B., 2010, 'Philanthropy in Africa: Functions, Status, Challenges and Opportunities' in MacDonald, N. and de Borms, L.T. (eds.) *Global Philanthropy* London: MF Publishing.

Mukandala, R., Yahya-Othman, S., Mushi, S.S. and Ndumbaro, J. (eds.), 2006, *Justice, Rights and Worship: Religion and Politics in Tanzania,* Dar es Salaam: E&D Publishers.

Munro, L.T., 2003, 'A Social Safety Net for the Chronically Poor? Zimbabwe's Public Assistance in the 1990s'. Paper prepared for the International Conference on Chronic Poverty and Development Policy, University of Manchester, 27 February 2003.

Murphy, E.J., 1976, *Creative Philanthropy: Carnegie Corporation and Africa, 1953–1973* New York: Teachers' Press, Columbia University.

Mushi, S.S. et al., 2001, *Tanzania's Political Culture: A Baseline Survey,* Dar es Salaam: Department of Political Science and Public Administration, Univ. of Dar es Salaam.

Mustapha, A.R., 2000, 'Rethinking Africanist Political Science' in *The Study of Africa: Volume 1 – Disciplinary and Interdisciplinary Encounters,* Dakar: CODESRIA.

Mutume, G., 2005, 'Workers' Remittances: a Boon to Development. Money Sent Home by African Migrants Rivals Development Aid' *Africa Renewal* 19/3.

Muzondidya, J., 2006, 'Makwerekwere: Citizenship, Nationhood and Identity among Diaspora Zimbabweans in South Africa', *Zimbabwe Review* 6/4.

Muzondidya, J., 2008, 'Majoni-joni: Survival Strategies among Zimbabwean Immigrants in South Africa', Paper presented at the International Conference on the Political Economies of Displacement in Zimbabwe, Wits University, South Africa, 9–11 June.

Muzondidya, J., 2010, 'Makwekwere: Migration, Citizenship and Identity among Zimbabweans in South Africa', in Macgregor, J. and Promorac, R., eds., *Zimbabwe's New Diaspora: Displacement and the Cultural Politics of Survival*, New York and Oxford, Berghahn Books.

Mwaikusa, J.T., 1995, 'Towards Responsible Democratic Government: Executive Powers and Constitutional Practice in Tanzania, 1962–1992', PhD dissertation, SOAS, University of London.

National Committee for Responsible Philanthropy, 2003, 'Social Justice Philanthropy: The Latest Trend or a Lasting Lens for Grantmaking?' National Committee for Responsible Philanthropy. Available www.ncrp.org [25 March 2007].

National Committee for Responsible Philanthropy, 2003, 'Understanding Social Justice Philanthropy.' National Committee for Responsible Philanthropy. [Online], Available www.ncrp.org [25 March 2007].

Nelson, K., 2002, 'An Overview of the Tax Campaign: 2000–2002' Paper prepared for the Non-Profit Partnership.

Ng'ethe, N. and Owina, W. (eds.), 1995, *From Sessional Paper No. 10 to Structural Adjustment: Towards Indigenizing the Policy Debate,* Nairobi: Institute of Policy Analysis and Research.

Ngondi-Houghton, C., 2008, *Promoting Philanthropy in Kenya: The Case for Tax Law Reform,* Nairobi: Allavida.

Ngunyi, M. and Gathiaka, K., 1993, 'Markets, Civil Society and Democracy in Africa' in Gibbon, P. (ed.) *Social Change and Economic Reforms in Africa* Uppsala: Nordic Africa Institute.

Nimtz, A.H., 1980, *Islam and Politics in East Africa: The Sufi Order in Tanzania,* Minneapolis: University of Minnesota Press.

Nketia, J.H., 1949, *Akanfo Nnwom Bi,* Oxford: Oxford University Press.

Nketia, J.H., 1974, *Ayan,* Tema: Ghana Publishing Corporation.

Norris, P., 1978, *Dickens and Charity,* London: Macmillan.

Nyar, A., 2004, 'Organised Philanthropy: Toward an understanding of Community Foundations in South Africa'. ISTR Sixth International Conference, Toronto, 11–14 July.

O'Halloran, K., 2007, *Charity Law and Social Inclusion: An International Study,* London, New York: Routledge.

Oliver, R.A., 1965, *The Missionary Factor in East Africa,* Second Edition. London: Longmans.

Olson, M., 1971, *The Logic of Collective Action: Public Goods and the Theory of Groups',* Harvard Economic Studies 124, Cambridge, MA: Harvard University Press.

Opiniano, J.M., 2002, 'The Dynamics of Transnational Philanthropy by Migrant Workers to their Communities of Origin: The Case of Pozorrubio, Philippines'. Paper presented to the Fifth International Society for Third Sector Research (ISTR) International Conference, University of Cape Town, South Africa, July 2011.

Orford, M., 2004, *Rural Voice: The Social Change Assistance Trust 1984–2004,* Cape Town: David Philip.

Ostrom, E., 1990, *Governing the Commons: The Evolution of Institutions for Collective Action. Political Economy of Institutions and Decisions,* Cambridge, New York: Cambridge University Press.

Özden, Ç. and Schiff, M.W., 2006, *International Migration, Remittances, and the Brain Drain. Trade and Development Series* Washington, DC: World Bank.

Page, B., 2007, 'Slow Going: The Mortuary, Modernity and the Hometown Association in Bali-Nyonga, Cameroon', *Africa: Journal of the International African Institute* 77/3.

Page, J. and Plaza, S., 2006, 'Migration Remittances and Development: A Review of Global Evidence', *Journal of African Economies* 15/S2.

Patterson, R., 2007, *African Brain Circulation: Beyond the Drain–Gain Debate. International Studies in Sociology and Social Anthropology* 105. Leiden: Brill.

Payton, R., 1987, 'American Values and Private Philanthropy' in Thompson, K.W. (ed.) *Philanthropy – Private Means, Public Ends.* Lanham: University Press of America.

Philp, R., Ntshingila, F., Sukhraj, P., Gules, N., and van der Merwe, J., 2004, 'Glory Hallelujah!', *Sunday Times* 22 December.

Pieterse, E., 1998, 'Development and Community Participation: Decoding the Conceptual "Stock and Trade" of the Voluntary Sector', *Development Update* 2/1 SANGOCO and INTERFUND.

Pieterse, E. and van Donk, M., 2002, 'Capacity Building for Poverty Eradication', unpublished concept paper produced for the Sedibeng Centre.

Pieterse, E. and Meintjies, F. (eds), 2004, *Voices of Transition: The Politics, Poetics and Practices of Social Change in South Africa,* Oxford: Heinemann.

Polzer, T. 2007, 'Responding to Zimbabwean Migration to South Africa – Evaluating Options'. Paper prepared for Meeting of the Lawyers for Human Rights and Wits Forced Migration Studies Program, Witwatersrand University, 27 November 2007.

Porter, M. E. and Kramer, M. R., 1999, 'Philanthropy's New Agenda: Creating Value', *Harvard Business Review* Nov/Dec.

Possi, M., 2001, 'Provision of Education: Infrastructure and Resources'. Paper presented at a Conference on Religion and Democracy in Tanzania, Dar es Salaam.

Possi, M., 2003, 'Islamic Philanthropy: A Research Report on Arusha, Dar es Salaam and Kilimanjaro' Unpublished paper.

Pourtier R., 2003, *Afrique centrale et les régions transfrontalières: perspectives de reconstruction et d'intégration,* Paris: INICA/OCDE.

Pouwels, R.L., 1987, *Horn and Crescent: Cultural Change and Traditional Islam on the East African Coast, 800–1900.* African Studies Series 53, Cambridge, New York: Cambridge University Press.

Powell, F., 2007, *The Politics of Civil Society, Neoliberalism or Social Left?,* Bristol: The Policy Press.

Powell, W.W. and Steinberg, R., 2006, *The Nonprofit Sector: A Research Handbook.* 2nd ed. New Haven: Yale University Press.

Prowse, M., 2002, 'Charity Begins – but it Doesn't Go Far,' *Financial Times Weekend* Dec. 1.

Punch, K., 2000, *Developing Effective Research Proposals.* Essential Resources for Social Research. London, Thousand Oaks CA: Sage.

Putnam, R.D., 1993, 'The Prosperous Community', *Current* 356/10.

Putnam, R.D., 2000, *Bowling Alone: The Collapse and Revival of American Community,* New York: Simon & Schuster.

Ractliffe, T., 2010, 'South African Social Investment – A Giving Model Beyond "Philanthropy"' in MacDonald, N. and De Borms, L.T., eds., *Global Philanthropy,* London: MF Publishing.

Rakita, S., 2005, 'African Diaspora Philanthropy' Draft paper.

Rakodi, C., 1997, *The Urban Challenge in Africa: Growth and Management of its Large Cities,* Tokyo: United Nations University Press.

Ramdas, K., 2004, 'Interview with the CEO of the Global Fund for Women' *Alliance* 9/3 London: Alliance Publishing Trust.

Ranger, T., 1970, *The African Voice in Southern Rhodesia*, Evanston IL: Northwestern University Press.

Ranger, T., 1989, 'Missionaries, Migrants and the Manyika: The invention of ethnicity in Zimbabwe' in L. Vail, ed., *The Creation of Tribalism in Southern Africa,* London: James Currey.

Ratha, D., 2004, 'Understanding the importance of remittances' http://www.migrationinformation.org/Feature/display.cfm?id=256

Rattray, R.S., 1929, *Religion and Art in Ashanti.* Oxford: Clarendon Press.

Rattray, R.S., 1952, *Ashanti Proverbs: the Primitive Ethics of a Savage People,* Oxford: Clarendon Press.

Rattray, R.S., 1959, *Religion and Art in Ashanti,* Accra: Presbyterian Book Depot.

Rattray, R.S., 1969, *Ashanti Law and Constitution,* Oxford: Clarendon Press.

Rawls, J., 1971, *A Theory of Justice,* Cambridge, MA: Belknap Press of Harvard University Press.

Reid, D., Budlender, G., Cuthburt, D., Kinghorn, J., Kleinschmidt, H. & Mogotsi, L., 1993, 'Fundraising, Volunteering and Giving,' Paper prepared as part of the Independent Study for an Enabling Environment for NGOs. Joburg: Development Resource Centre.

Reindorf, C.C., 1895, *History of the Gold Coast and Asante Based on Traditions and Historical Facts Comprising a Period of More Than Three Centuries from About 1500 to 1860,* Basel: Basel Mission Book Depot.

Republic of Kenya, 1965, *African Socialism and Its Application to Planning in Kenya.*

Republic of Kenya 2003, *Report of the Task Force on Public Collections or 'Harambees'.*

Riggs, F.W., 1998, *The Modernity of Ethnic Identity and Conflict,* www.hawaii.edu/~fredr/riggs.htm.

Rist, G., 2007, 'Development as a Buzzword', *Development in Practice* 17. London: Routledge.

Ritchie, J., 1988, *Fundraising for the New Millennium.* Cape Town: Papillon/Nedcor Community Development Fund.

Robinson, D.W., 1963, 'The Church in Tanganyika', *African Ecclesiastical Review* 5/3 Kampala: Pastrol Institute of Eastern Africa.

Robinson, J. (ed.), 2002, *Displacement and Development,* Oxford: Oxford University Press.

Rockey, V. (ed.), 2001, *The Corporate Social Investment Handbook,* Trialogue: Johannesburg, South Africa.

Rockey, V., 2003, *The Corporate Social Investment Handbook*, Johannesburg: Trialogue.

Rooney, P. and Sherman, L.(eds.), 2005, *Exploring Black Philanthropy: New Directions for Philanthropic Fundraising,* No. 48 New York: Jossey Bass Inc.

Rosaldo, M. Z., Lamphere, L. and Bamberger, J., 1974, *Woman, Culture, and Society,* Stanford, CA: Stanford University Press.

Rousseau, J.-J. and Glover, A.S.B., 1980, *The Confessions of Jean-Jacques Rousseau: The Anonymous Translation into English of 1783 & 1790*, Revised Edition (The 100 Greatest Books Ever Written) Norwalk, CT: The Easton Press.

Roux, J. 2001, 'SAGA Community Foundations Programme: Evaluation Report', Cape Town.

Rudebeck, L., Törnquist, O. and Rojas, V., 1998, *Democratization in the Third World: Concrete Cases in Comparative and Theoretical Perspective,* International Political Economy Series, Basingstoke: Macmillan Press.

Rushdie, S., 2005, 'Beware Those Who Seek to Deny Us Our Right to Freedom From Religion', *The Sunday Times* 27 March.

Rutherford, B. and Addison, L., 2007, 'Zimbabwean Farm Workers in Northern South Africa', *Review of African Political Economy* 34/114.

Rzepka, C. J., 1995, *Sacramental Commodities: Gift, Text, and the Sublime in De Quincey.* Amherst: University of Massachusetts Press.

Sacks, E., 2004, *Community Foundations Global Status Report,* New York: Worldwide Initiative for Grantmaker Support (WINGS).

Safran, W., 1991, 'Diasporas in Modern Societies: Myths of Homeland and Return', *Diaspora* 1 Toronto: University of Toronto Press.

Said, M., 1998, *The Life and Times of Abdulwahid Sykes (1924–1968): The Untold Story of the Muslim Struggle against British Colonialism in Tanganyika,* London: Minerva Press.

Salole, G., 1991, 'Not Seeing the Wood for the Trees: Searching for Indigenous Non-Government Organisations in the Forest of Voluntary Self Help Associations' *Journal of Social Development in Africa* 6/1 Addis Ababa: OSSREA.

Sarpong, P. A., 1974, *Ghana in Retrospect – Some Aspects of Ghanaian Culture* Tema: Ghana Publishing Corporation.

Schatzberg, M. G., 1987, *The Political Economy of Kenya. A SAIS Study on Africa,* New York: Praeger.

Schervish P.G., and Ostrander S., 1990, 'Giving and Getting: Philanthropy as a Social Relation' in *Critical Issues in American Philanthropy: Strengthening Theory and Practice',* Jossey Bass, San Francisco.

Schervish, P.G., 1998, 'Philanthropy' in Wuthnow, R. (ed.) *The Encyclopedia of Politics and Religion. Volume II,* Washington DC: CQ Press.

Schwettman, J., 2011, 'Capacity Building for Africa's Cooperatives and Social Economy Orgnisations'. Paper prepared for the Expert Group Meeting on Cooperatives in Social Development: Beyond 2012. Mongolia.

Seekings, J. and Nattrass, N., 2005, *Class, Race, and Inequality in South Africa,* New Haven: Yale University Press.

Selby, A., 2006, 'Commercial Farmers and the State: Interest Group Politics and Land Reform in Zimbabwe' D.Phil. Thesis, Oxford University.

Selinger, L., 2004, 'The Forgotten Factor: The Uneasy Relationship Between Religion and Development', *Social Compass* 51/4.

Sen, A., 2000, 1999, *Development as Freedom,* New York: Anchor Books.

Setkova, L., 2004, 'Social Justice Philanthropy: A Strategic Framework for Philanthropic Organisations', MSc in Development Management.

Sexwale, T., 2005, 'BEE is Very Simple – It's About Fixing Up the Mess', *Sunday Times* 6 March.

Shaw, A., 2002, *Social Justice Philanthropy: An Overview.* http://www.synergos.org/knowledge/philanthropyissues [22 April 2007].

Sheffer, G., 1986, *Modern Diasporas in International Politics* New York: St. Martin's Press.

Shivji, I. G., 1976, *Class Struggles in Tanzania.* London: Heinemann.

Shuval, J. T., 2000, 'Diaspora Migration: Definitional Ambiguities and a Theoretical Paradigm, *International Migration* 38/5.

Sikod, F, and Tchouassi, G., 2007, 'Diaspora Remittances and the Financing of Basic Social Services and Infrastructure in Francophone Africa South of the Sahara' in Rubin Paterson (eds) *Africa Brain Drain Circulation: Beyond the Drain-Gain Debate,* Boston: Brill.

Sisulu, E., Moyo, B. and Tshuma, N., 2007, 'The Zimbabwean Community in South Africa', in Roger Southall et al., eds., *State of the Nation; South Africa, 2006–2007*, Pretoria: HSRC Press.

Sithole, M.P., 2005. 'Non-Arithmetic Giving: The Ethnography of Giving Amongst the Shembe and Zionist Followers in KwaZulu-Natal and Mpumulanga', Natal: Centre for Civil Society, University of Kwazulu-Natal.

Sivalon, J. C., 1990, 'Roman Catholicism and the Defining of Tanzanian Socialism in 1953–1985: An Analysis of the Social Ministry of the Roman Catholic Church in Tanzania' Ph.D. dissertation, Department of Theology, University of St. Michael's College, Toronto.

Slim, H., 2002, 'Not philanthropy But Rights: The Proper Politicization of Humanitarian Philosophy', *International Journal of Human Rights* 6/2.

Smillie, I. and Minear, L., 2004, *The Charity of Nations: Humanitarian Action in a Calculating World,* Bloomfield, CT: Kumarian Press.

Smith, B., 2004, 'New Southern Africa Trust Launched', *Alliance* 9/2 London: Alliance Publishing Trust.

Smith, B.K., 2003, 'Philanthropy, Accountability and Social Justice'. Lecture given at the University of Bologna April 7.

Soghayroun, I.E., 1992, *Islam, Christian Missions and the Colonial Administration in East Africa: A Documentary Study with Special Emphasis on Uganda,* Muscat: Sultan Qaboos University.

Sookraj, R., 2005, 'The State of Giving in South Africa: A Hindu Perspective' Natal: Centre for Civil Society, University of Kwazulu Natal.

SpringerLink, 2009, *International Encyclopedia of Civil Society,* New York: Springer.

Stewart, C. (Mott Foundation), 1998, 'Community Foundations: Building a New South Africa Through Community', *Philanthropy and Community Development,* Flint, MI.

Stiglitz, J.E., Sen, A. and Fitoussi, J.P., 2009, 'Report by the Commission on the Measurement of Economic Performance and Social Progress' www.stiglitz-sen-fitoussi.fr

Svanberg, I. and Westerlund, D., 1999, *Islam Outside the Arab World,* Richmond: Curzon.

Sweetman, C., 1999, Editorial *Gender and Development,* 7:2–6.

Swilling, M. and Russell, B., 2002, *The Size and Scope of the Non Profit Sector in South Africa,* Johannesburg, Durban: University of the Witwatersrand and University of Natal.

Synergos. Undated. *Social Justice Philanthropy: Perspectives from Five Countries.* [Online], Available http://www.synergos.org/knowledge/philanthropyissues [22 April 2007].

Taylor, J.E., 1999, 'The New Economics of Labor Migration and the Role of Remittances', *International Migration,* Vol. 37(1), pp. 63-86.

Tchouassi G., 2004, 'Migrations et envois d'argent des migrants en Afrique au Sud du Sahara', *Techniques Financières et Développement* 76.

TGNP - Tanzania Gender Networking Programme, 2004, *Gender Budget Analysis in Tanzania: 1997–2000,* Dar es Salaam: TGNP.

TEMCO, 2006, Papers presented at Dissemination Conference on 2005 General Elections. 20-21 February. Dar es Salaam.

Terreblanche, S.J., 2002, *A History of Inequality in South Africa, 1652–2002,* Pietermaritzburg: University of Natal Press.

Tevera, D. and Zinyama, L. (eds.), 2002, *Zimbabweans Who Move: Perspectives on International Migration in Zimbabwe.* Migration Policy Series No 25 Cape Town: Southern Africa Migration Project.

Tevera, D. & Crush, J., 2003, *The New Brain Drain from Zimbabwe* (Migration Policy Series, no. 29).

Tobin, G.A., 2000, 'The Transition of Communal Values and Behavior in Jewish Philanthropy'. Paper presented at the Forum on Philanthropy, Public Policy and the Economy, UCLA.

Tostensen, A., Tvedten, I. and Vaa, M. (eds.), 2001, *Associational Life in African Cities: Popular Responses to the Urban Crisis,* Uppsala: Nordic African Institute.

Trager, L., 1998, 'Home-Town Linkages and Local Development in South-Western Nigeria Whose Agenda? What Impact?', *Africa: Journal of the International African Institute* 68/3.

Transparency International Kenya, 2001, *Harambee: Pooling Together or Pulling Apart,* Nairobi: Transparency International Kenya.

Tronca, L., 2003, 'Building a Network Theory of Social Capital', *Sociologia e Politiche Sociali* 6/3.

Tyndale, W., 2003, 'Idealism and Practicality: The Role of Religion in Development', *Development,* 46.

UNESCO (ed.), 1974, *Two Studies of Ethnic Group Relations in Africa: Senegal and the United Republic of Tanzania, Part Two: Ethnic Group Relations in the United Republic of Tanzania* Paris: UNESCO.

United Nations, 2005, *The Inequality Predicament: Report on the World Social Situation 2005.* New York: United Nations.

Uphoff, N.T., 1992, *Learning From Gal Oya: Possibilities for Participatory Development and Post-Newtonian Social Science* Ithaca: Cornell University Press.

Van Til, J., 1990, *Critical Issues in American Philanthropy: Strengthening Theory and Practice,* Jossey-Bass Nonprofit Sector Series, San Francisco: Jossey-Bass.

Viederman, S., 2002, 'The Future of Philanthropy', *Souls: A Critical Journal of Black Politics, Culture and Society,* New York: Institute for Research on African-American Studies at Columbia University.

Voigt-Graf, C., 1998, *Asian Communities in Tanzania: A Journey Through Past and Present Times.* Hamburg African Studies 7, Hamburg: Institut für Afrika-Kunde.

Von Troll, M., 1993, *Changing Paradigms in Development – South, East, West: A Meeting of Minds in Africa,* Uppsala: The Scandinavian Institute for African Studies.

Vygotskiǐ, L.S., Kozulin, A. and MITCogNet, 1986, *Thought and Language,* Cambridge, MA: MIT Press.

Wanyonyi, P. K., 2004, 'Harambee Self Help in Kenya: An Interplay Between Global and Local' in Aina, T.A., Chachage, C.S.L. and Annan-Yao, E. (eds.) *Globalization and Social Policy in Africa,* Dakar: CODESRIA.

Weiss, H., 2002, *Social Welfare in Muslim Societies in Africa* Uppsala: Nordic Africa Institute.

Westerlund, D., 1980, *Ujamaa na Dini: A Study of Some Aspects of Society and Religion, 1961–1977,* Stockholm: Stockholm Studies in Comparative Religion.

White, D. E., 2010, *The Nonprofit Challenge: Integrating Ethics into the Purpose and Promise of Our Nation's Charities* New York: Palgrave Macmillan.

Whittington Banda, Gill, 2006, 'Improving Corporate Responses to HIV and AIDs', *CSI Handbook, Ninth Edition.*

Wilkinson-Maposa, S., 2005, 'The Rich Not the Only Ones Who Can Help the Poor', *Sunday Times Business Section,* 13 February.

Wilkinson-Maposa, S., Fowler, A., Oliver-Evans, C. and Mulenga, C.F.N., 2006, *The Poor Philanthropist: How And Why The Poor Help And Give Each Other,* Cape Town: Compress.

Wilks, I., 1975, *Asante in the Nineteenth Century: The Structure and Evolution of a Political Order.* African Studies Series 13, London, New York: Cambridge University Press.

Williams, R. and Cawthra, G. (eds.), 2003, *Ourselves to Know: Civil–Military Relations and Defense Transformation in Southern Africa,* Pretoria: ISS.

Williams, R., 2006, 'A Conversation with Barry Gaberman', *Foundation News & Commentary* 47/2 Washington DC: Council on Foundations.

Wilson, E. W., 2001, *Building Credibility, the Foundation for Fundraising,* The Netherlands: KIT Publishers.

Woolcock, M., 1998, 'Social Capital and Economic Development: Toward a Theoretical Synthesis and Policy Framework' *Theory and Society* 27/2.

Woolcock, M. and Narayan, D., 1999, 'Social Capital: Implications for Development Theory, Research and Policy'. Paper submitted to the World Bank Research Observer, World Bank, February.

Wright, K., 2001, 'Generosity vs. Altruism: Philanthropy and Charity in the United States and United Kingdom', *Voluntas: International Journal of Voluntary & Nonprofit Organizations* 12/4.

Wrong, M., 2000, *In the Footsteps of Mr. Kurz: Living on the Brink of Disaster in Congo,* London, New York: Fourth Estate.

Wrong, M., 2005, *I Didn't Do It For You: How the World Betrayed a Small African Nation.* London, New York: Fourth Estate.

Wuthnow, R., 1998, *The Encyclopedia of Politics and Religion,* Washington DC: Congressional Quarterly.

Wyngaard, R., 2002, 'The Tax Laws for Non-Profit Organisations: Comparing the Old and the New Provisions of the Income Tax Act' Unpublished paper prepared for the Non-Profit Legal Support Project of the Legal Resources Centre.

Yahya-Othman, S., 2001, 'Education Perfomance'. Paper presented at a Conference on Religion and Democracy in Tanzania, Dar es Salaam.

Yahya-Othman, S., 2006, 'Educational Performance' in Mukandala, R., Yahya-Othman, S., Mushi, S.S. and Ndumbaro, J. (eds.), 2006, *Justice, Rights and Worship: Religion and Politics in Tanzania,* Dar es Salaam: E&D Publishers.

Young, N. and Shih, J. 2003, 'The Chinese Diaspora and Philanthropy'. Paper prepared for the *Workshop on Diaspora Philanthropy from China to India.* Global Equity Initiative, Harvard University.

Young, S., 2003, *Philanthropy for Social Change: Four Decades of Ford Foundation Grant Making in Eastern Africa,* Nairobi: the Ford Foundation Office for Eastern Africa.

Yusuf, I., 1990, 'Islam and African Socialism: A Study of the Interactions between Islam and Ujamaa Socialism in Tanzania' Ph.D. dissertation, Temple University, Philadelphia.

Zabala, G. 1999, 'Reviving Indigenous Philanthropic Institutions and Social Support Systems', Southern African Grantmakers Association (SAGA), Second International Conference Proceedings, Durban.

Zanzibar Revolutionary Government, 2001, *Ripoti ya Kuangalia Hali ya Waqf na Mali ya Amana*.

Zeleza, P.T., 1993, *A Modern Economic History of Africa*, Dakar: CODESRIA.

Zeleza, P.T. (ed.), 2004, *Human Rights, the Rule of Law, and Development in Africa,* Philadelphia: University of Pennsylvania Press.

Zubeir, H., 2003, 'Misikiti Katika Mji Mkongwe Zanzibar' in Maarifa, Zanzibar.

INDEX